HOTOTO-GISU. COUGH-ING UP BLOOD, FOR THE FANS. THINK I WON'T DO IT?

和月伸宏

NOBUHIRO WATSUKI

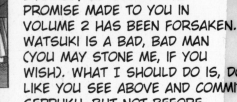

# WATSUKI LIES FOR THE THIRD TIME!

I AM SO, SO SORRY. THE PROMISE MADE TO YOU IN VOLUME 2 HAS BEEN FORSAKEN. WATSUKI IS A BAD, BAD MAN (YOU MAY STONE ME, IF YOU WISH). WHAT I SHOULD DO IS, DO LIKE YOU SEE ABOVE AND COMMIT SEPPUKU, BUT NOT BEFORE FINISHING RUROKEN AND NOT BEFORE FINISHING SHIN (NEW) SAMURAI SPIRITS. INSTEAD I'LL SUCK IT UP, TIGHTEN THE KNOT ON MY HACHIMAKI, AND RESOLVE TO DO MY BEST. PLEASE DON'T ABANDON ME...PLEASE....

*Rurouni Kenshin*, which has found fans not only in Japan but around the world, first made its appearance in 1992, as an original short story in *Weekly Shonen Jump Special*. Later rewritten and published as a regular, continuing *Jump* series in 1994, *RUROUNI KENSHIN* ended serialization in 1999 but continued in popularity, as evidenced by the 2000 publication of **Yahiko no Sakabatô** (Yahiko's Reversed-Edge Sword)" in **Weekly Shonen Jump**. His most current work, *Busô Renkin* ("Armored Alchemist"), began publication this June, also in *Jump*.

**RUROUNI KENSHIN**
VOL. 4: DUAL CONCLUSIONS
**The SHONEN JUMP Graphic Novel Edition**

STORY AND ART BY
**NOBUHIRO WATSUKI**

English Adaptation/Gerard Jones
Translation/Kenichiro Yagi
Touch-Up Art & Lettering/Steve Dutro
Cover, Graphics & Layout/Sean Lee
Editor/Avery Gotoh

Supervising Editor/Kit Fox
Production Manager/Noboru Watanabe
Managing Editor/Annette Roman
Associate Managing Editor/Albert Totten
Editor in Chief/Hyoe Narita
Sr. Director of Licensing and Acquisitions/Rika Inouye
V.P. of Marketing/Liza Coppola
V.P. of Strategic Development/Yumi Hoashi
Publisher/Seiji Horibuchi

PARENTAL ADVISORY
**Rurouni Kenshin** contains violence.
It is rated "T+" for older teens.

Printed in the USA.

Published by VIZ, LLC
P.O. Box 77010 • San Francisco, CA 94107

SHONEN JUMP Graphic Novel Edition
10 9 8 7 6 5 4 3 2 1
First printing, March 2004

www.viz.com

THE WORLD'S
MOST POPULAR MANGA

www.shonenjump.com

SHONEN JUMP GRAPHIC NOVEL

# Rurouni Kenshin™

## MEIJI SWORDSMAN ROMANTIC STORY
## Vol. 4: DUAL CONCLUSIONS

STORY AND ART BY
NOBUHIRO WATSUKI

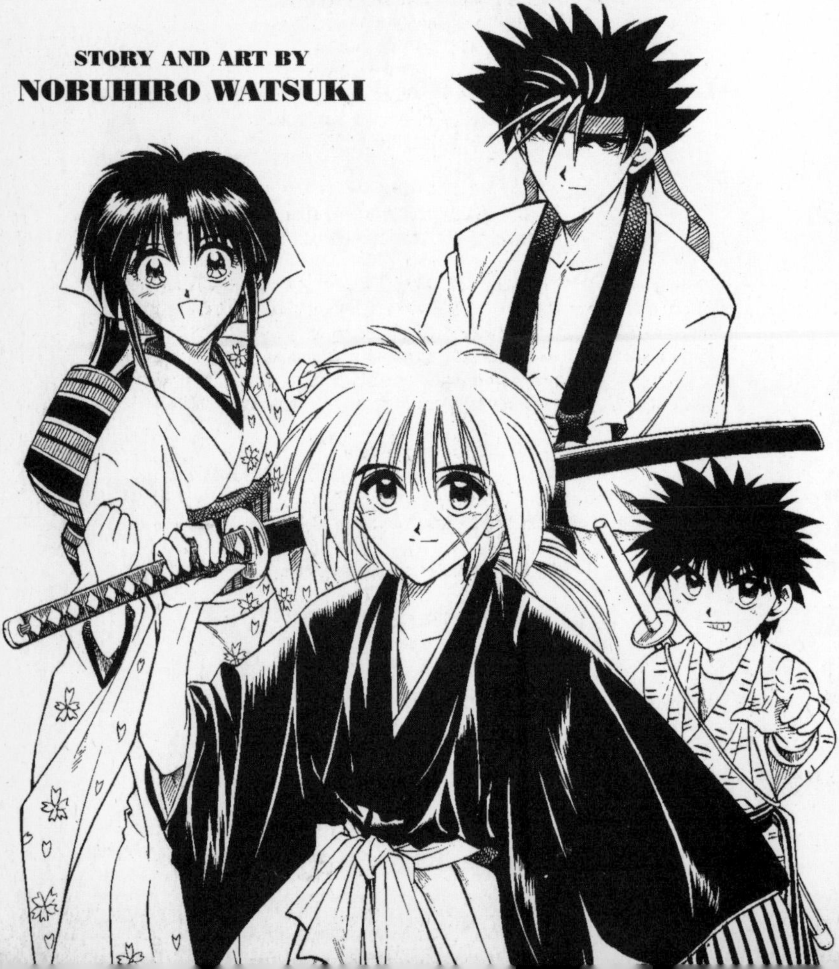

# CAST

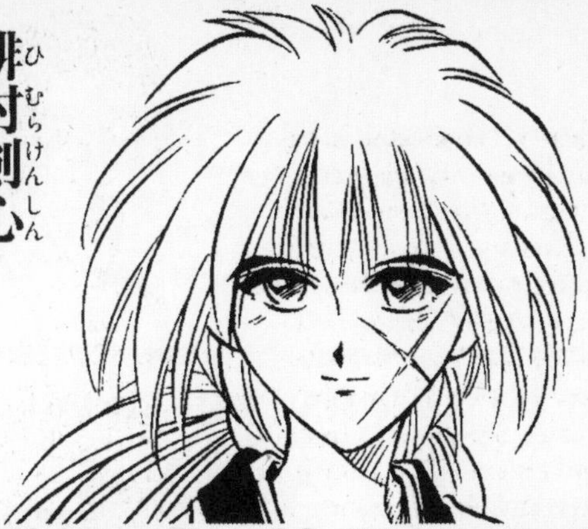

緋村剣心（人斬り抜刀斎）

**Himura Kenshin (Hitokiri Battōsai)**

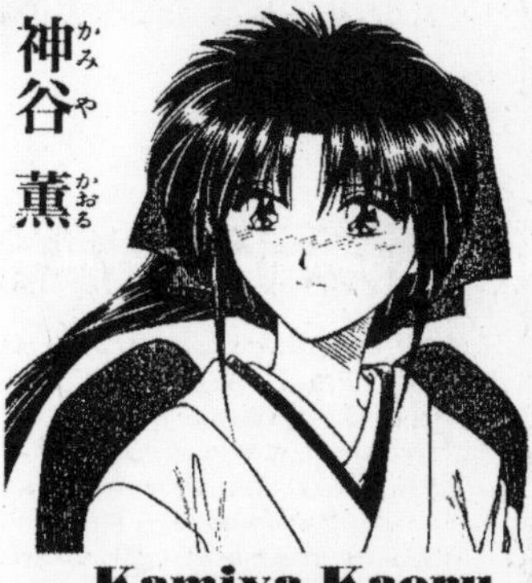

神谷薫

**Kamiya Kaoru**

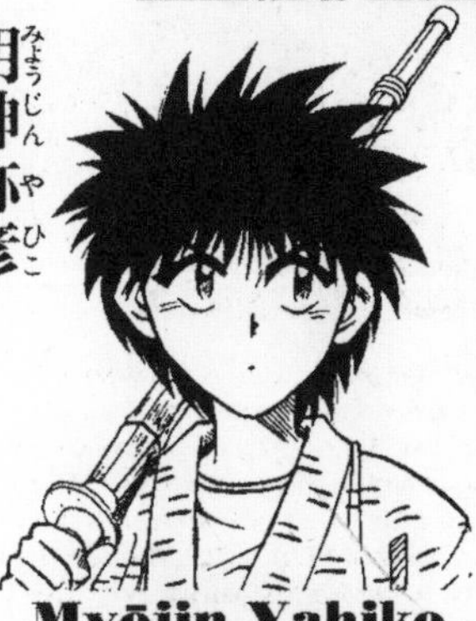

明神弥彦

**Myōjin Yahiko**

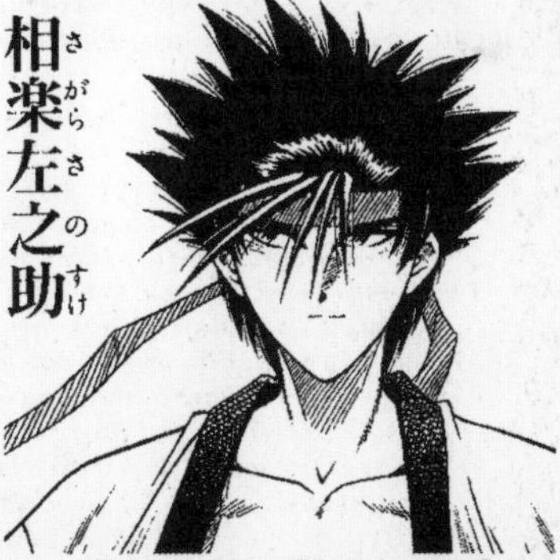

相楽左之助

**Sagara Sanosuke**

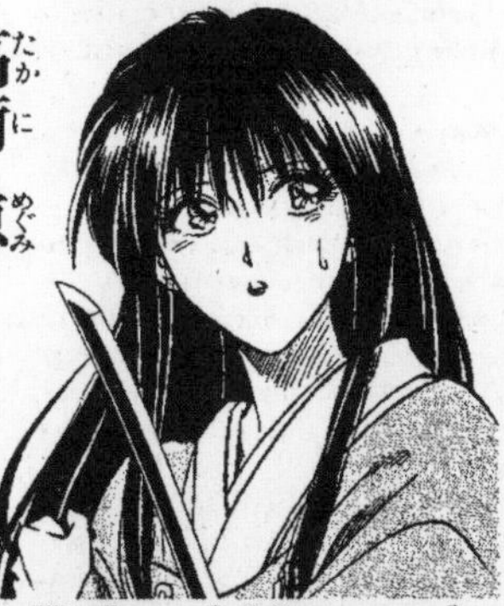

高荷恵

**Takani Megumi**

るろうに剣心

和月伸宏

**Himura Kenshin, once known as "Himura Battōsai"--a *hitokiri* legendary among the pro-Imperialist patriots who fought to create the Meiji Era. Now a guest of the Kamiya dojo, former assassin Kenshin carries only a *sakabatō*, a reversed-edge sword, to prohibit himself from taking life, ever again.**

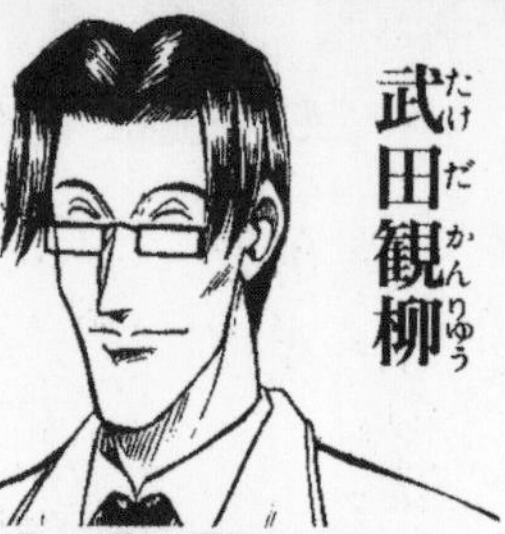

武田観柳

**Takeda Kanryū**

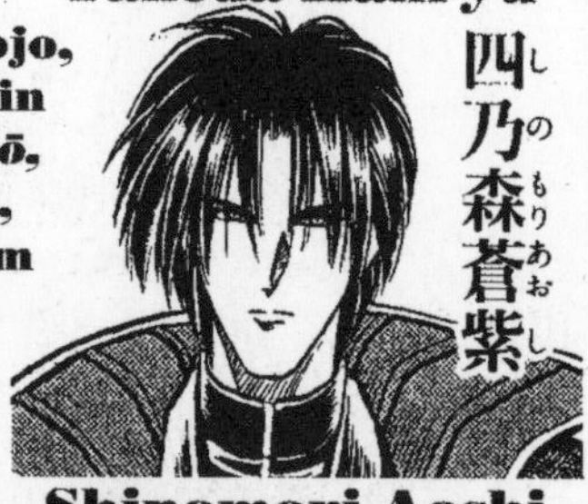

四乃森蒼紫

**Shinomori Aoshi**

## THUS FAR

**Recently, Kenshin saved Takani Megumi from the private army of grasping young industrialist Takeda Kanryū. Megumi, daughter of the Takani family of Aizu honored for its achievements in medicine, was separated from her family during the Aizu War and came to Tokyo as assistant to a doctor. That doctor, however, was working with Kanryū to sell a new form of opium, and Megumi began unknowingly to assist him. Captured upon the doctor's death by Kanryū, Megumi was forced to continue producing the new opium--she (perhaps not accidentally) being the only one familiar with its production.**

**After an escape from Kanryū, Megumi was to have stayed with Kenshin and the others at the Kamiya dojo. Instead, she disappears, leaving only a letter stating that she's returning to Aizu. The truth, though, is that Kanryū--who's since discovered Kenshin's past--has threatened her in order to avoid a confrontation with the legendary *hitokiri*. Sensing that Megumi has for her own reasons returned to Kanryū, Kenshin heads out with Yahiko and Sanosuke to rescue her. His private army annihilated, Kanryū tries to buy off Kenshin, but the *rurouni* wants no part of it. That's good news to Aoshi--head of Kanryū's elite force, the Oniwabanshū--as a fight with Kenshin is what the battle-hungry Aoshi would like most of all. Now in Kanryū Manor, Han'nya, the first of the Oniwabanshū, appears...**

# CONTENTS

**Rurouni Kenshin**
Meiji Swordsman Romantic Story
BOOK FOUR: DUAL CONCLUSIONS

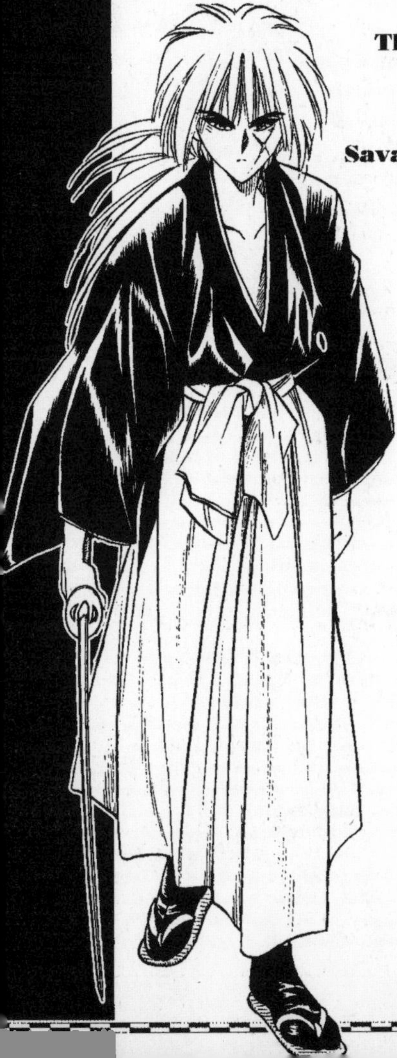

READ THIS WAY

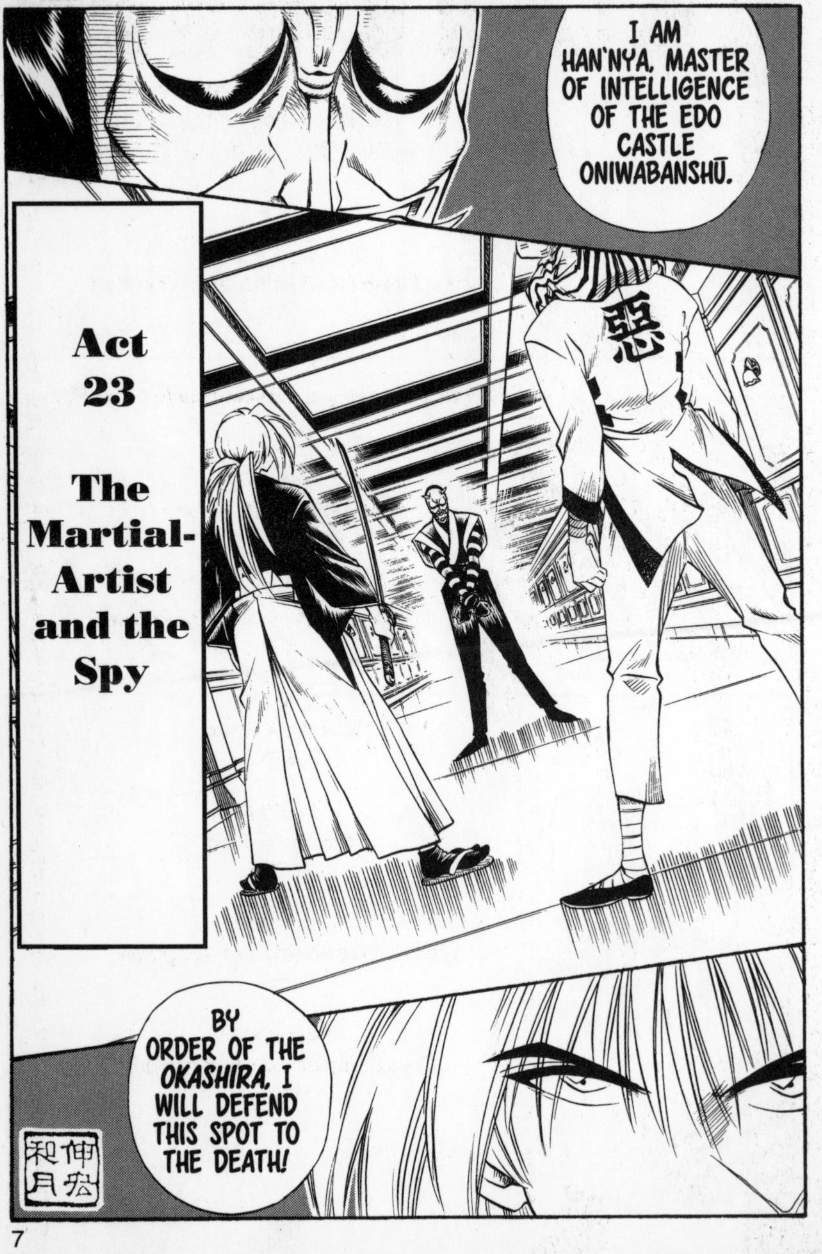
I AM HAN'NYA, MASTER OF INTELLIGENCE OF THE EDO CASTLE ONIWABANSHŪ.
Act 23
The Martial-Artist and the Spy
惡
BY ORDER OF THE *OKASHIRA*, I WILL DEFEND THIS SPOT TO THE DEATH!
伸宏和月

READ THIS WAY

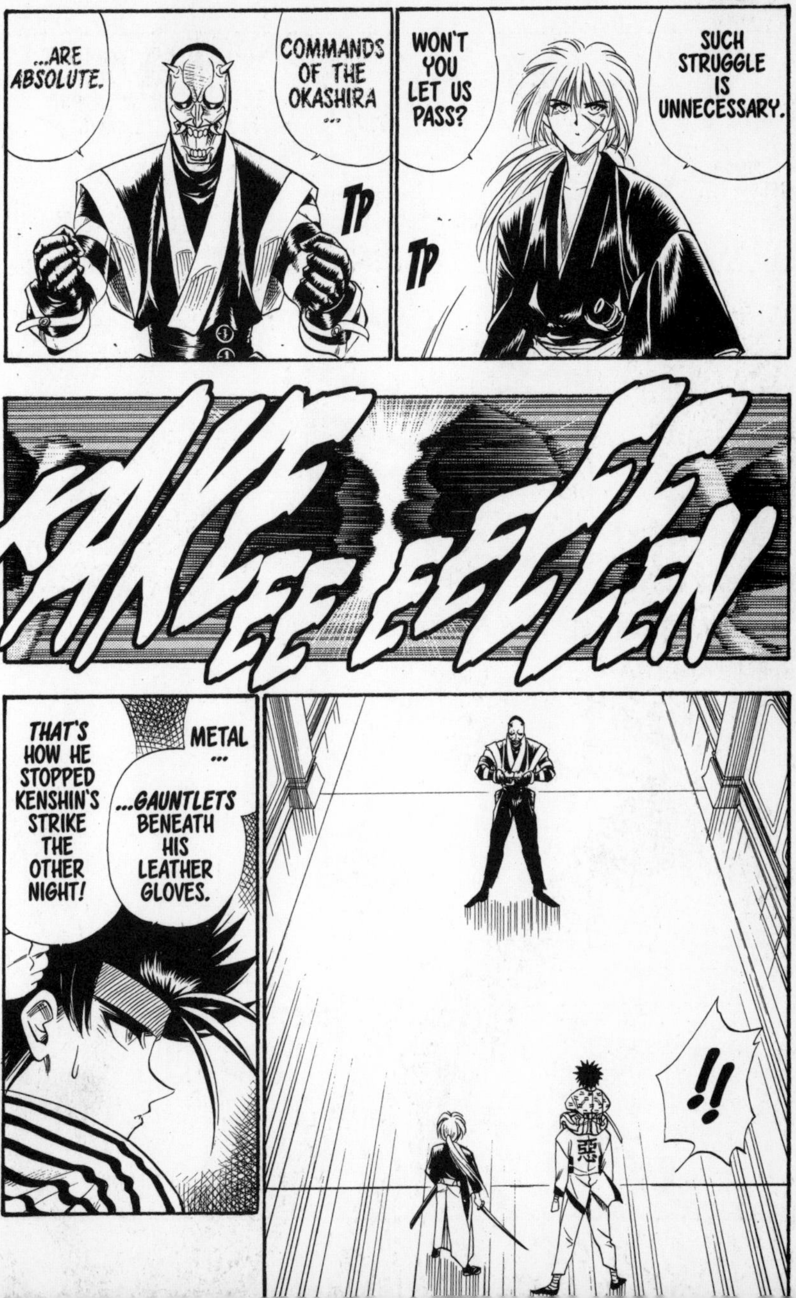
SUCH STRUGGLE IS UNNECESSARY.
WON'T YOU LET US PASS?
TP
TP
COMMANDS OF THE OKASHIRA ...
...ARE ABSOLUTE.
!!
METAL ...
...GAUNTLETS BENEATH HIS LEATHER GLOVES.
THAT'S HOW HE STOPPED KENSHIN'S STRIKE THE OTHER NIGHT!

READ THIS WAY

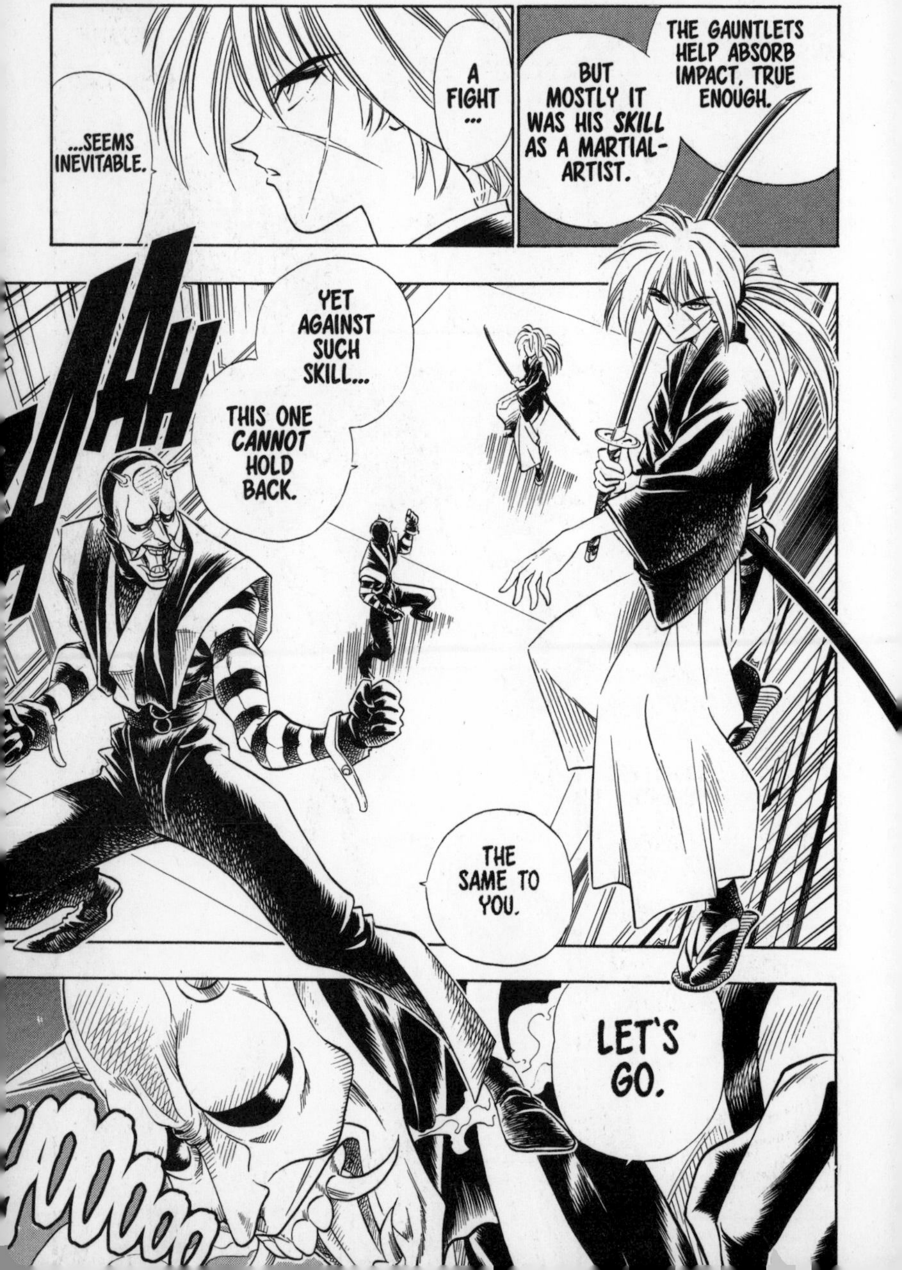
THE GAUNTLETS HELP ABSORB IMPACT, TRUE ENOUGH.
BUT MOSTLY IT WAS HIS *SKILL* AS A MARTIAL-ARTIST.
A FIGHT ...
...SEEMS INEVITABLE.
YET AGAINST SUCH SKILL...
THIS ONE *CANNOT* HOLD BACK.
THE SAME TO YOU.
LET'S GO.

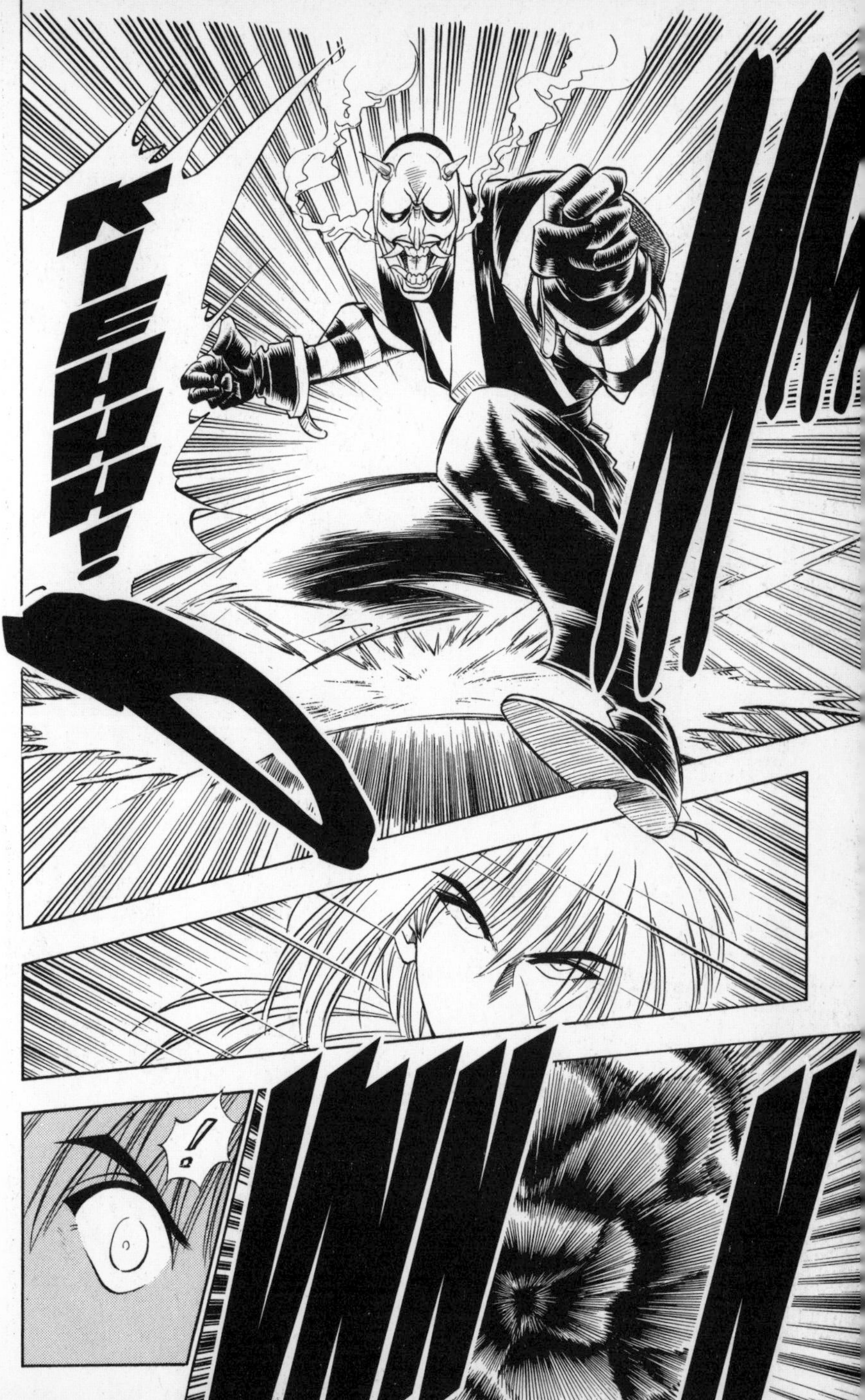
KIEHHH!
!

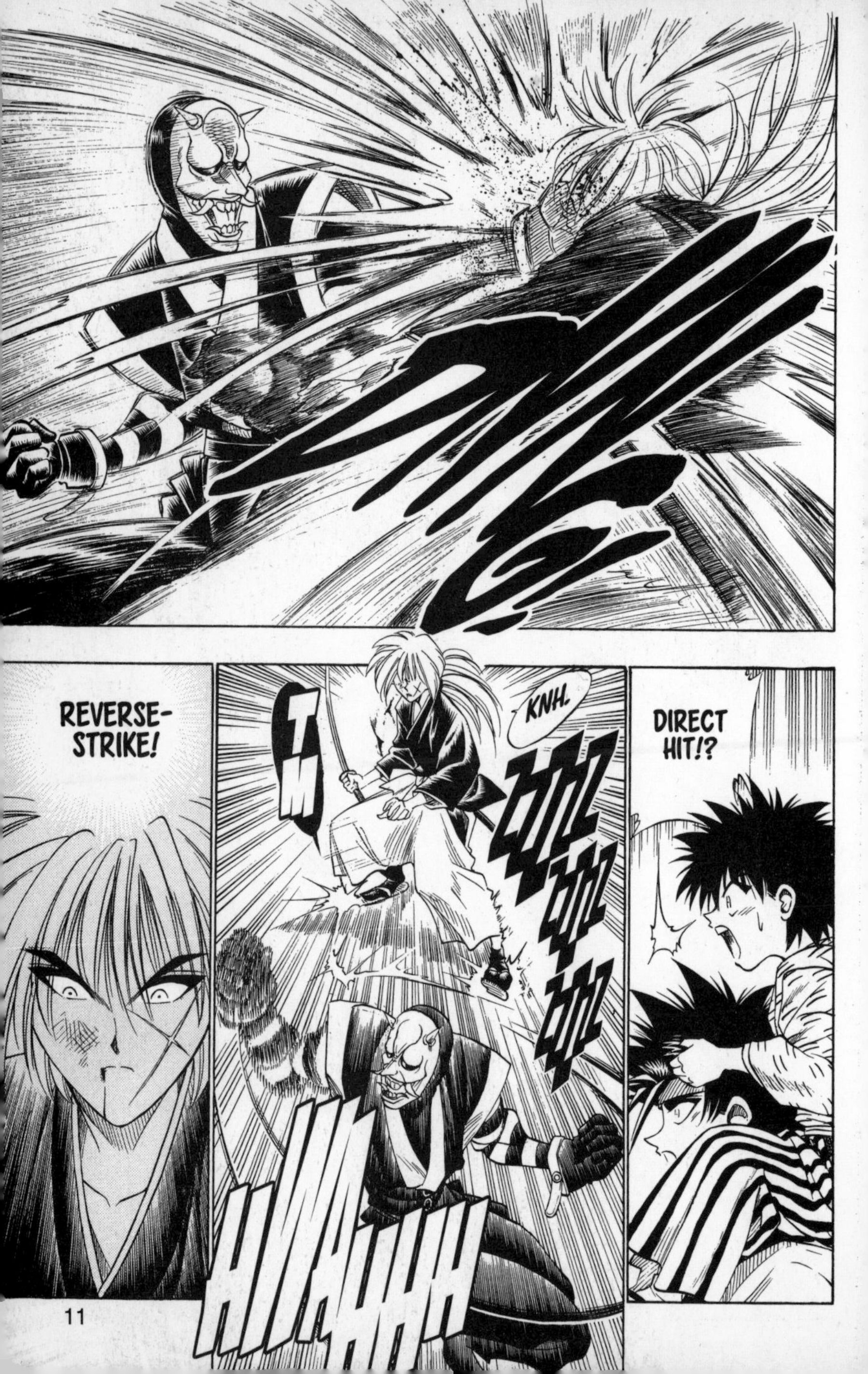
DIRECT HIT!?
KNH.
REVERSE-STRIKE!

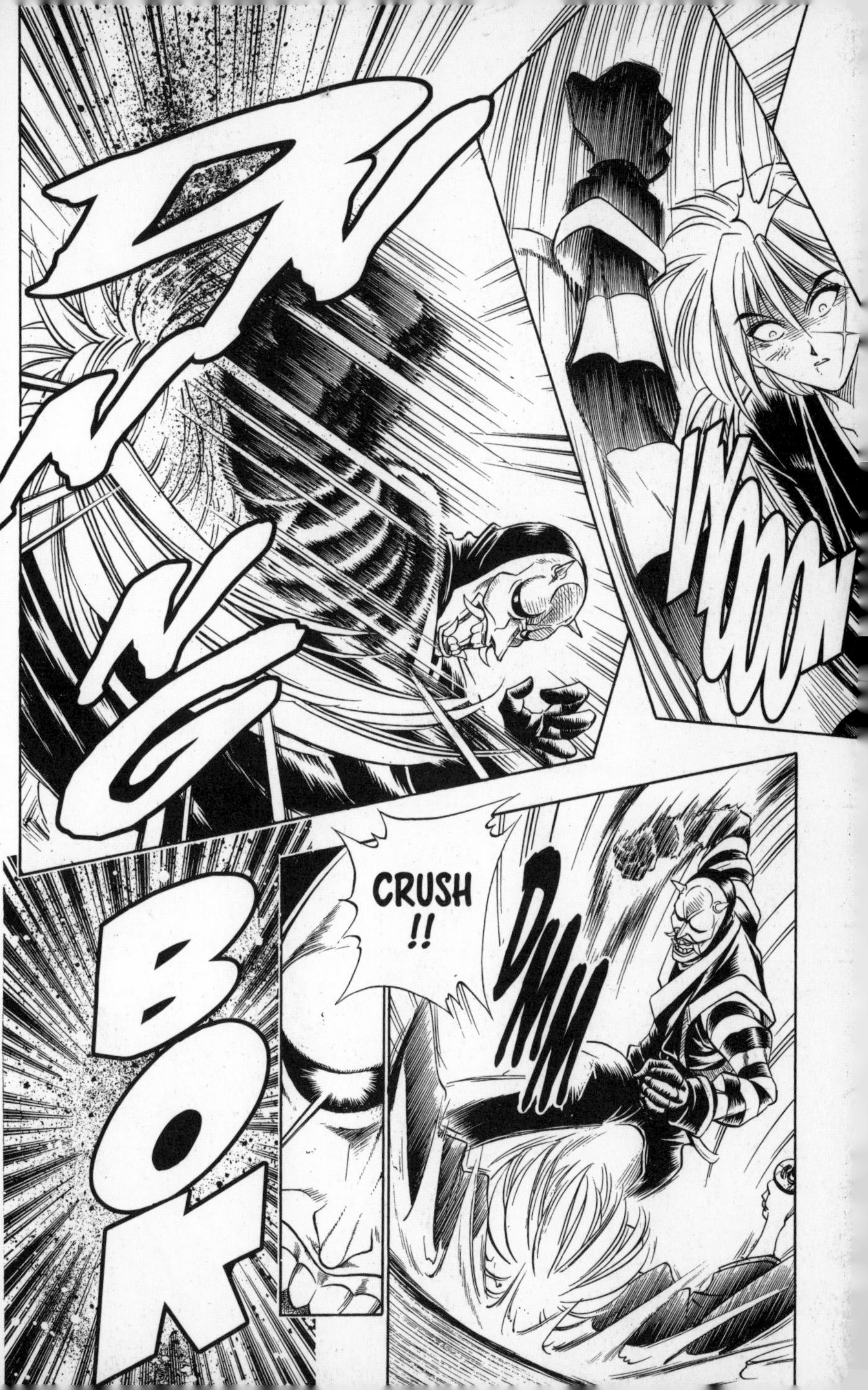
VWOOM
CRUSH !!
BOK

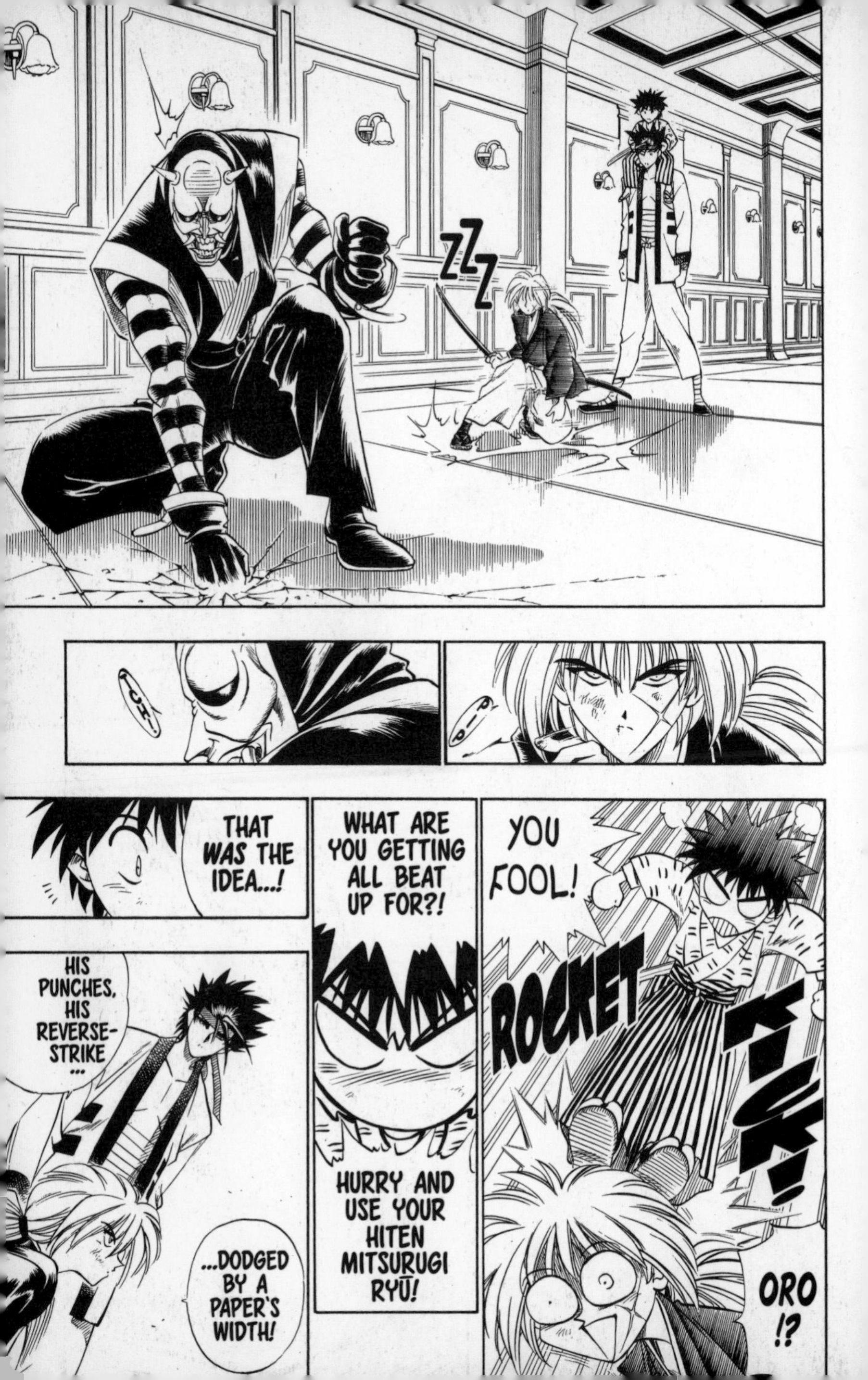
ZZZ
P-P
TCH!
YOU FOOL!
ROCKET
KICK!
ORO!?
WHAT ARE YOU GETTING ALL BEAT UP FOR?!
HURRY AND USE YOUR HITEN MITSURUGI RYŪ!
THAT WAS THE IDEA...!
HIS PUNCHES, HIS REVERSE-STRIKE ...
...DODGED BY A PAPER'S WIDTH!

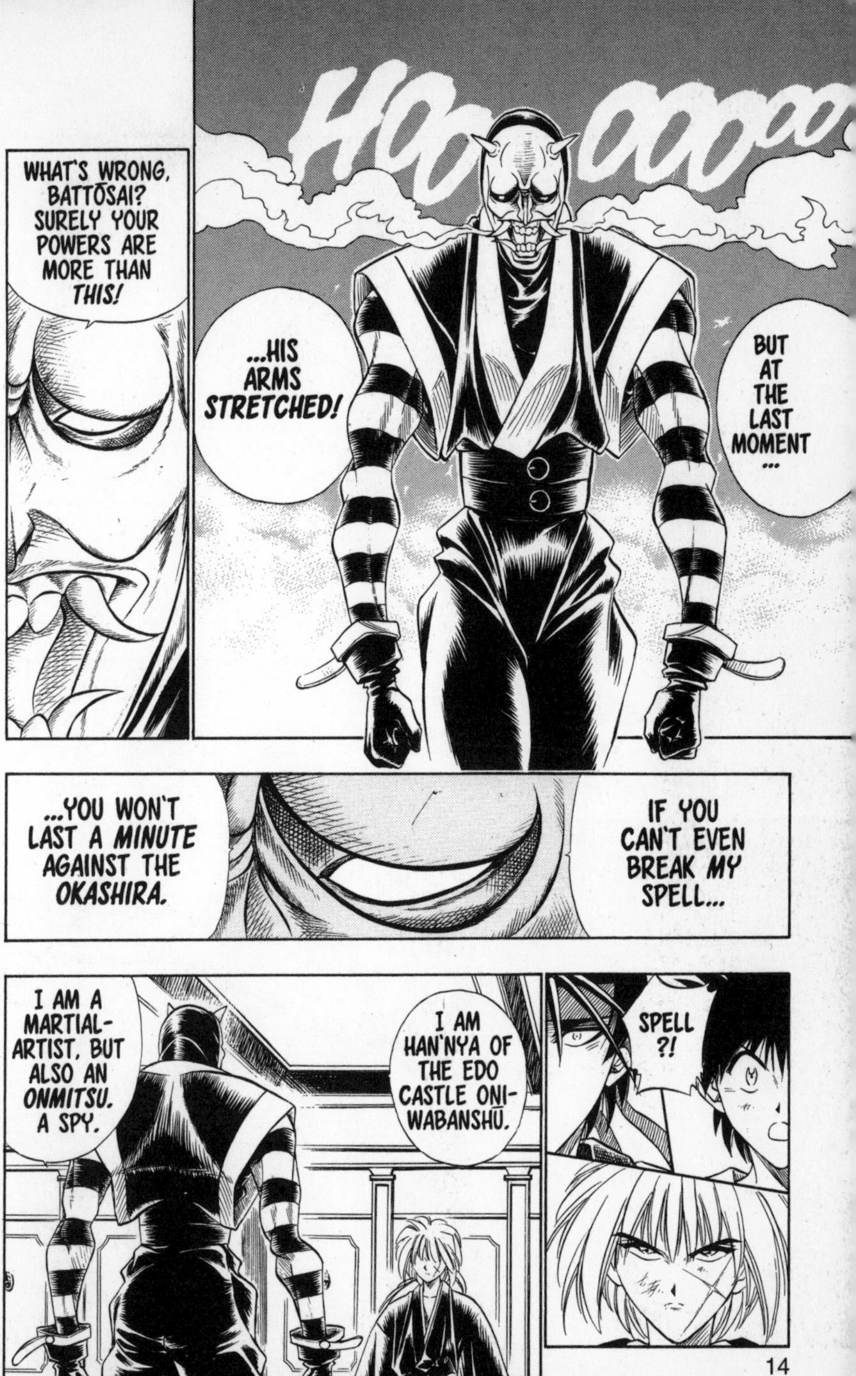
HOOOOOO
BUT AT THE LAST MOMENT...
...HIS ARMS STRETCHED!
WHAT'S WRONG, BATTŌSAI? SURELY YOUR POWERS ARE MORE THAN THIS!
IF YOU CAN'T EVEN BREAK MY SPELL...
...YOU WON'T LAST A MINUTE AGAINST THE OKASHIRA.
SPELL ?!
I AM HAN'NYA OF THE EDO CASTLE ONI-WABANSHŪ.
I AM A MARTIAL-ARTIST, BUT ALSO AN ONMITSU. A SPY.

READ THIS WAY

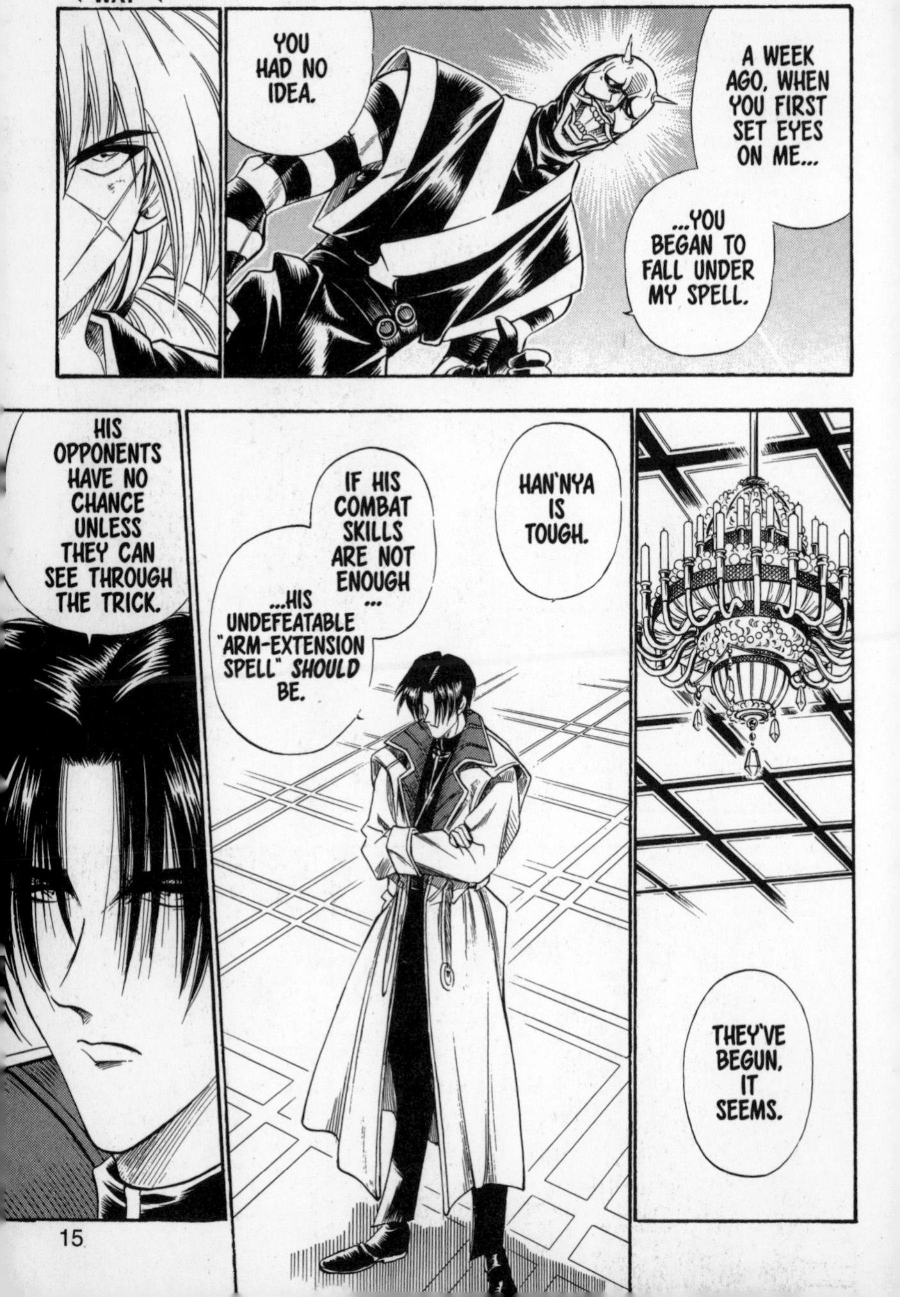

A WEEK AGO, WHEN YOU FIRST SET EYES ON ME...
...YOU BEGAN TO FALL UNDER MY SPELL.
YOU HAD NO IDEA.
THEY'VE BEGUN, IT SEEMS.
HAN'NYA IS TOUGH.
IF HIS COMBAT SKILLS ARE NOT ENOUGH...
...HIS UNDEFEATABLE "ARM-EXTENSION SPELL" SHOULD BE.
HIS OPPONENTS HAVE NO CHANCE UNLESS THEY CAN SEE THROUGH THE TRICK.

READ THIS WAY

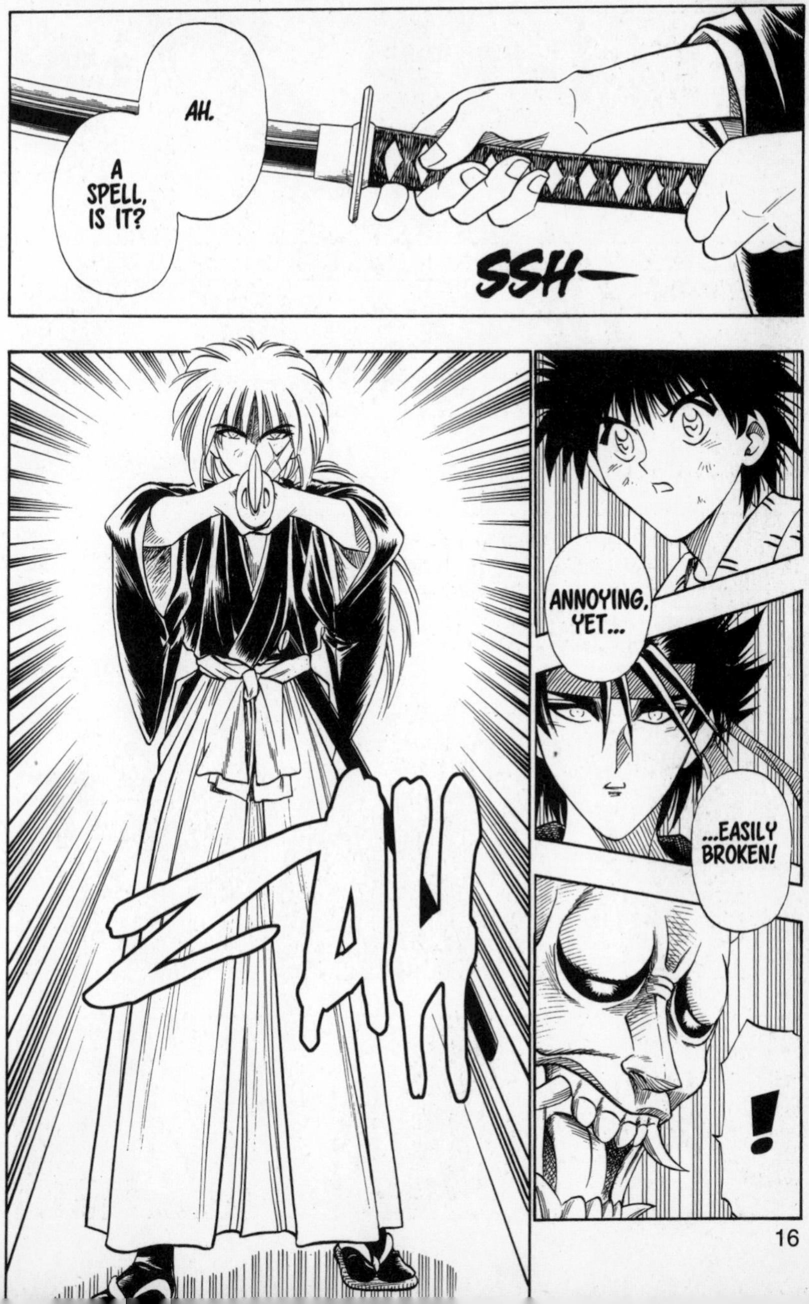
AH.
A SPELL, IS IT?
SSH—
ANNOYING, YET...
...EASILY BROKEN!
!
ZAN

READ THIS WAY

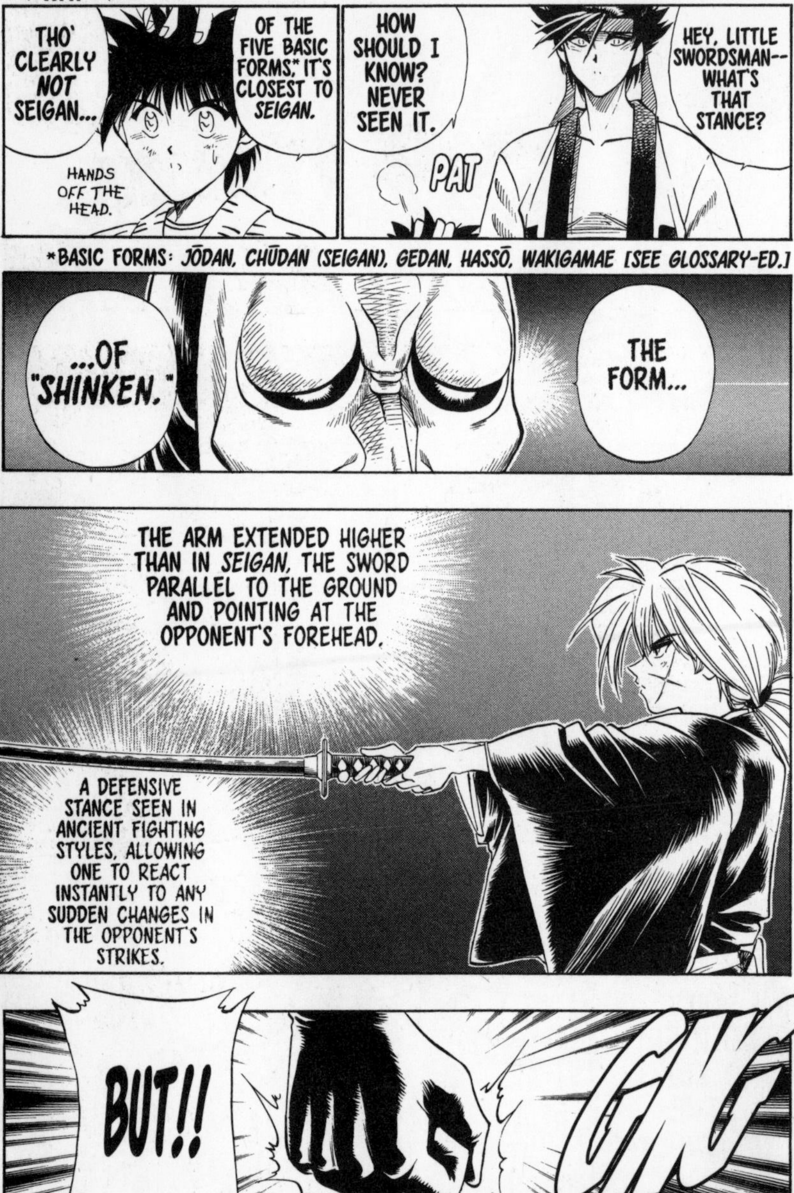
HEY, LITTLE SWORDSMAN-- WHAT'S THAT STANCE?
HOW SHOULD I KNOW? NEVER SEEN IT.
PAT
OF THE FIVE BASIC FORMS,* IT'S CLOSEST TO SEIGAN.
THO' CLEARLY NOT SEIGAN...
HANDS OFF THE HEAD.
*BASIC FORMS: JŌDAN, CHŪDAN (SEIGAN), GEDAN, HASSŌ, WAKIGAMAE [SEE GLOSSARY-ED.]
THE FORM...
...OF "SHINKEN."
THE ARM EXTENDED HIGHER THAN IN SEIGAN, THE SWORD PARALLEL TO THE GROUND AND POINTING AT THE OPPONENT'S FOREHEAD.
A DEFENSIVE STANCE SEEN IN ANCIENT FIGHTING STYLES, ALLOWING ONE TO REACT INSTANTLY TO ANY SUDDEN CHANGES IN THE OPPONENT'S STRIKES.
GN
BUT!!

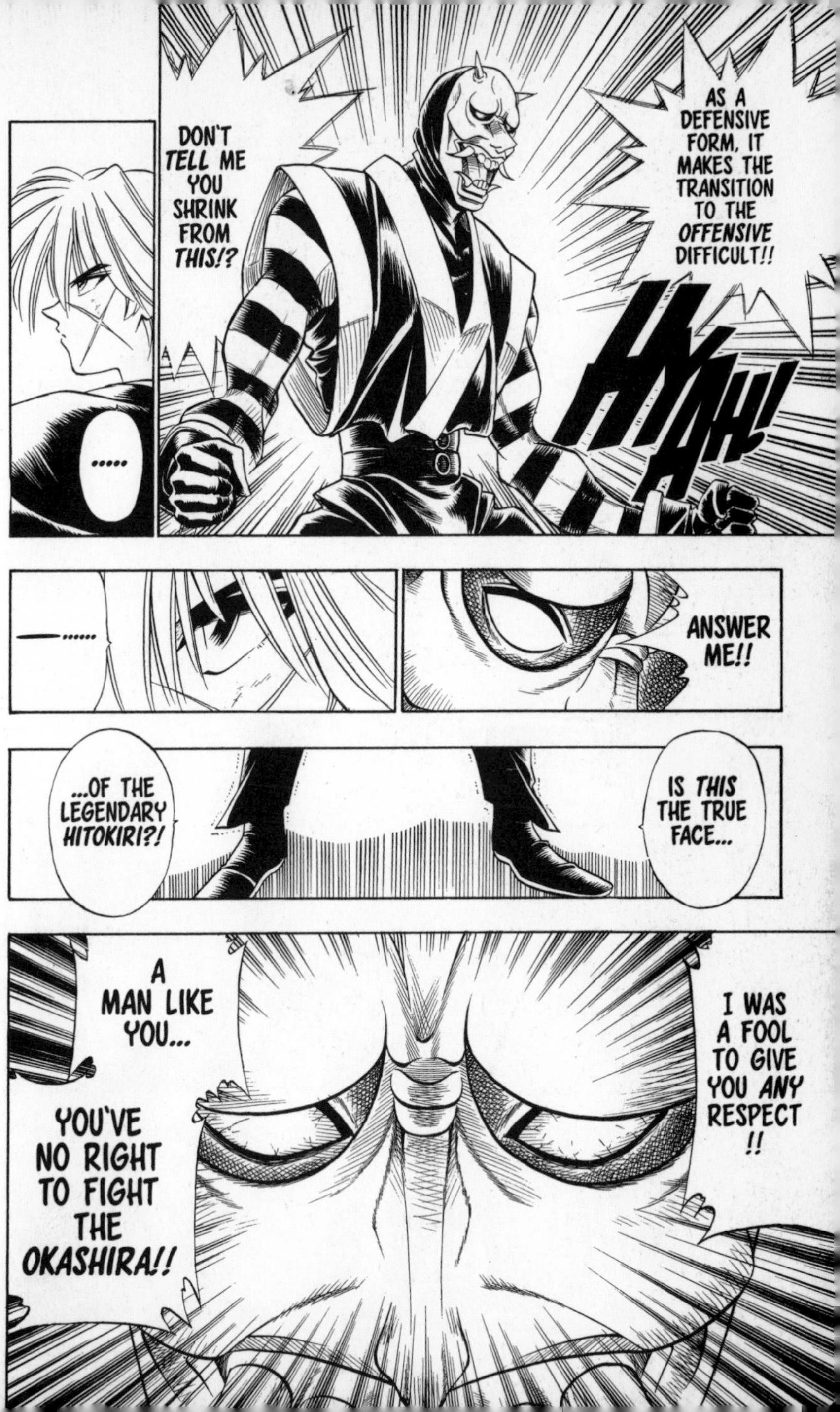
AS A DEFENSIVE FORM, IT MAKES THE TRANSITION TO THE OFFENSIVE DIFFICULT!!
HYAH!!
DON'T TELL ME YOU SHRINK FROM THIS!?
......
ANSWER ME!!
—......
IS THIS THE TRUE FACE...
...OF THE LEGENDARY HITOKIRI?!
I WAS A FOOL TO GIVE YOU ANY RESPECT!!
A MAN LIKE YOU...
YOU'VE NO RIGHT TO FIGHT THE OKASHIRA!!

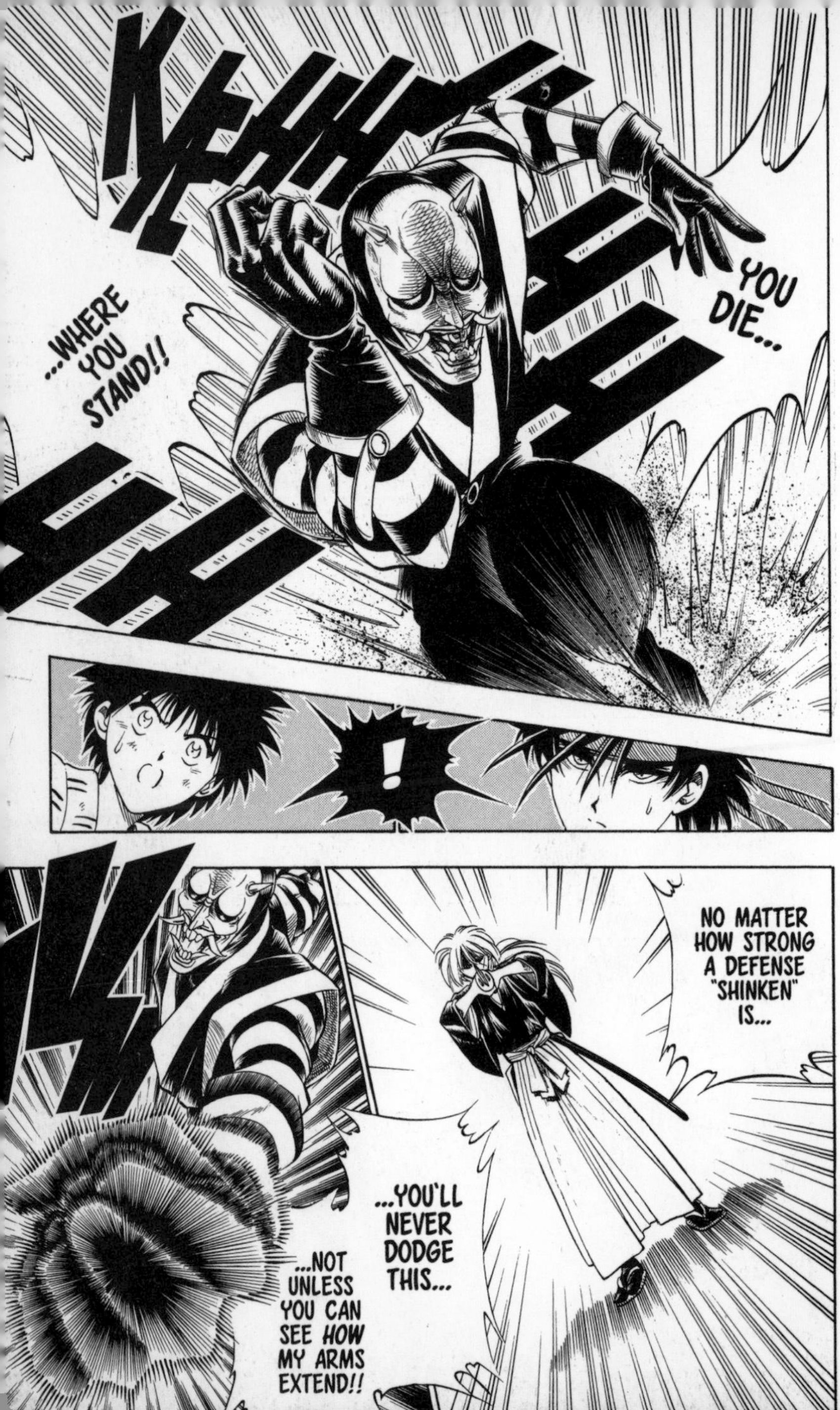
YOU DIE...
...WHERE YOU STAND!!
!
NO MATTER HOW STRONG A DEFENSE "SHINKEN" IS...
...YOU'LL NEVER DODGE THIS...
...NOT UNLESS YOU CAN SEE *HOW* MY ARMS EXTEND!!

READ THIS WAY

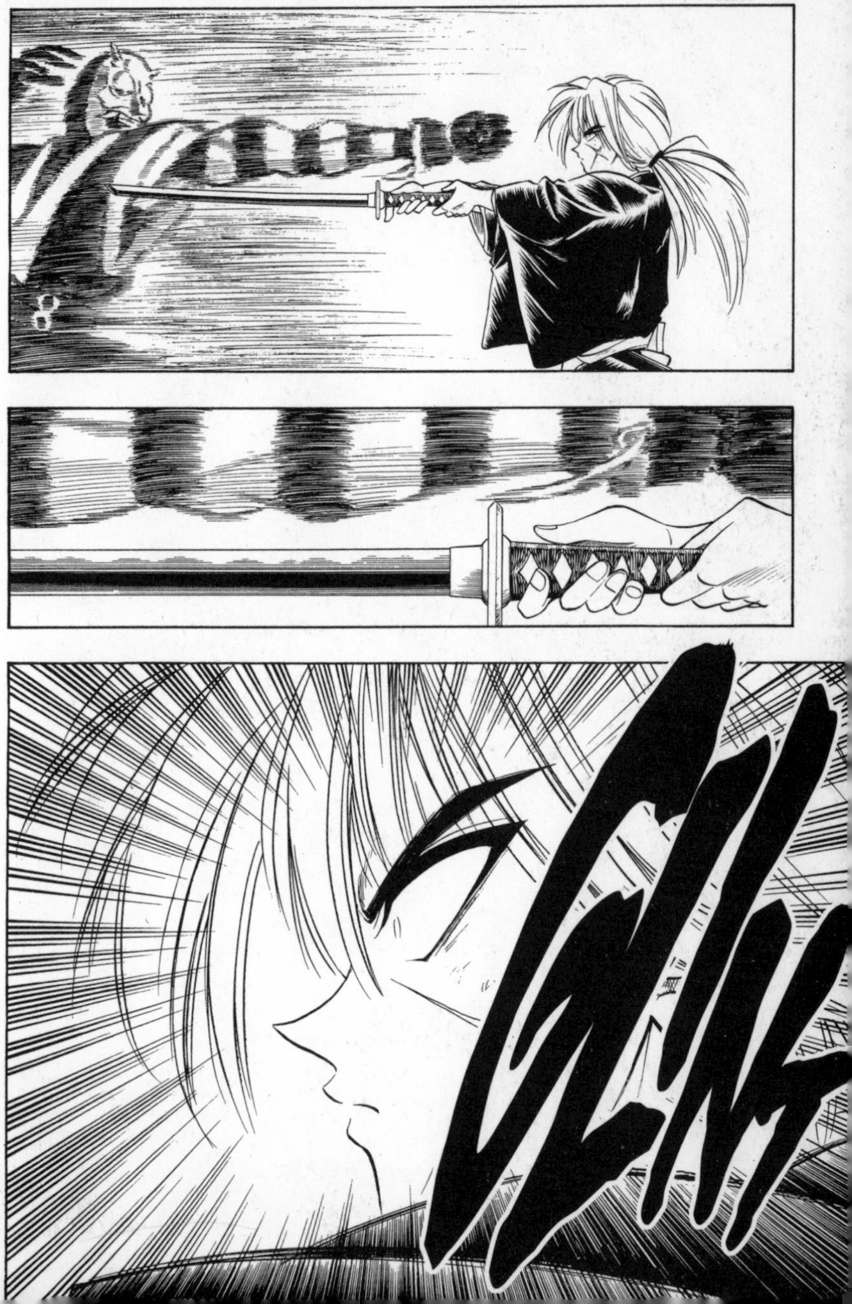

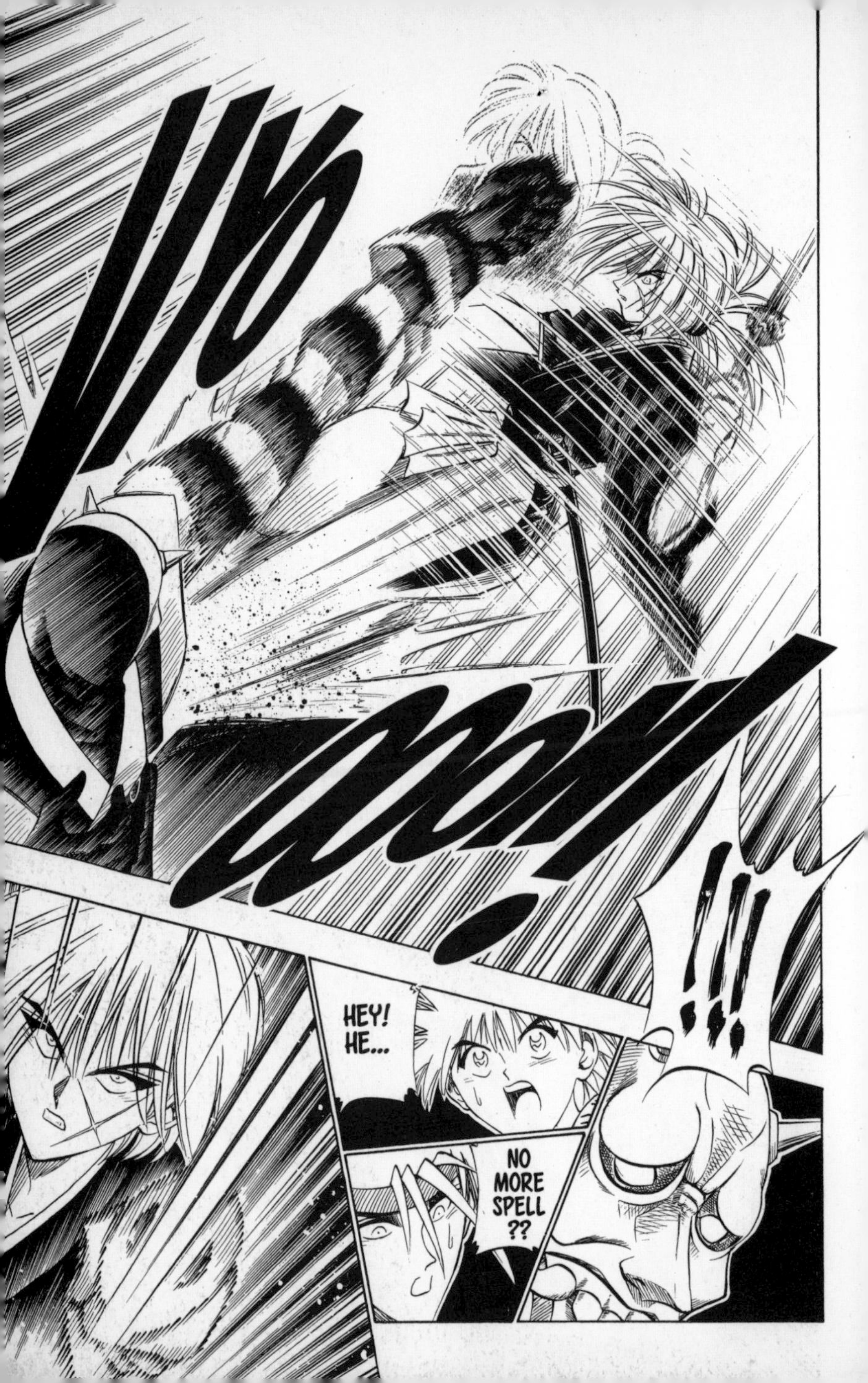
HEY! HE...
NO MORE SPELL ??

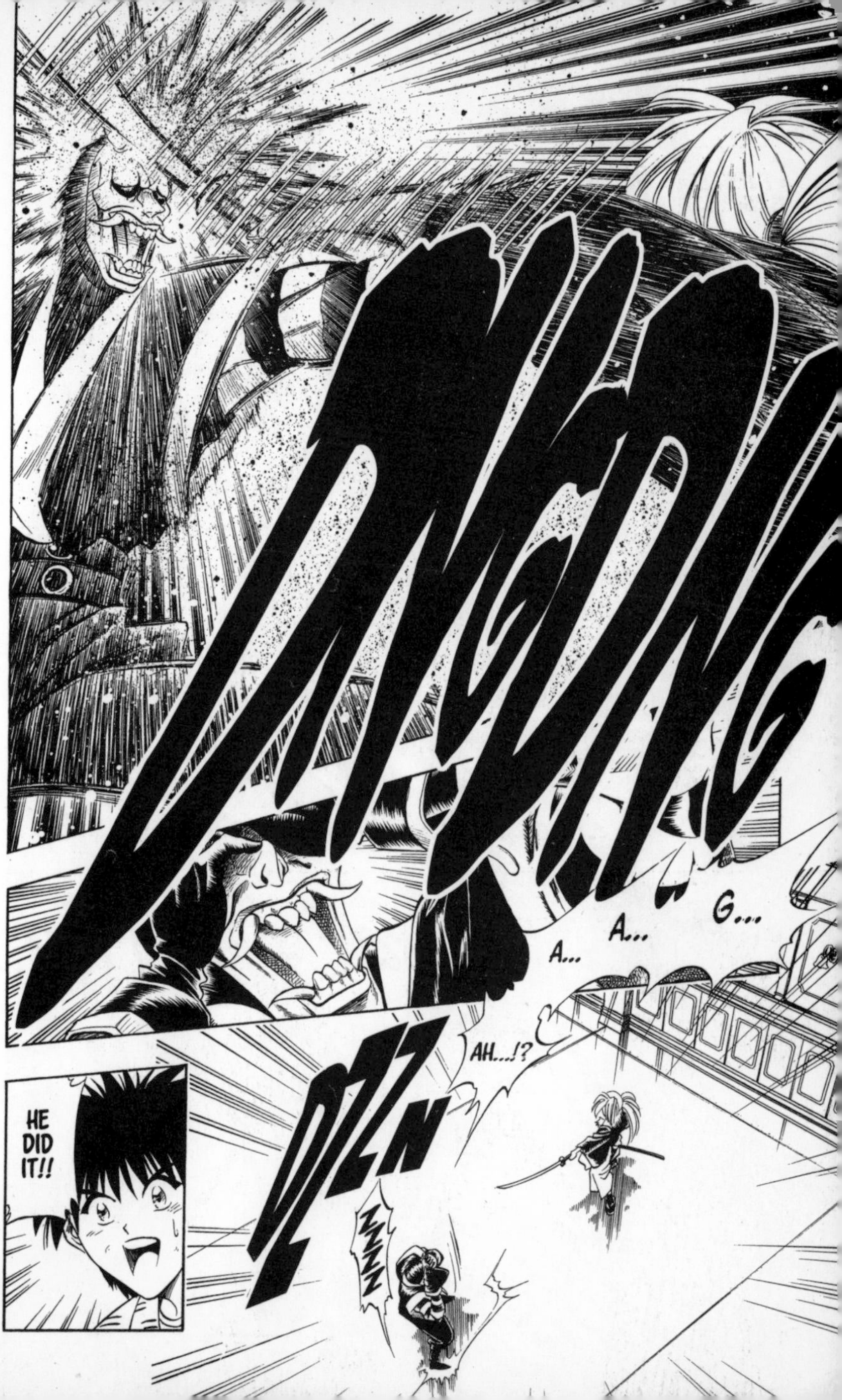
G...
A...
A...
AH...!?
HE DID IT!!

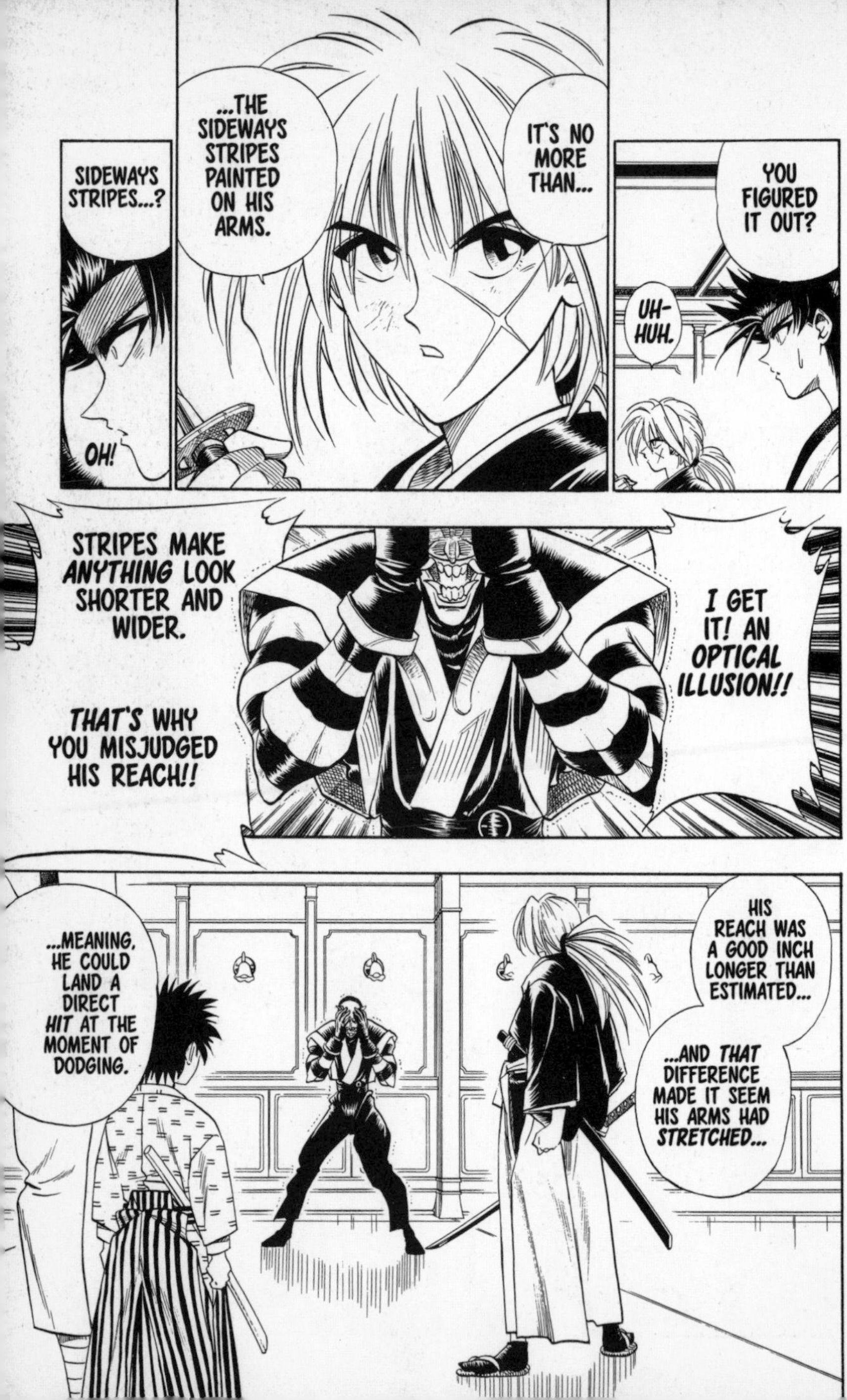
YOU FIGURED IT OUT?
UH-HUH.
IT'S NO MORE THAN...
...THE SIDEWAYS STRIPES PAINTED ON HIS ARMS.
SIDEWAYS STRIPES...?
OH!
I GET IT! AN OPTICAL ILLUSION!!
STRIPES MAKE *ANYTHING* LOOK SHORTER AND WIDER.
*THAT'S* WHY YOU MISJUDGED HIS REACH!!
HIS REACH WAS A GOOD INCH LONGER THAN ESTIMATED...
...AND *THAT* DIFFERENCE MADE IT SEEM HIS ARMS HAD *STRETCHED*...
...MEANING, HE COULD LAND A DIRECT *HIT* AT THE MOMENT OF DODGING.

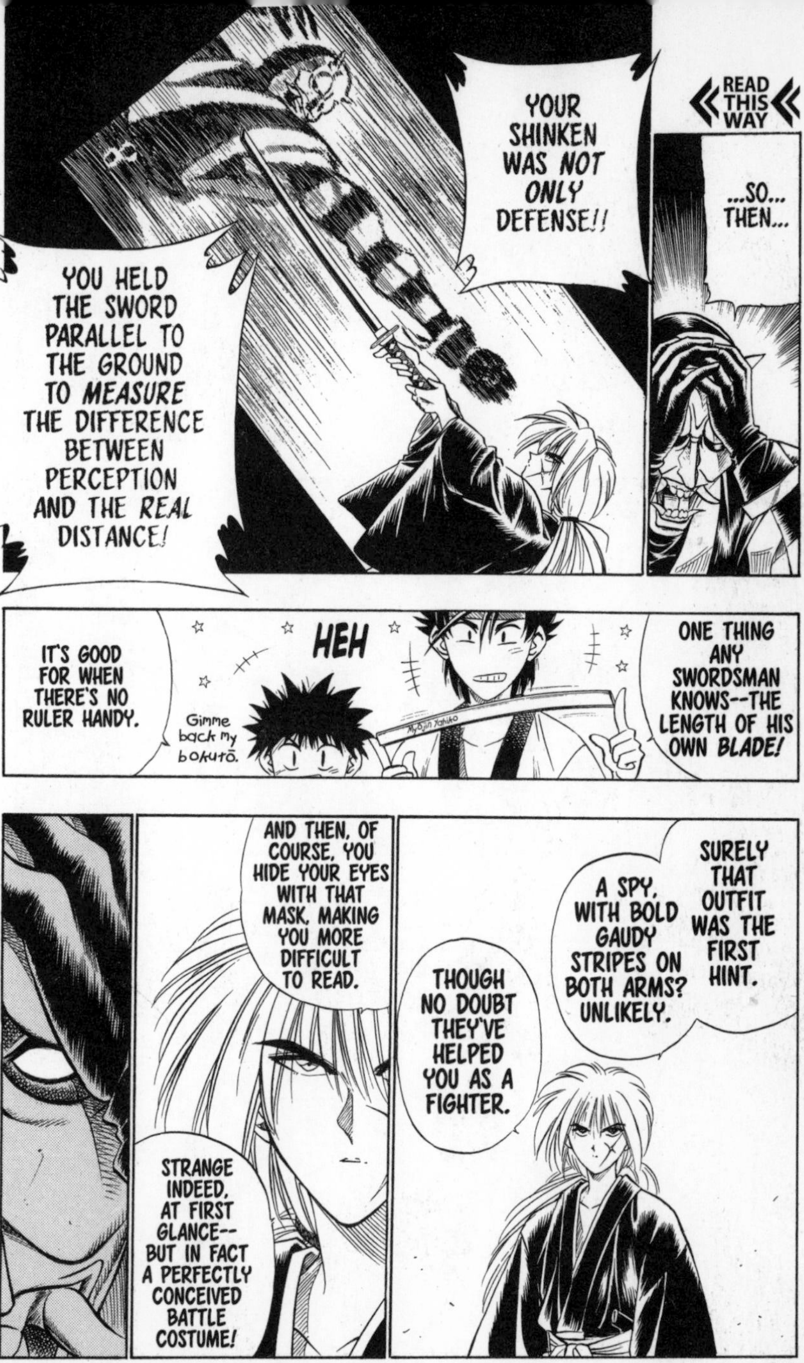

READ THIS WAY
...SO... THEN...
YOUR SHINKEN WAS NOT ONLY DEFENSE!!
YOU HELD THE SWORD PARALLEL TO THE GROUND TO MEASURE THE DIFFERENCE BETWEEN PERCEPTION AND THE REAL DISTANCE!
ONE THING ANY SWORDSMAN KNOWS--THE LENGTH OF HIS OWN BLADE!
HEH
Gimme back my bokutō.
IT'S GOOD FOR WHEN THERE'S NO RULER HANDY.
SURELY THAT OUTFIT WAS THE FIRST HINT.
A SPY, WITH BOLD GAUDY STRIPES ON BOTH ARMS? UNLIKELY.
THOUGH NO DOUBT THEY'VE HELPED YOU AS A FIGHTER.
AND THEN, OF COURSE, YOU HIDE YOUR EYES WITH THAT MASK, MAKING YOU MORE DIFFICULT TO READ.
STRANGE INDEED, AT FIRST GLANCE--BUT IN FACT A PERFECTLY CONCEIVED BATTLE COSTUME!

READ THIS WAY

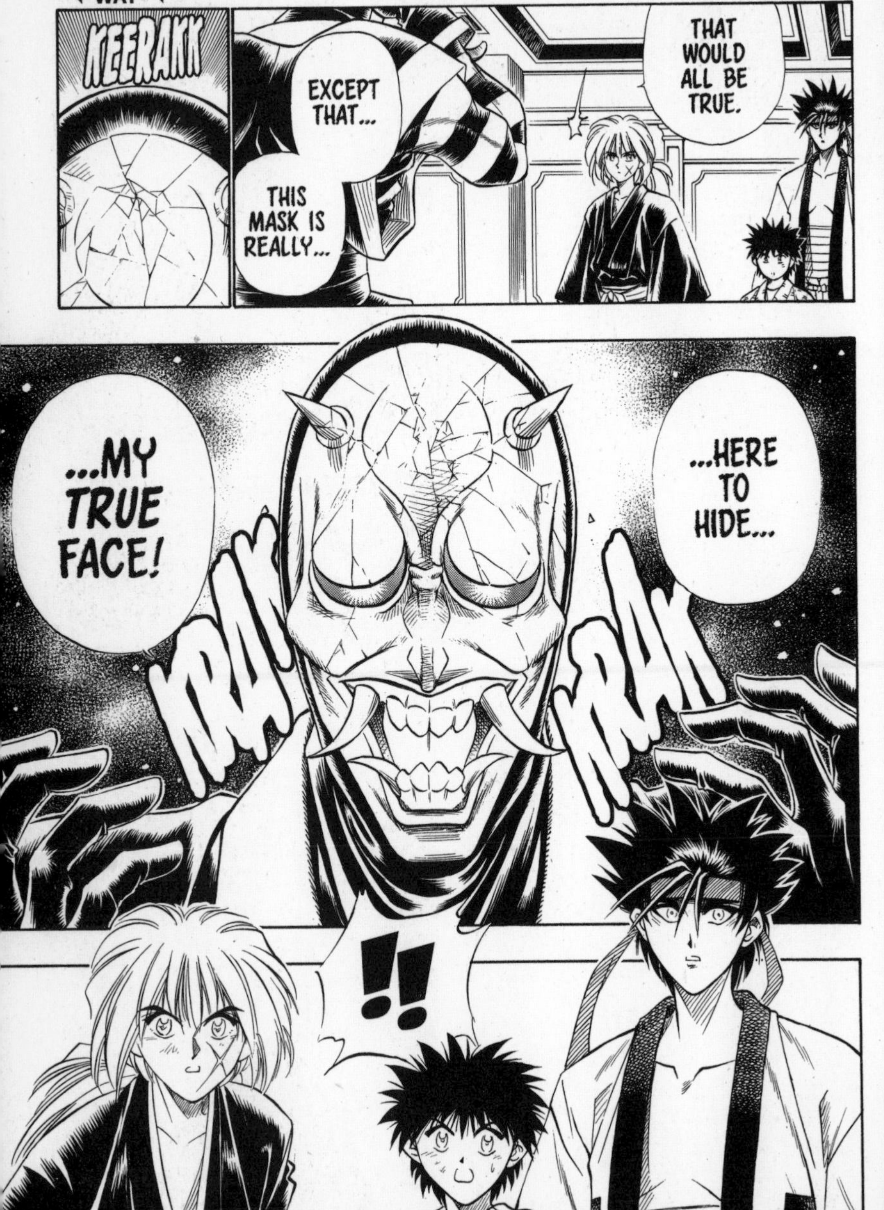

THAT WOULD ALL BE TRUE.
EXCEPT THAT...
THIS MASK IS REALLY...
KEERAKK
...HERE TO HIDE...
...MY TRUE FACE!
KRAK
KRAK
!!

Rurouni Kenshin

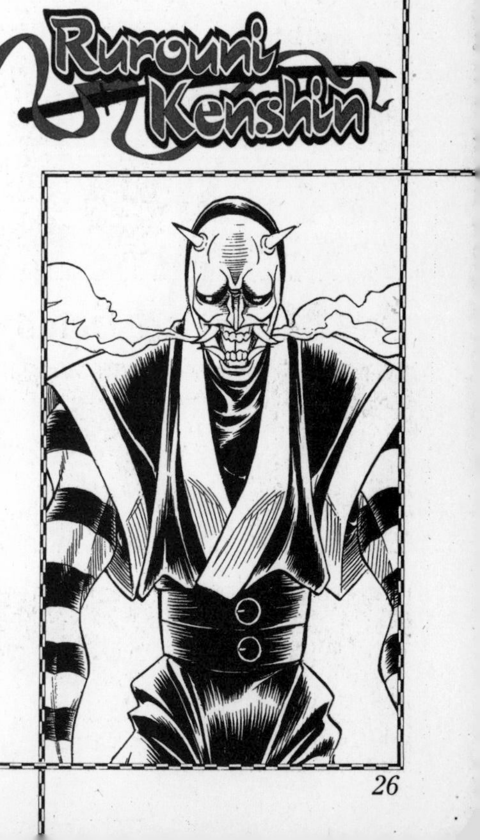

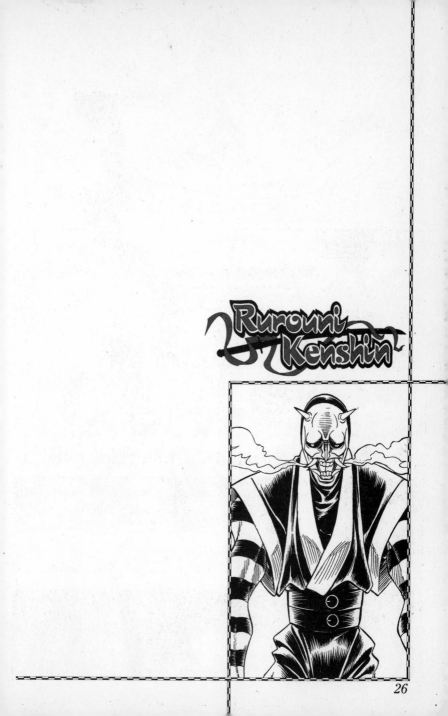

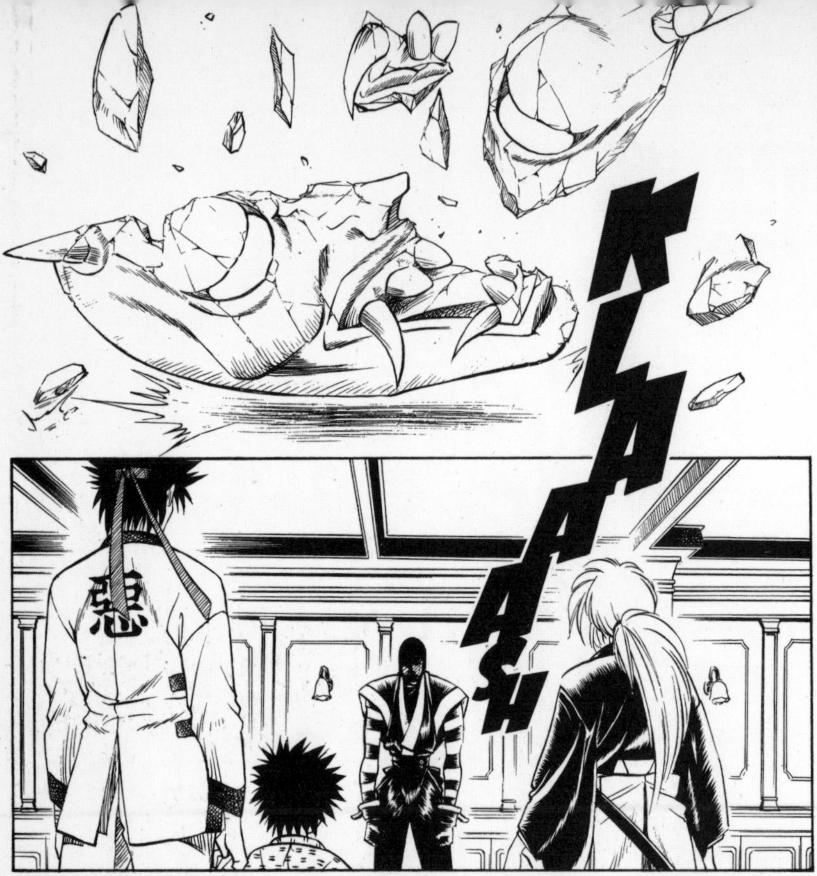

## Act 24 Savage Han'nya, Honorable Shikijō

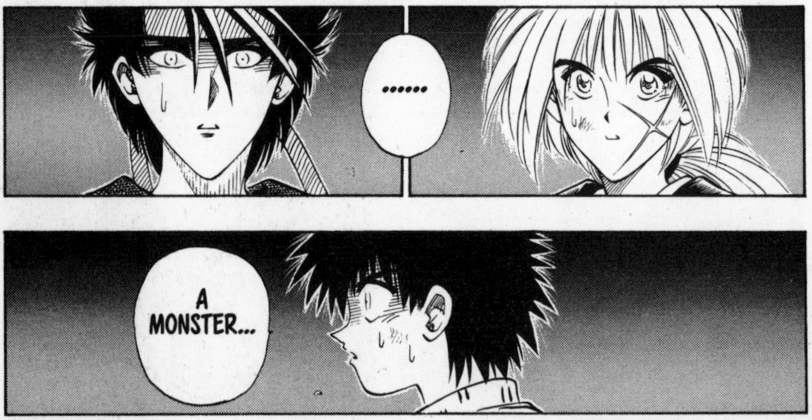
......
A MONSTER...

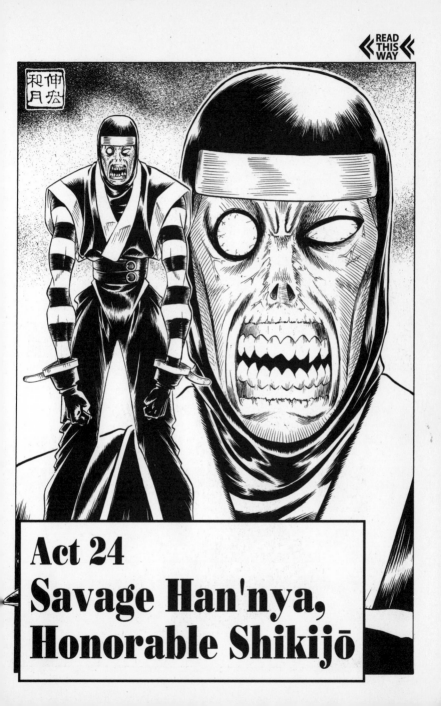

# Act 24
# Savage Han'nya,
# Honorable Shikijō

READ THIS WAY

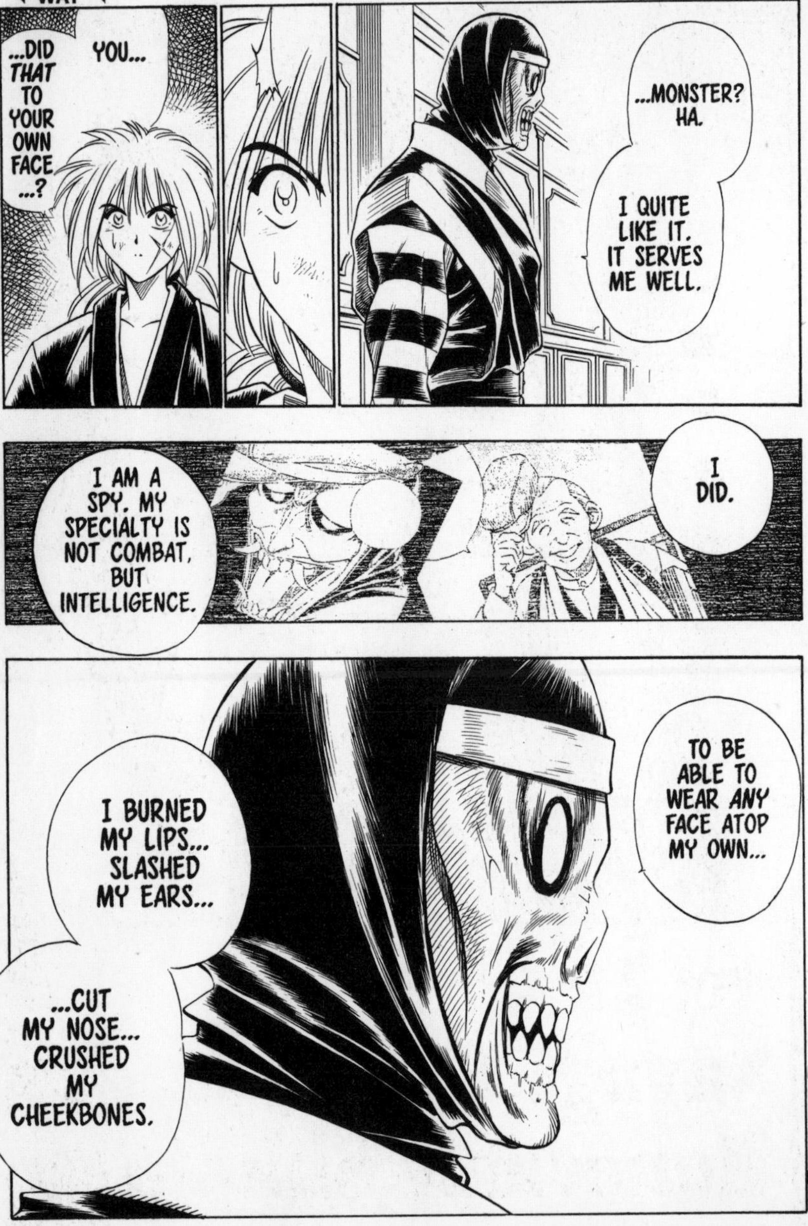

...MONSTER? HA.
I QUITE LIKE IT. IT SERVES ME WELL.
YOU...
...DID *THAT* TO YOUR OWN FACE ...?
I DID.
I AM A SPY. MY SPECIALTY IS NOT COMBAT, BUT INTELLIGENCE.
TO BE ABLE TO WEAR *ANY* FACE ATOP MY OWN...
I BURNED MY LIPS... SLASHED MY EARS...
...CUT MY NOSE... CRUSHED MY CHEEKBONES.

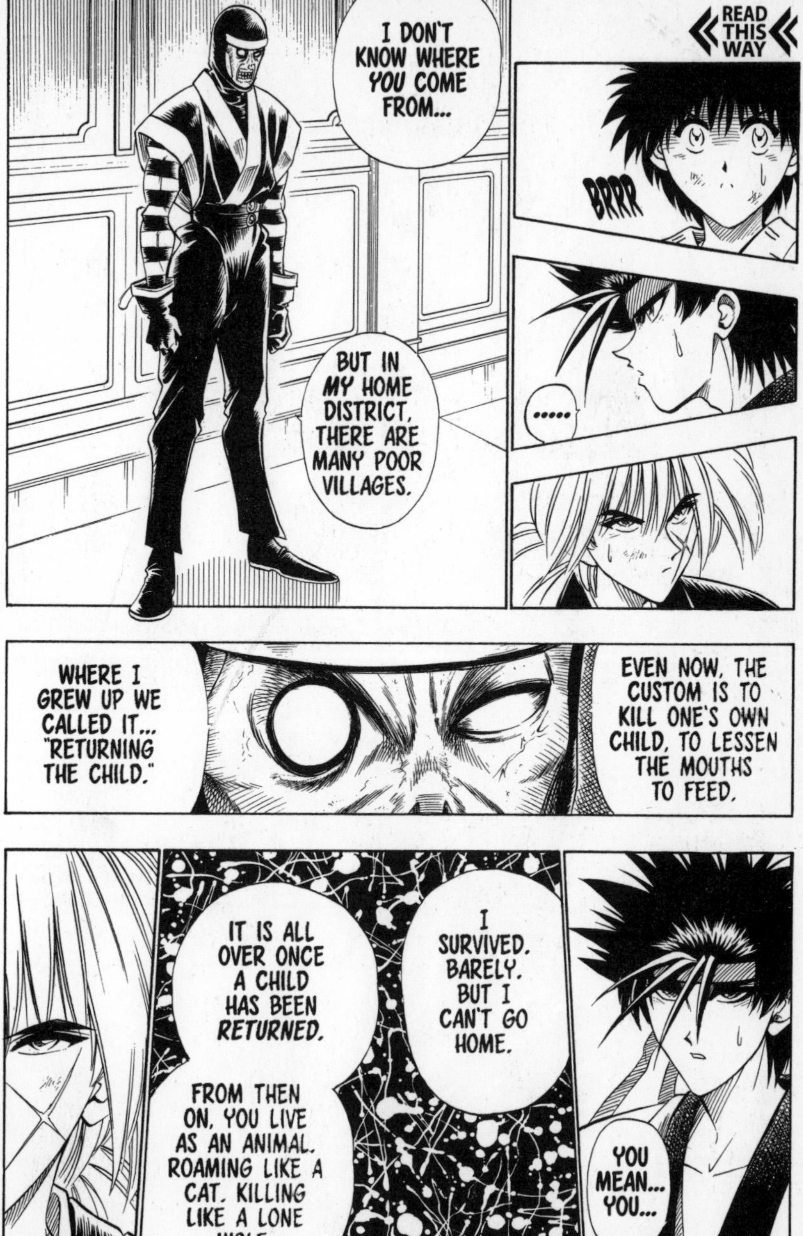
READ THIS WAY
BRRR
.....
I DON'T KNOW WHERE *YOU* COME FROM...
BUT IN *MY* HOME DISTRICT, THERE ARE MANY POOR VILLAGES.
EVEN NOW, THE CUSTOM IS TO KILL ONE'S OWN CHILD, TO LESSEN THE MOUTHS TO FEED.
WHERE I GREW UP WE CALLED IT... "RETURNING THE CHILD."
YOU MEAN... YOU...
I SURVIVED. BARELY. BUT I CAN'T GO HOME.
IT IS ALL OVER ONCE A CHILD HAS BEEN *RETURNED.*
FROM THEN ON, YOU LIVE AS AN ANIMAL. ROAMING LIKE A CAT. KILLING LIKE A LONE WOLF.

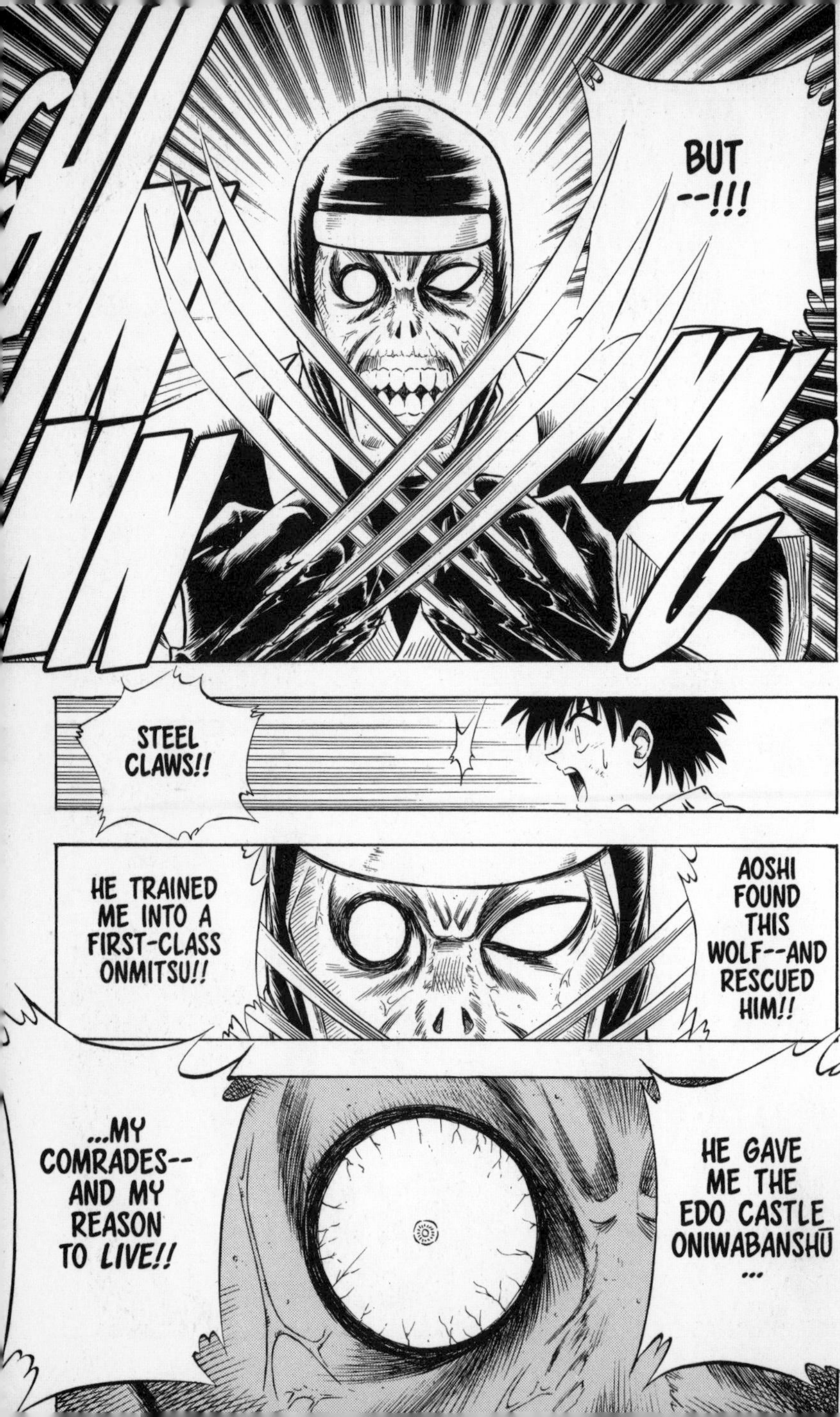
BUT --!!!
STEEL CLAWS!!
AOSHI FOUND THIS WOLF--AND RESCUED HIM!!
HE TRAINED ME INTO A FIRST-CLASS ONMITSU!!
HE GAVE ME THE EDO CASTLE ONIWABANSHŪ ...
...MY COMRADES-- AND MY REASON TO LIVE!!

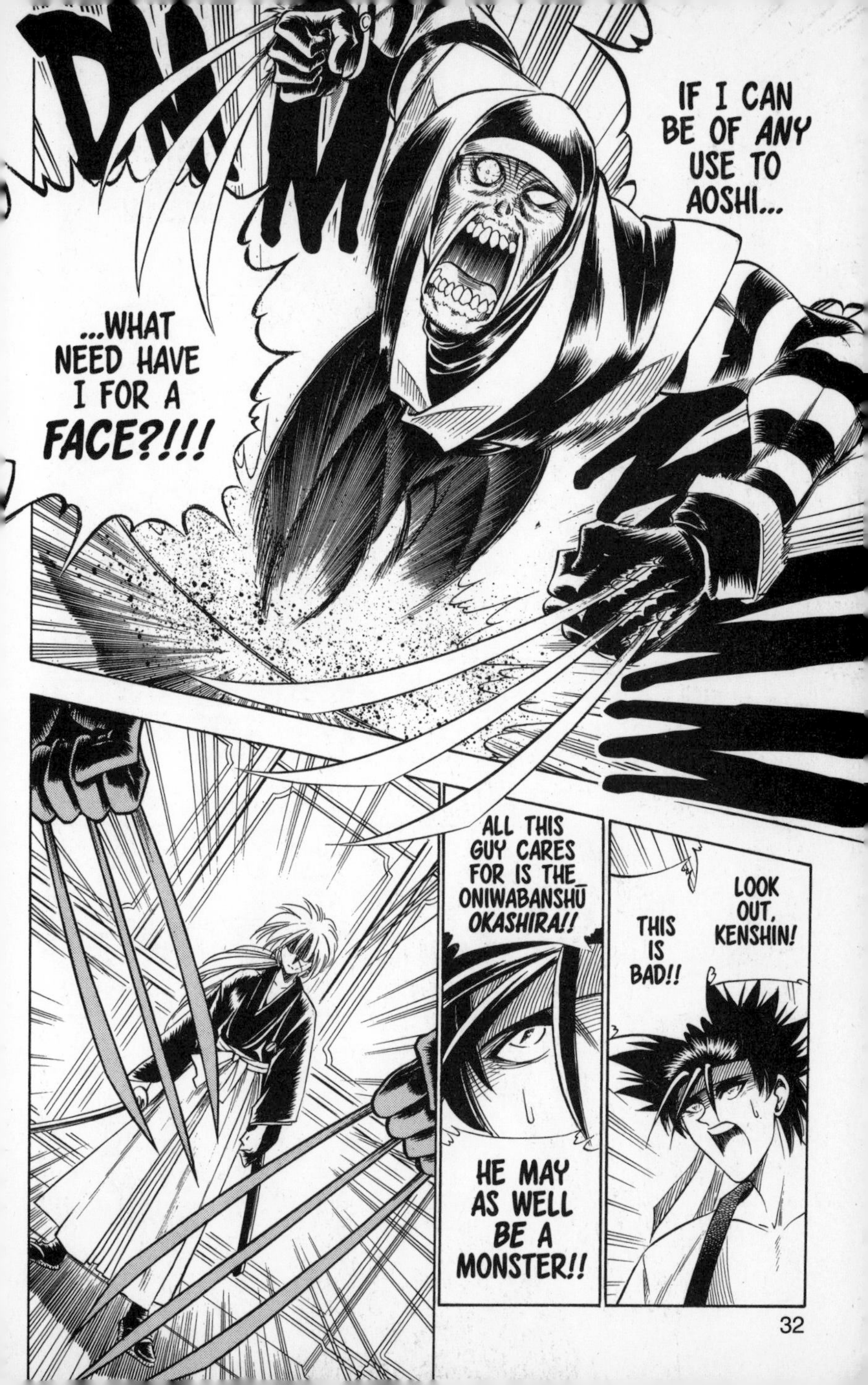
IF I CAN BE OF ANY USE TO AOSHI...
...WHAT NEED HAVE I FOR A FACE?!!!
LOOK OUT, KENSHIN!
THIS IS BAD!!
ALL THIS GUY CARES FOR IS THE ONIWABANSHŪ OKASHIRA!!
HE MAY AS WELL BE A MONSTER!!

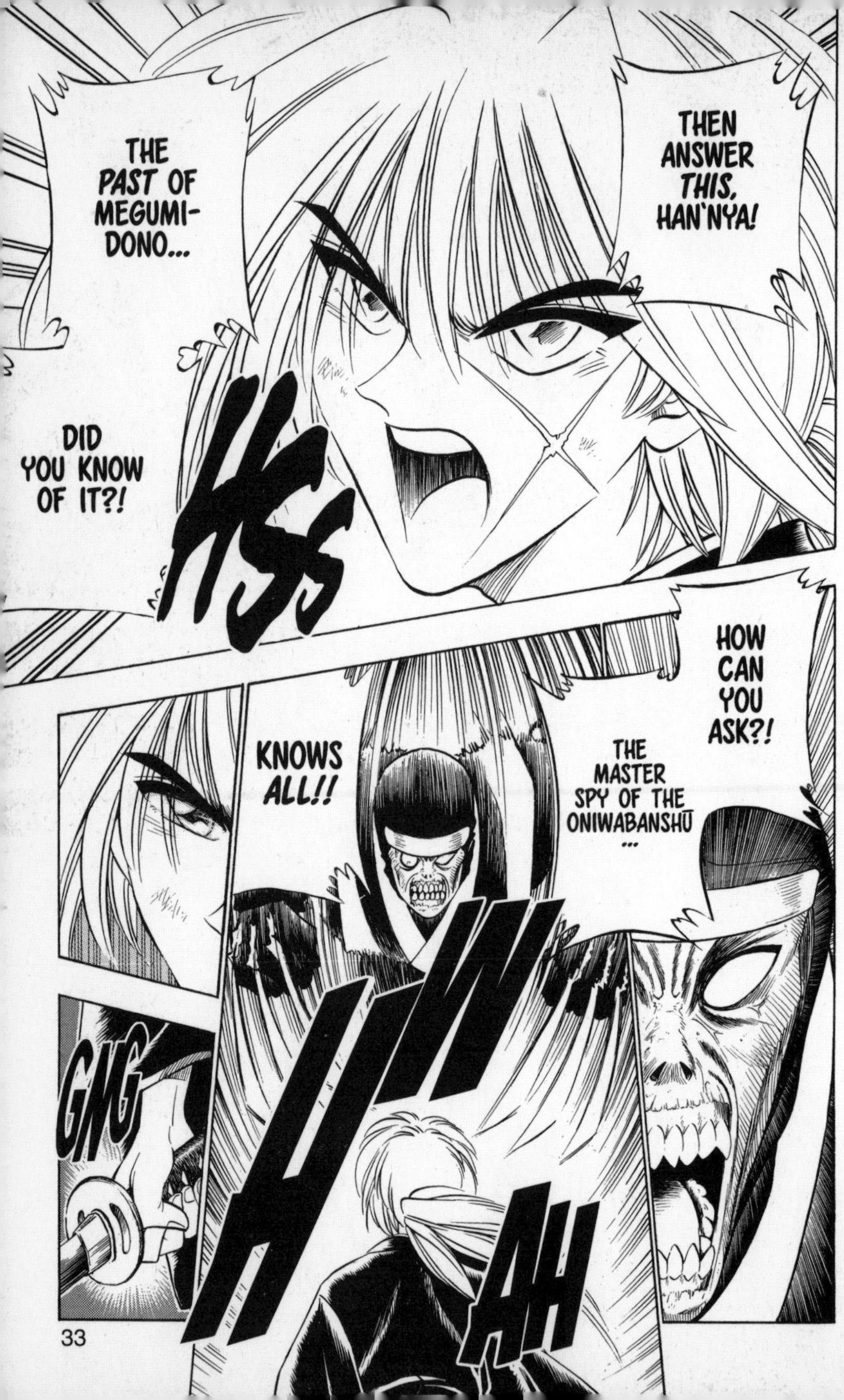
THEN ANSWER THIS, HAN'NYA!
THE PAST OF MEGUMI-DONO...
DID YOU KNOW OF IT?!
HSS
HOW CAN YOU ASK?!
THE MASTER SPY OF THE ONIWABANSHŪ ...
KNOWS ALL!!
HAH
GNG

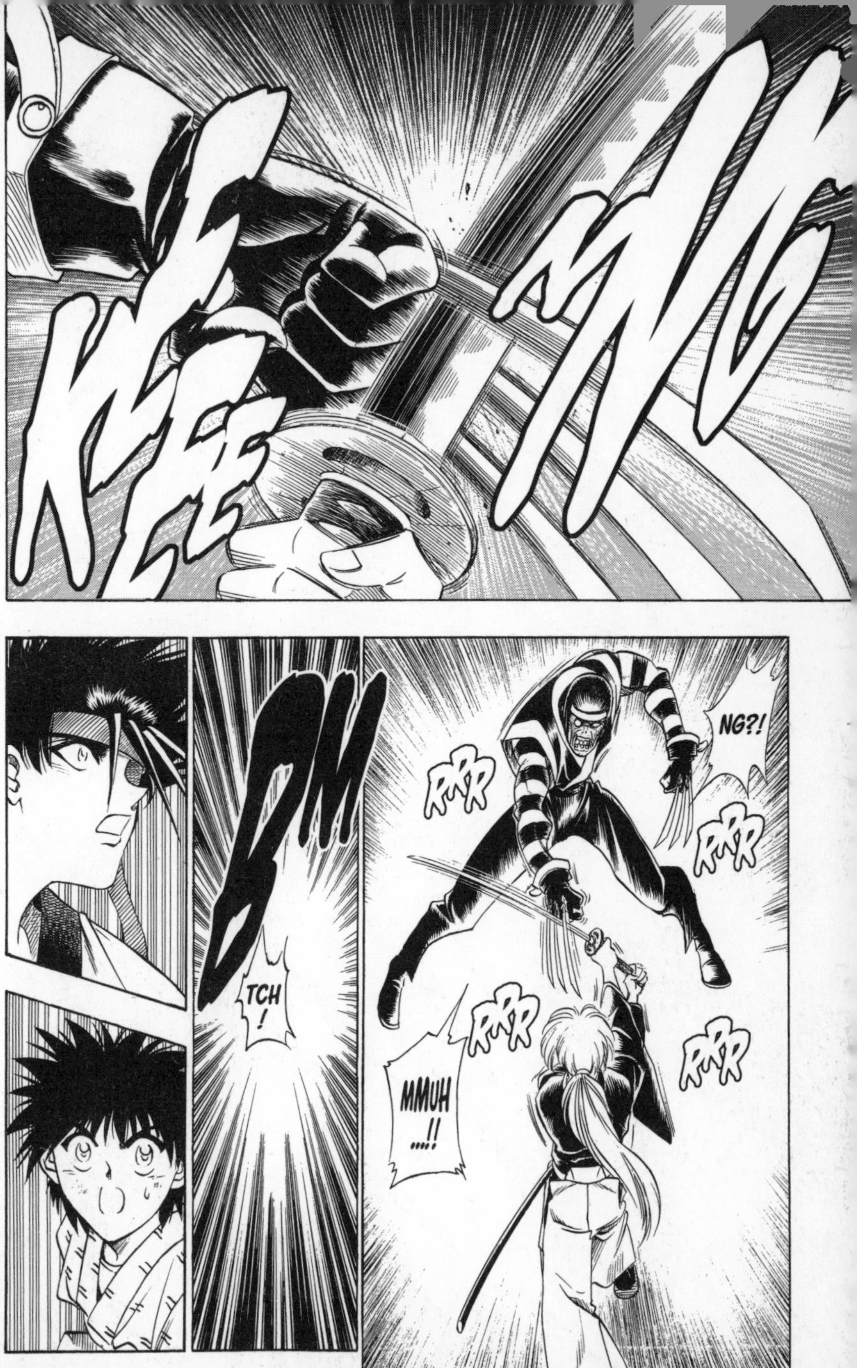
NG?!
RRR
RRR
RRR
RRR
MMUH ...!!
TCH!

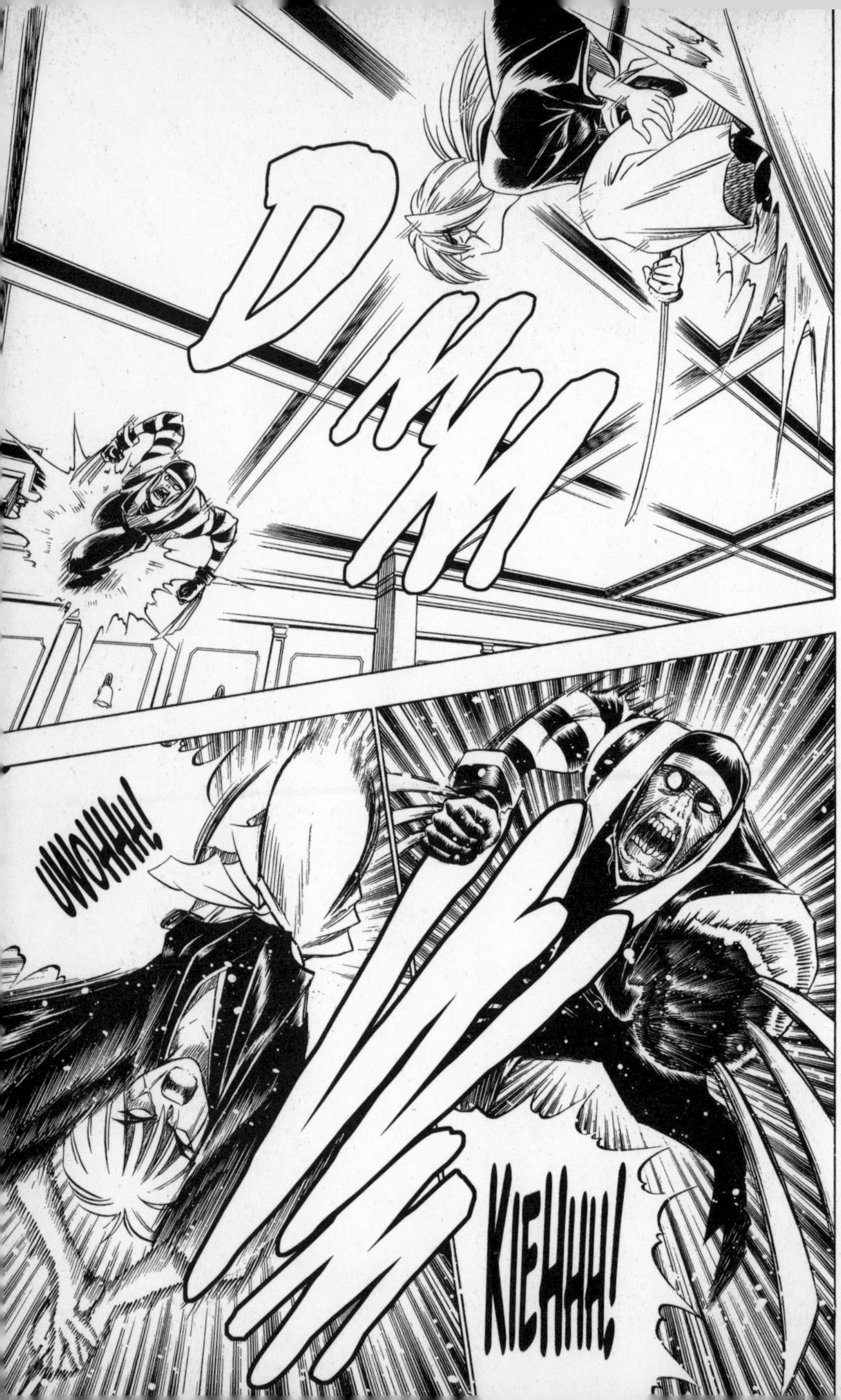

DMM
UWOHHH!
KIEHHH!

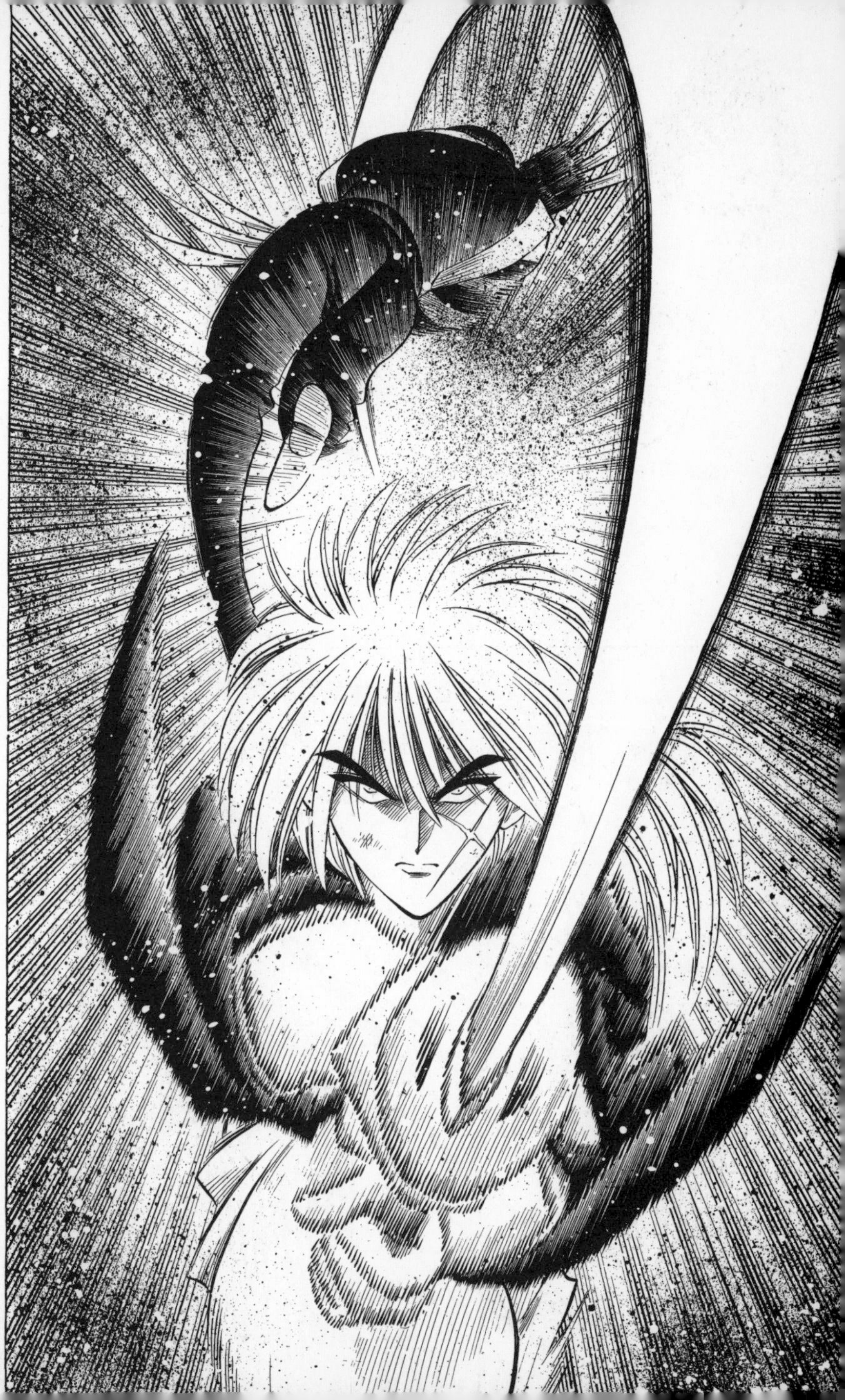

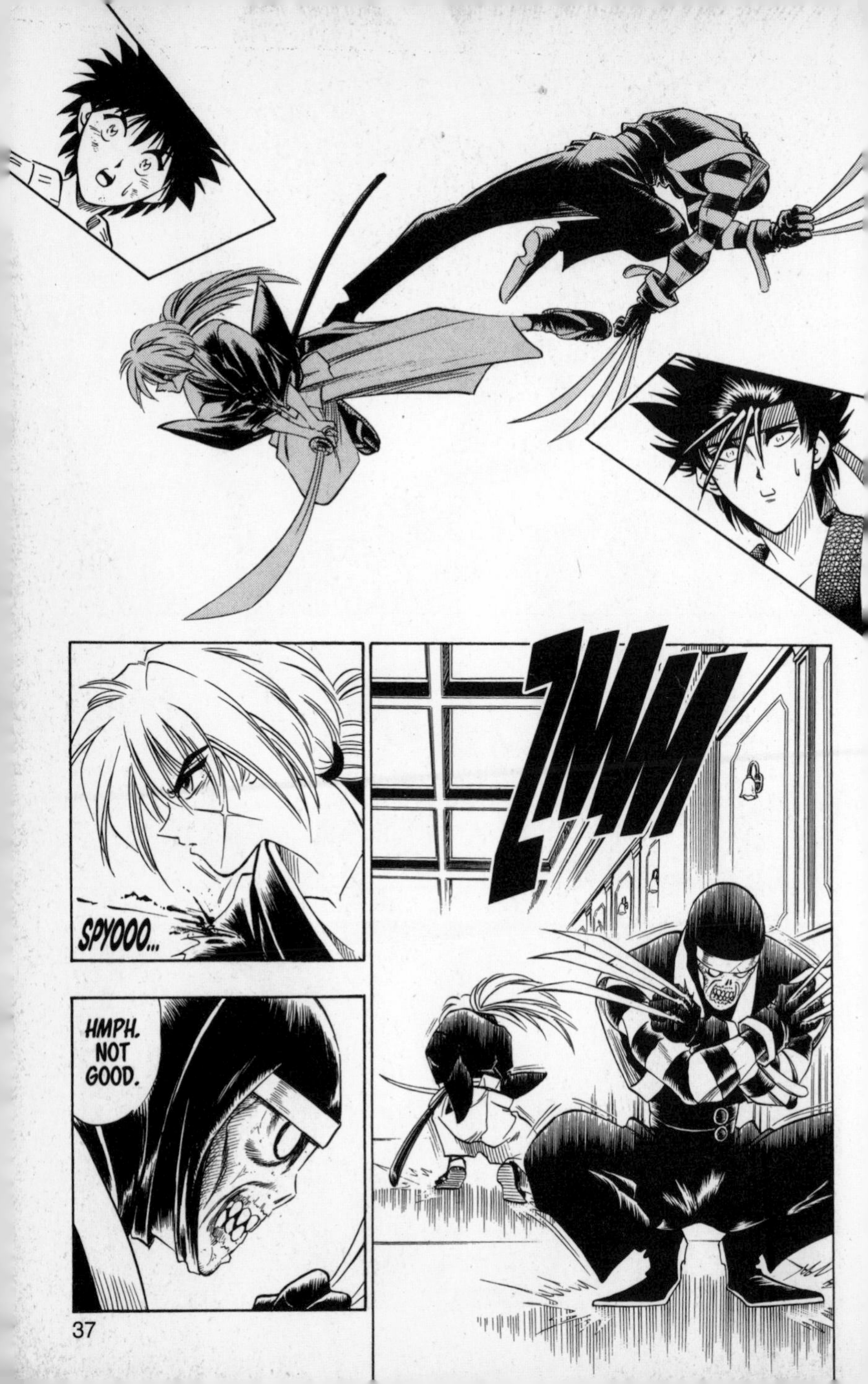
SPYOOO...
HMPH. NOT GOOD.

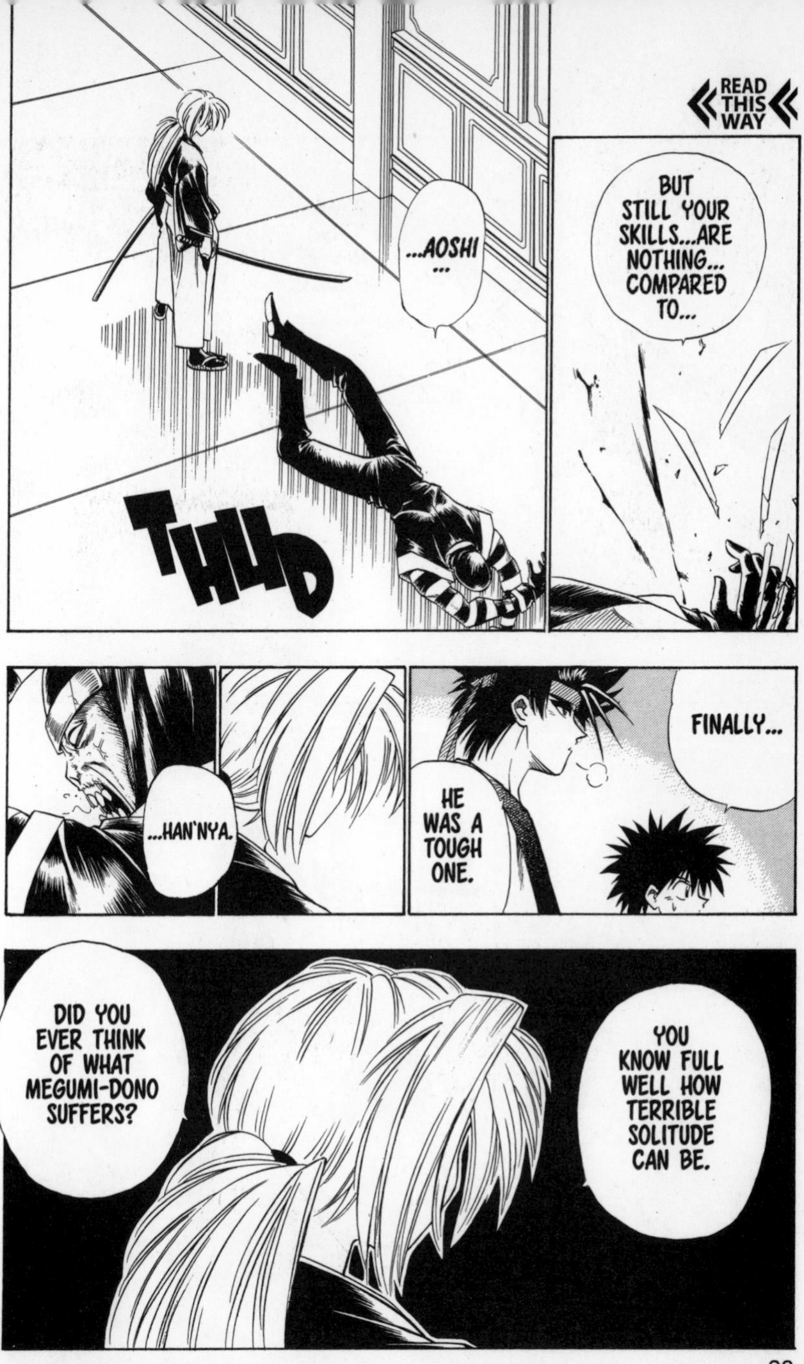
READ THIS WAY
BUT STILL YOUR SKILLS...ARE NOTHING... COMPARED TO...
...AOSHI ...
THUD
FINALLY...
HE WAS A TOUGH ONE.
...HAN'NYA.
YOU KNOW FULL WELL HOW TERRIBLE SOLITUDE CAN BE.
DID YOU EVER THINK OF WHAT MEGUMI-DONO SUFFERS?

KEEEN

MEGUMI-DONO MAY BE IN NEED.

LET'S HURRY.

KENSHIN...

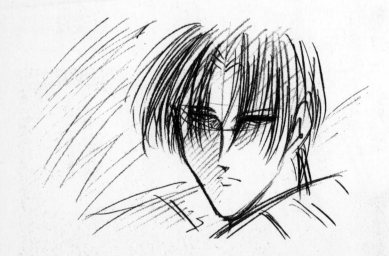

READ THIS WAY

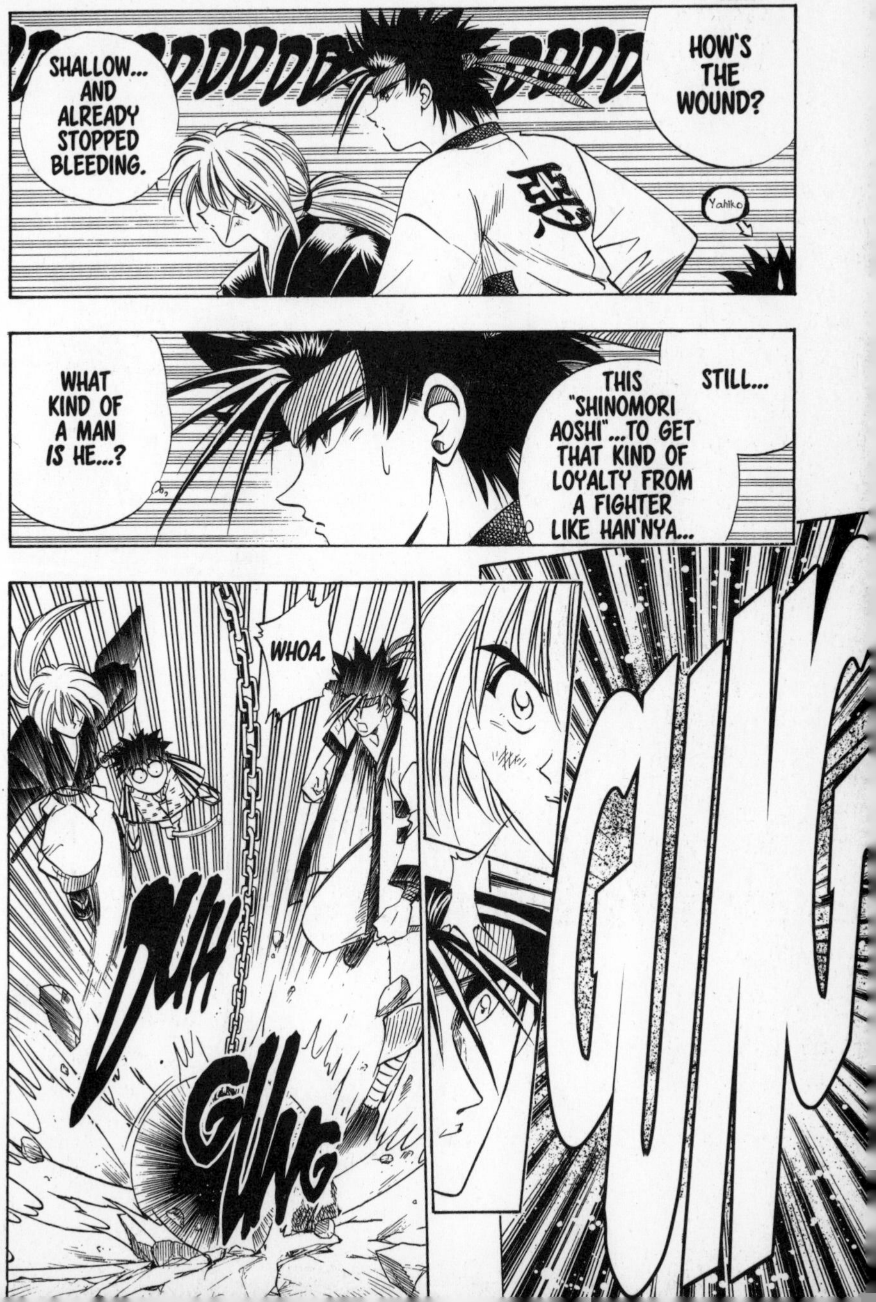
HOW'S THE WOUND?
Yahiko
SHALLOW... AND ALREADY STOPPED BLEEDING.
STILL...
THIS "SHINOMORI AOSHI"...TO GET THAT KIND OF LOYALTY FROM A FIGHTER LIKE HAN'NYA...
WHAT KIND OF A MAN IS HE...?
WHOA.

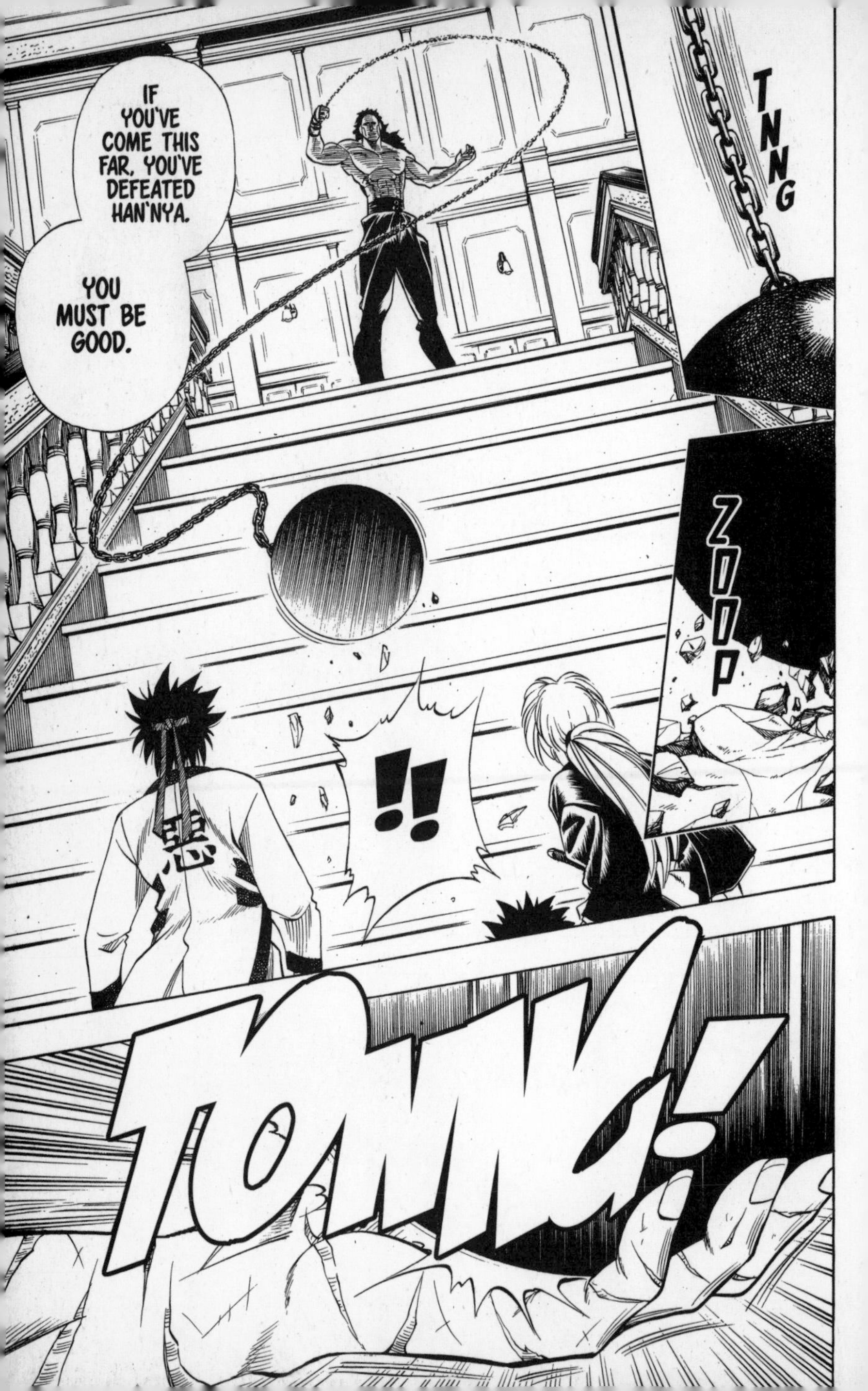
TNNG
ZOOOP
IF YOU'VE COME THIS FAR, YOU'VE DEFEATED HAN'NYA.
YOU MUST BE GOOD.
!!
TOMM!

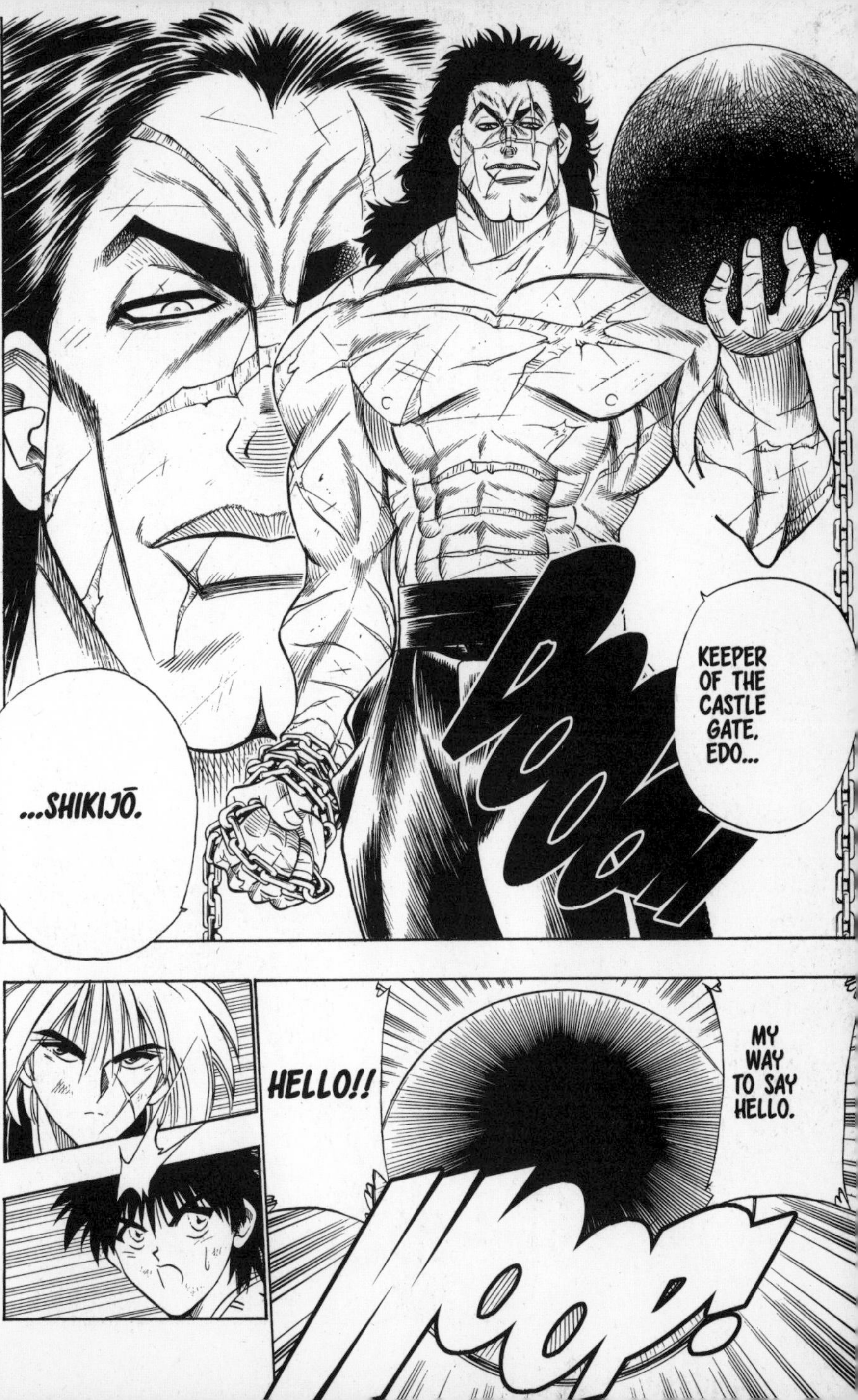
KEEPER OF THE CASTLE GATE, EDO...
...SHIKIJŌ.
MY WAY TO SAY HELLO.
HELLO!!

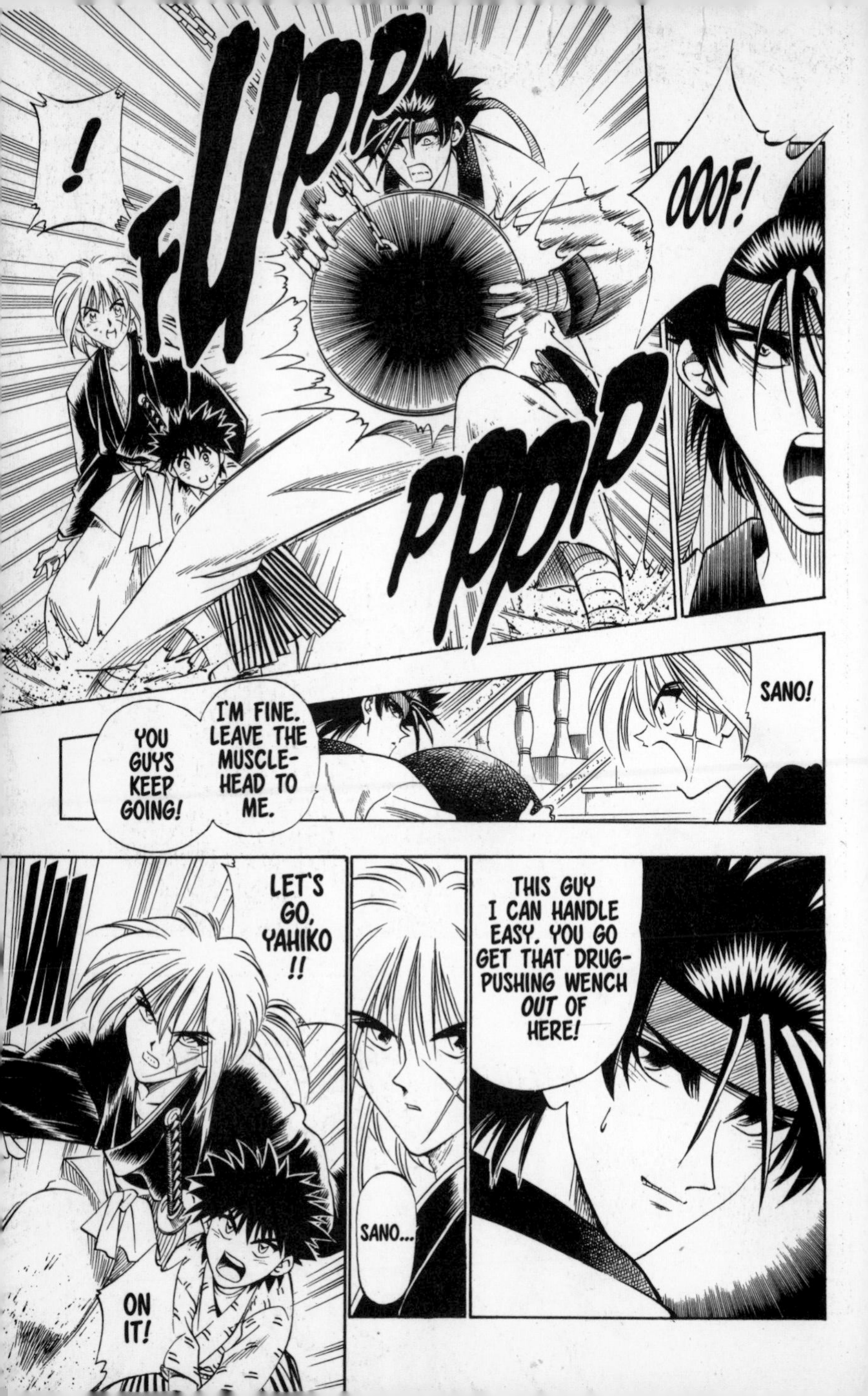
OOOF!
FLIPP
!
PPPP
SANO!
I'M FINE. LEAVE THE MUSCLE-HEAD TO ME.
YOU GUYS KEEP GOING!
THIS GUY I CAN HANDLE EASY. YOU GO GET THAT DRUG-PUSHING WENCH OUT OF HERE!
SANO...
LET'S GO, YAHIKO !!
ON IT!

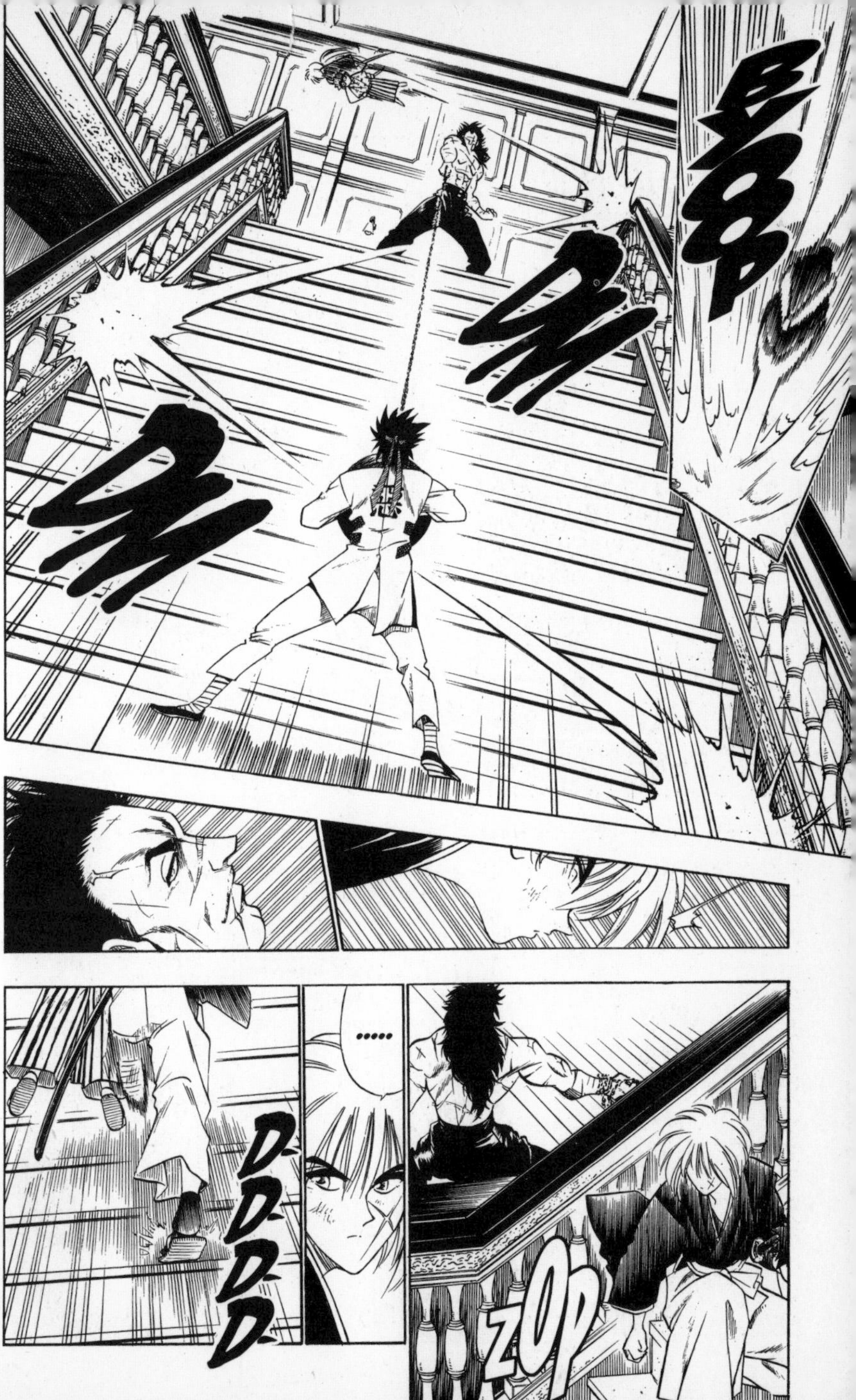
ZOP
.....
D-D-D-D-D-

READ THIS WAY

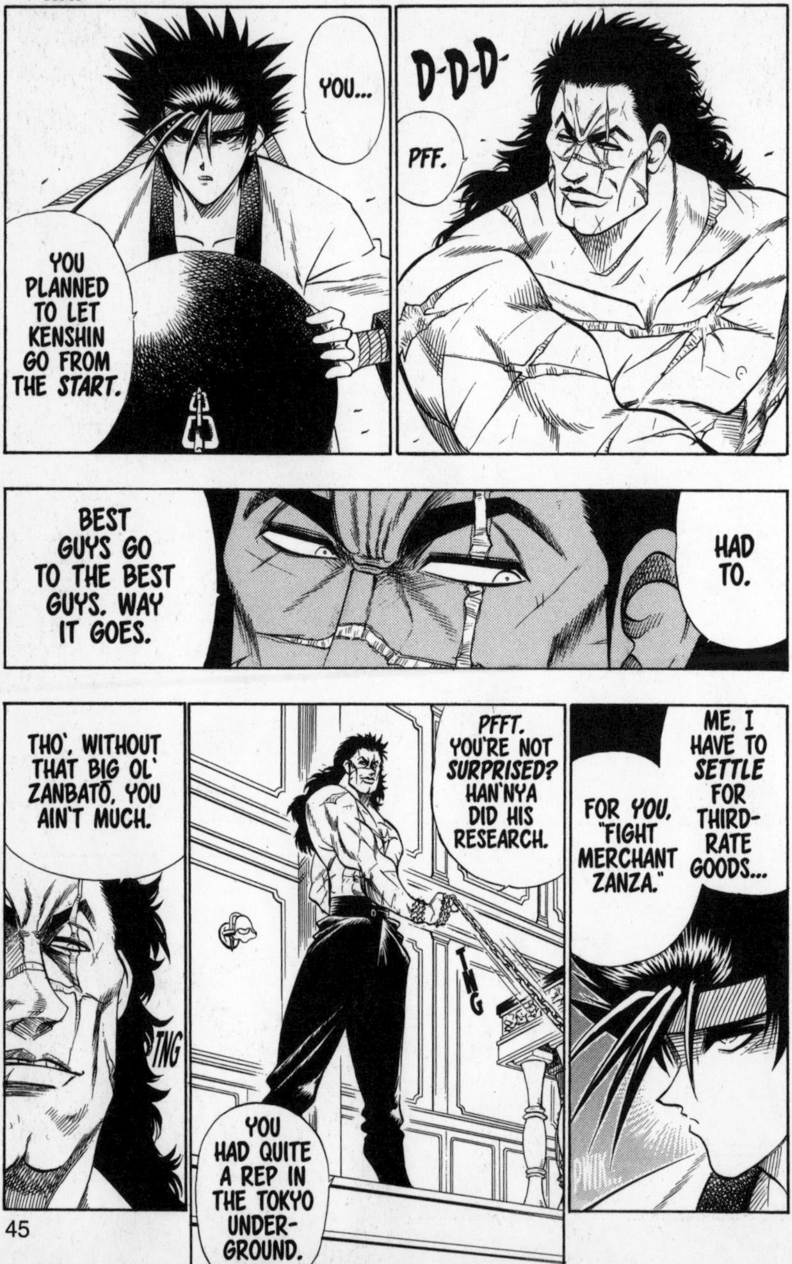

D-D-D
PFF.
YOU...
YOU PLANNED TO LET KENSHIN GO FROM THE *START.*
HAD TO.
BEST GUYS GO TO THE BEST GUYS. WAY IT GOES.
ME, I HAVE TO *SETTLE* FOR THIRD-RATE GOODS...
FOR *YOU,* "FIGHT MERCHANT ZANZA."
PWIK...
PFFT. YOU'RE NOT *SURPRISED?* HAN'NYA DID HIS RESEARCH.
TNG
YOU HAD QUITE A REP IN THE TOKYO UNDER-GROUND.
THO', WITHOUT THAT BIG OL' ZANBATŌ, YOU AIN'T MUCH.
TNG

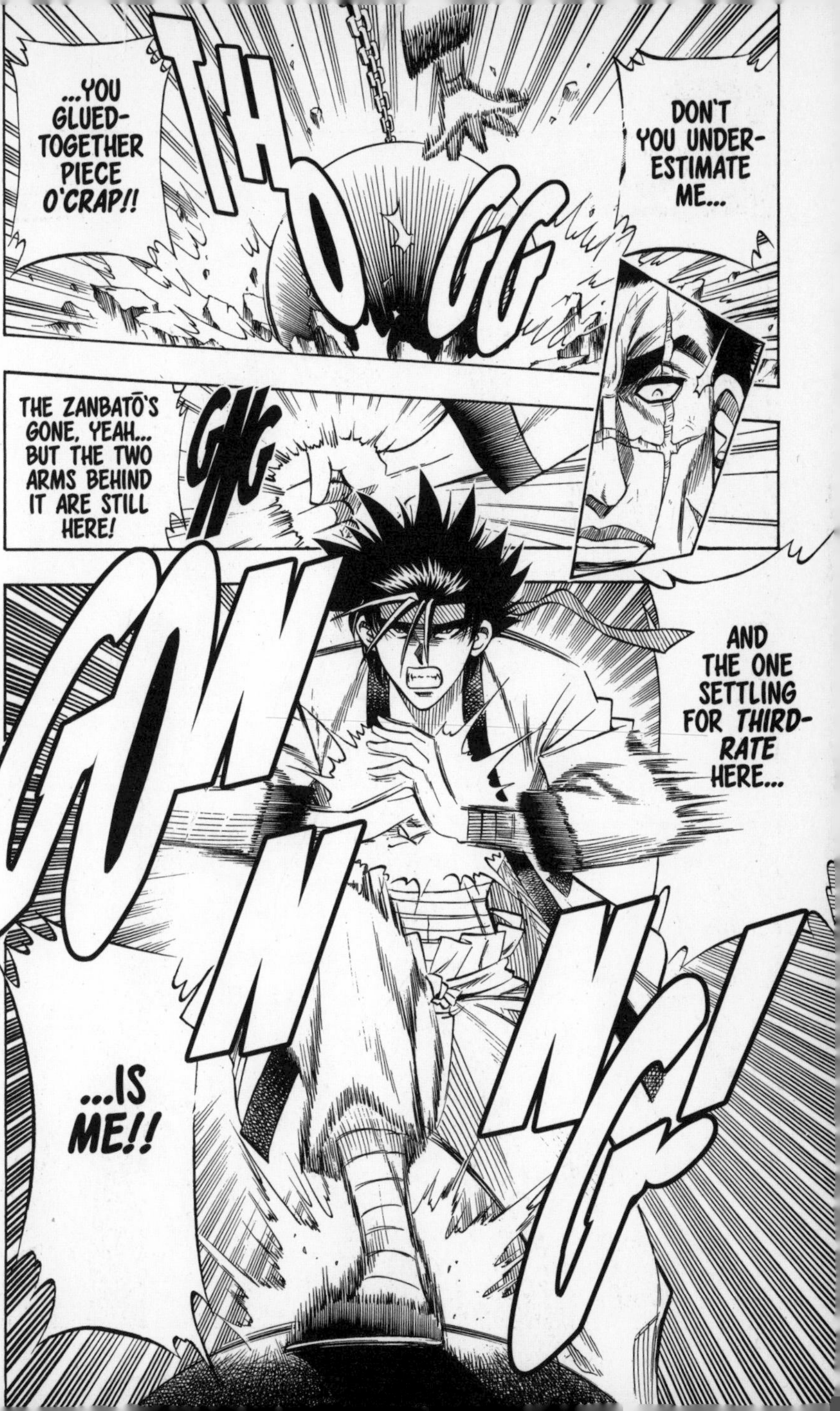
DON'T YOU UNDER-ESTIMATE ME...
...YOU GLUED-TOGETHER PIECE O'CRAP!!
THOGG
THE ZANBATŌ'S GONE, YEAH... BUT THE TWO ARMS BEHIND IT ARE STILL HERE!
AND THE ONE SETTLING FOR *THIRD-RATE* HERE...
...IS **ME!!**

READ THIS WAY

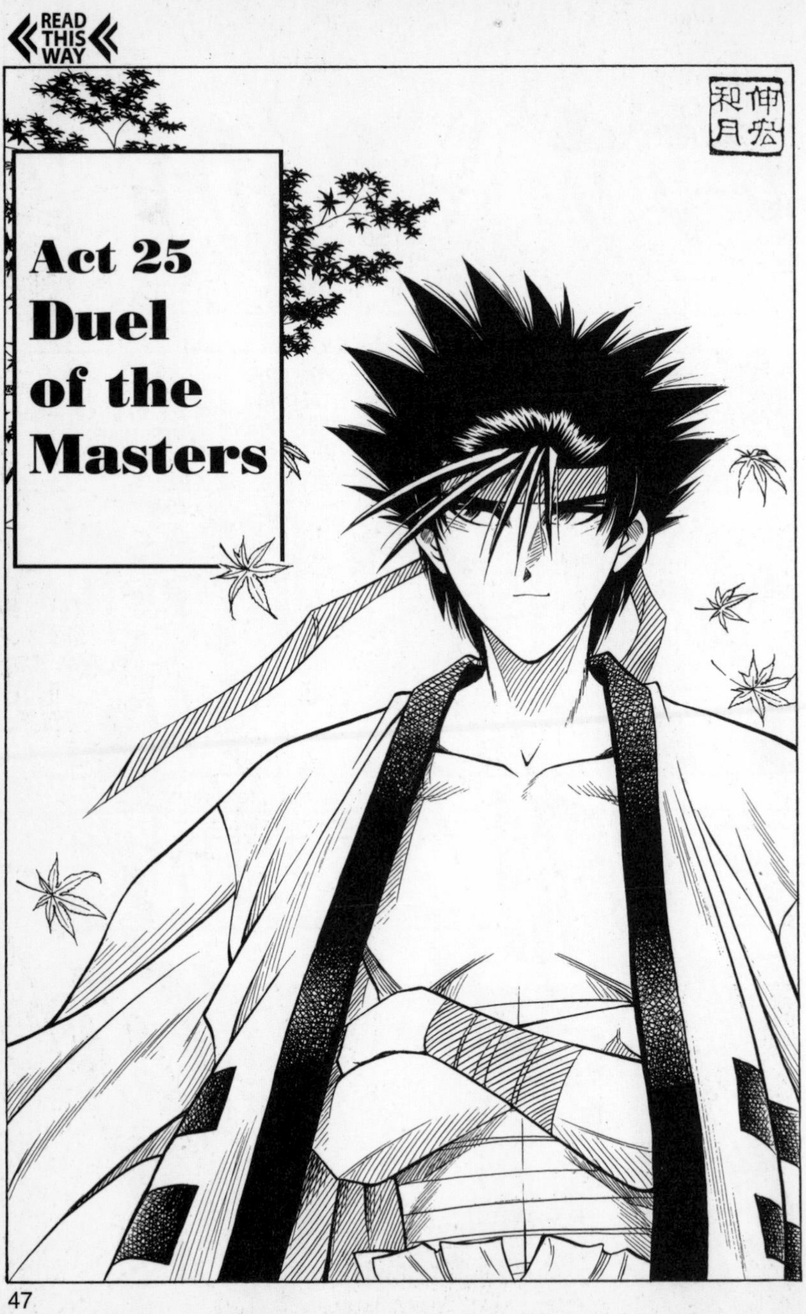

Act 25
Duel of the Masters
伸宏 和月

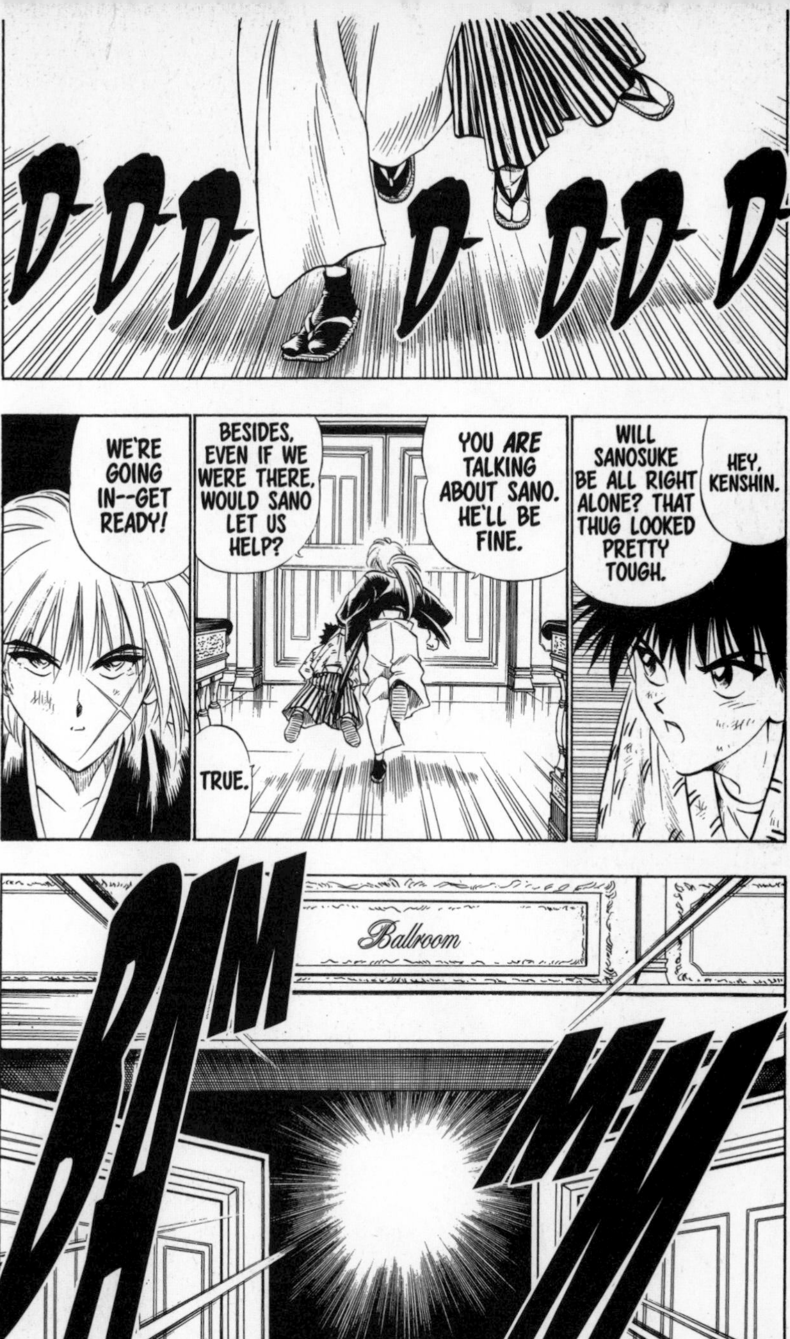
DDDDDDD
HEY, KENSHIN.
WILL SANOSUKE BE ALL RIGHT ALONE? THAT THUG LOOKED PRETTY TOUGH.
YOU *ARE* TALKING ABOUT SANO. HE'LL BE FINE.
BESIDES, EVEN IF WE WERE THERE, WOULD SANO LET US HELP?
TRUE.
WE'RE GOING IN--GET READY!
Ballroom
BAMMM

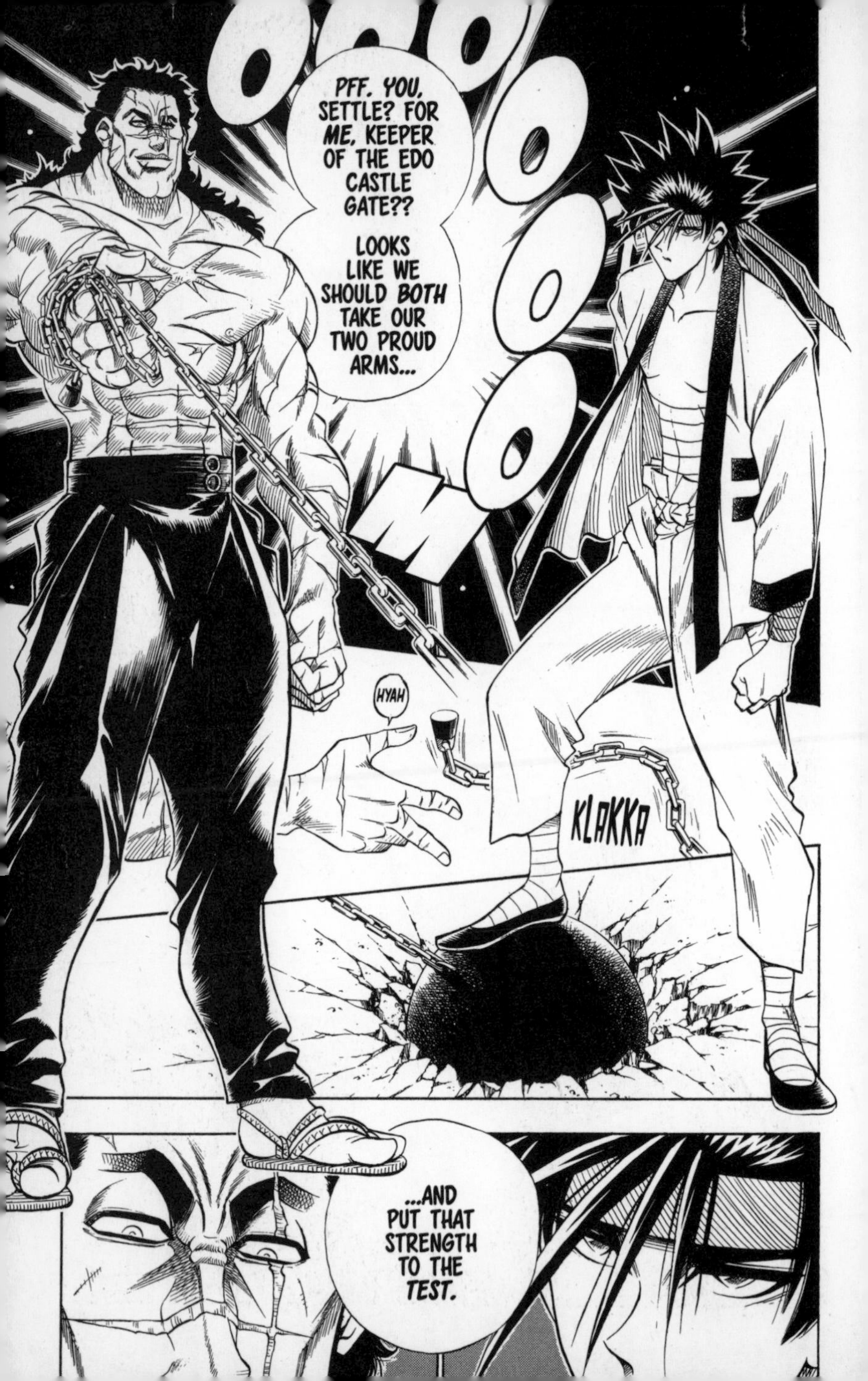
PFF. YOU, SETTLE? FOR *ME*, KEEPER OF THE EDO CASTLE GATE??
LOOKS LIKE WE SHOULD *BOTH* TAKE OUR TWO PROUD ARMS...
OOOOOOOOM
KLAKKA
HYAH
...AND PUT THAT STRENGTH TO THE *TEST*.

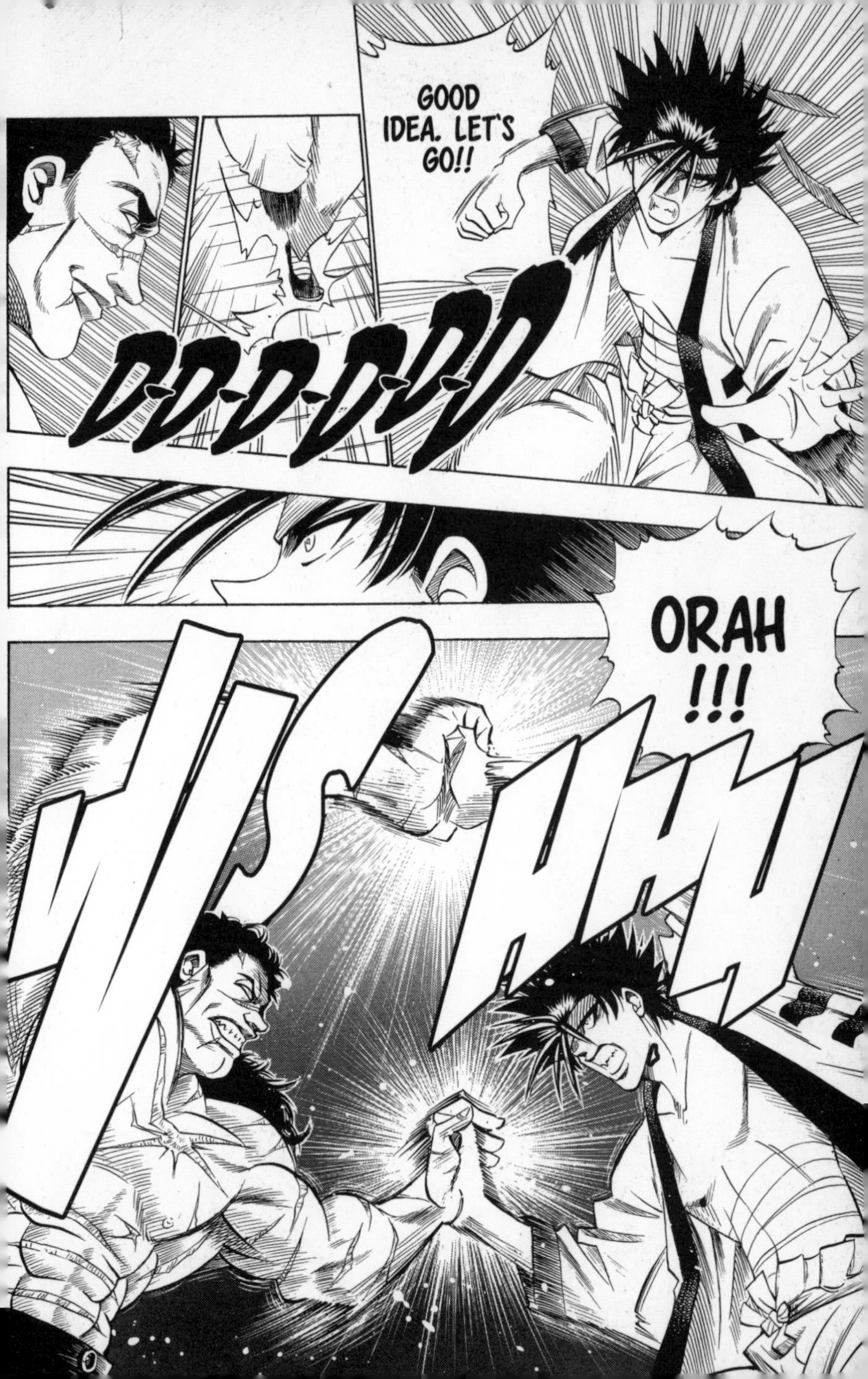
GOOD IDEA. LET'S GO!!
ORAH !!!

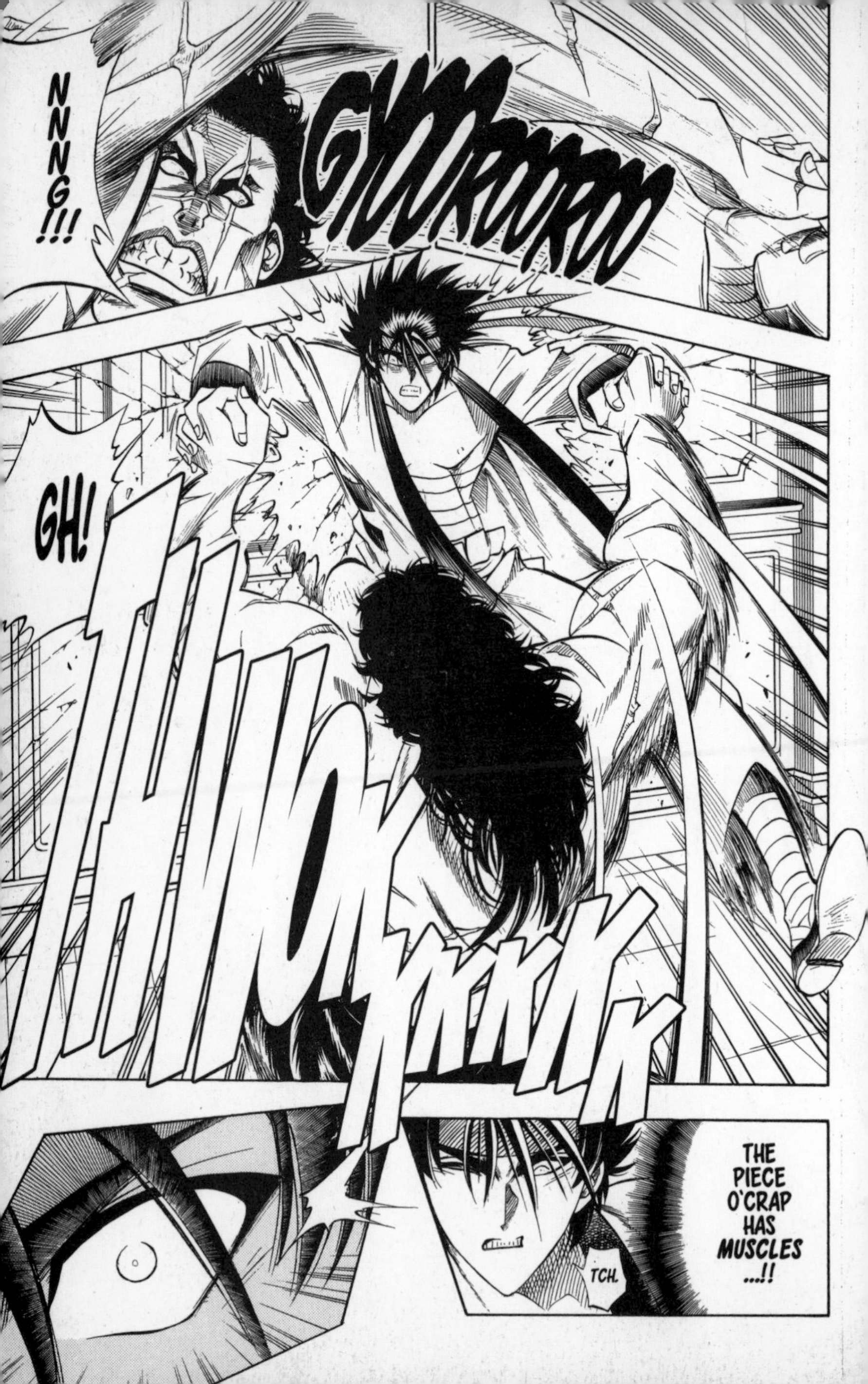
GYURORORO
NNNG!!!
THUNKKKK
GH!
THE PIECE O'CRAP HAS MUSCLES ...!!
TCH.

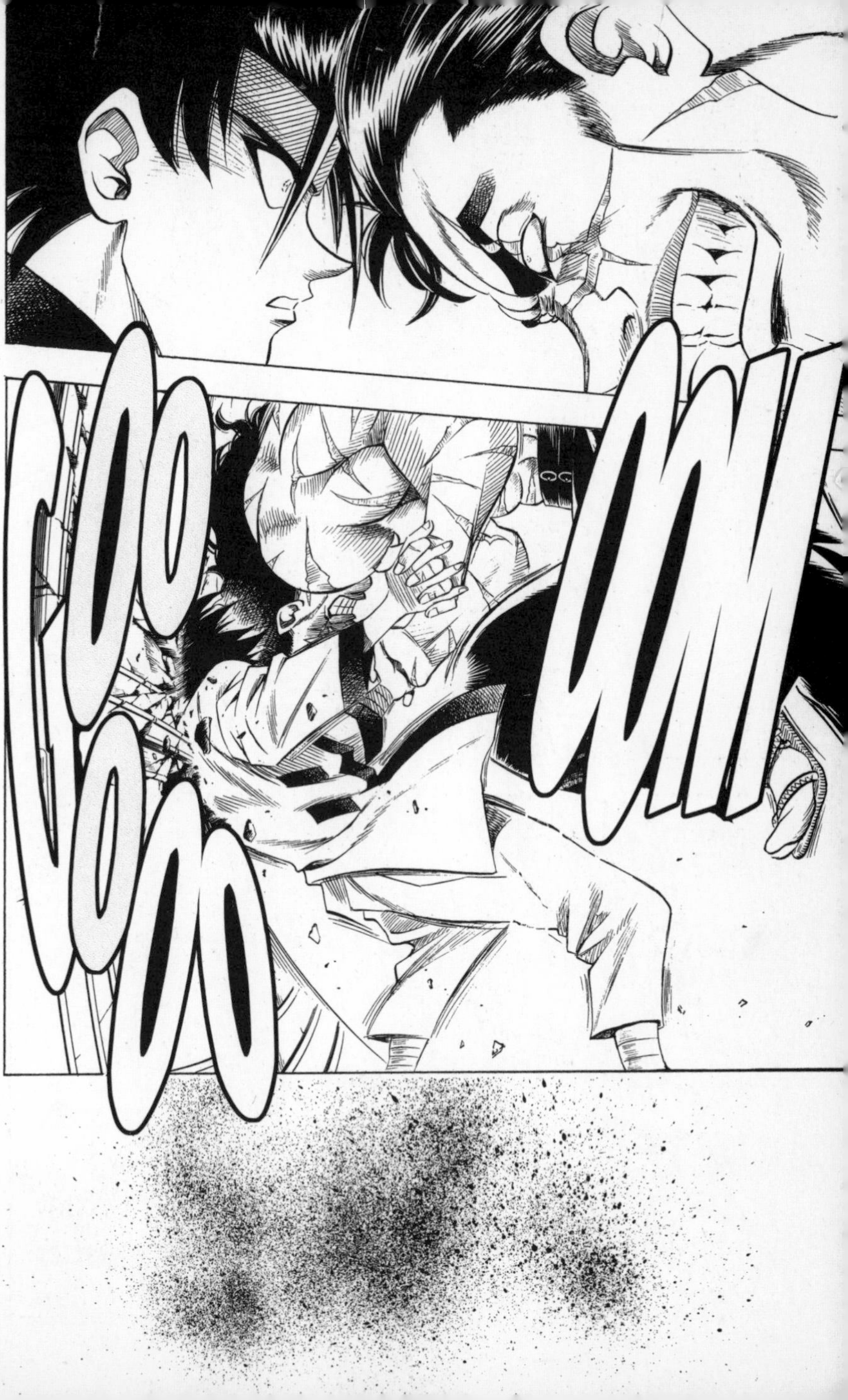
GOOOOOOM

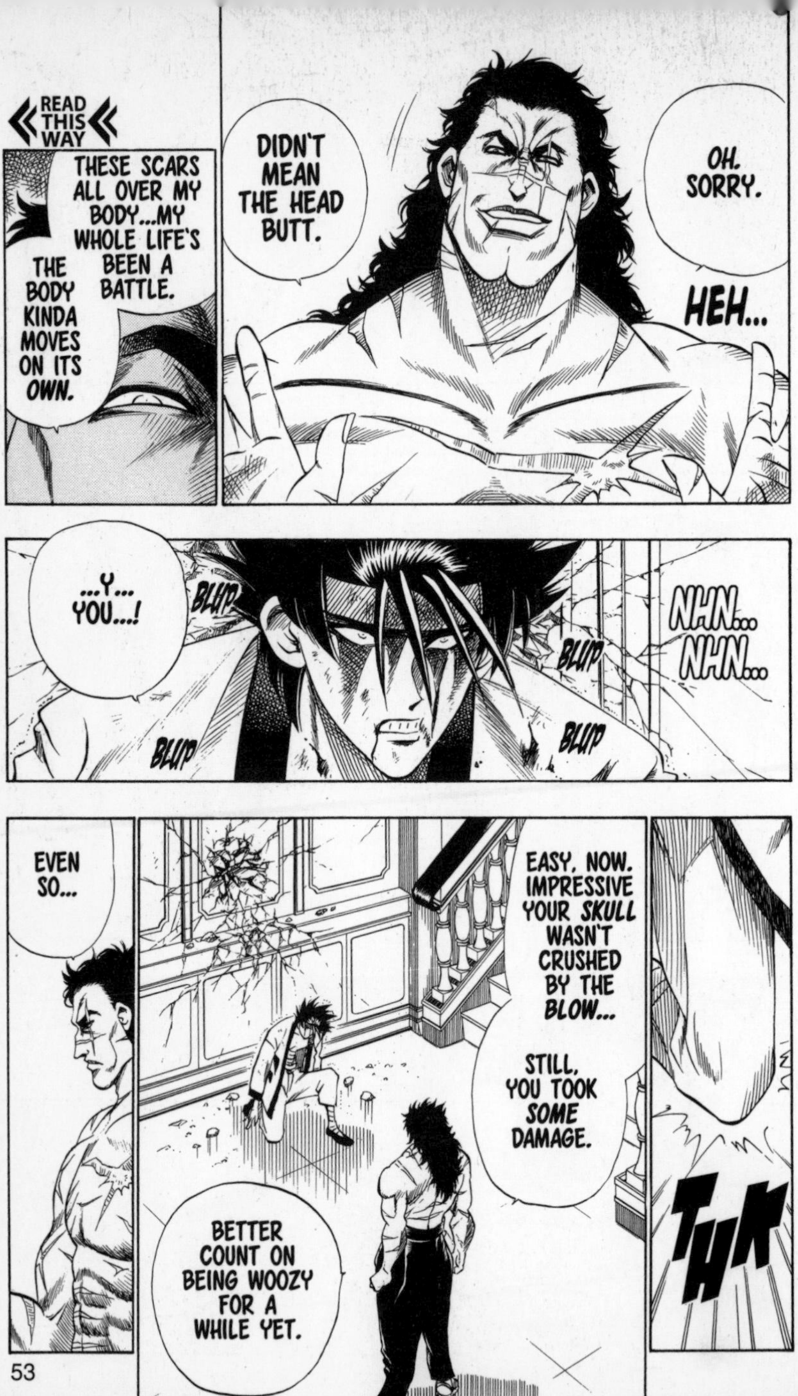
READ THIS WAY
OH. SORRY.
HEH...
DIDN'T MEAN THE HEAD BUTT.
THESE SCARS ALL OVER MY BODY...MY WHOLE LIFE'S BEEN A BATTLE.
THE BODY KINDA MOVES ON ITS OWN.
NHN... NHN...
BLUP
BLUP
BLUP
BLUP
...Y... YOU...!
THK
EASY, NOW. IMPRESSIVE YOUR SKULL WASN'T CRUSHED BY THE BLOW...
STILL, YOU TOOK SOME DAMAGE.
BETTER COUNT ON BEING WOOZY FOR A WHILE YET.
EVEN SO...

READ THIS WAY

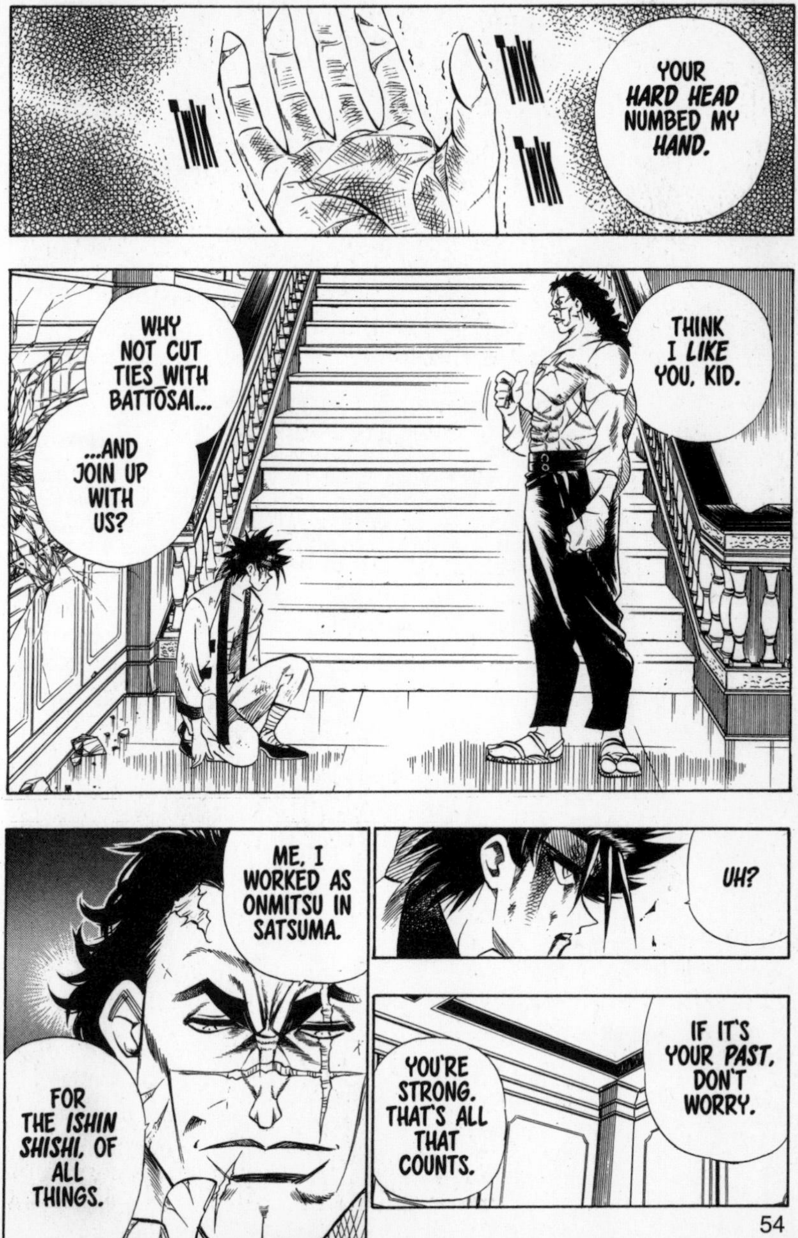
YOUR *HARD HEAD* NUMBED MY *HAND.*
TWIK
TWIK
TWIK
THINK I *LIKE* YOU, KID.
WHY NOT CUT TIES WITH BATTŌSAI...
...AND JOIN UP WITH US?
UH?
IF IT'S YOUR *PAST,* DON'T WORRY.
YOU'RE STRONG. THAT'S ALL THAT COUNTS.
ME, I WORKED AS ONMITSU IN SATSUMA.
FOR THE *ISHIN SHISHI,* OF ALL THINGS.

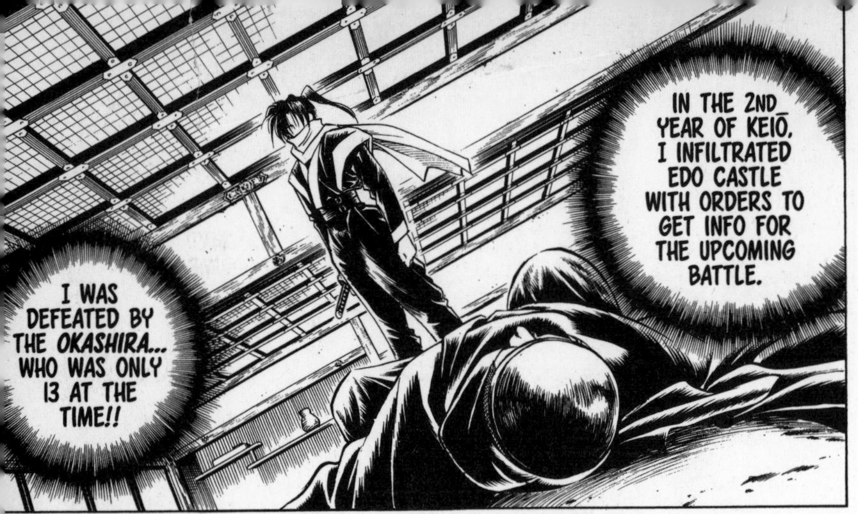
IN THE 2ND YEAR OF KEIŌ, I INFILTRATED EDO CASTLE WITH ORDERS TO GET INFO FOR THE UPCOMING BATTLE.
I WAS DEFEATED BY THE *OKASHIRA*... WHO WAS ONLY 13 AT THE TIME!!

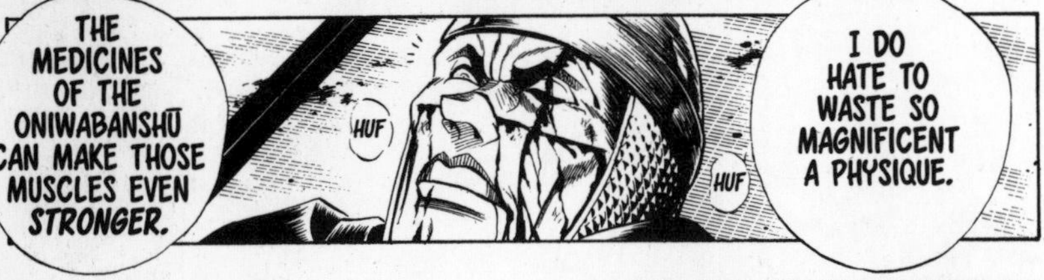
I DO HATE TO WASTE SO MAGNIFICENT A PHYSIQUE.
HUF
HUF
THE MEDICINES OF THE ONIWABANSHŪ CAN MAKE THOSE MUSCLES EVEN *STRONGER.*

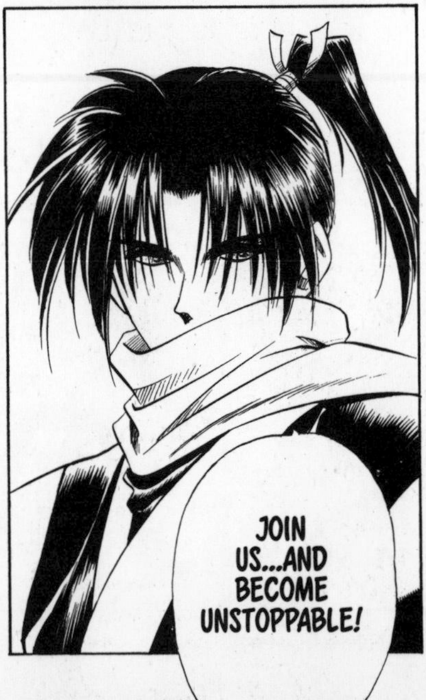
JOIN US...AND BECOME UNSTOPPABLE!

Young Aoshi. Although the design was initially for a different character, I tried him out here and he was a big hit (with women, at least...). His bangs, though—man, are they a pain. Man.

伸宏和月

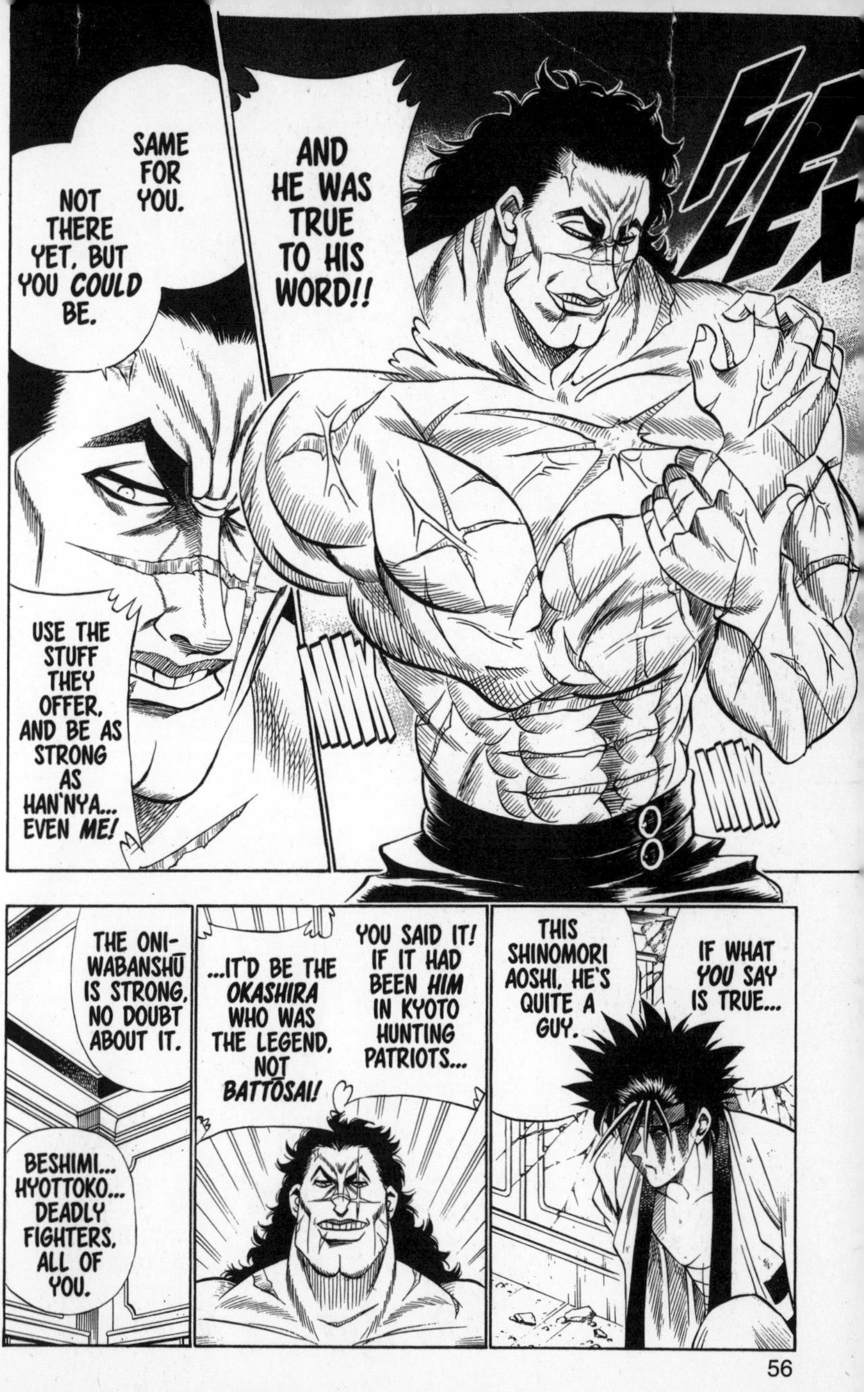
AND HE WAS TRUE TO HIS WORD!!
NOT THERE YET, BUT YOU COULD BE. SAME FOR YOU.
USE THE STUFF THEY OFFER, AND BE AS STRONG AS HAN'NYA... EVEN ME!
IF WHAT YOU SAY IS TRUE...
THIS SHINOMORI AOSHI, HE'S QUITE A GUY.
YOU SAID IT! IF IT HAD BEEN HIM IN KYOTO HUNTING PATRIOTS...
...IT'D BE THE OKASHIRA WHO WAS THE LEGEND, NOT BATTOSAI!
THE ONI-WABANSHŪ IS STRONG, NO DOUBT ABOUT IT.
BESHIMI... HYOTTOKO... DEADLY FIGHTERS, ALL OF YOU.

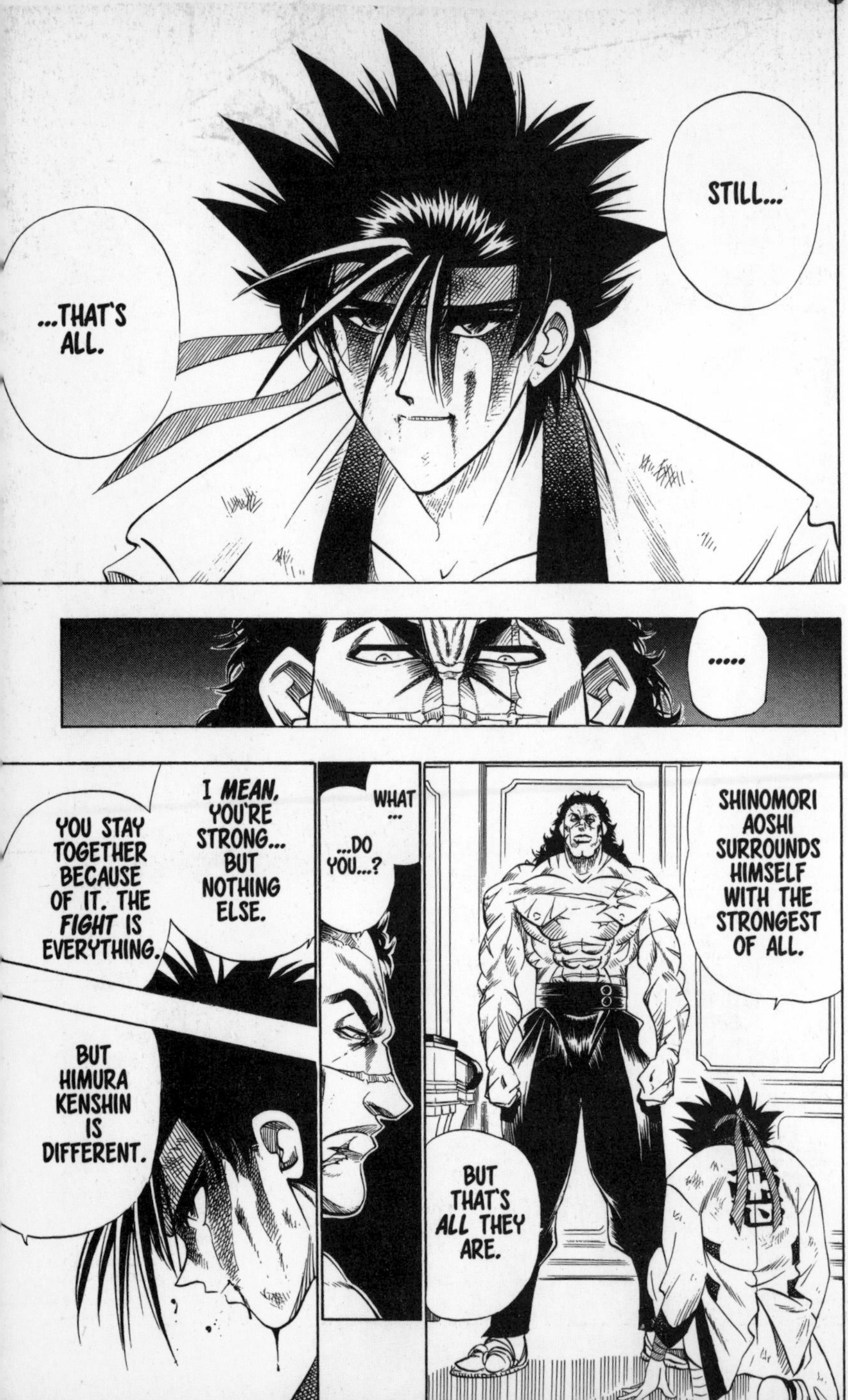
STILL...
...THAT'S ALL.
.....
SHINOMORI AOSHI SURROUNDS HIMSELF WITH THE STRONGEST OF ALL.
BUT THAT'S *ALL* THEY ARE.
WHAT ...
...DO YOU...?
I *MEAN*, YOU'RE STRONG... BUT NOTHING ELSE.
YOU STAY TOGETHER BECAUSE OF IT. THE *FIGHT* IS EVERYTHING.
BUT HIMURA KENSHIN IS DIFFERENT.

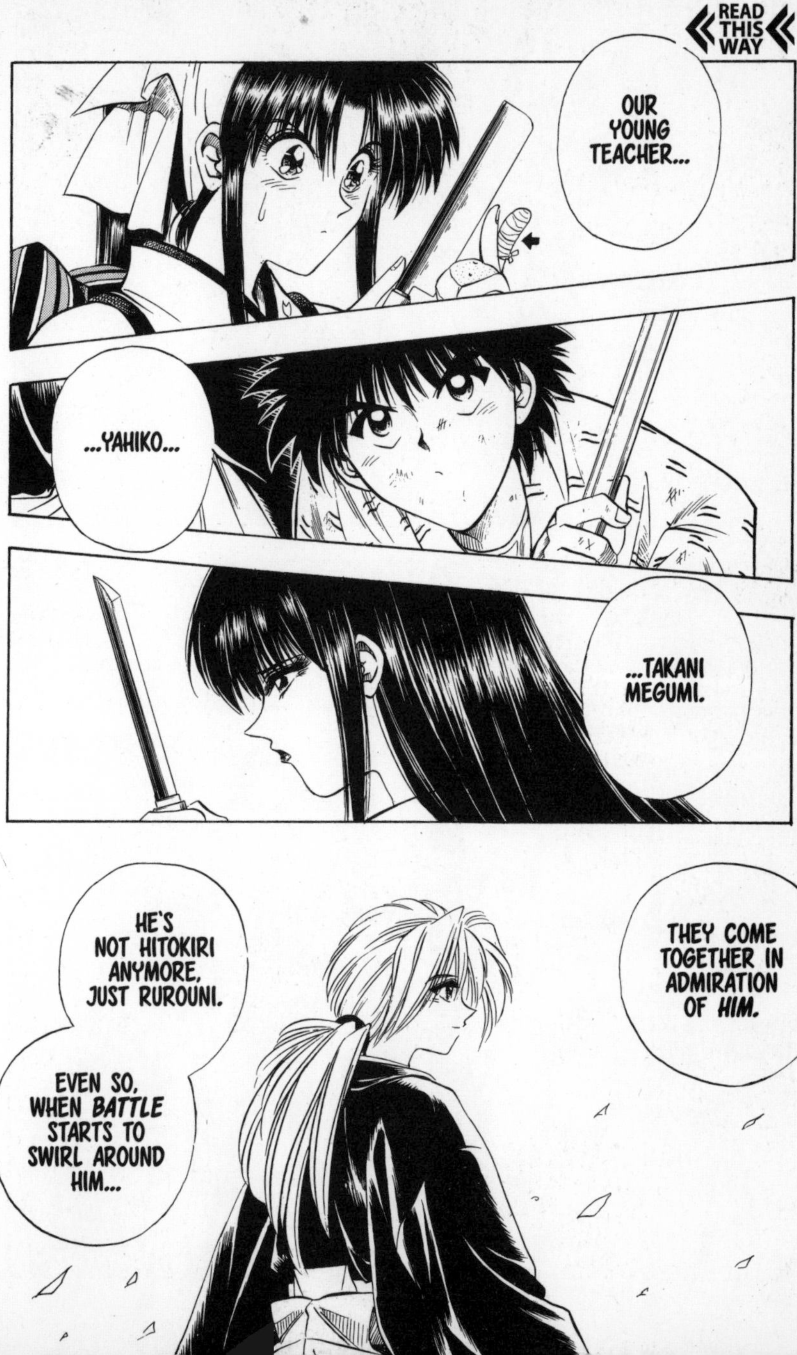
READ THIS WAY
OUR YOUNG TEACHER...
...YAHIKO...
...TAKANI MEGUMI.
THEY COME TOGETHER IN ADMIRATION OF *HIM*.
HE'S NOT HITOKIRI ANYMORE, JUST RUROUNI.
EVEN SO, WHEN *BATTLE* STARTS TO SWIRL AROUND HIM...

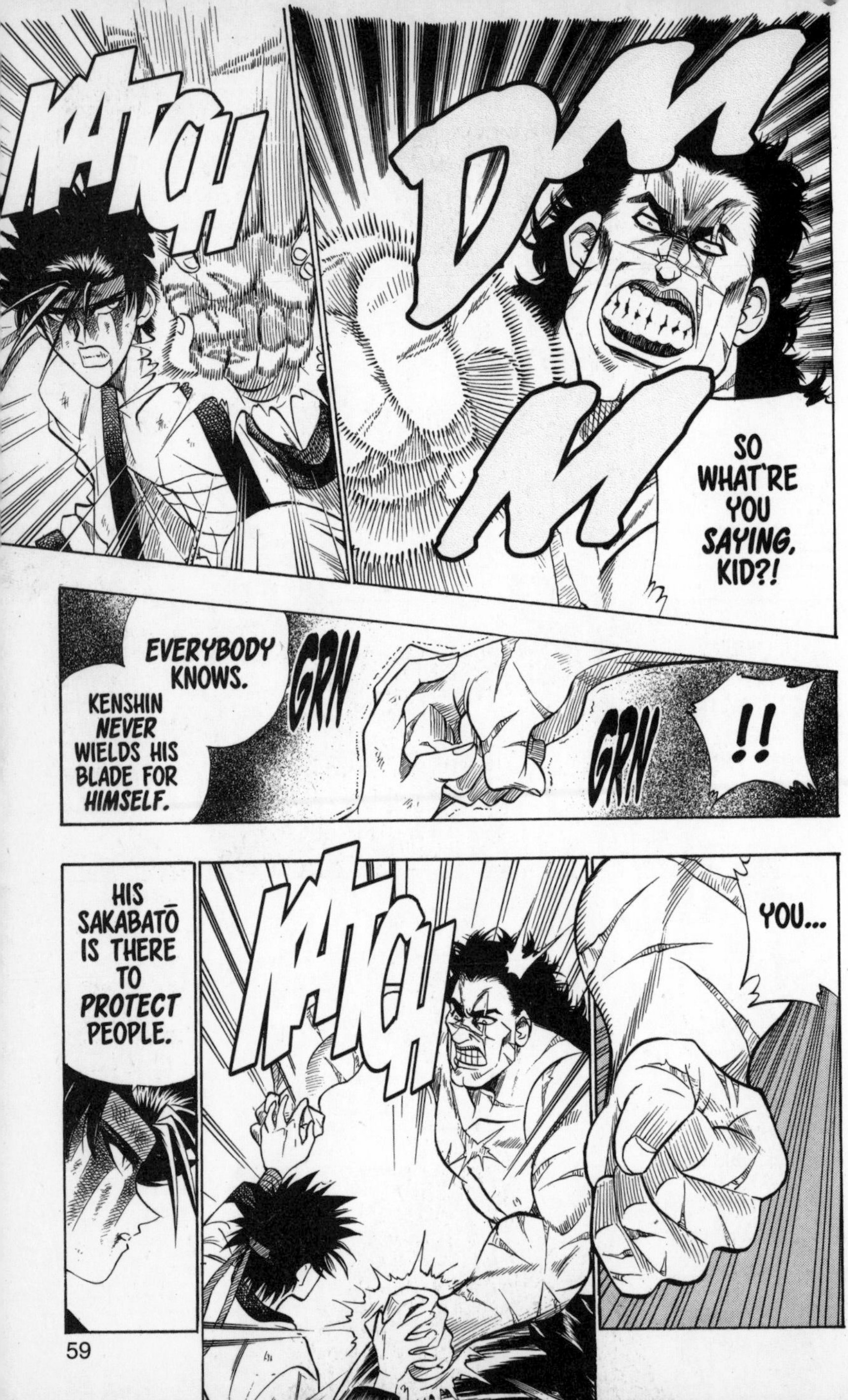
DMM
SO WHAT'RE YOU SAYING, KID?!
KATCH
!!
GRN
GRN
EVERYBODY KNOWS.
KENSHIN NEVER WIELDS HIS BLADE FOR HIMSELF.
YOU...
KATCH
HIS SAKABATŌ IS THERE TO PROTECT PEOPLE.

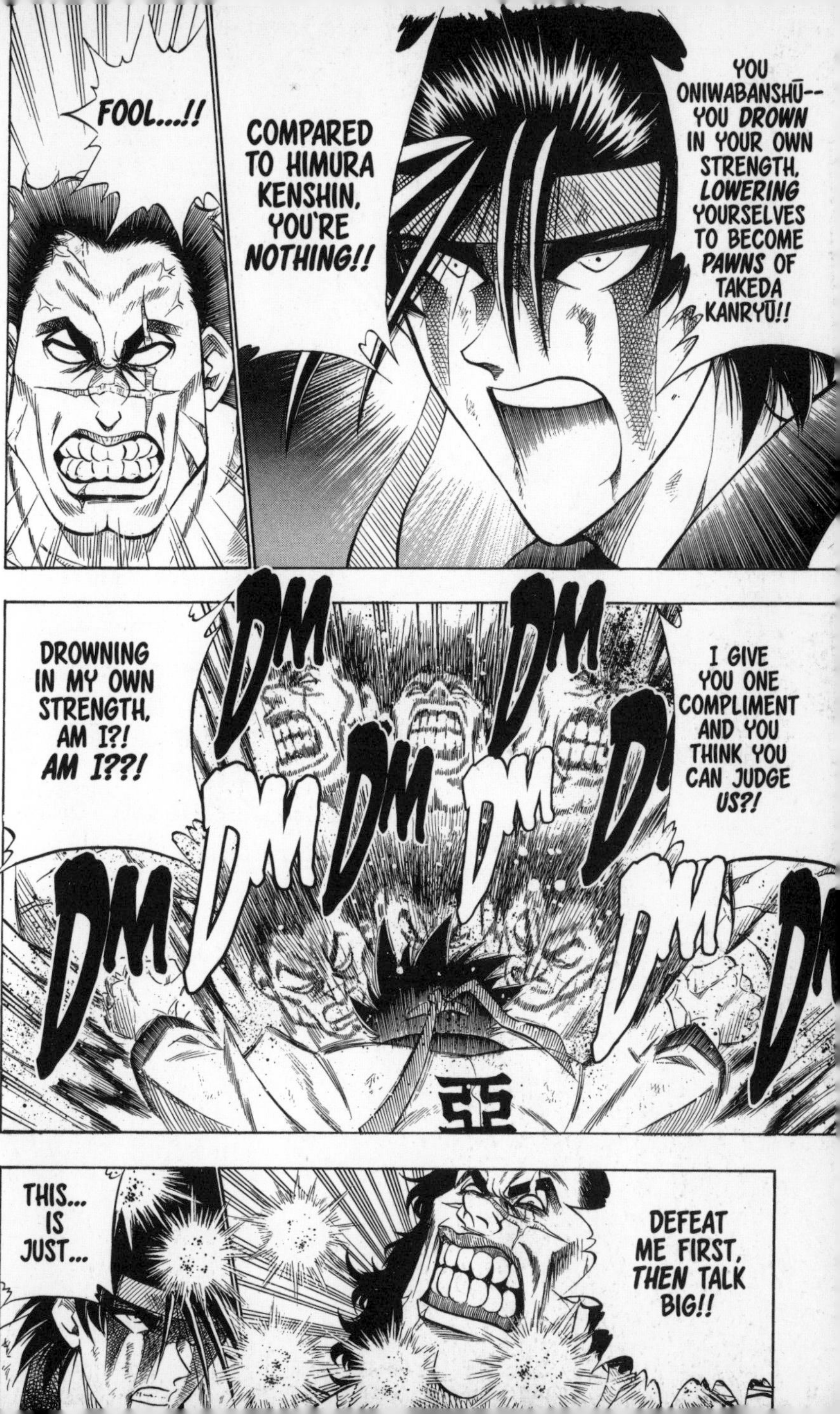
YOU ONIWABANSHŪ-- YOU *DROWN* IN YOUR OWN STRENGTH, *LOWERING* YOURSELVES TO BECOME *PAWNS* OF TAKEDA KANRYŪ!!
COMPARED TO HIMURA KENSHIN, YOU'RE *NOTHING!!*
FOOL...!!
DM DM
I GIVE YOU ONE COMPLIMENT AND YOU THINK YOU CAN JUDGE *US?!*
DROWNING IN MY OWN STRENGTH, AM I?! *AM I??!*
DM DM DM DM DM DM DM
DEFEAT ME FIRST, THEN TALK BIG!!
THIS... IS JUST...

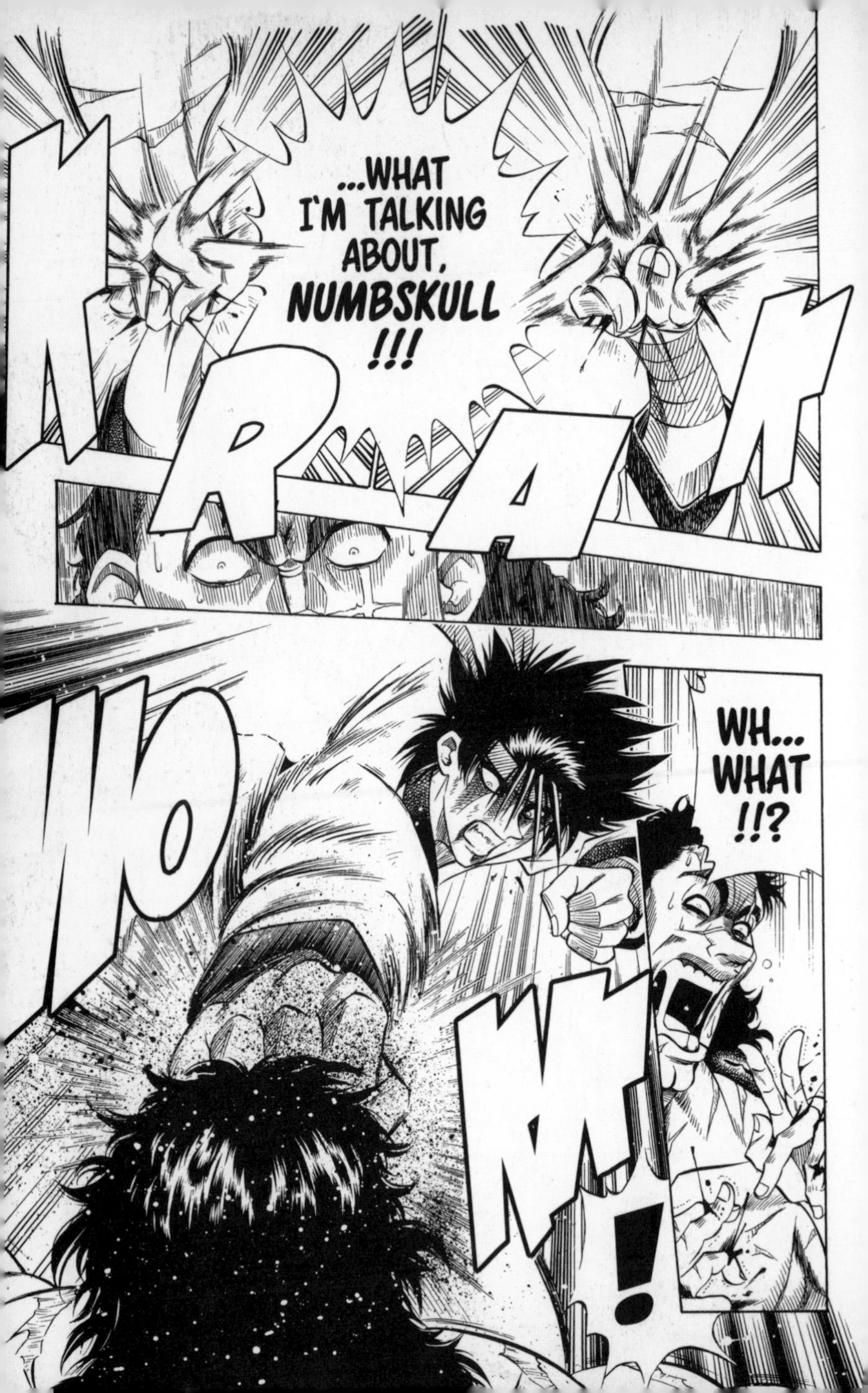

...WHAT I'M TALKING ABOUT, NUMBSKULL !!!
WH... WHAT !!?

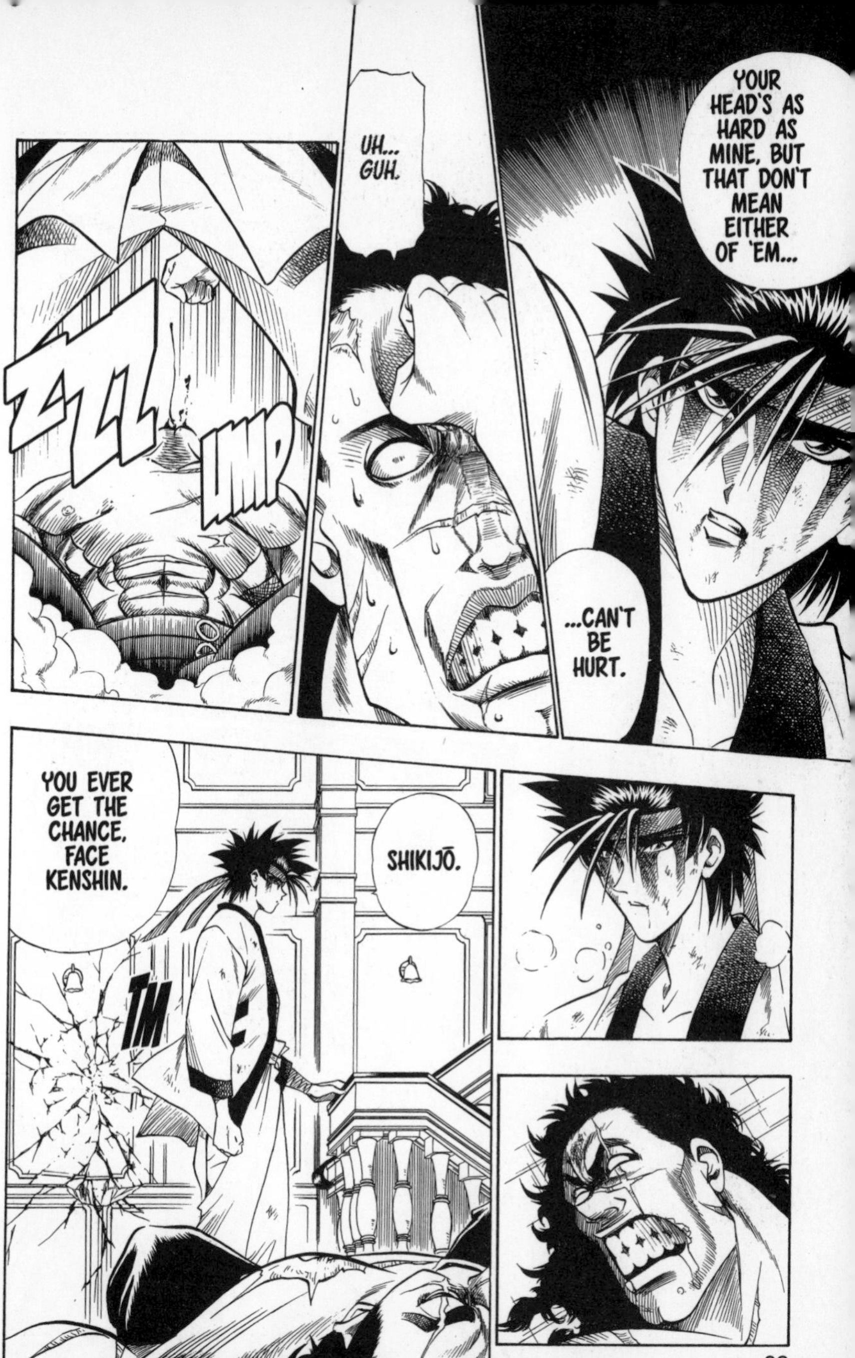
YOUR HEAD'S AS HARD AS MINE, BUT THAT DON'T MEAN EITHER OF 'EM...
...CAN'T BE HURT.
UH... GUH.
ZZLUMP
SHIKIJŌ.
YOU EVER GET THE CHANCE, FACE KENSHIN.
TM

READ THIS WAY

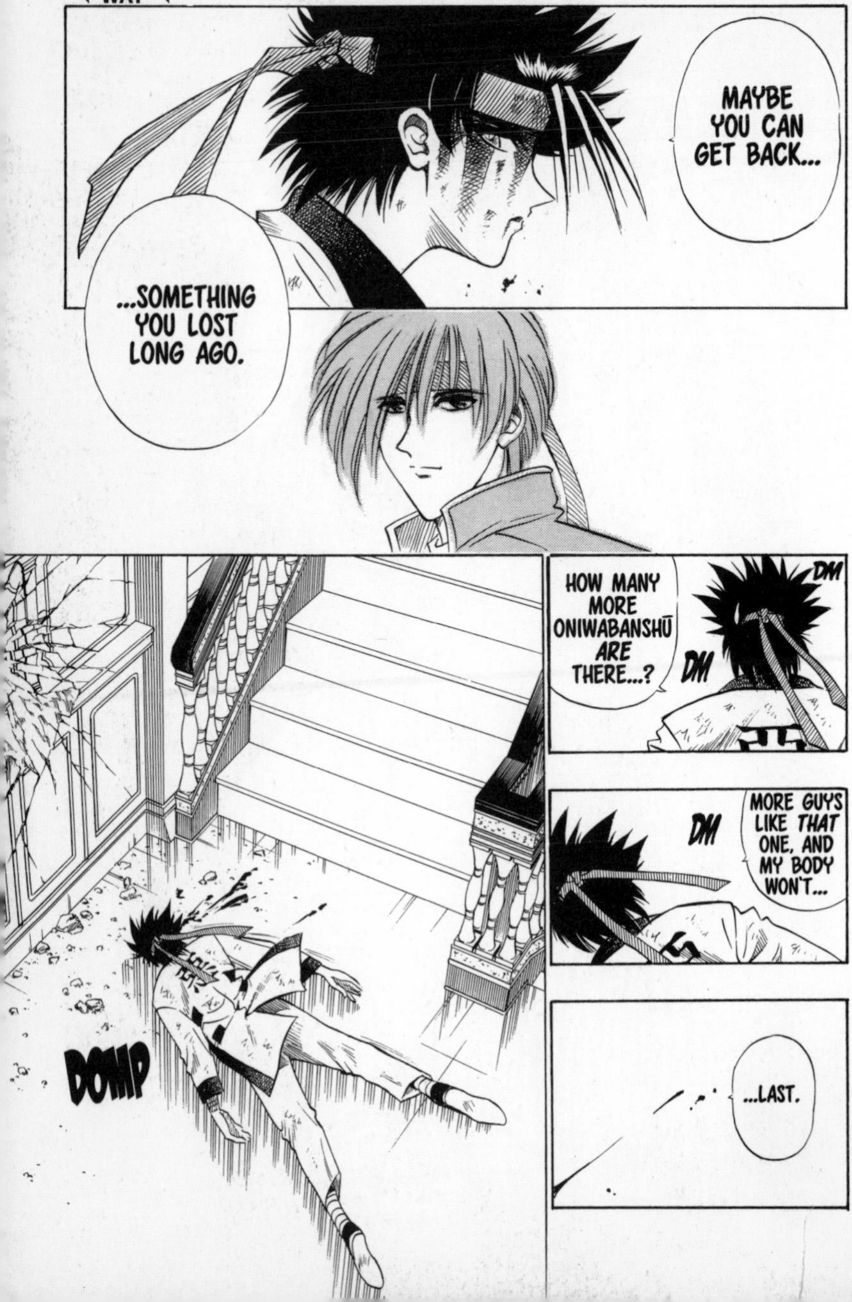
MAYBE YOU CAN GET BACK...
...SOMETHING YOU LOST LONG AGO.
DM
HOW MANY MORE ONIWABANSHŪ ARE THERE...?
DM
MORE GUYS LIKE THAT ONE, AND MY BODY WON'T...
DM
...LAST.
DOMP

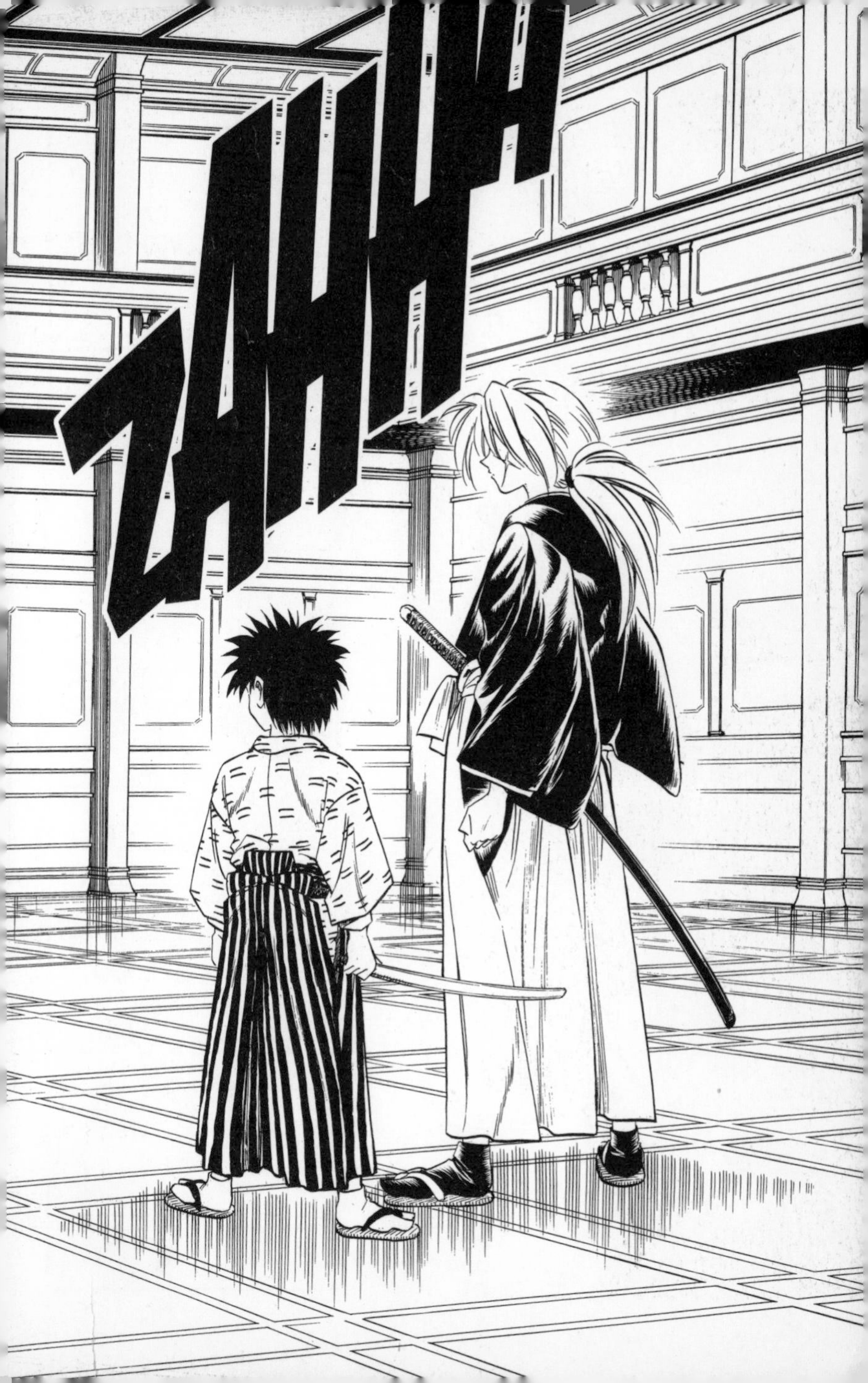
ZAHH

READ THIS WAY

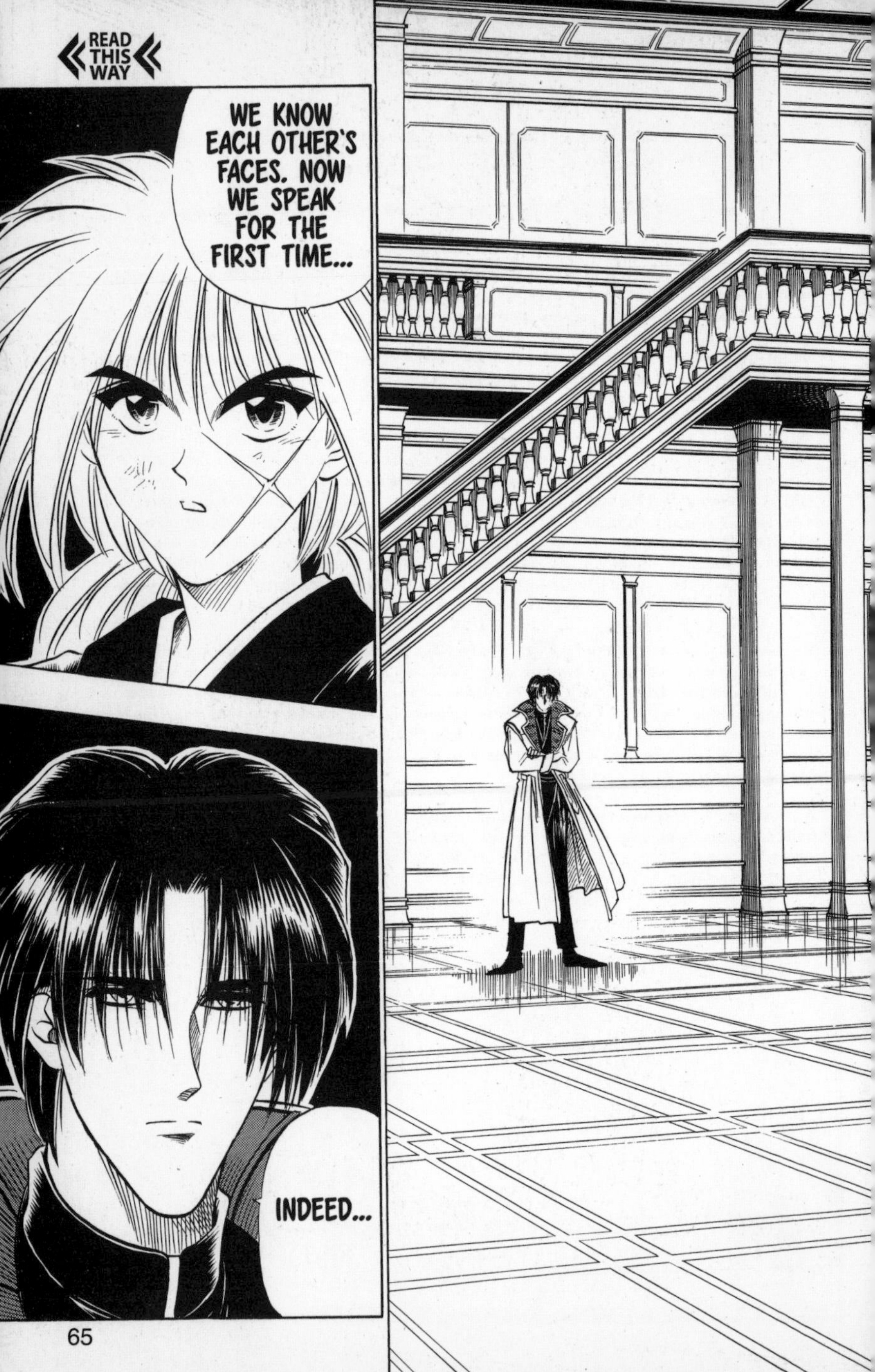
WE KNOW EACH OTHER'S FACES. NOW WE SPEAK FOR THE FIRST TIME...
INDEED...

## The Secret Life of Characters (10)

# —Oniwabanshū • Han'nya—

He's not "Masked Ninja [Akakage]," if that's what you're thinking (LAUGH). Han'nya's forebears are more like the "Elephant Man." Originally, his face was to have been congenitally deformed. Like the Elephant Man, the idea was for him to have been stepped on while still in his mother's body. He would have been treated not as a human being, but as a monster, and would have lived deep in the mountains, in solitude. He'd be discovered by Aoshi, join the Oniwabanshū. He'd be a tragic figure who tells himself, "Only in the Oniwabanshū am I able to live as a human being." Only in battle would he find his raison d'être.

When it came to writing all this up, though, my editor and I got into a discussion about how it might be interpreted to mean "the shape of one's life is determined by how one is born." After a long conversation about whether such a message is even appropriate in a young men's magazine (I think it was the longest discussion ever, since the start of *Rurouni*), I came to the conclusion that a change needed to be made. As an author, Han'nya was really a challenging character for me in that I was aware for perhaps the first time of the responsibility of writing for young people.

Personality-wise, he's based on Yamazaki Susumu of the Shinsengumi. Many readers proposed that, beneath the mask, he was secretly handsome, or was *kagemusha* for Aoshi (his twin brother, say!), or even *kunoichi* (a female ninja). There were lots of interesting guesses. For whatever reason, the idea of a *kunoichi* being part of the Oniwabanshū never entered my head; I find it interesting. Maybe she'll appear as a new character in the future—not that there are any plans as of yet.

The model in terms of design was nothing more than a skeleton. That the left and right eyes are of different shape and size is a remnant of the original concept. As a side note, Han'nya's outfit became more and more blocky as I drew it, leading my assistants to call it "robot," "mobile suit," you name it.

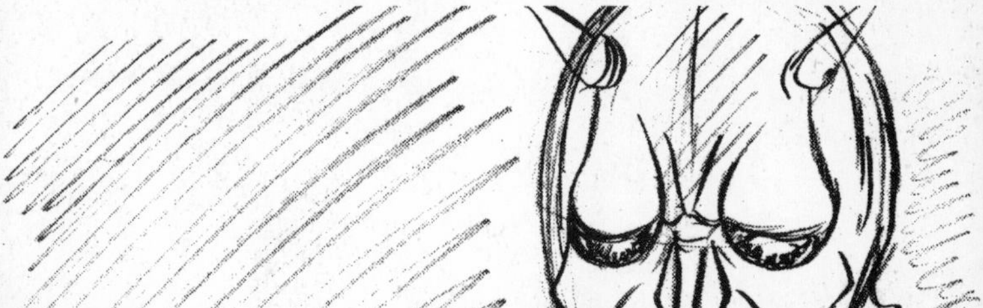

伸宏
和月

READ THIS WAY

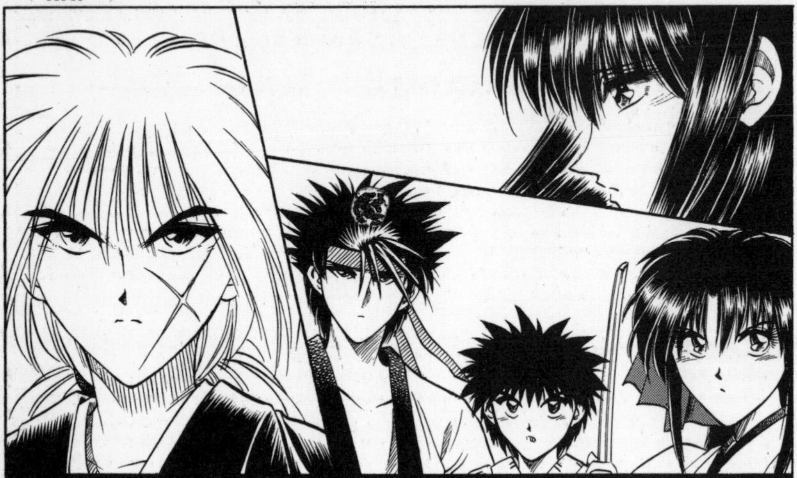

和月伸宏

# Act 26
# Shinomori Aoshi, Okashira

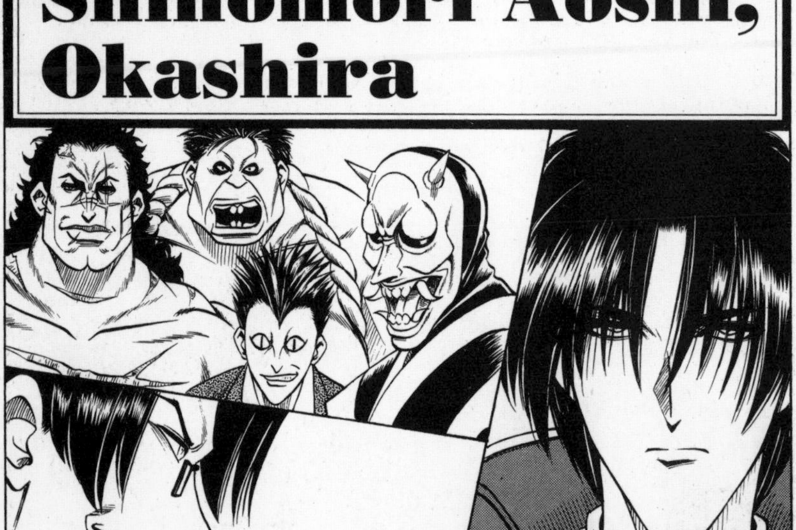

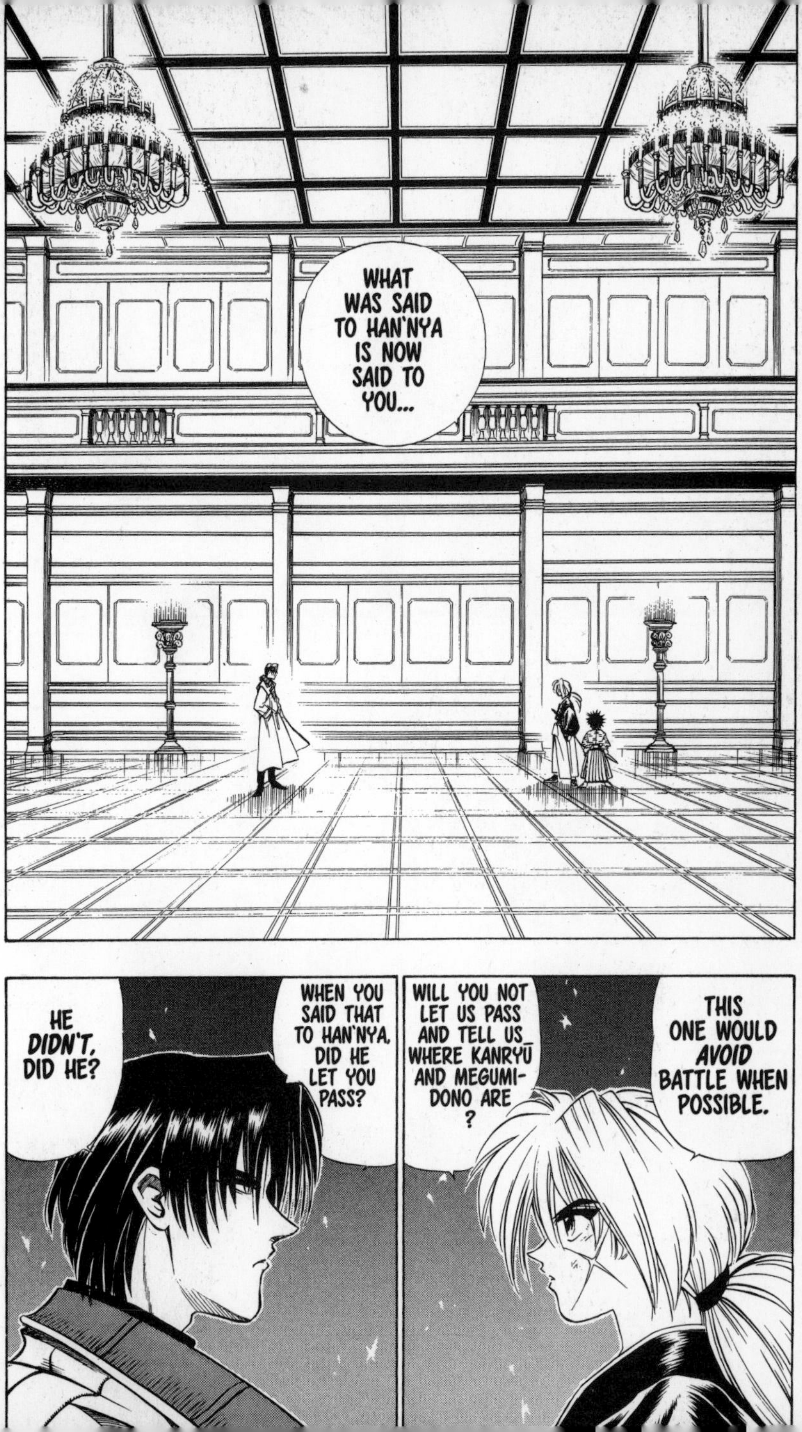
WHAT WAS SAID TO HAN'NYA IS NOW SAID TO YOU...
THIS ONE WOULD *AVOID* BATTLE WHEN POSSIBLE.
WILL YOU NOT LET US PASS AND TELL US WHERE KANRYŪ AND MEGUMI-DONO ARE?
WHEN YOU SAID THAT TO HAN'NYA, DID HE LET YOU PASS?
HE *DIDN'T*, DID HE?

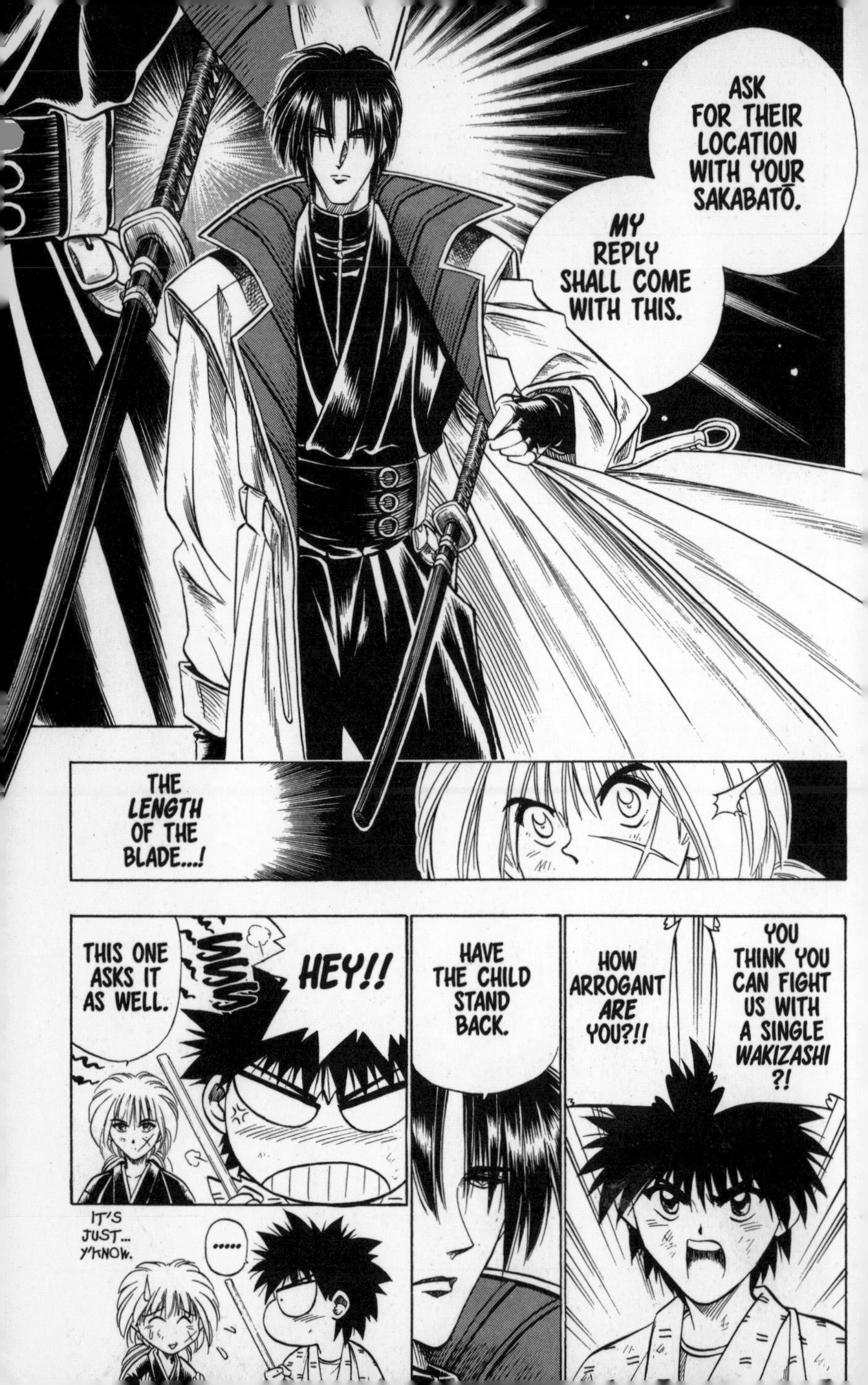
ASK FOR THEIR LOCATION WITH YOUR SAKABATŌ.
MY REPLY SHALL COME WITH THIS.
THE LENGTH OF THE BLADE...!
YOU THINK YOU CAN FIGHT US WITH A SINGLE WAKIZASHI ?!
HOW ARROGANT ARE YOU?!!
HAVE THE CHILD STAND BACK.
THIS ONE ASKS IT AS WELL.
HEY!!
......
IT'S JUST... Y'KNOW.

READ THIS WAY

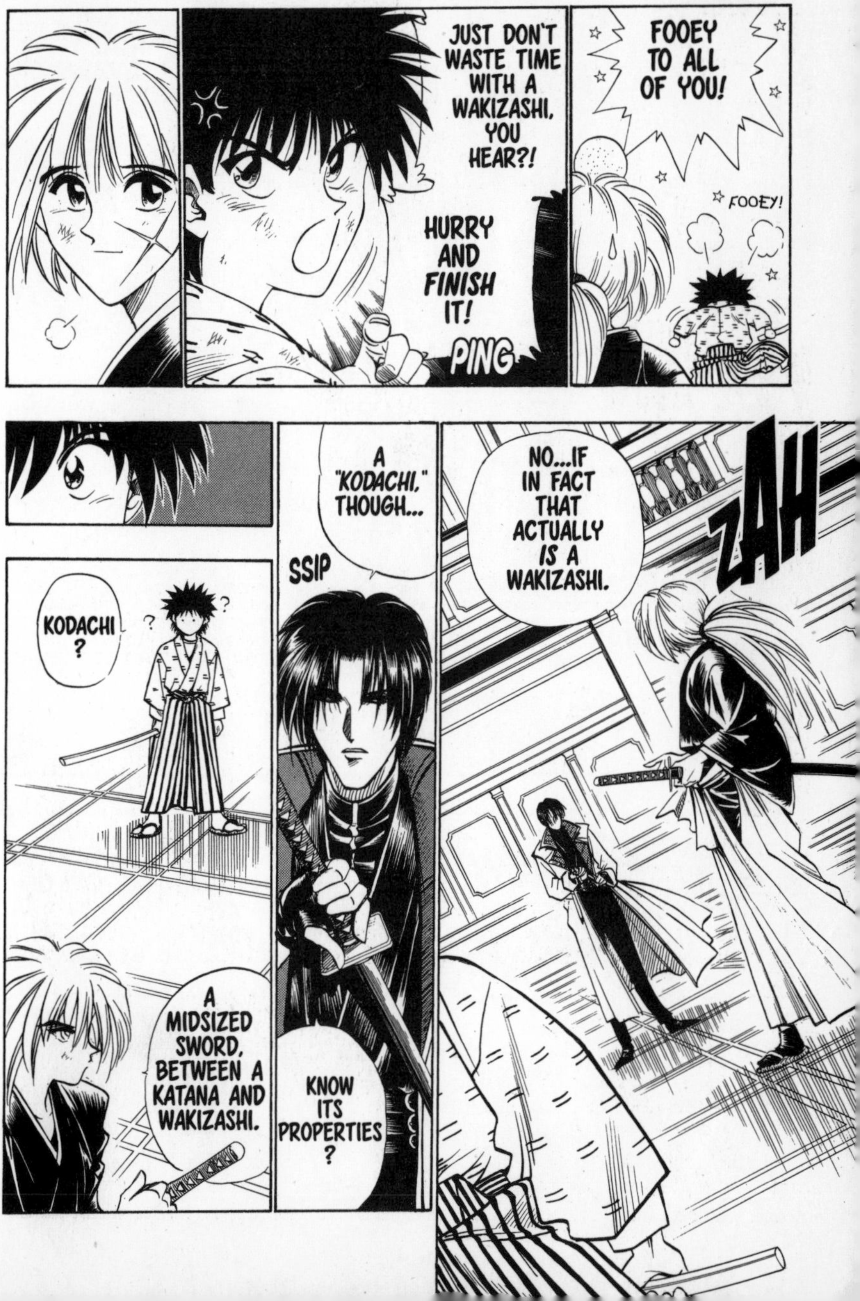
FOOEY TO ALL OF YOU!
FOOEY!
JUST DON'T WASTE TIME WITH A WAKIZASHI, YOU HEAR?!
HURRY AND FINISH IT!
PING
ZAH
NO...IF IN FACT THAT ACTUALLY IS A WAKIZASHI.
A "KODACHI," THOUGH...
SSIP
KNOW ITS PROPERTIES?
KODACHI?
A MIDSIZED SWORD, BETWEEN A KATANA AND WAKIZASHI.

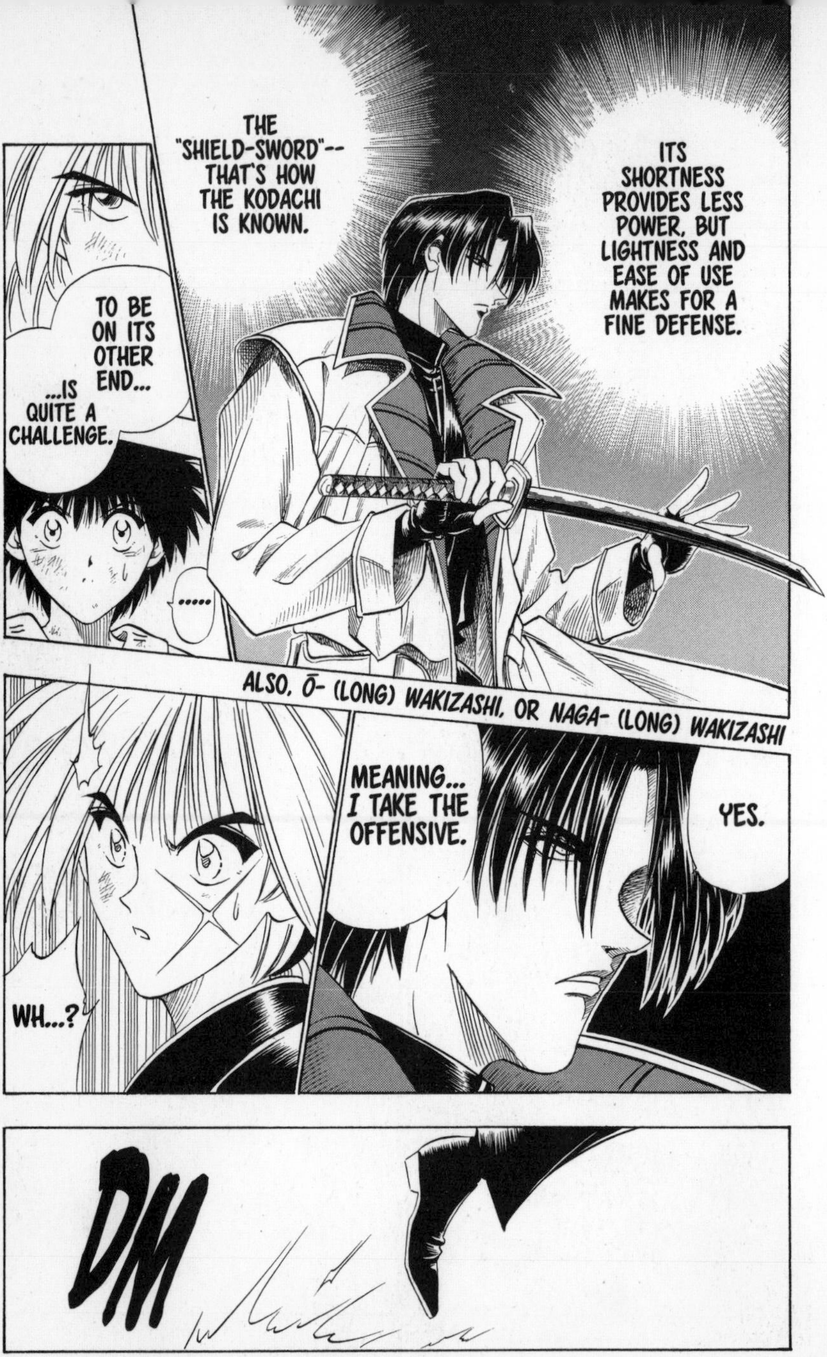
ITS SHORTNESS PROVIDES LESS POWER, BUT LIGHTNESS AND EASE OF USE MAKES FOR A FINE DEFENSE.
THE "SHIELD-SWORD"-- THAT'S HOW THE KODACHI IS KNOWN.
TO BE ON ITS OTHER END...
...IS QUITE A CHALLENGE.
.....
ALSO, Ō- (LONG) WAKIZASHI, OR NAGA- (LONG) WAKIZASHI
YES.
MEANING... I TAKE THE OFFENSIVE.
WH...?
DM

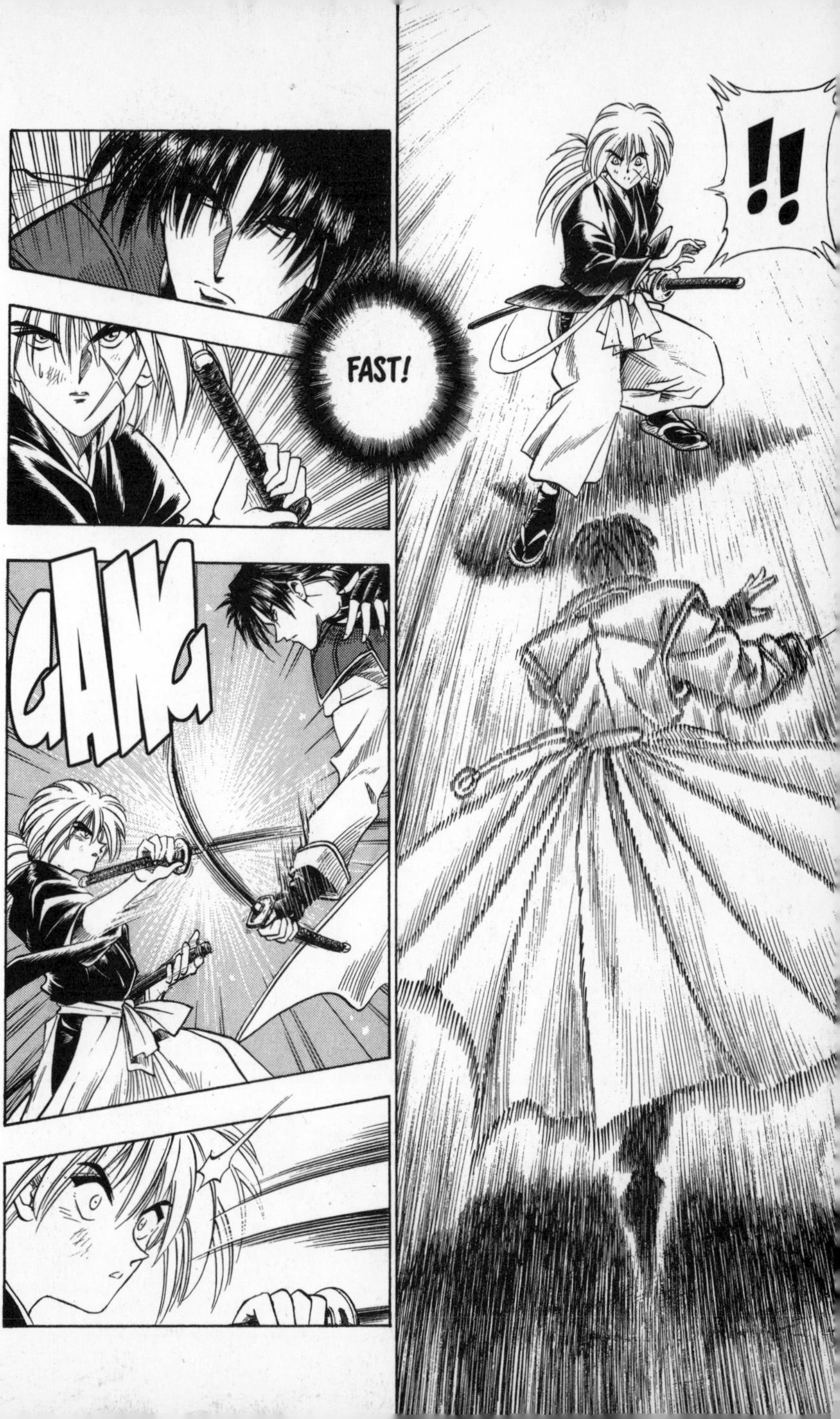
!!
FAST!
GANG

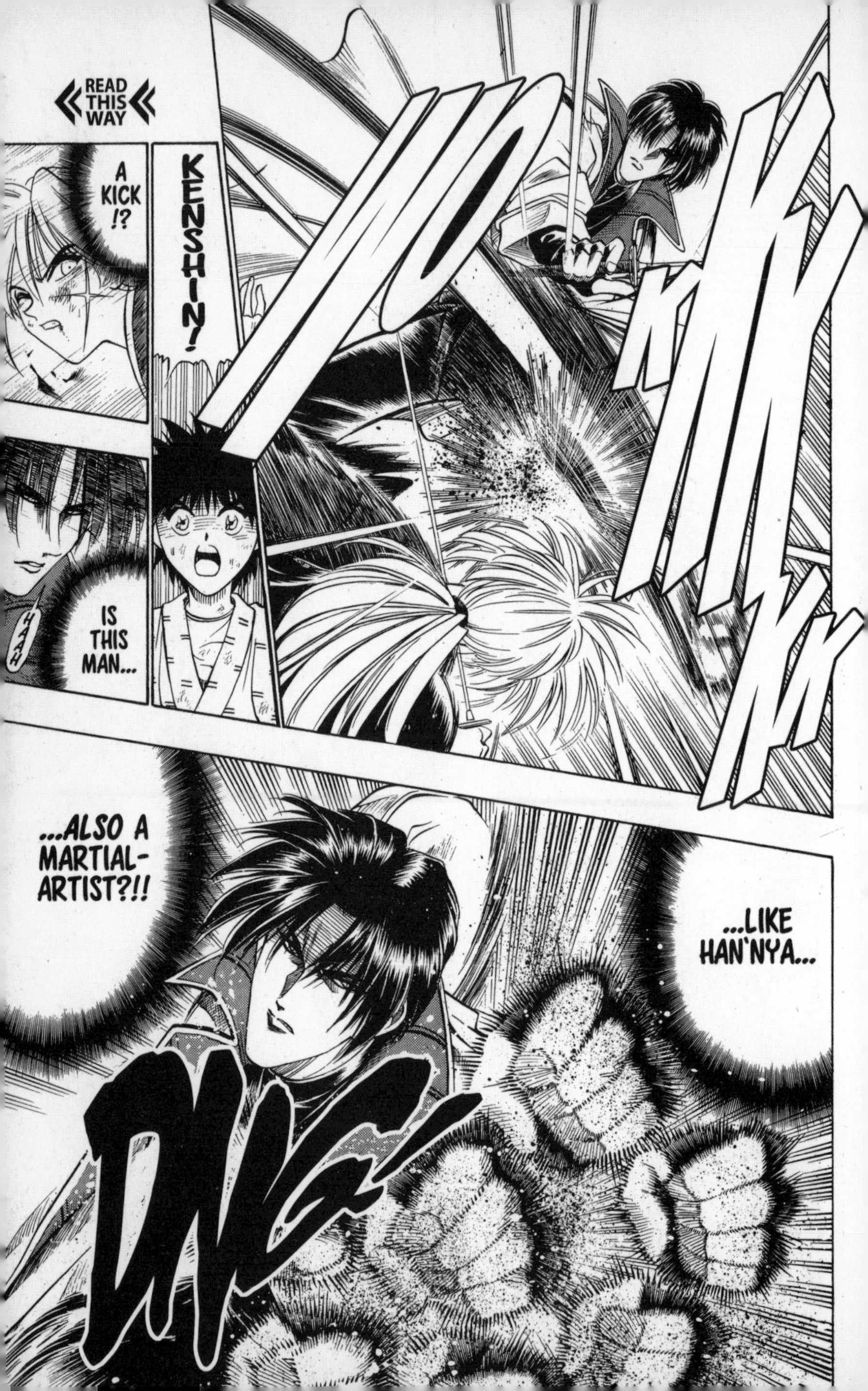
READ THIS WAY
KENSHIN!
A KICK!?
IS THIS MAN...
HAAH
...LIKE HAN'NYA...
...ALSO A MARTIAL-ARTIST?!!

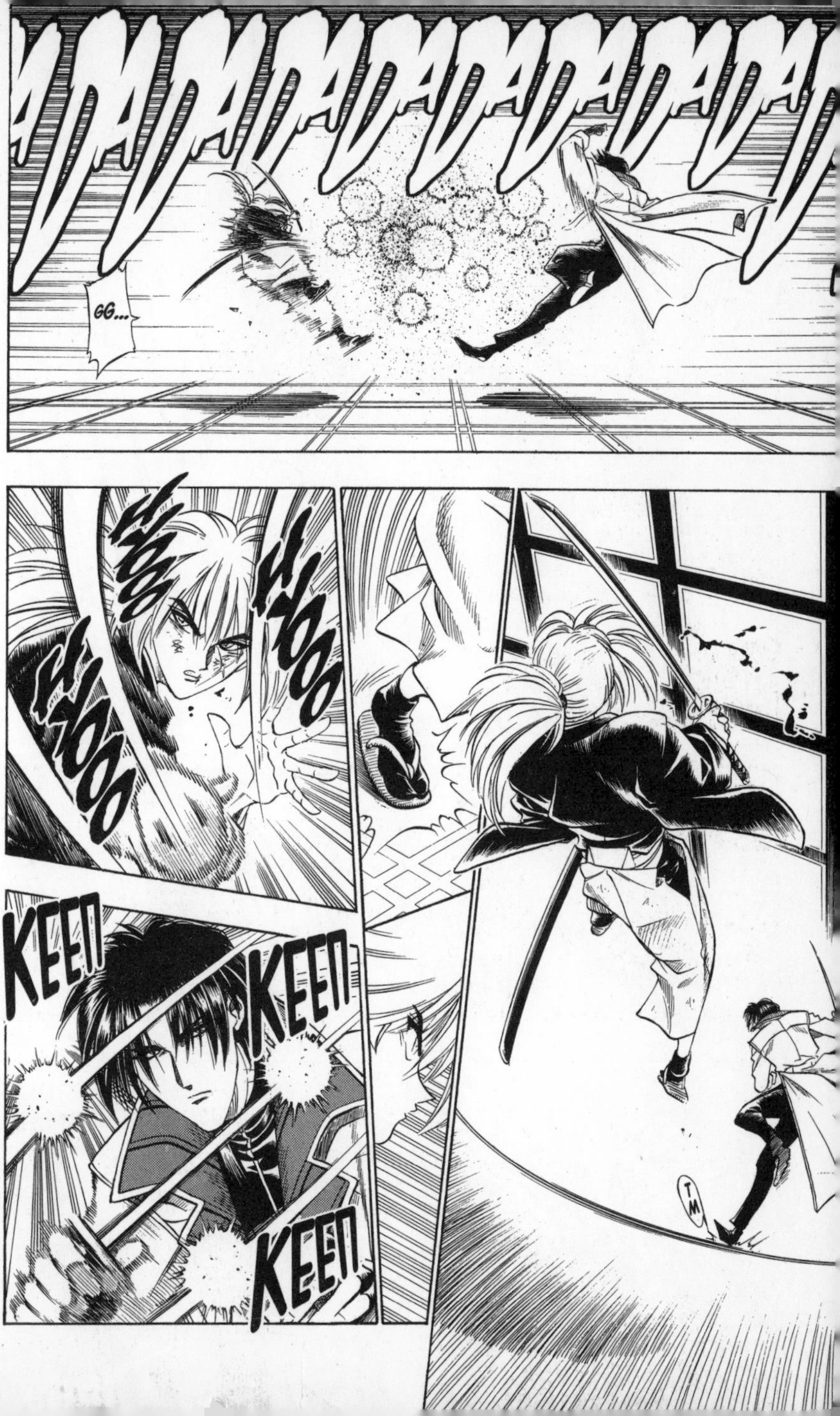
ADADADADADADADA
GG...
TM
WHOOO
WHOOO
WHOOO
KEEN
KEEN
KEEN

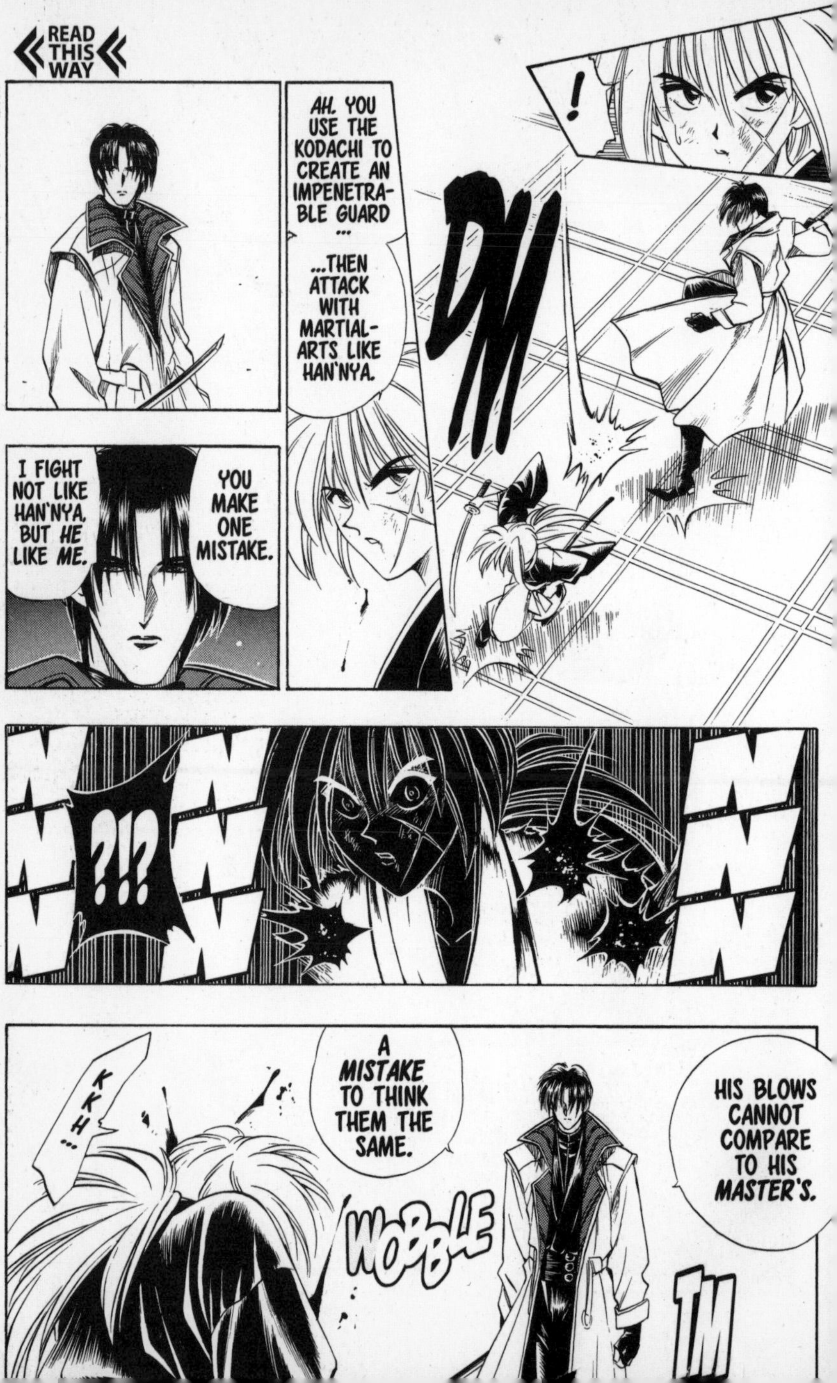
READ THIS WAY
!
DM
AH. YOU USE THE KODACHI TO CREATE AN IMPENETRABLE GUARD ...
...THEN ATTACK WITH MARTIAL-ARTS LIKE HAN'NYA.
YOU MAKE ONE MISTAKE.
I FIGHT NOT LIKE HAN'NYA, BUT *HE* LIKE *ME*.
?!?
HIS BLOWS CANNOT COMPARE TO HIS *MASTER'S*.
A *MISTAKE* TO THINK THEM THE SAME.
KKH ...
WOBBLE
TM

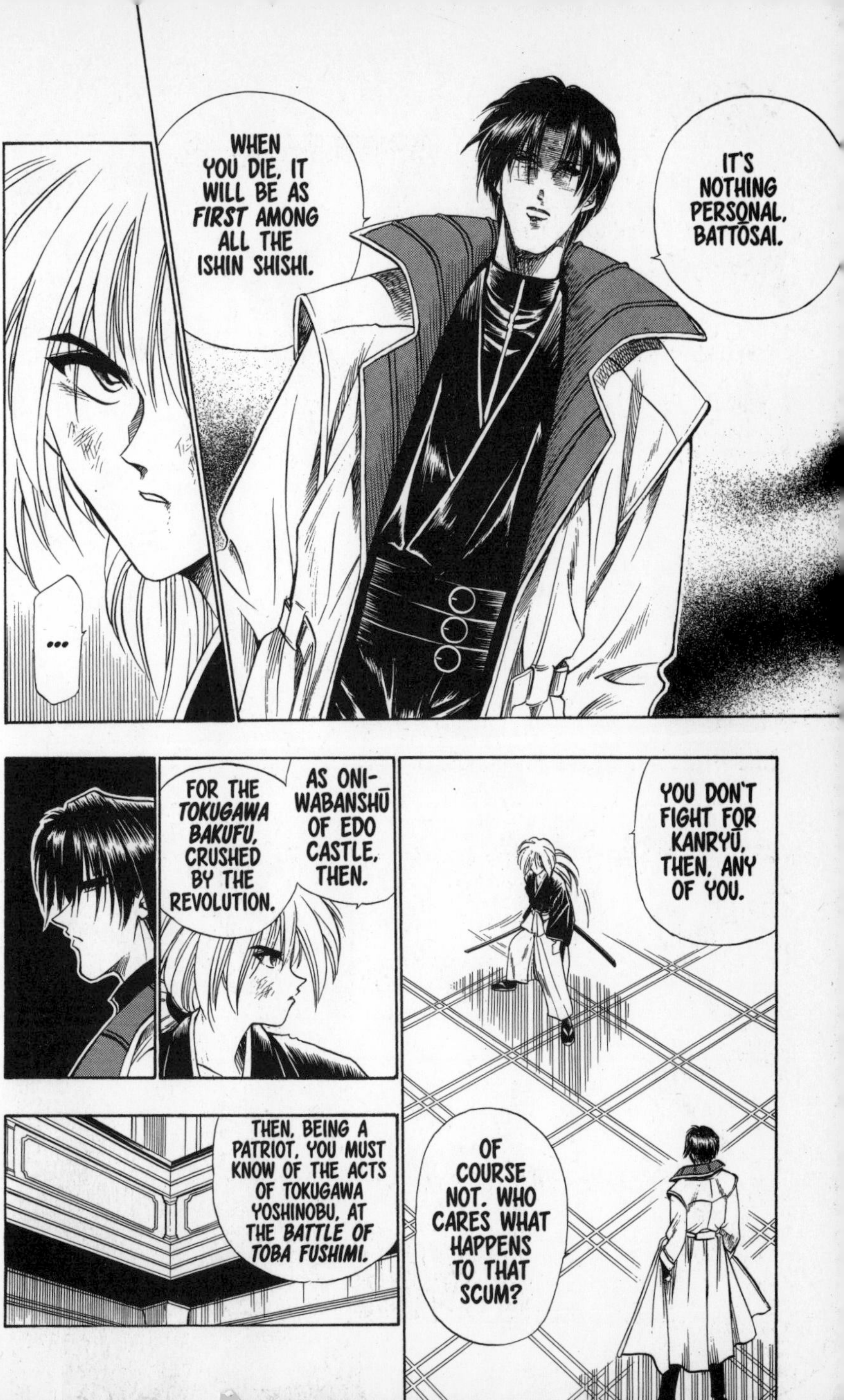
IT'S NOTHING PERSONAL, BATTŌSAI.
WHEN YOU DIE, IT WILL BE AS *FIRST* AMONG ALL THE ISHIN SHISHI.
...
YOU DON'T FIGHT FOR KANRYŪ, THEN, ANY OF YOU.
OF COURSE NOT. WHO CARES WHAT HAPPENS TO THAT SCUM?
AS ONIWABANSHŪ OF EDO CASTLE, THEN.
FOR THE *TOKUGAWA BAKUFU,* CRUSHED BY THE REVOLUTION.
THEN, BEING A PATRIOT, YOU MUST KNOW OF THE ACTS OF TOKUGAWA YOSHINOBU, AT THE *BATTLE OF TOBA FUSHIMI.*

READ THIS WAY

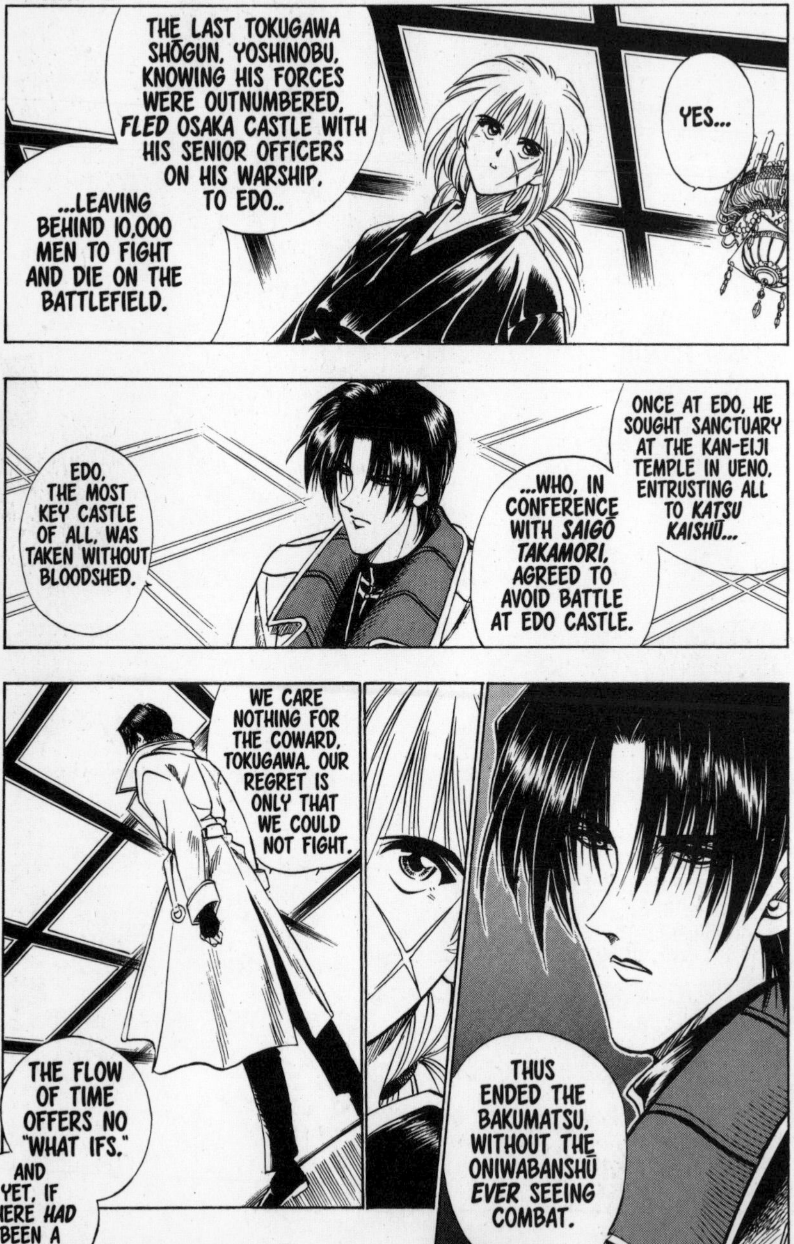
YES...
THE LAST TOKUGAWA SHŌGUN, YOSHINOBU, KNOWING HIS FORCES WERE OUTNUMBERED, *FLED* OSAKA CASTLE WITH HIS SENIOR OFFICERS ON HIS WARSHIP, TO EDO..
...LEAVING BEHIND 10,000 MEN TO FIGHT AND DIE ON THE BATTLEFIELD.
ONCE AT EDO, HE SOUGHT SANCTUARY AT THE KAN-EIJI TEMPLE IN UENO, ENTRUSTING ALL TO *KATSU KAISHŪ*...
...WHO, IN CONFERENCE WITH *SAIGŌ TAKAMORI*, AGREED TO AVOID BATTLE AT EDO CASTLE.
EDO, THE MOST KEY CASTLE OF ALL, WAS TAKEN WITHOUT BLOODSHED.
THUS ENDED THE BAKUMATSU, WITHOUT THE ONIWABANSHŪ *EVER* SEEING COMBAT.
WE CARE NOTHING FOR THE COWARD, TOKUGAWA. OUR REGRET IS ONLY THAT WE COULD NOT FIGHT.
THE FLOW OF TIME OFFERS NO "WHAT IFS."
AND YET, IF THERE *HAD* BEEN A BATTLE...

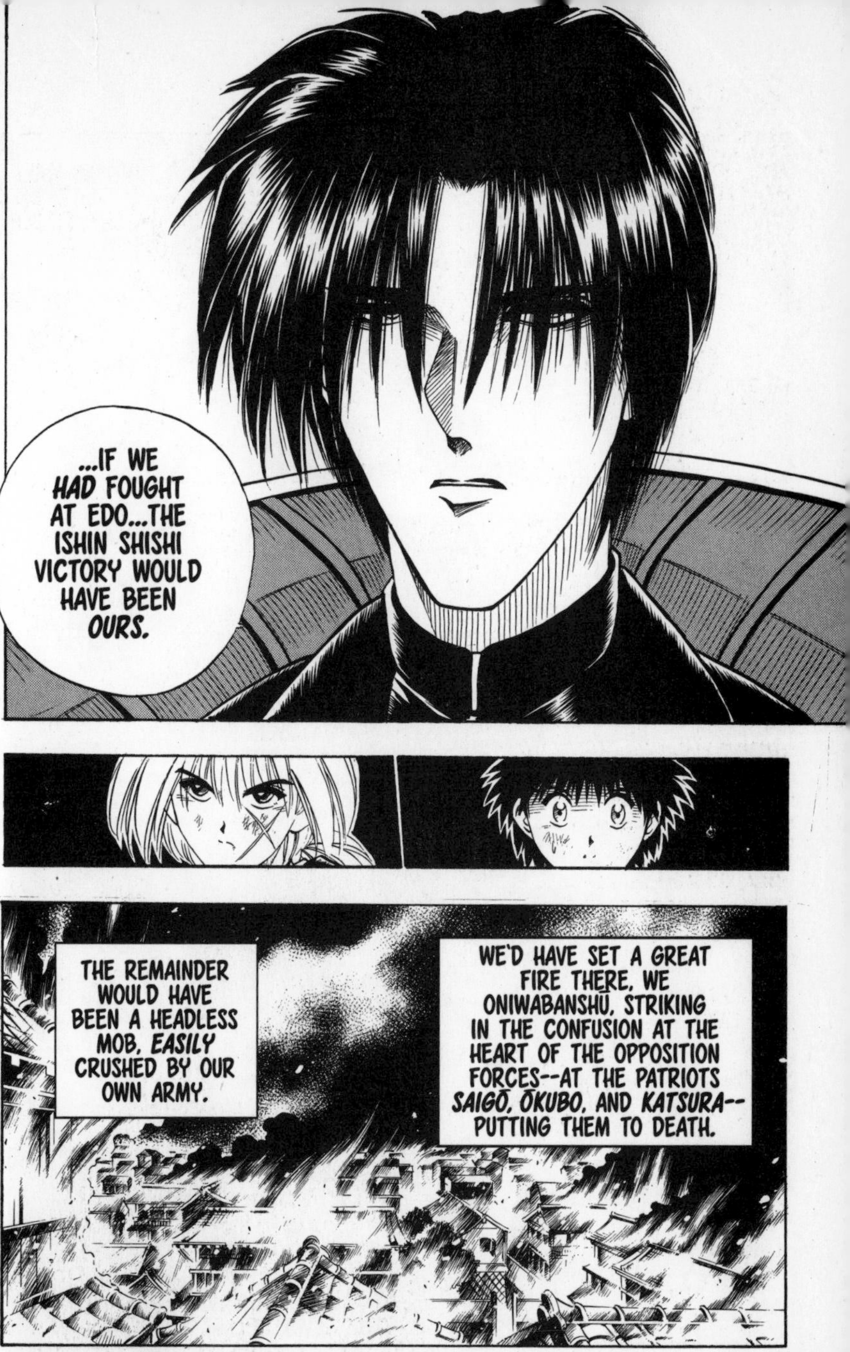
...IF WE HAD FOUGHT AT EDO...THE ISHIN SHISHI VICTORY WOULD HAVE BEEN OURS.
WE'D HAVE SET A GREAT FIRE THERE, WE ONIWABANSHŪ, STRIKING IN THE CONFUSION AT THE HEART OF THE OPPOSITION FORCES--AT THE PATRIOTS SAIGŌ, ŌKUBO, AND KATSURA--PUTTING THEM TO DEATH.
THE REMAINDER WOULD HAVE BEEN A HEADLESS MOB, EASILY CRUSHED BY OUR OWN ARMY.

READ THIS WAY

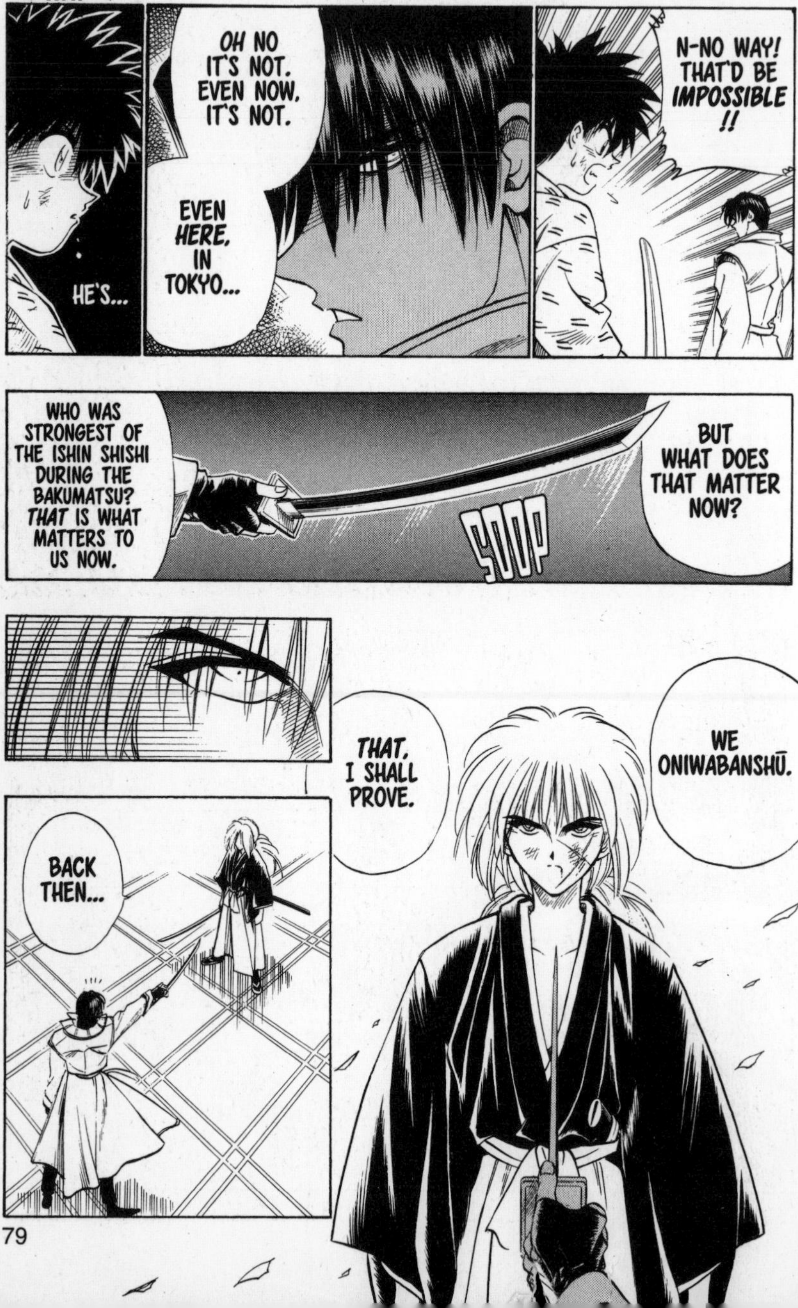
N-NO WAY! THAT'D BE IMPOSSIBLE !!
OH NO IT'S NOT. EVEN NOW, IT'S NOT.
EVEN HERE, IN TOKYO...
HE'S...
BUT WHAT DOES THAT MATTER NOW?
WHO WAS STRONGEST OF THE ISHIN SHISHI DURING THE BAKUMATSU? THAT IS WHAT MATTERS TO US NOW.
SOOP
WE ONIWABANSHŪ.
THAT, I SHALL PROVE.
BACK THEN...

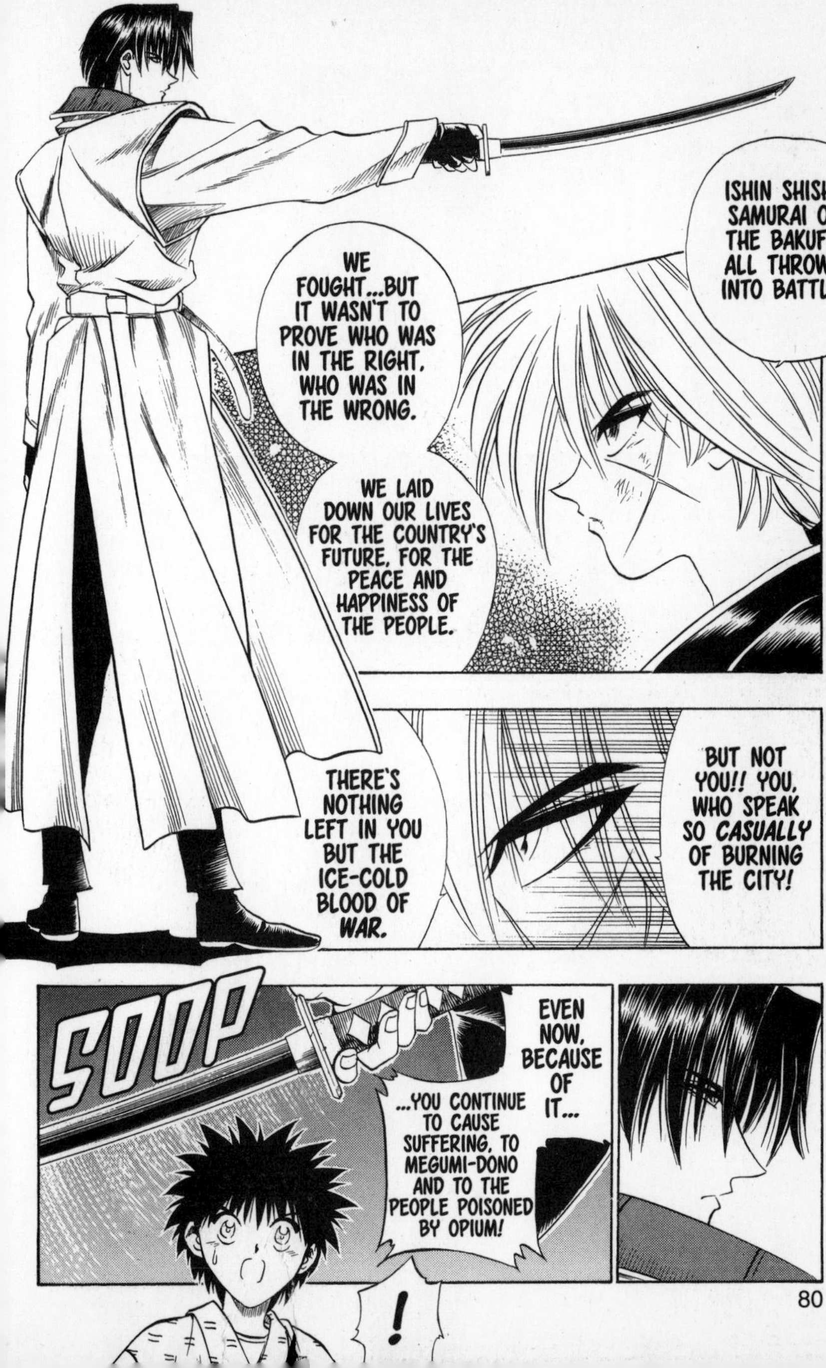
ISHIN SHISHI, SAMURAI OF THE BAKUFU, ALL THROWN INTO BATTLE.
WE FOUGHT...BUT IT WASN'T TO PROVE WHO WAS IN THE RIGHT, WHO WAS IN THE WRONG.
WE LAID DOWN OUR LIVES FOR THE COUNTRY'S FUTURE, FOR THE PEACE AND HAPPINESS OF THE PEOPLE.
BUT NOT YOU!! YOU, WHO SPEAK SO *CASUALLY* OF BURNING THE CITY!
THERE'S NOTHING LEFT IN YOU BUT THE ICE-COLD BLOOD OF *WAR.*
EVEN NOW, BECAUSE OF IT...
...YOU CONTINUE TO CAUSE SUFFERING, TO MEGUMI-DONO AND TO THE PEOPLE POISONED BY OPIUM!
SOOP
!

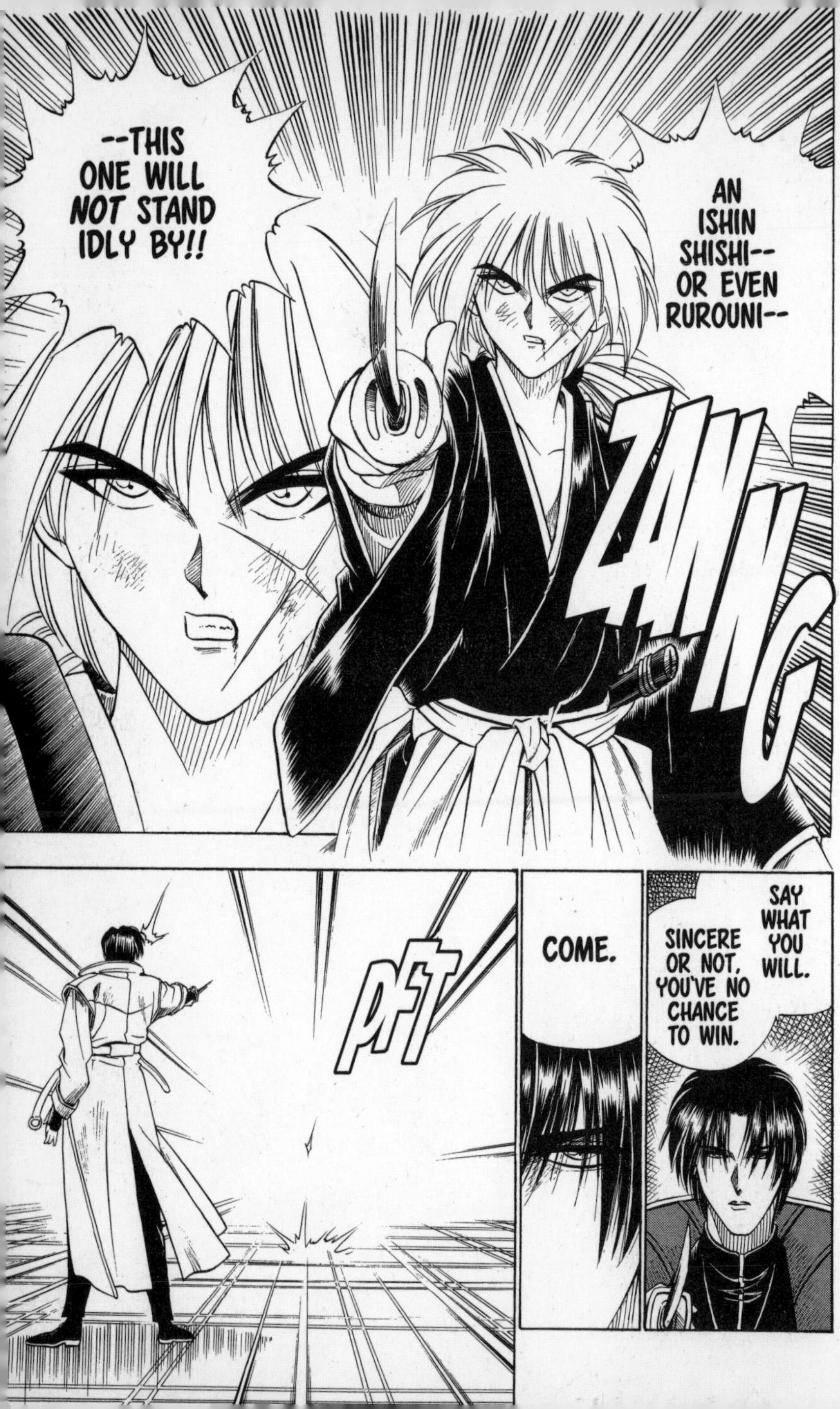
AN ISHIN SHISHI-- OR EVEN RUROUNI--
--THIS ONE WILL NOT STAND IDLY BY!!
ZANNG
SAY WHAT YOU WILL.
SINCERE OR NOT, YOU'VE NO CHANCE TO WIN.
COME.
pft

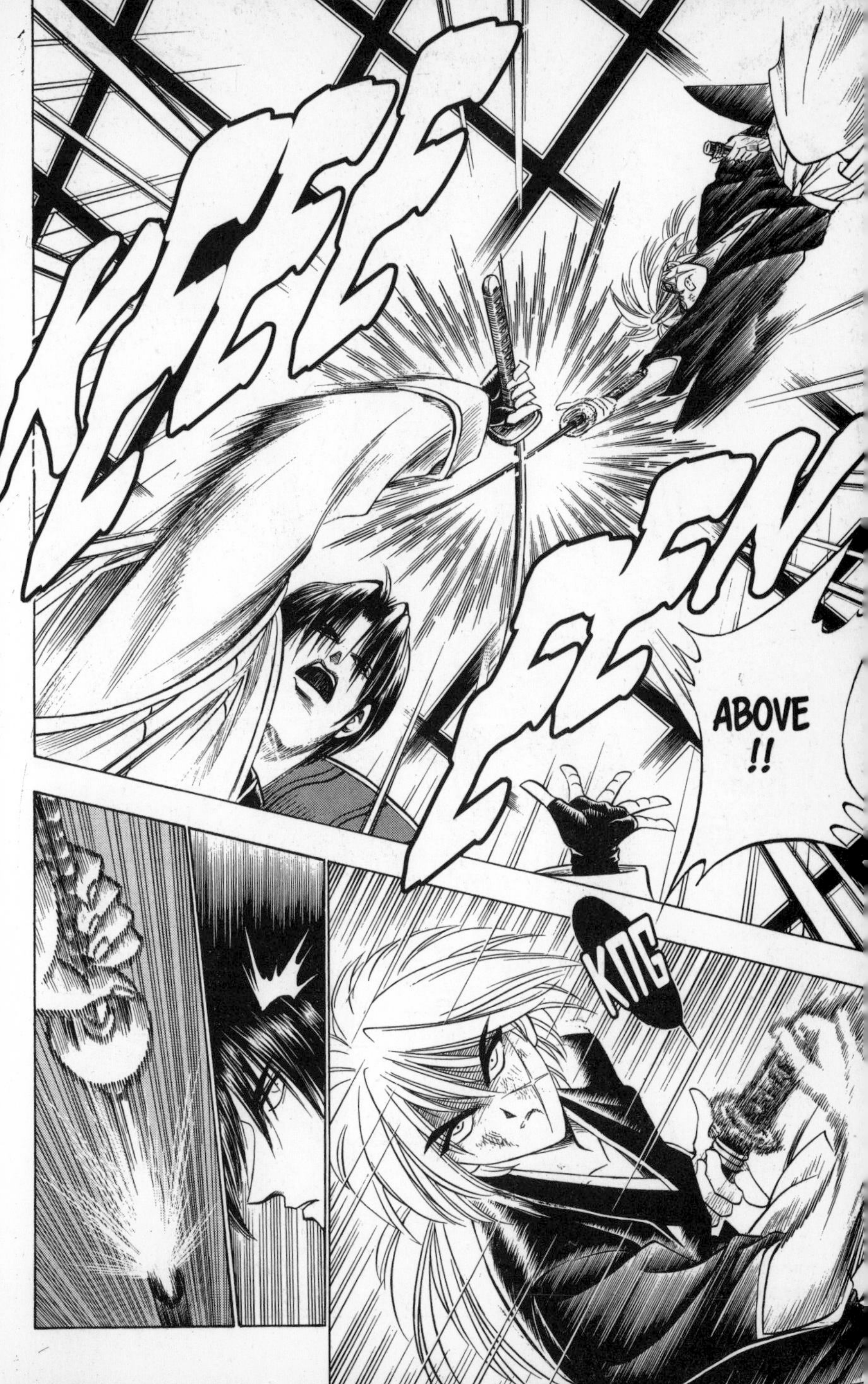
ABOVE !!
KNG

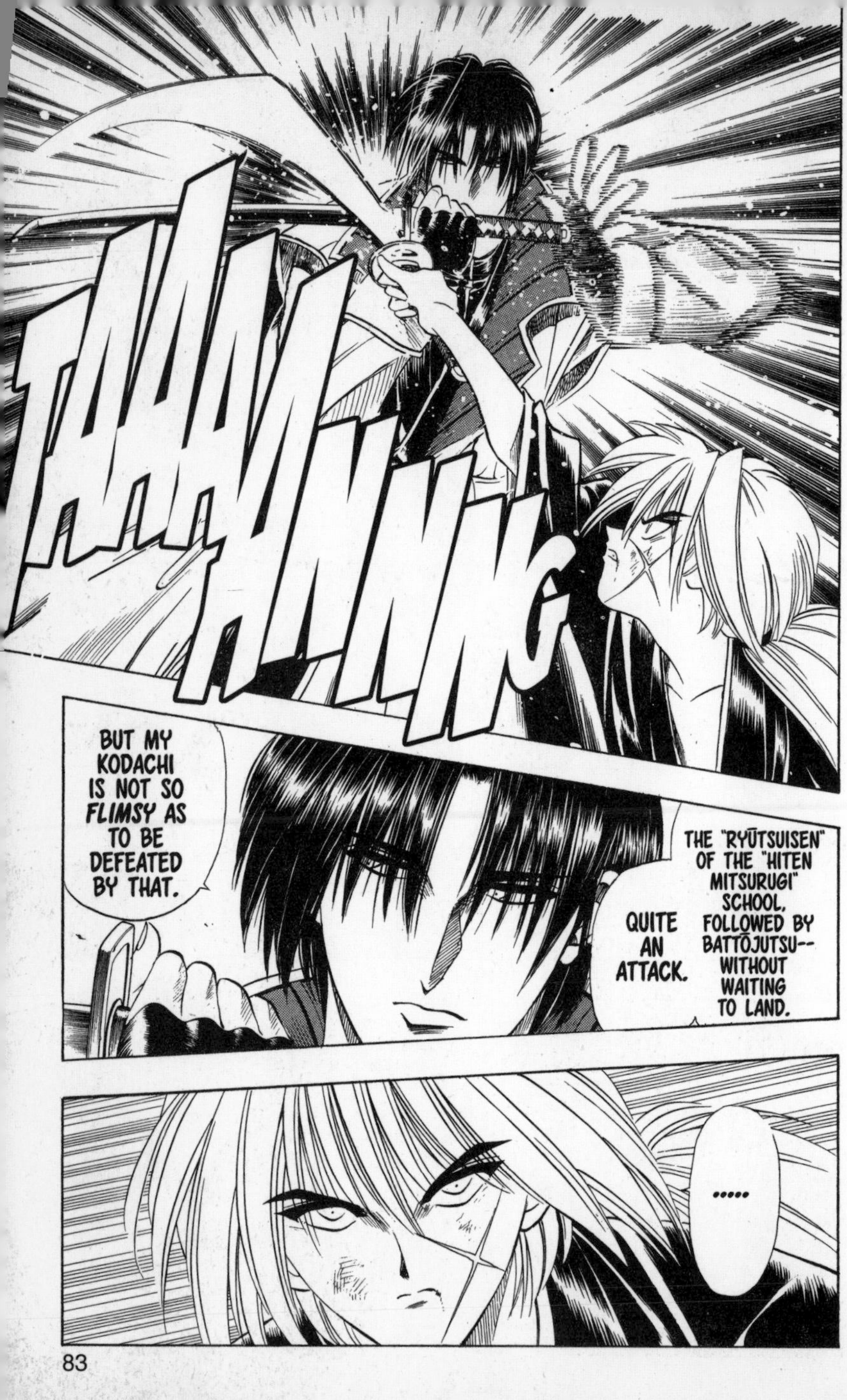
TAAAANNNNG
THE "RYŪTSUISEN" OF THE "HITEN MITSURUGI" SCHOOL, FOLLOWED BY BATTŌJUTSU-- WITHOUT WAITING TO LAND.
QUITE AN ATTACK.
BUT MY KODACHI IS NOT SO *FLIMSY* AS TO BE DEFEATED BY THAT.
......

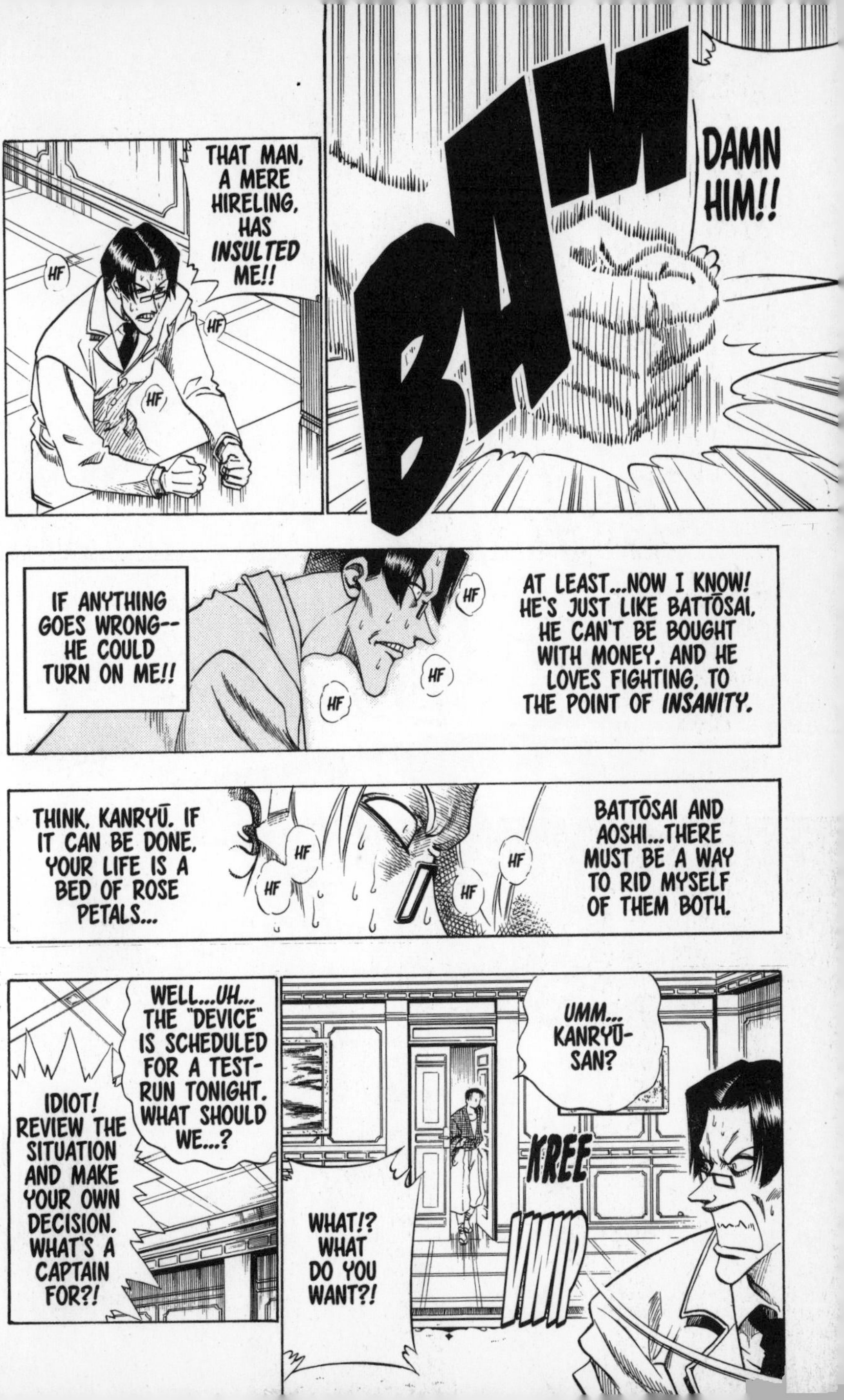
DAMN HIM!!
BAM
THAT MAN, A MERE HIRELING, HAS *INSULTED* ME!!
HF
HF
HF
AT LEAST...NOW I KNOW! HE'S JUST LIKE BATTŌSAI. HE CAN'T BE BOUGHT WITH MONEY. AND HE LOVES FIGHTING, TO THE POINT OF *INSANITY*.
HF
HF
HF
IF ANYTHING GOES WRONG-- HE COULD TURN ON ME!!
BATTŌSAI AND AOSHI...THERE MUST BE A WAY TO RID MYSELF OF THEM BOTH.
HF
HF
HF
HF
THINK, KANRYŪ. IF IT CAN BE DONE, YOUR LIFE IS A BED OF ROSE PETALS...
UMM... KANRYŪ-SAN?
KREE
WHAT!? WHAT DO YOU WANT?!
WELL...*UH*... THE "DEVICE" IS SCHEDULED FOR A TEST-RUN TONIGHT. WHAT SHOULD WE...?
IDIOT! REVIEW THE SITUATION AND MAKE YOUR OWN DECISION. WHAT'S A CAPTAIN FOR?!

READ THIS WAY

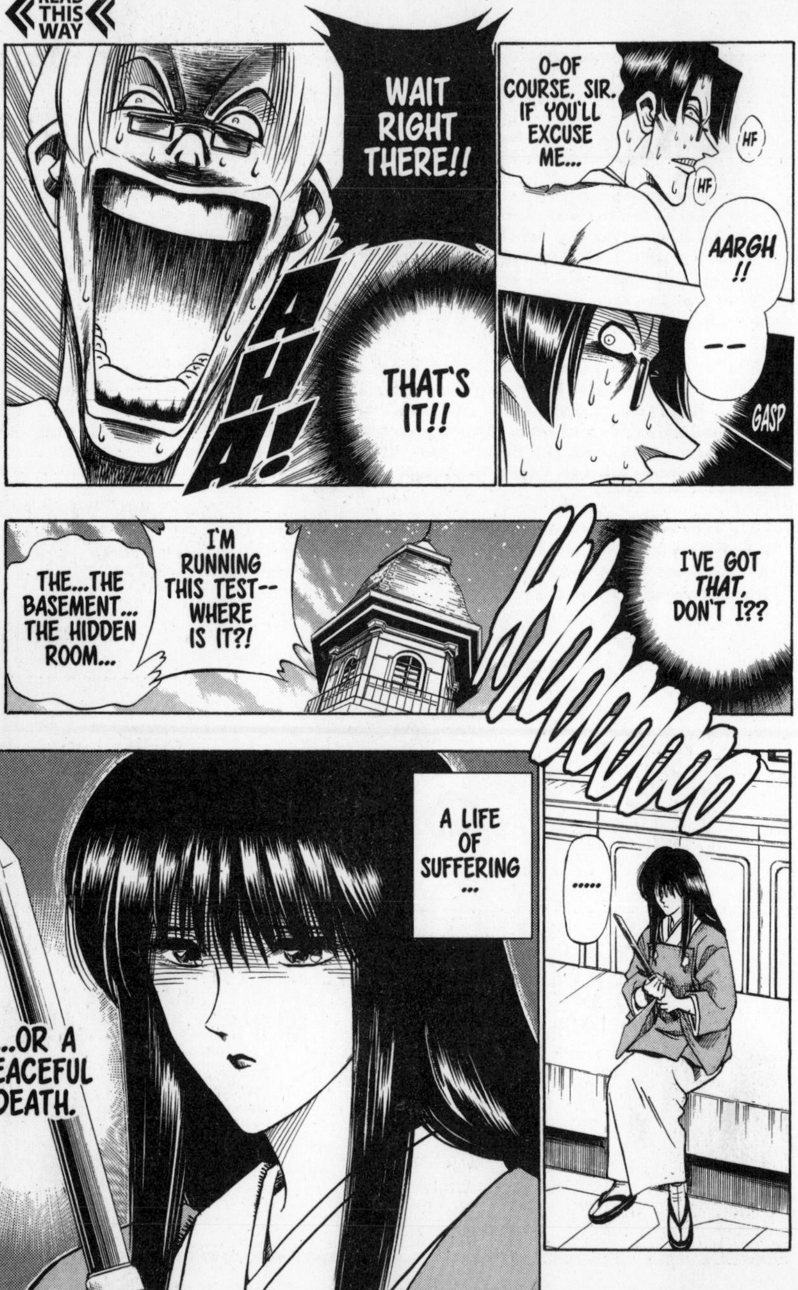
O-OF COURSE, SIR. IF YOU'LL EXCUSE ME...
HF
HF
AARGH!!
--
GASP
WAIT RIGHT THERE!!
AHA!
THAT'S IT!!
I'VE GOT THAT, DON'T I??
I'M RUNNING THIS TEST-- WHERE IS IT?!
THE...THE BASEMENT... THE HIDDEN ROOM...
......
A LIFE OF SUFFERING ...
...OR A PEACEFUL DEATH.

## The Secret Life of Characters (11)

# —Oniwabanshū • Shikijō—

**Shikijō's model is Sanosuke. Shocking to hear, perhaps, but true. His personality, then, is similar (cocksure and proud, but also generous), as is his fighting style (powerful), as well as philosophy (supportive of his "number one"). By putting them on opposite sides and having them fight, Shikijō and Sanosuke clearly embody the differences between the two sides. That was the idea behind the fight (which may or may not have worked, but...).**

**Han'nya wasn't a character you could describe as "evil," but even though Shikijō *was* setup as the complete villain, it was perhaps the noble manner of his death that transformed him into a pretty cool guy. He does have an enthusiastic group of fans...but, then again, so do all the Oniwabanshū. For this volume, though, the best response was for the young Aoshi. I guess what matters most in a man is his face (PAINED LAUGH).**

**For his design, there was no specific model. Since he's a "power fighter," I made him all muscles—but that didn't really make him strange-enough looking—so I also gave him scars all over, along with superhero-like exaggerated musculature.**

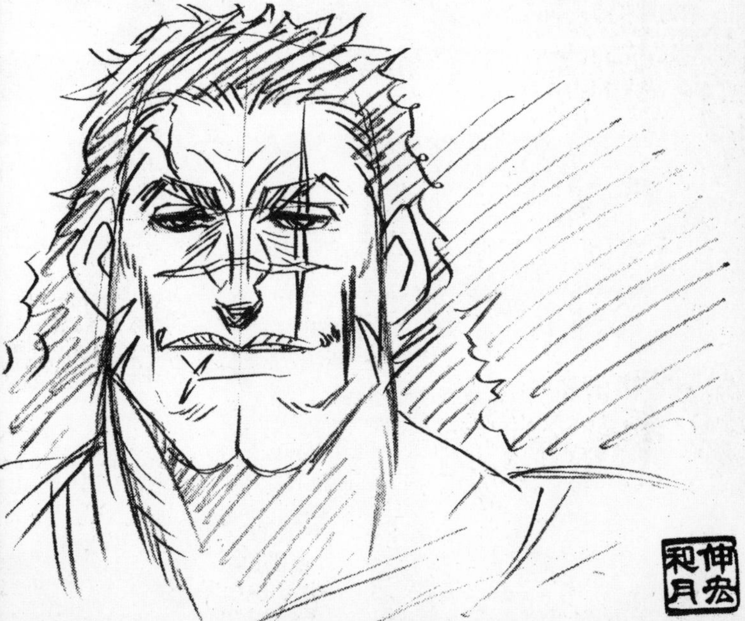
伸宏
和月

# Act 27 Battle's Heat

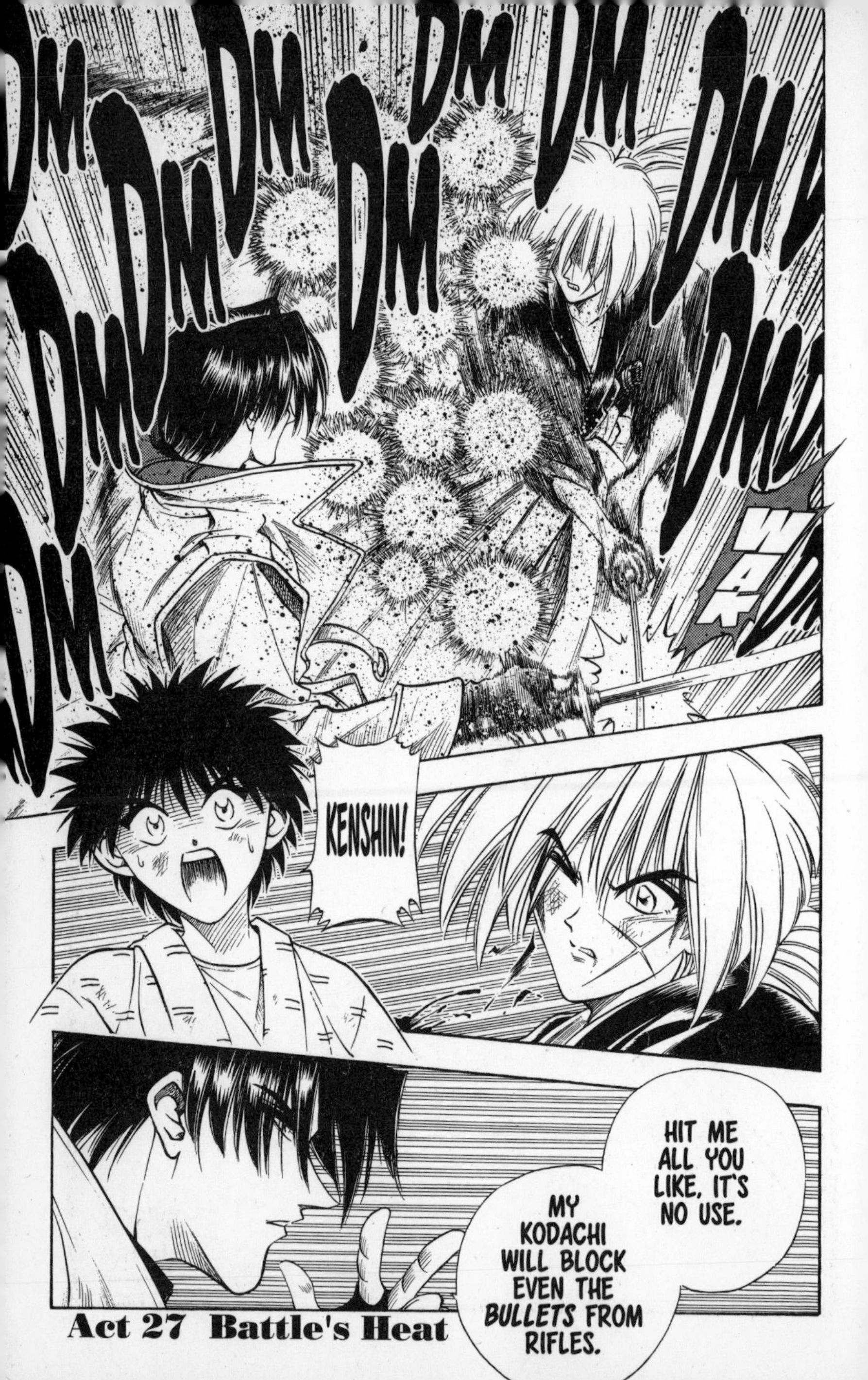
DM DM DM DM DM DM DM DM DM DM DM DM DM DM
WAK
KENSHIN!
HIT ME ALL YOU LIKE, IT'S NO USE.
MY KODACHI WILL BLOCK EVEN THE *BULLETS* FROM RIFLES.

READ THIS WAY

# Act 27
# Battle's Heat

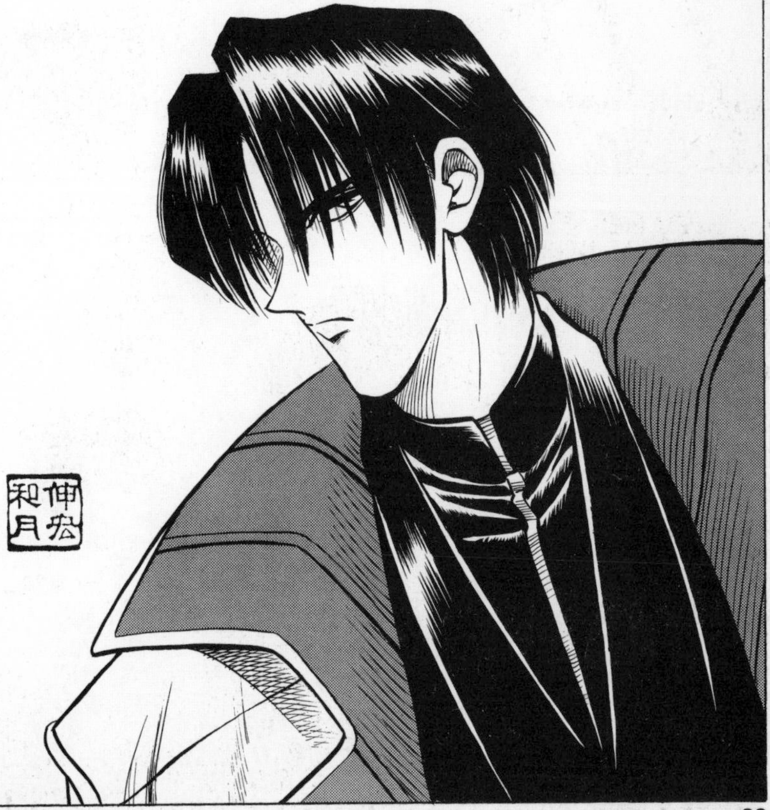
伸宏和月

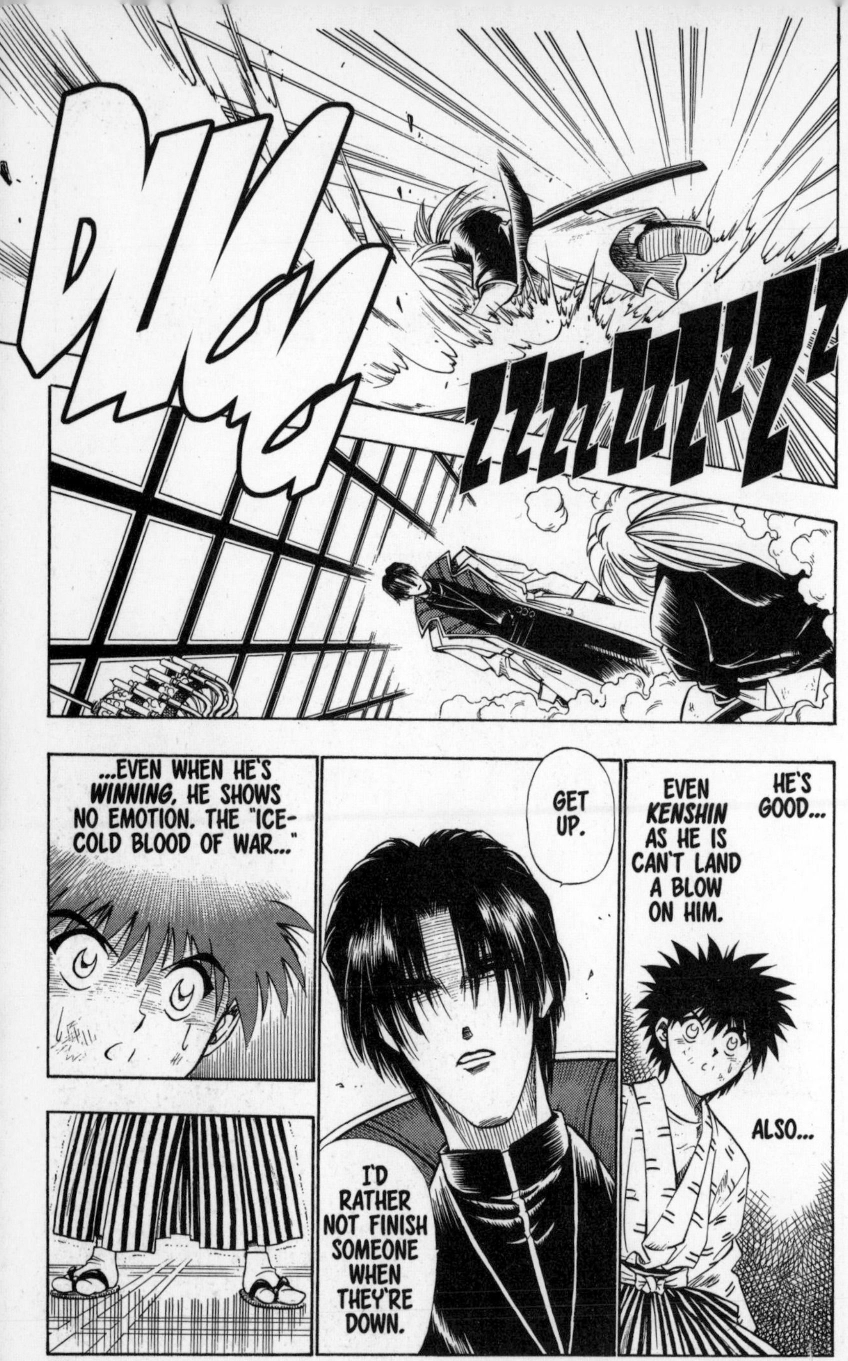
HE'S GOOD...
EVEN *KENSHIN* AS HE IS CAN'T LAND A BLOW ON HIM.
ALSO...
GET UP.
I'D RATHER NOT FINISH SOMEONE WHEN THEY'RE DOWN.
...EVEN WHEN HE'S *WINNING*, HE SHOWS NO EMOTION. THE "ICE-COLD BLOOD OF WAR..."

READ THIS WAY

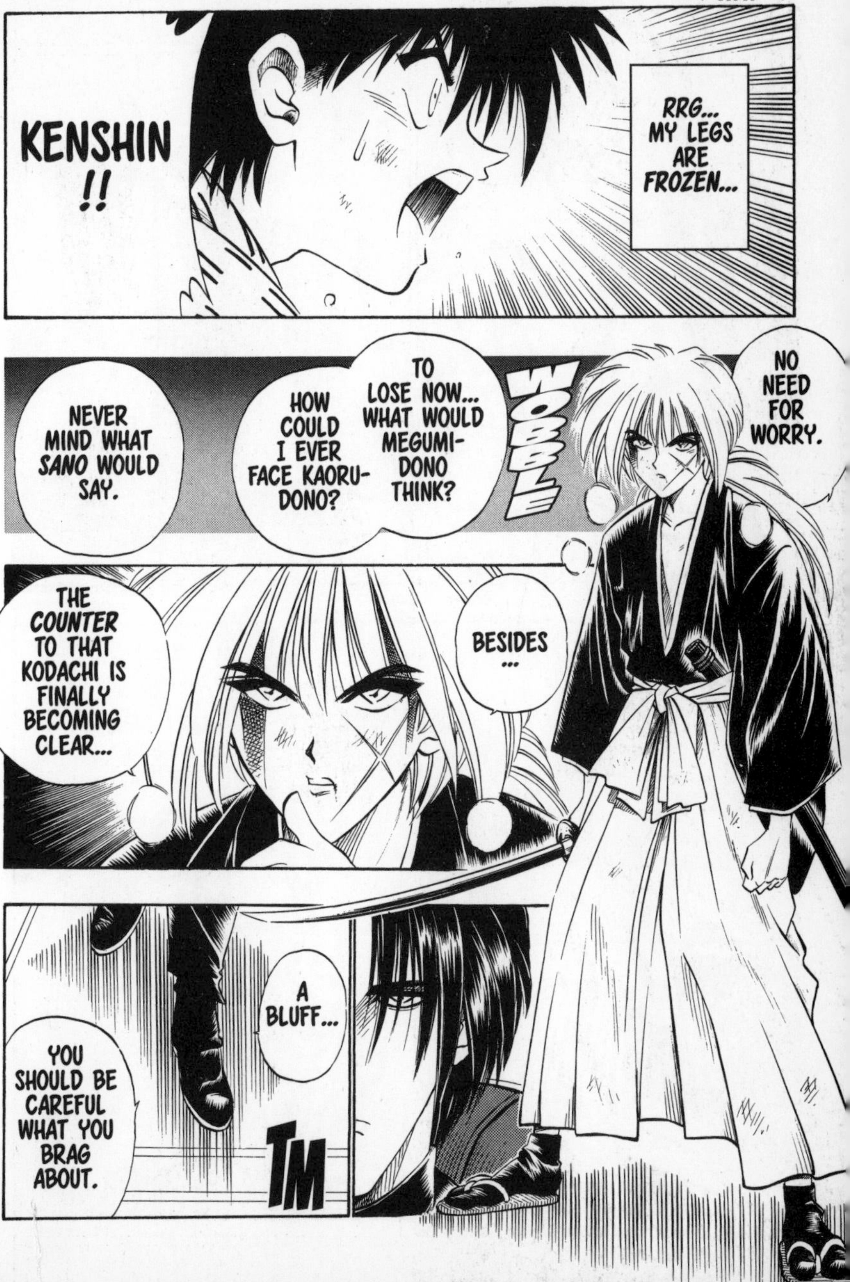

RRG... MY LEGS ARE FROZEN...
KENSHIN!!
NO NEED FOR WORRY.
WOBBLE
TO LOSE NOW... WHAT WOULD MEGUMI-DONO THINK?
HOW COULD I EVER FACE KAORU-DONO?
NEVER MIND WHAT *SANO* WOULD SAY.
BESIDES...
THE *COUNTER* TO THAT KODACHI IS FINALLY BECOMING CLEAR...
A BLUFF...
TM
YOU SHOULD BE CAREFUL WHAT YOU BRAG ABOUT.

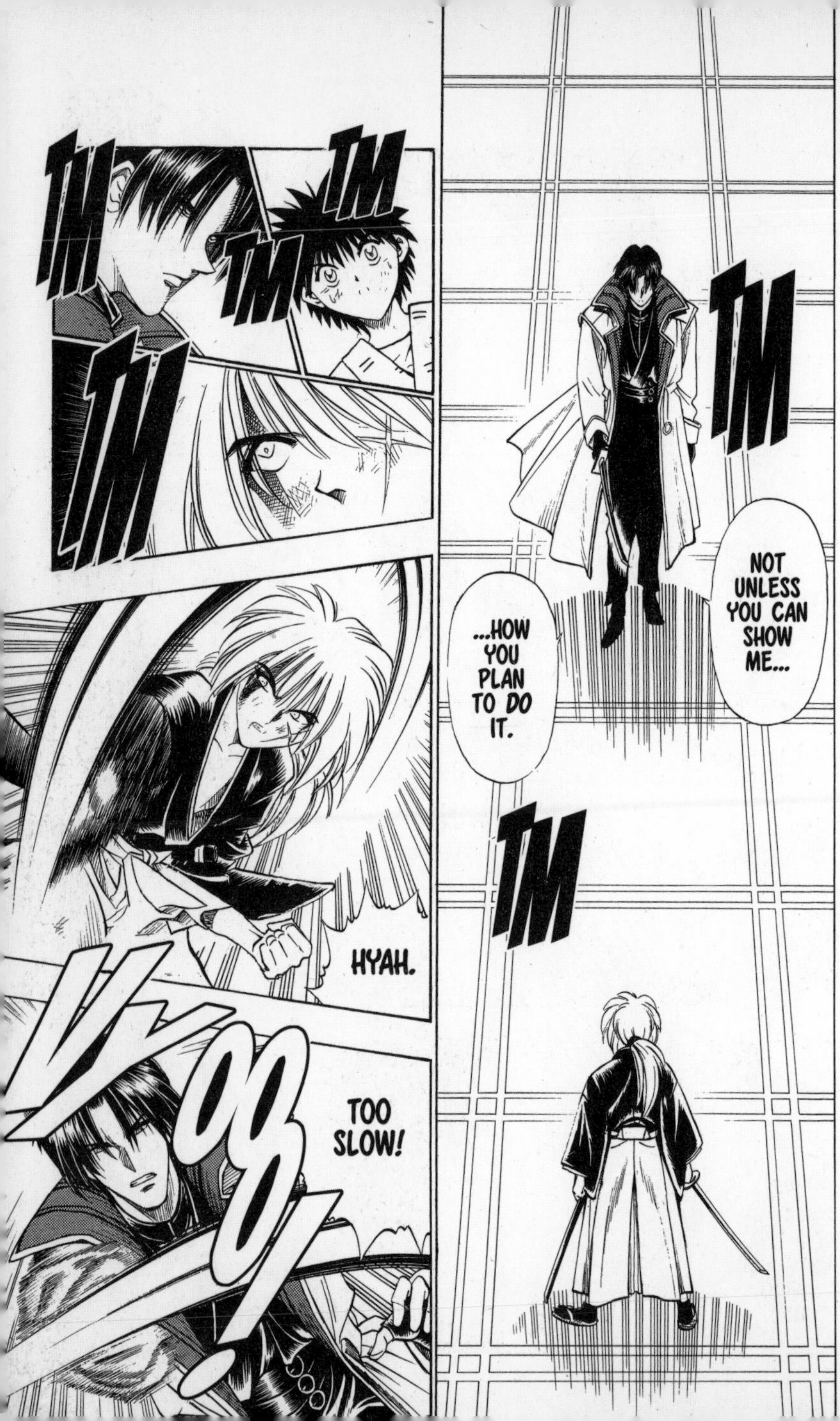
TM
NOT UNLESS YOU CAN SHOW ME...
...HOW YOU PLAN TO DO IT.
TM
TM
TM
TM
TM
HYAH.
VWOO
TOO SLOW!

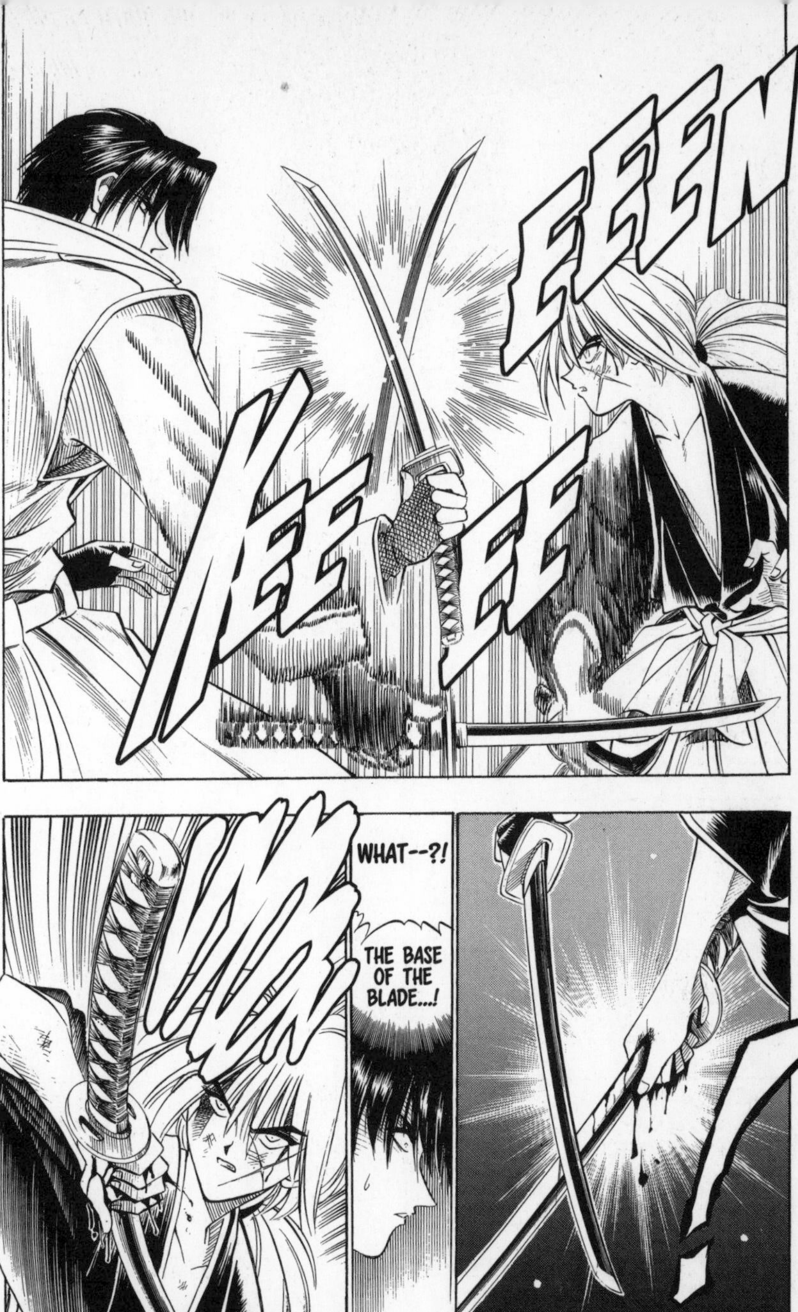
KEE EE EEEN
WHAT--?!
THE BASE OF THE BLADE...!

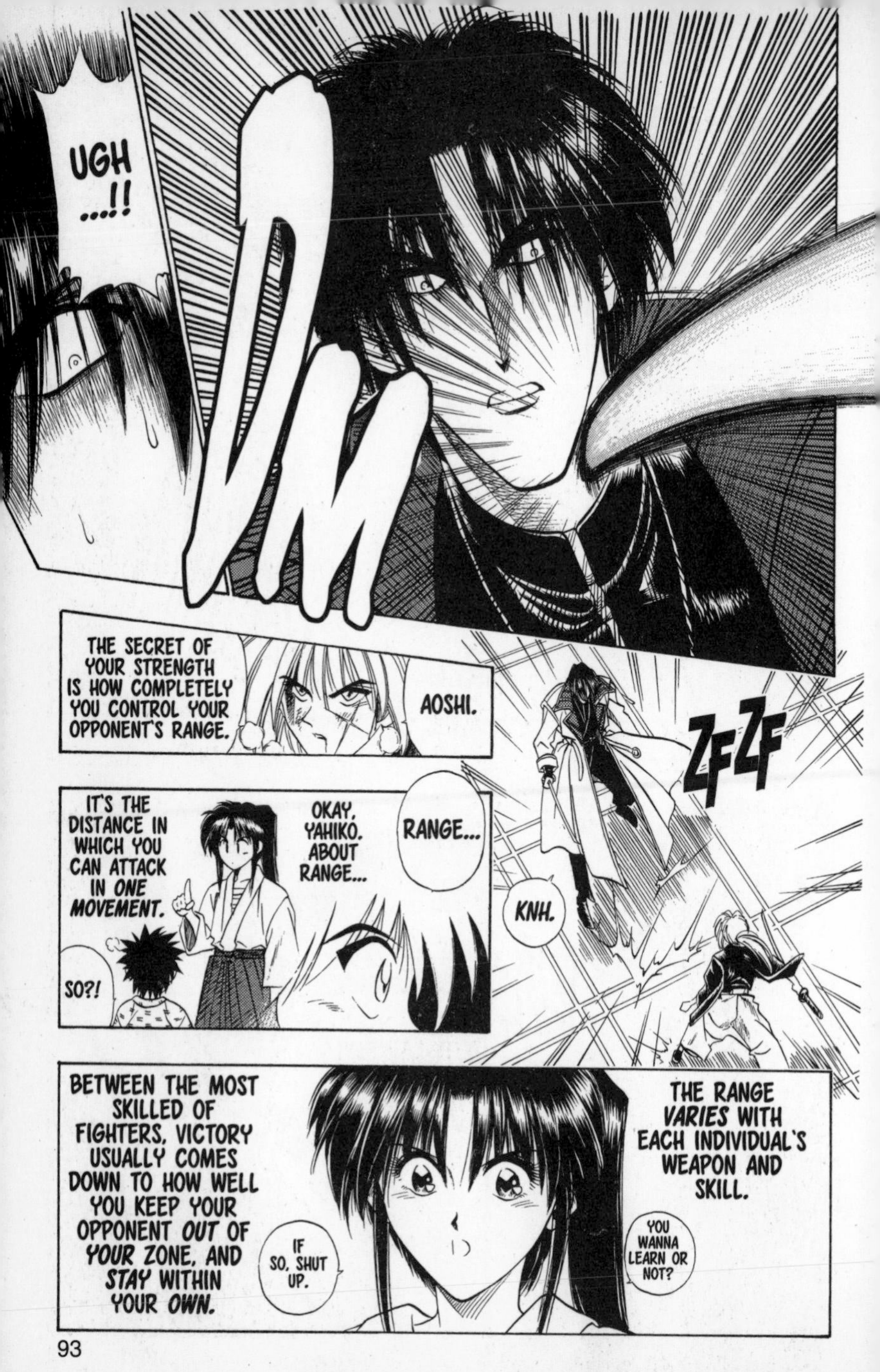
UGH ...!!
ZF ZF
KNH.
THE SECRET OF YOUR STRENGTH IS HOW COMPLETELY YOU CONTROL YOUR OPPONENT'S RANGE.
AOSHI.
RANGE...
OKAY, YAHIKO. ABOUT RANGE...
IT'S THE DISTANCE IN WHICH YOU CAN ATTACK IN *ONE MOVEMENT*.
SO?!
THE RANGE *VARIES* WITH EACH INDIVIDUAL'S WEAPON AND SKILL.
BETWEEN THE MOST SKILLED OF FIGHTERS, VICTORY USUALLY COMES DOWN TO HOW WELL YOU KEEP YOUR OPPONENT *OUT* OF *YOUR* ZONE, AND *STAY* WITHIN YOUR *OWN*.
YOU WANNA LEARN OR NOT?
IF SO, SHUT UP.

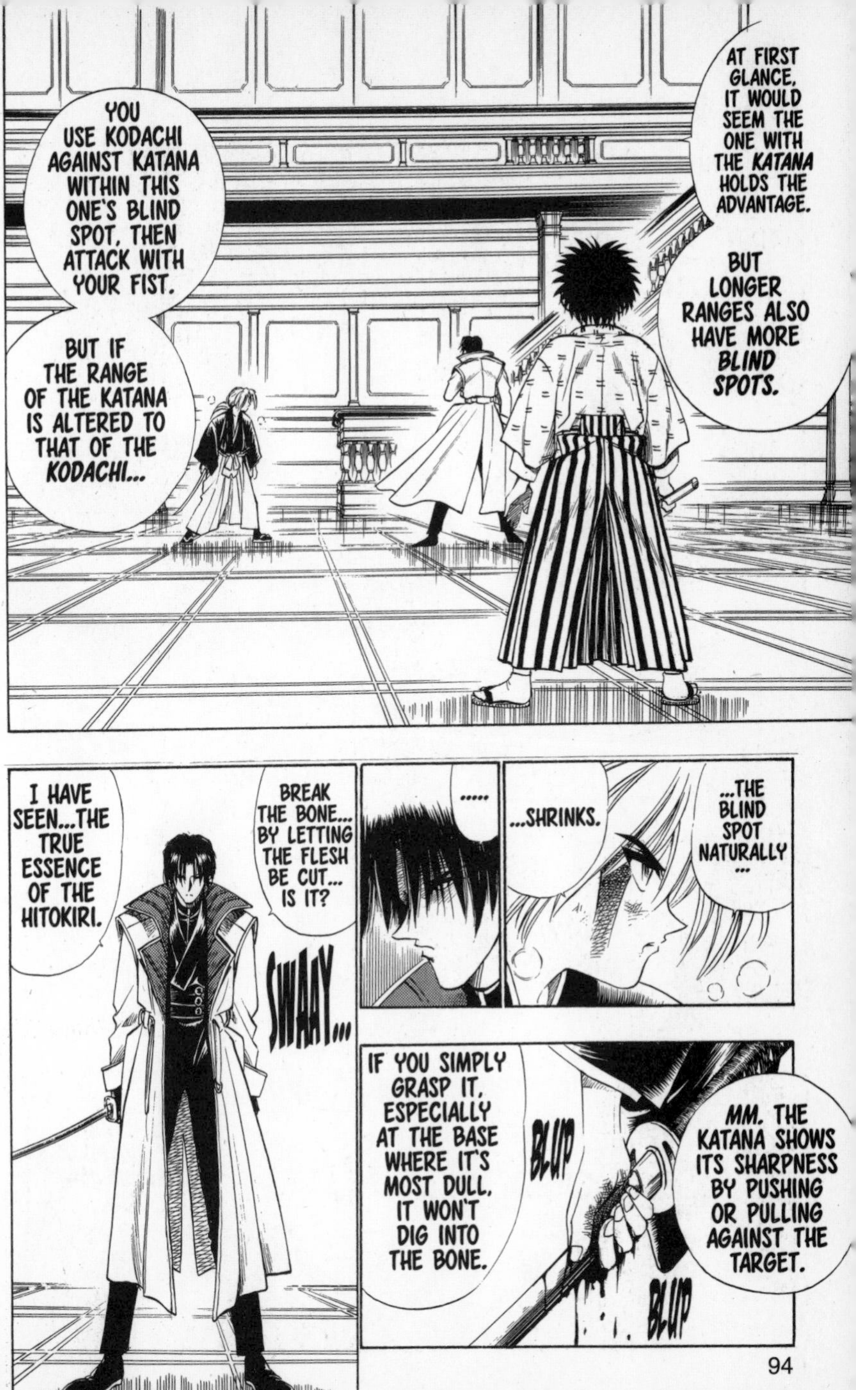
AT FIRST GLANCE, IT WOULD SEEM THE ONE WITH THE *KATANA* HOLDS THE ADVANTAGE.
BUT LONGER RANGES ALSO HAVE MORE *BLIND SPOTS.*
YOU USE KODACHI AGAINST KATANA WITHIN THIS ONE'S BLIND SPOT, THEN ATTACK WITH YOUR FIST.
BUT IF THE RANGE OF THE KATANA IS ALTERED TO THAT OF THE *KODACHI...*
...THE BLIND SPOT NATURALLY ...
...SHRINKS.
......
*MM.* THE KATANA SHOWS ITS SHARPNESS BY PUSHING OR PULLING AGAINST THE TARGET.
IF YOU SIMPLY GRASP IT, ESPECIALLY AT THE BASE WHERE IT'S MOST DULL, IT WON'T DIG INTO THE BONE.
BLUP
BLUP
BREAK THE BONE... BY LETTING THE FLESH BE CUT... IS IT?
I HAVE SEEN...THE TRUE ESSENCE OF THE HITOKIRI.
SWAAY...

READ THIS WAY

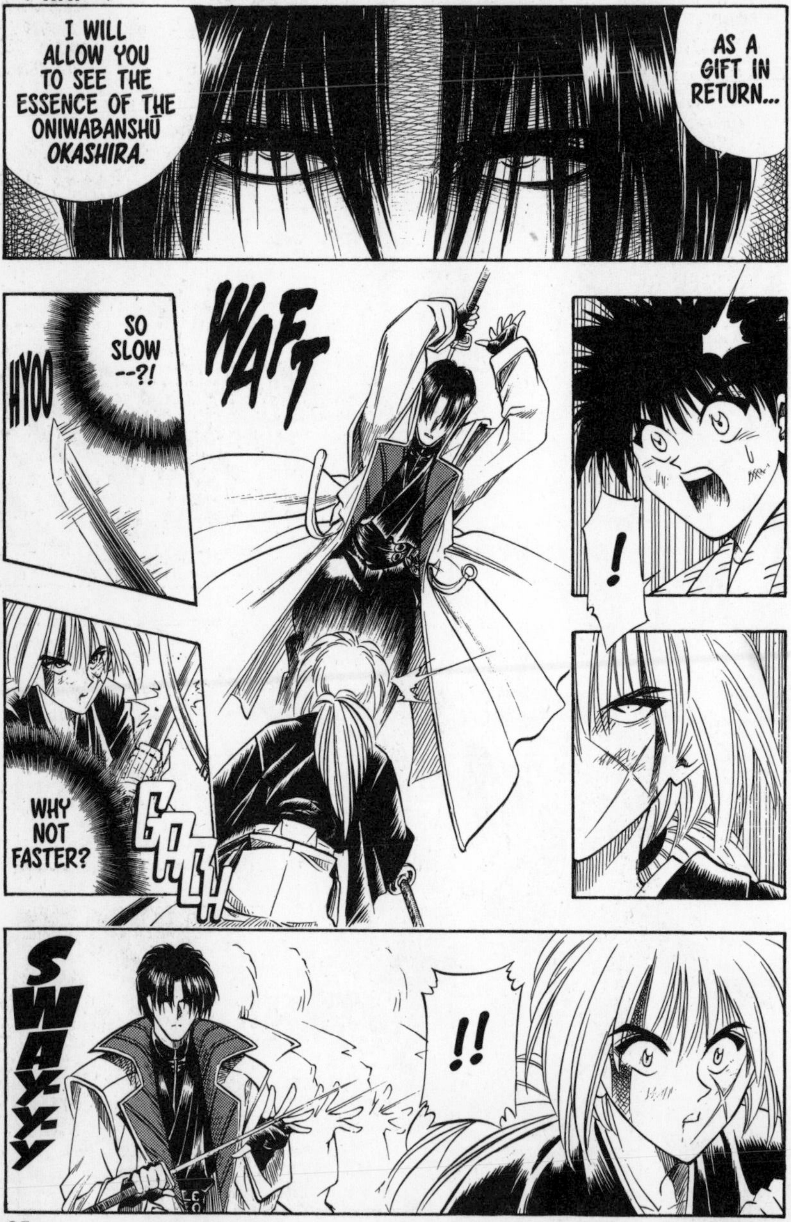

AS A GIFT IN RETURN...
I WILL ALLOW YOU TO SEE THE ESSENCE OF THE ONIWABANSHŪ *OKASHIRA.*
!
WAFT
GACH
HYOO
SO SLOW --?!
WHY NOT FASTER?
!!
SWAYYY

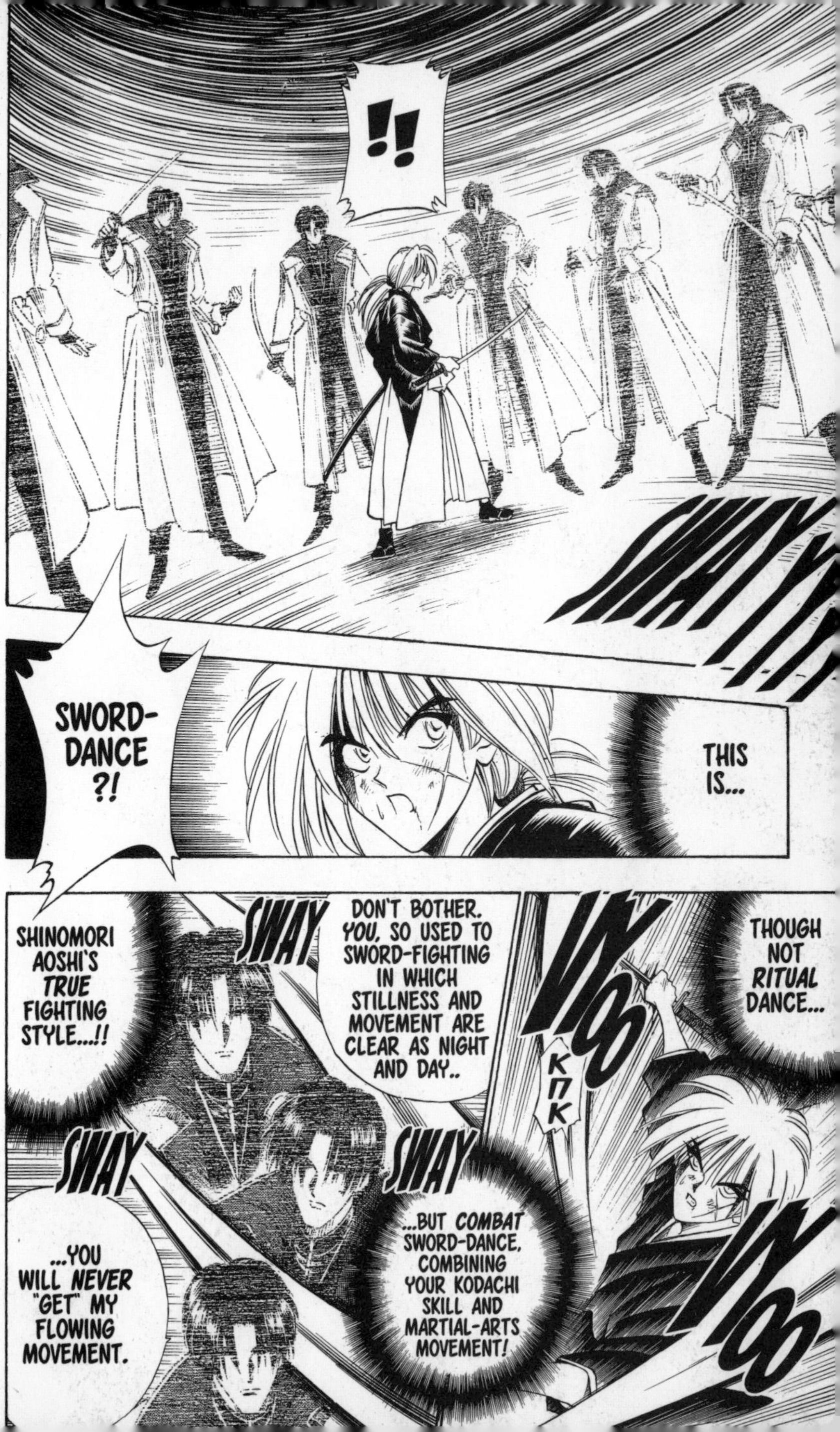
!!
SWAY
THIS IS...
SWORD-DANCE ?!
THOUGH NOT RITUAL DANCE...
...BUT COMBAT SWORD-DANCE, COMBINING YOUR KODACHI SKILL AND MARTIAL-ARTS MOVEMENT!
SHINOMORI AOSHI'S TRUE FIGHTING STYLE...!!
SWAY
DON'T BOTHER. YOU, SO USED TO SWORD-FIGHTING IN WHICH STILLNESS AND MOVEMENT ARE CLEAR AS NIGHT AND DAY..
SWAY
SWAY
...YOU WILL NEVER "GET" MY FLOWING MOVEMENT.

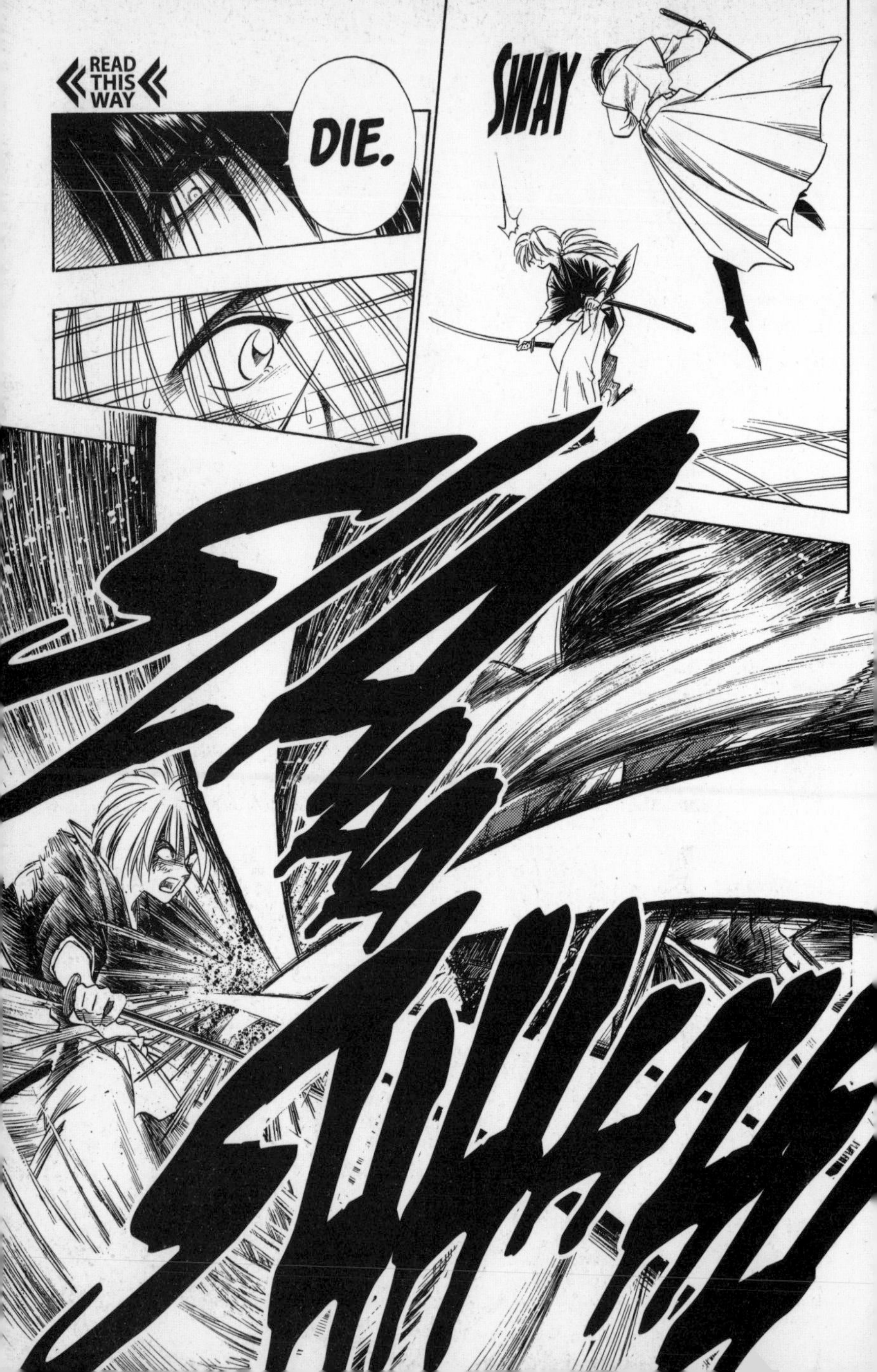
READ THIS WAY
SWAY
DIE.

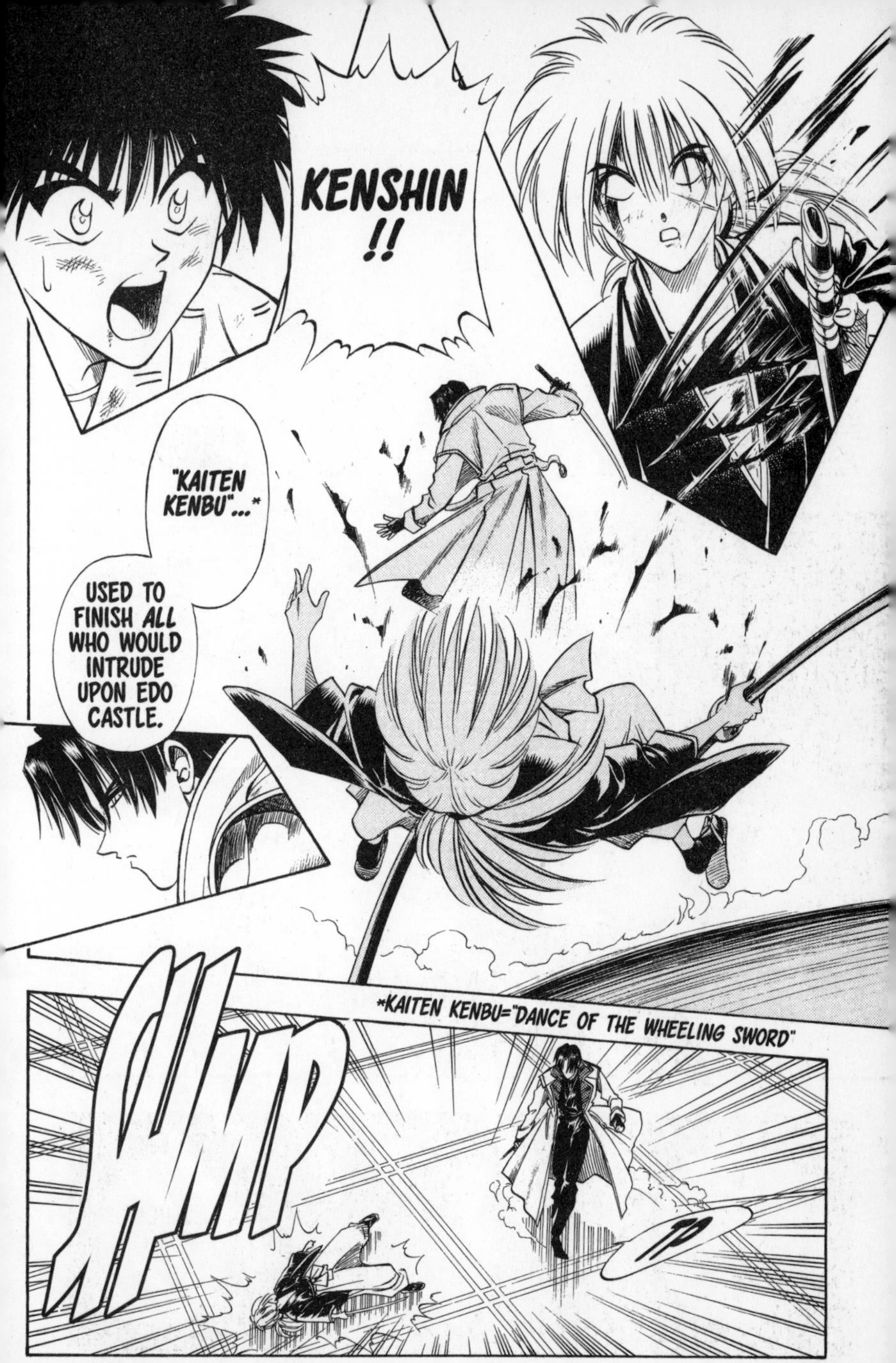
KENSHIN !!
"KAITEN KENBU"...*
USED TO FINISH ALL WHO WOULD INTRUDE UPON EDO CASTLE.
*KAITEN KENBU="DANCE OF THE WHEELING SWORD"

READ THIS WAY

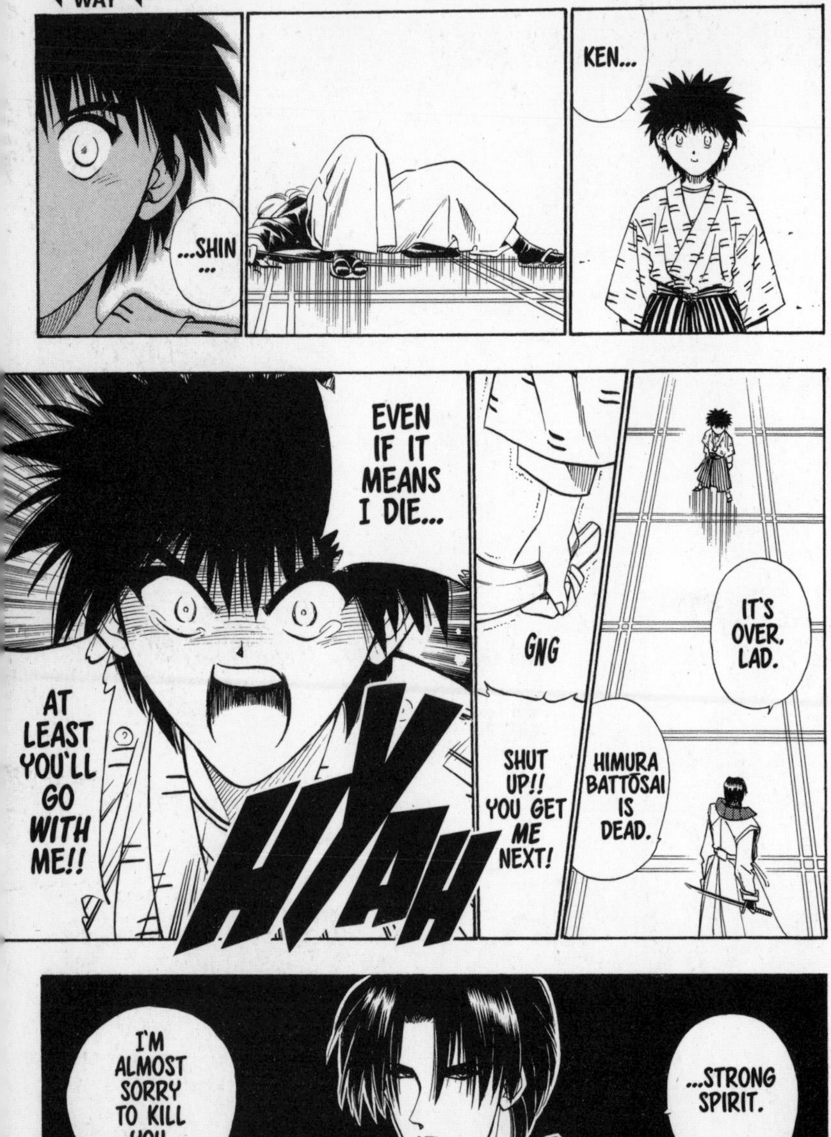
KEN...
...SHIN ...
IT'S OVER, LAD.
HIMURA BATTOSAI IS DEAD.
GNG
SHUT UP!! YOU GET ME NEXT!
EVEN IF IT MEANS I DIE...
AT LEAST YOU'LL GO WITH ME!!
HIYAH
...STRONG SPIRIT.
I'M ALMOST SORRY TO KILL YOU.

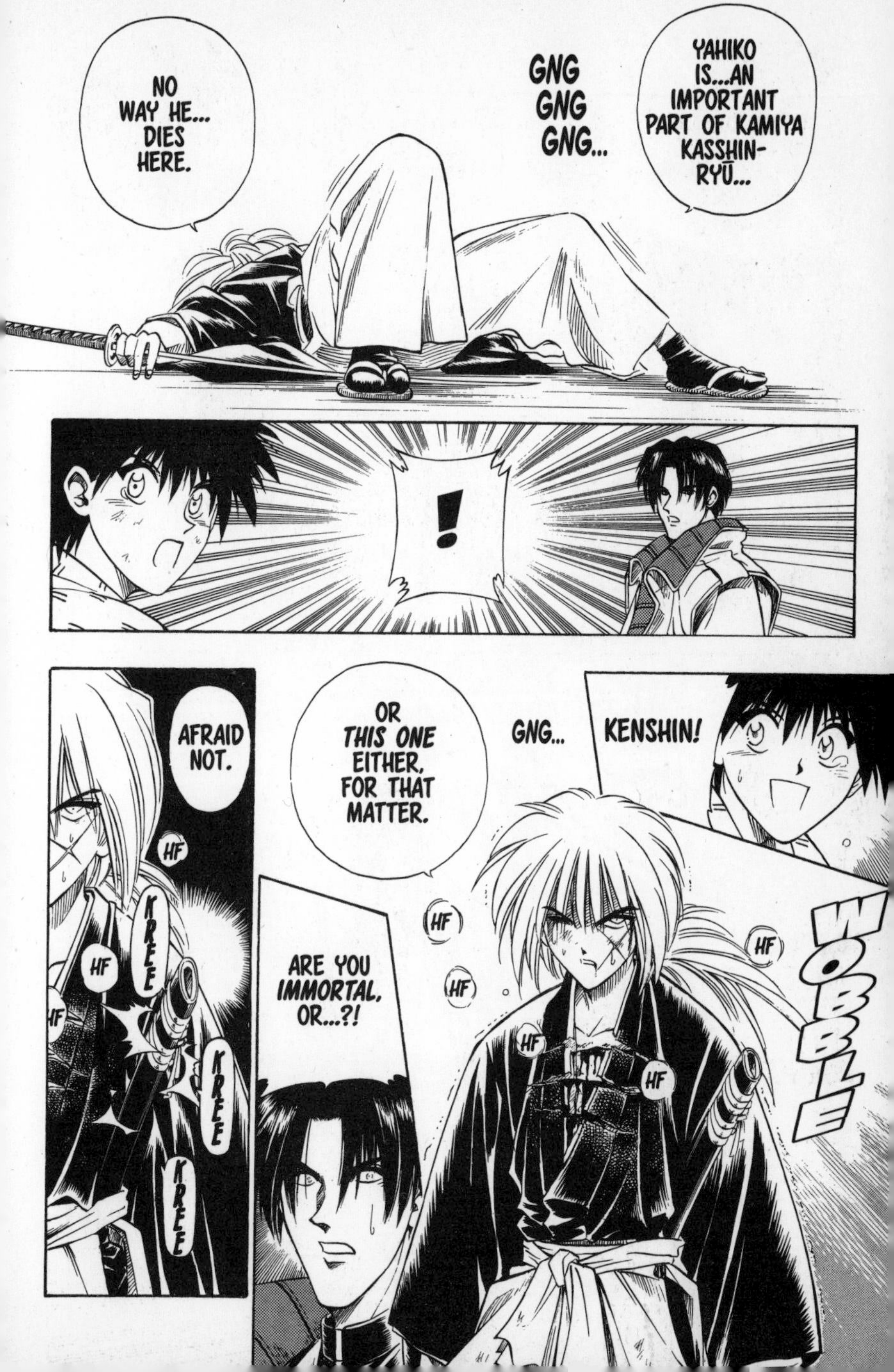
YAHIKO IS...AN IMPORTANT PART OF KAMIYA KASSHIN-RYŪ...
GNG GNG GNG...
NO WAY HE... DIES HERE.
!
KENSHIN!
WOBBLE
HF
GNG...
OR THIS ONE EITHER, FOR THAT MATTER.
HF
HF
HF
HF
ARE YOU IMMORTAL, OR...?!
AFRAID NOT.
HF
KREE
HF
HF
KREE
KREE

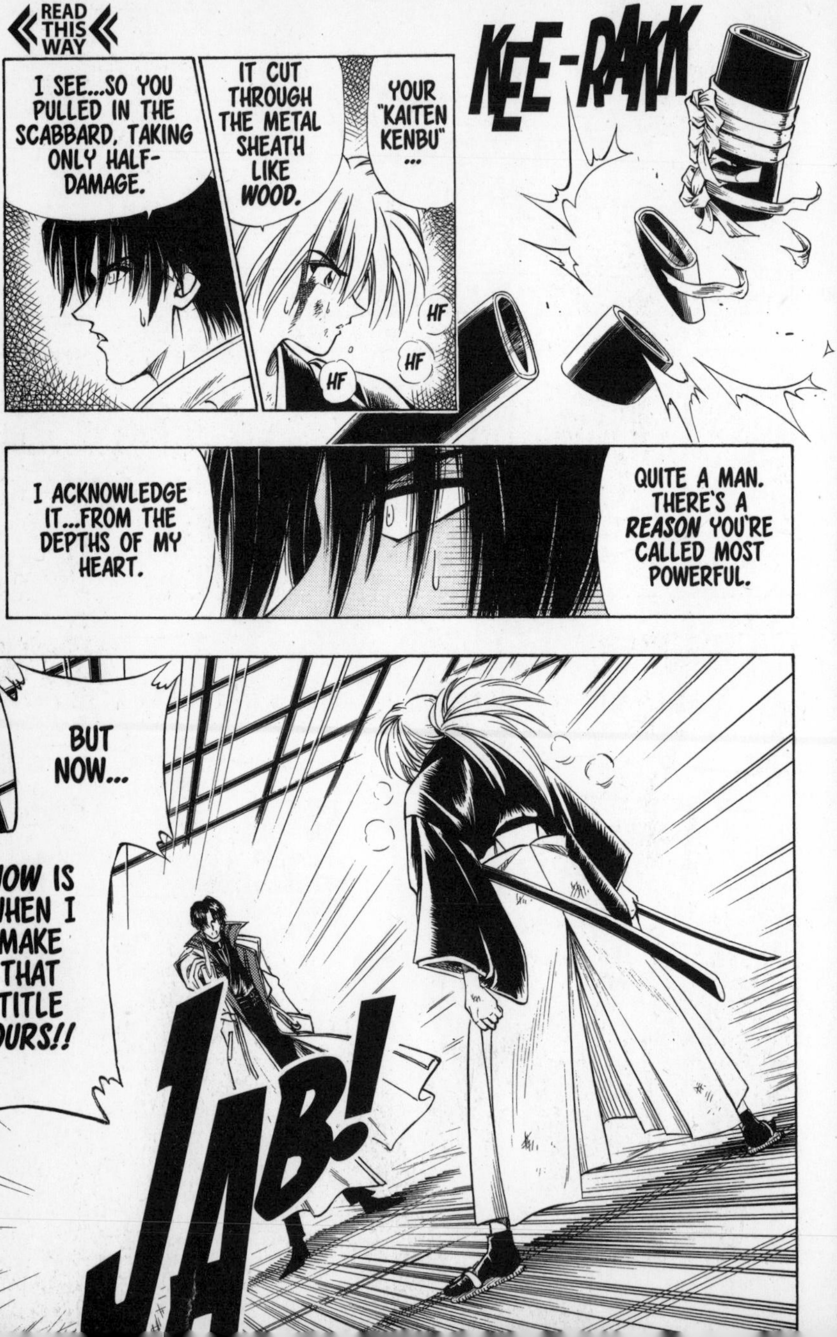
READ THIS WAY
KEE-RAKK
YOUR "KAITEN KENBU"...
IT CUT THROUGH THE METAL SHEATH LIKE WOOD.
HF
HF
HF
I SEE...SO YOU PULLED IN THE SCABBARD, TAKING ONLY HALF-DAMAGE.
QUITE A MAN. THERE'S A REASON YOU'RE CALLED MOST POWERFUL.
I ACKNOWLEDGE IT...FROM THE DEPTHS OF MY HEART.
BUT NOW...
NOW IS WHEN I MAKE THAT TITLE OURS!!
JAB!

READ THIS WAY

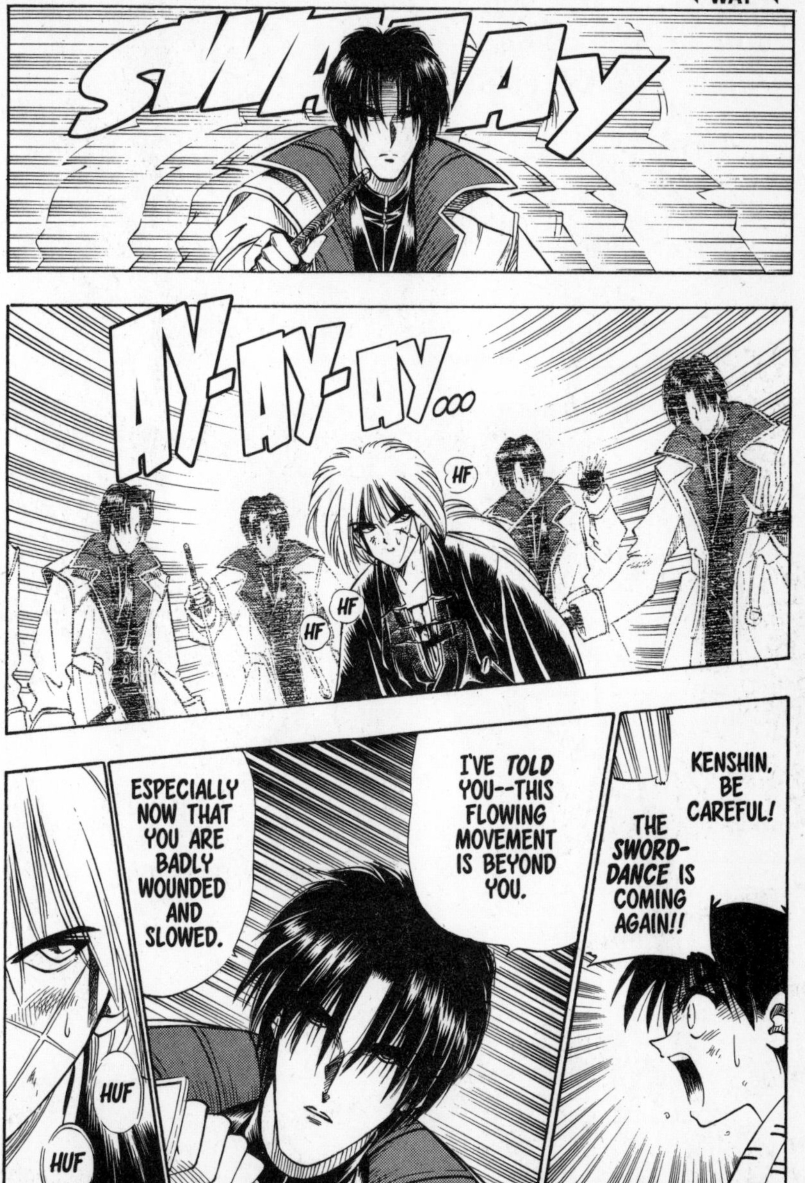

SWAAAY
AY-AY-AY...
HF
HF
HF
KENSHIN, BE CAREFUL!
THE SWORD-DANCE IS COMING AGAIN!!
I'VE *TOLD* YOU--THIS FLOWING MOVEMENT IS BEYOND YOU.
ESPECIALLY NOW THAT YOU ARE BADLY WOUNDED AND SLOWED.
HUF
HUF

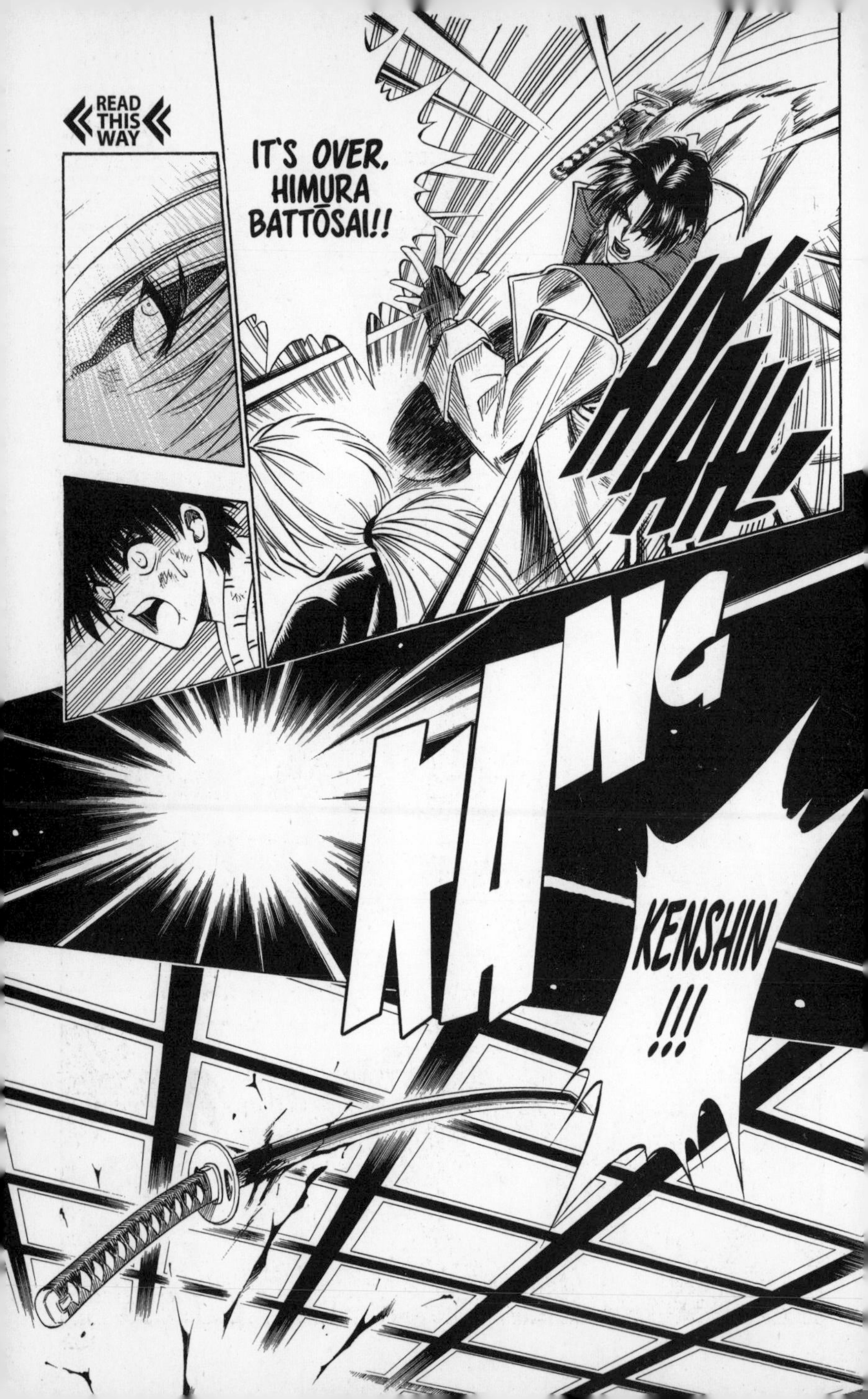
READ THIS WAY
IT'S OVER, HIMURA BATTŌSAI!!
HAH!
KANG
KENSHIN !!!

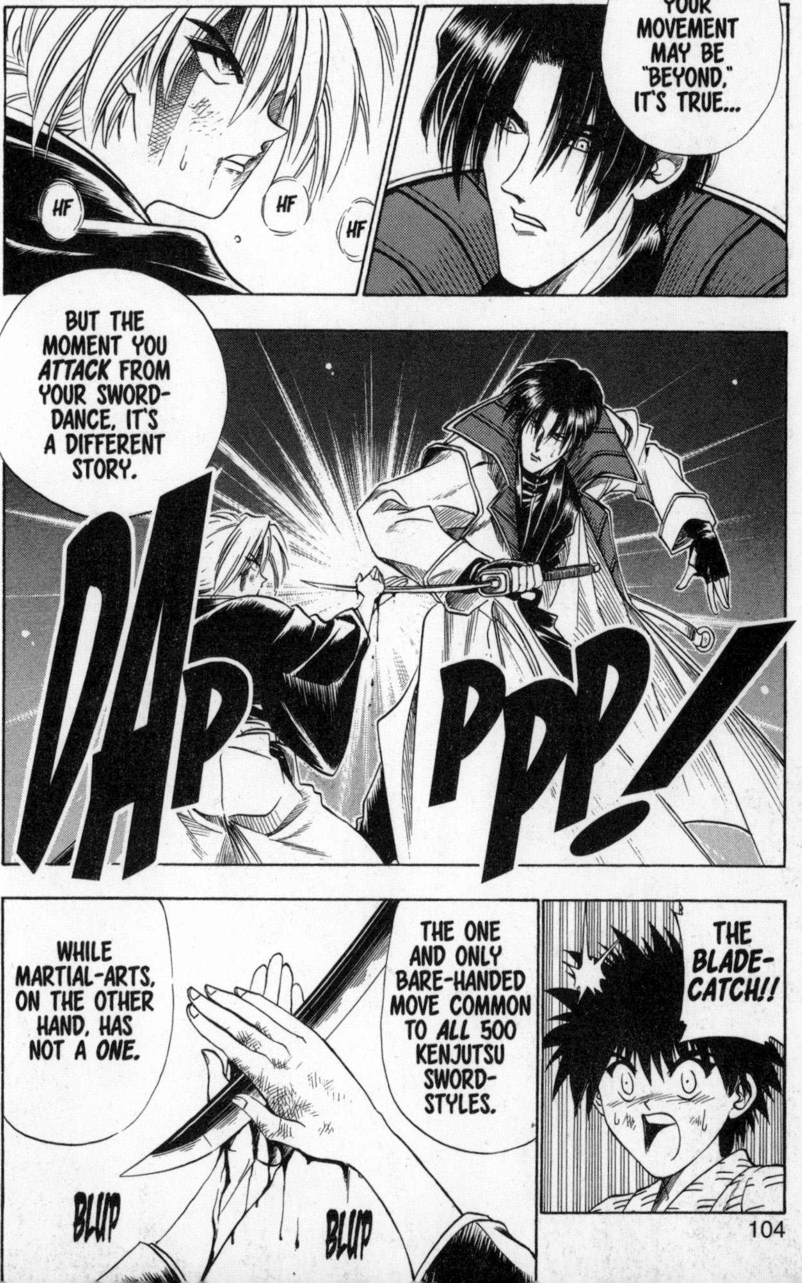
YOUR MOVEMENT MAY BE "BEYOND," IT'S TRUE...
HF
HF
HF
BUT THE MOMENT YOU *ATTACK* FROM YOUR SWORD-DANCE, IT'S A DIFFERENT STORY.
DAPPPP!
THE *BLADE-CATCH!!*
THE ONE AND ONLY BARE-HANDED MOVE COMMON TO *ALL* 500 KENJUTSU SWORD-STYLES.
WHILE MARTIAL-ARTS, ON THE OTHER HAND, HAS NOT A *ONE.*
BLUP
BLUP

READ THIS WAY

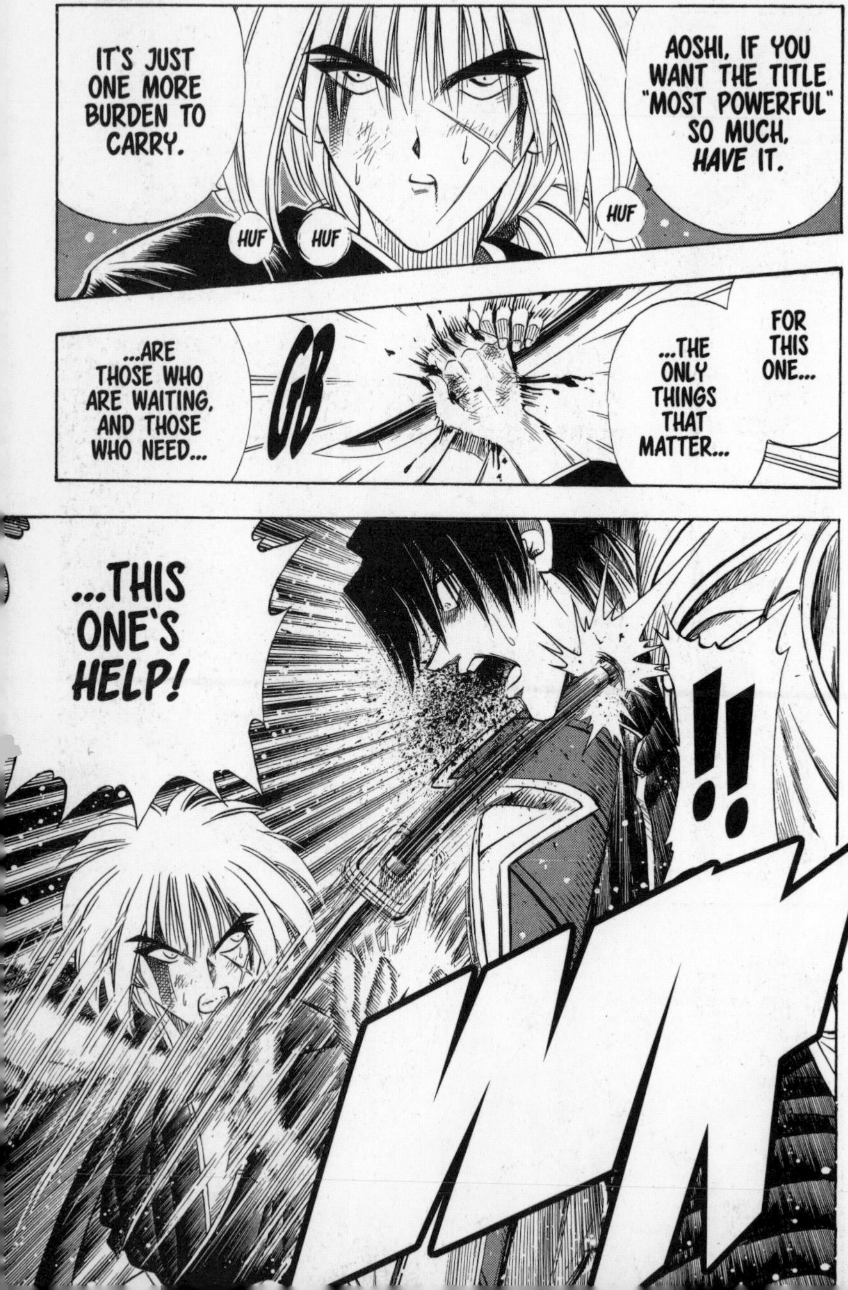
AOSHI, IF YOU WANT THE TITLE "MOST POWERFUL" SO MUCH, HAVE IT.
HUF
HUF
HUF
IT'S JUST ONE MORE BURDEN TO CARRY.
FOR THIS ONE...
...THE ONLY THINGS THAT MATTER...
GB
...ARE THOSE WHO ARE WAITING, AND THOSE WHO NEED...
!!
...THIS ONE'S HELP!
WHA

# Act 28
# Battle's End

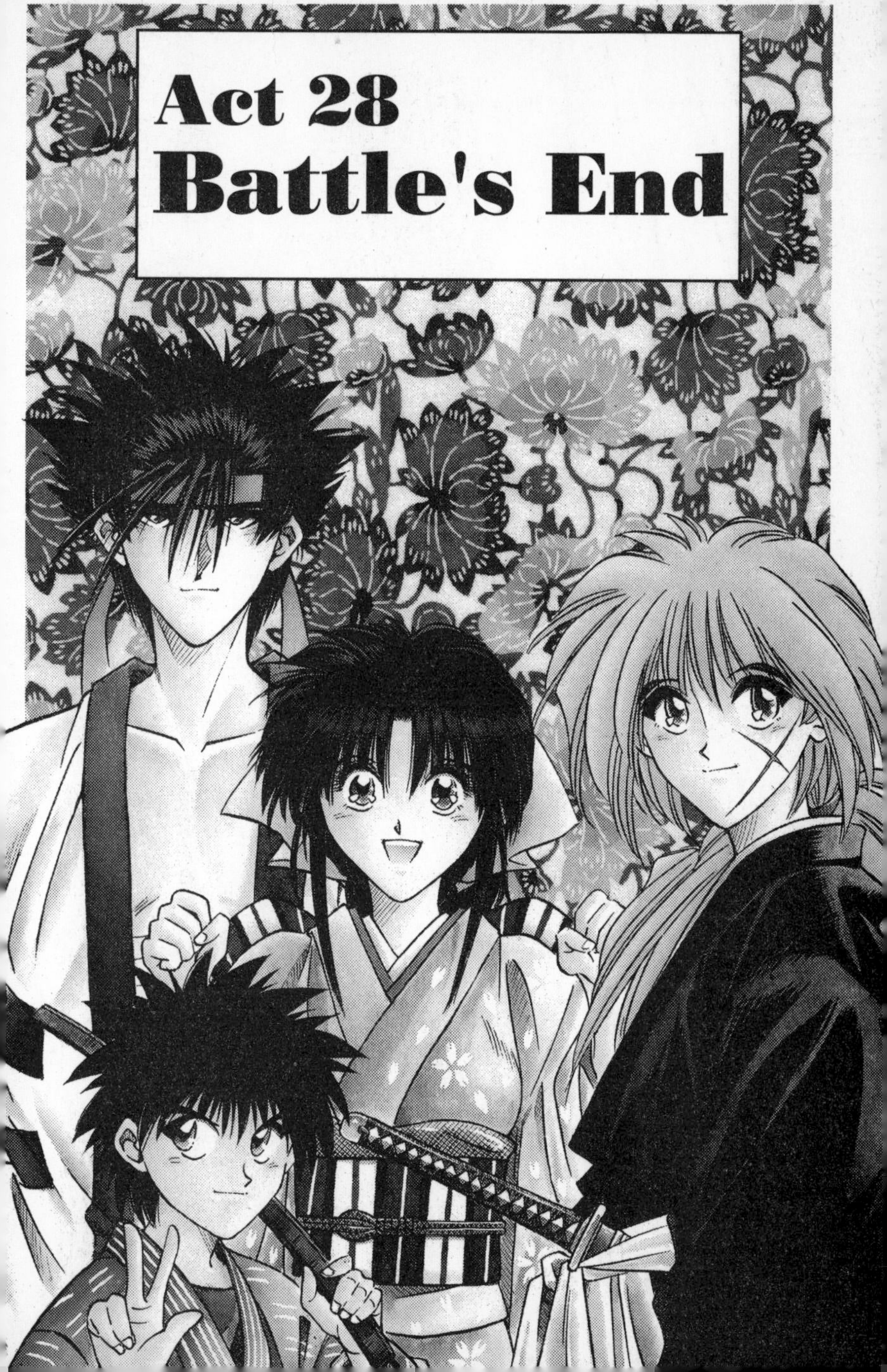

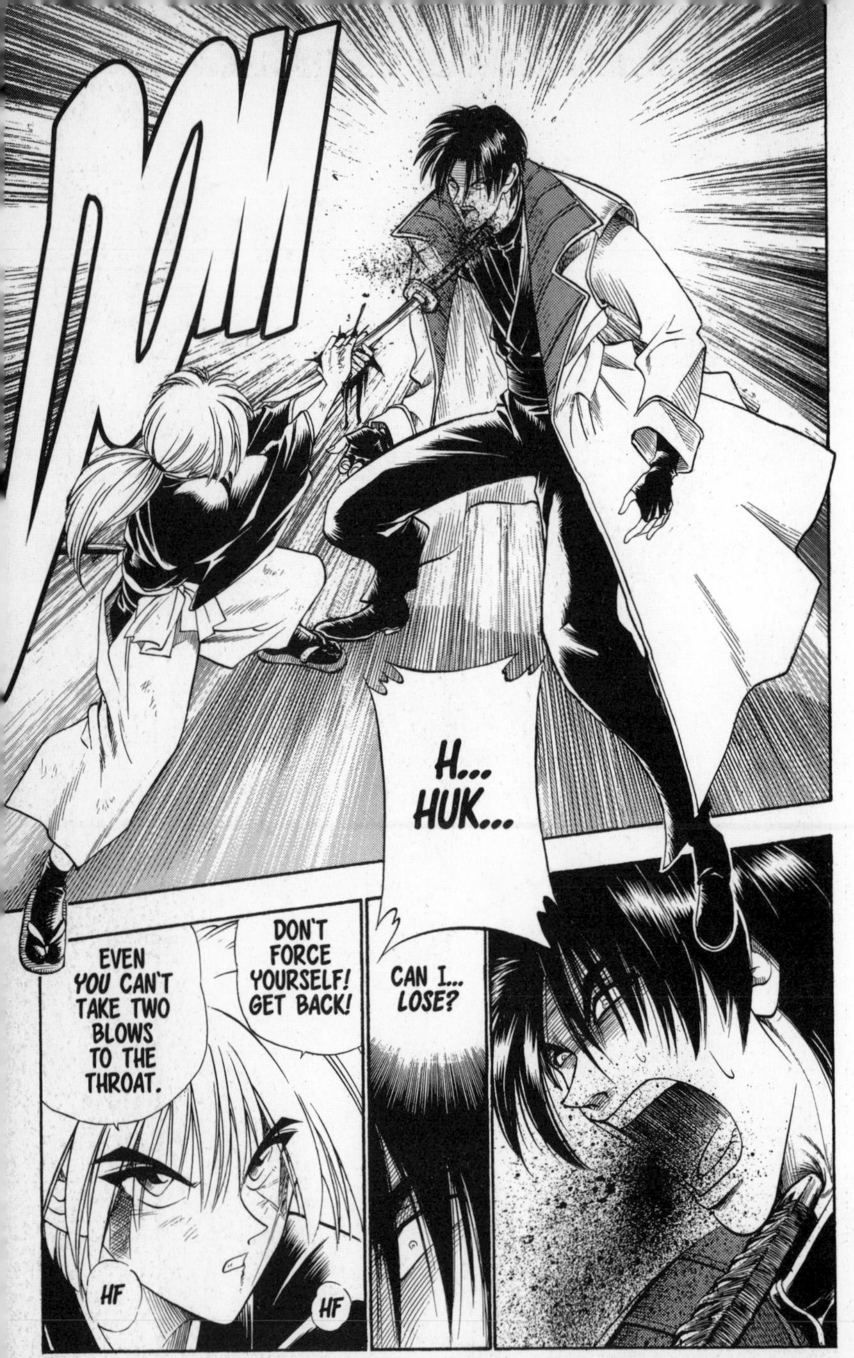
DOM
H... HUK...
CAN I... LOSE?
DON'T FORCE YOURSELF! GET BACK!
EVEN *YOU* CAN'T TAKE TWO BLOWS TO THE THROAT.
HF
HF

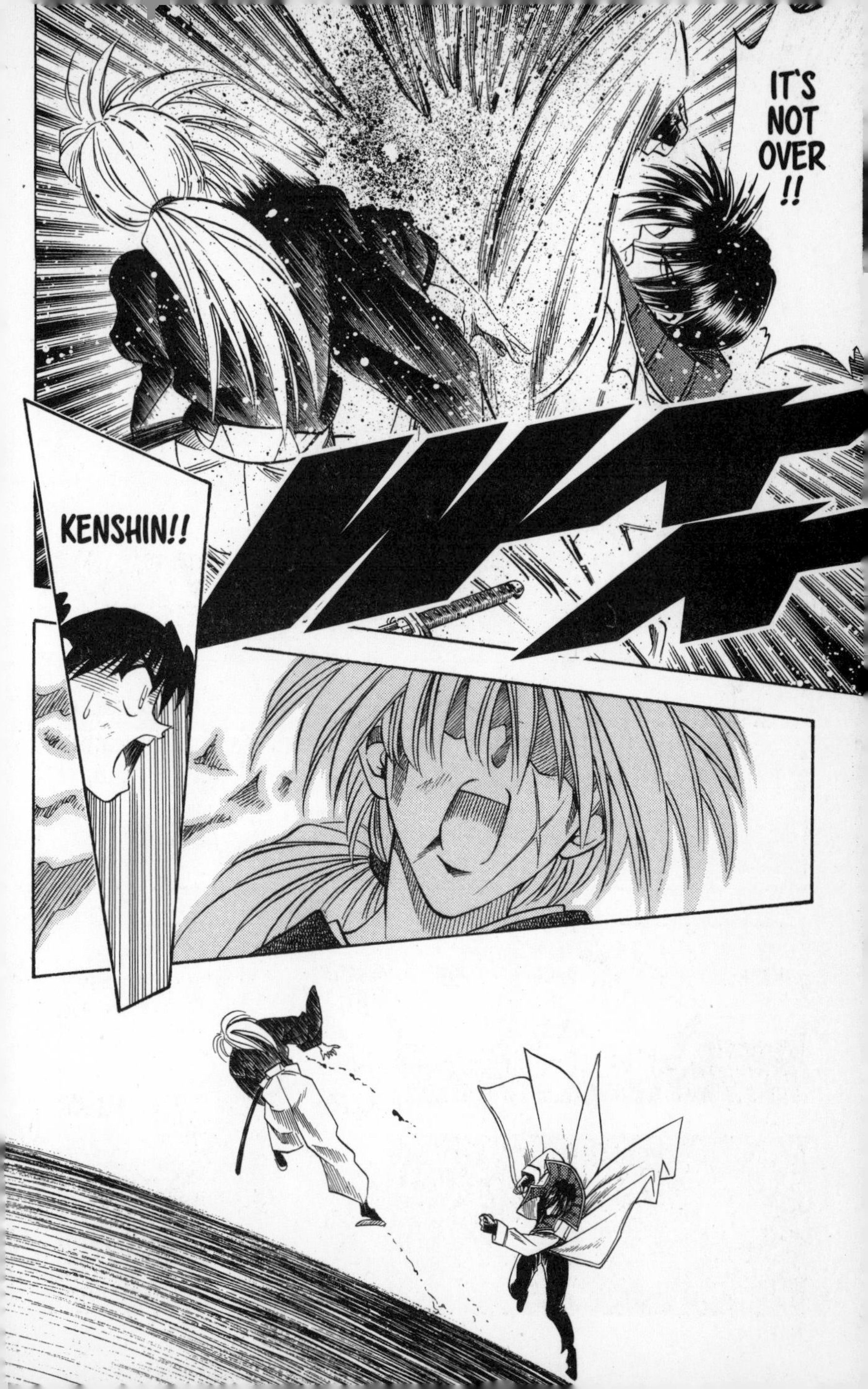
IT'S NOT OVER !!
KENSHIN!!

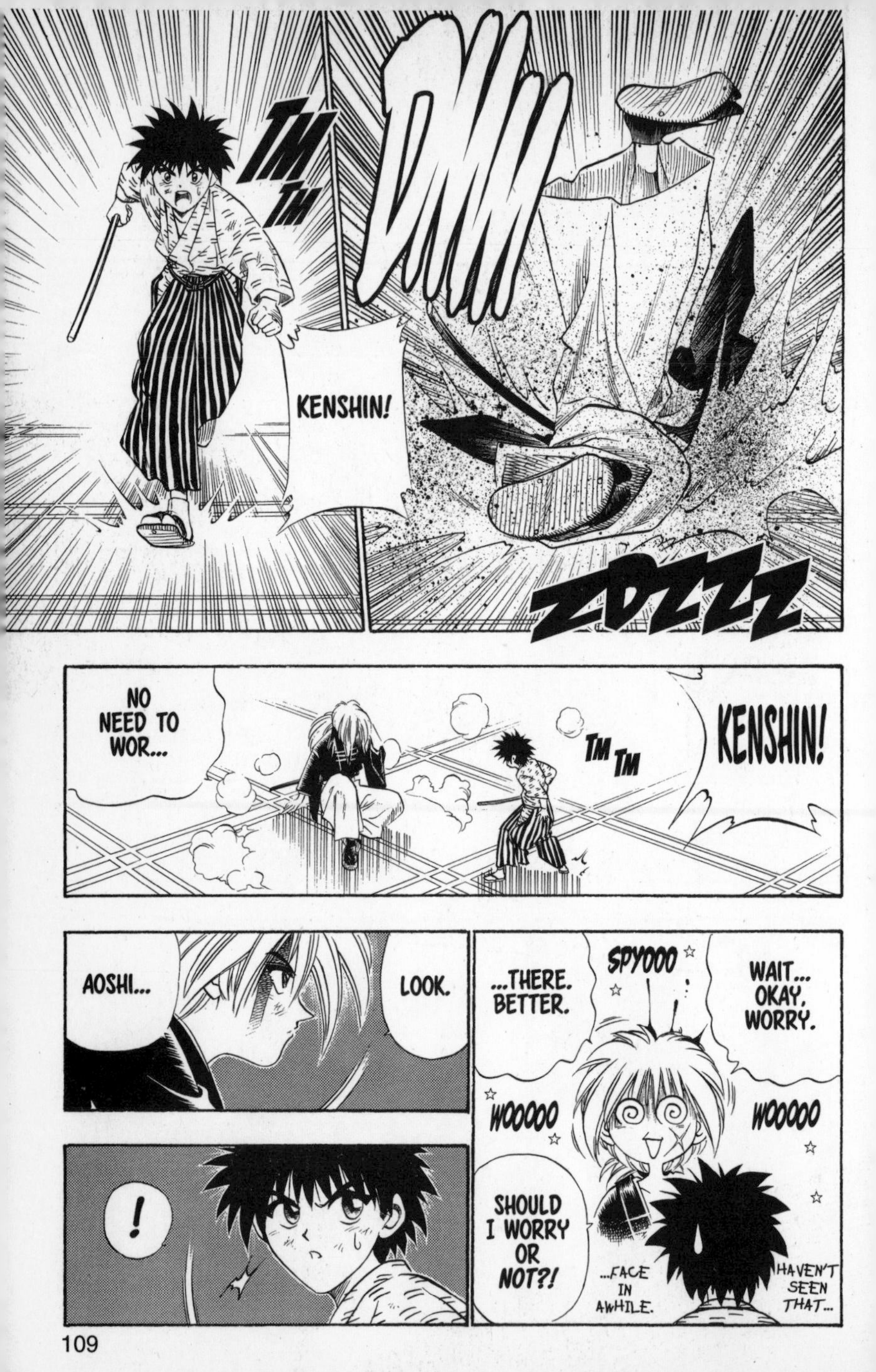
DMM
ZDZZZ
TM TM
KENSHIN!
KENSHIN!
TM TM
NO NEED TO WOR...
WAIT... OKAY, WORRY.
SPYOOO
...THERE. BETTER.
WOOOOO
WOOOOO
HAVEN'T SEEN THAT...
...FACE IN AWHILE.
SHOULD I WORRY OR NOT?!
LOOK.
AOSHI...
!

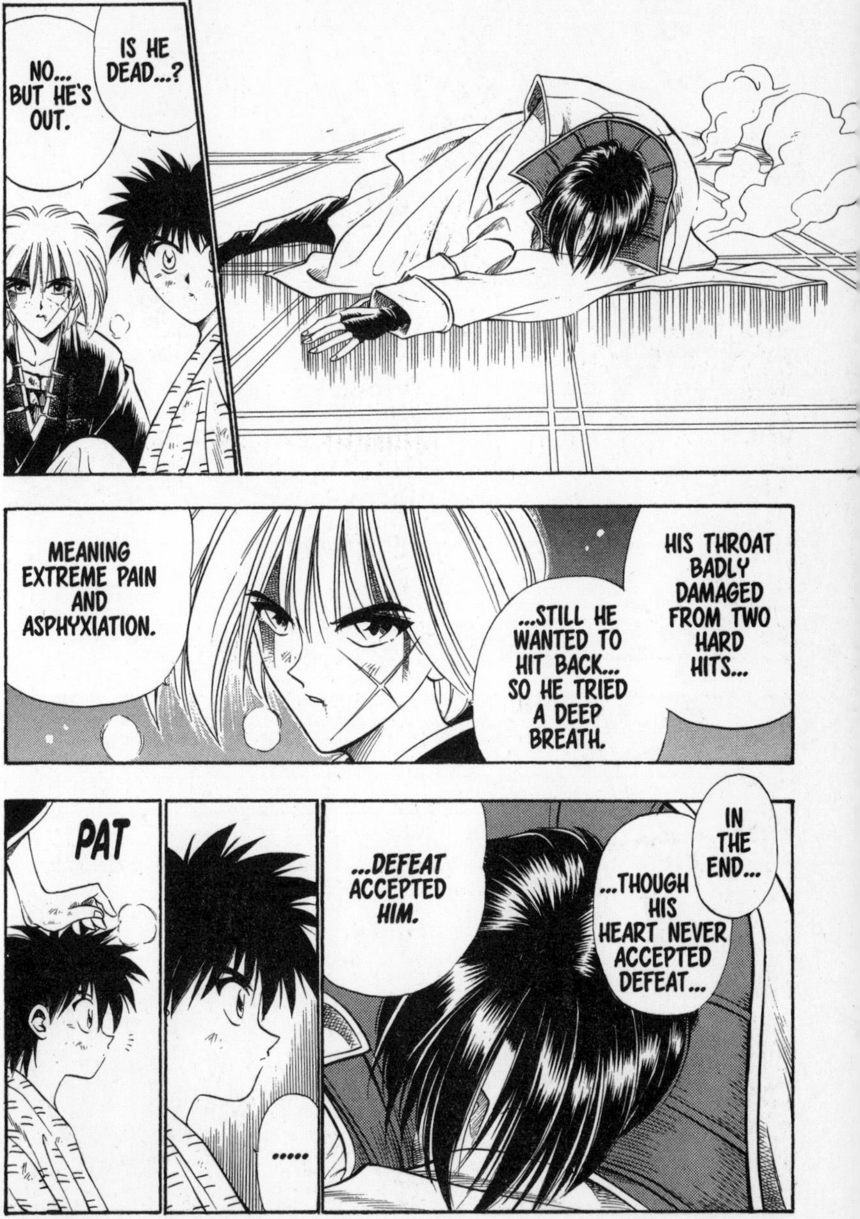
IS HE DEAD...?
NO... BUT HE'S OUT.
HIS THROAT BADLY DAMAGED FROM TWO HARD HITS...
...STILL HE WANTED TO HIT BACK... SO HE TRIED A DEEP BREATH.
MEANING EXTREME PAIN AND ASPHYXIATION.
IN THE END...
...THOUGH HIS HEART NEVER ACCEPTED DEFEAT...
...DEFEAT ACCEPTED HIM.
.....
PAT

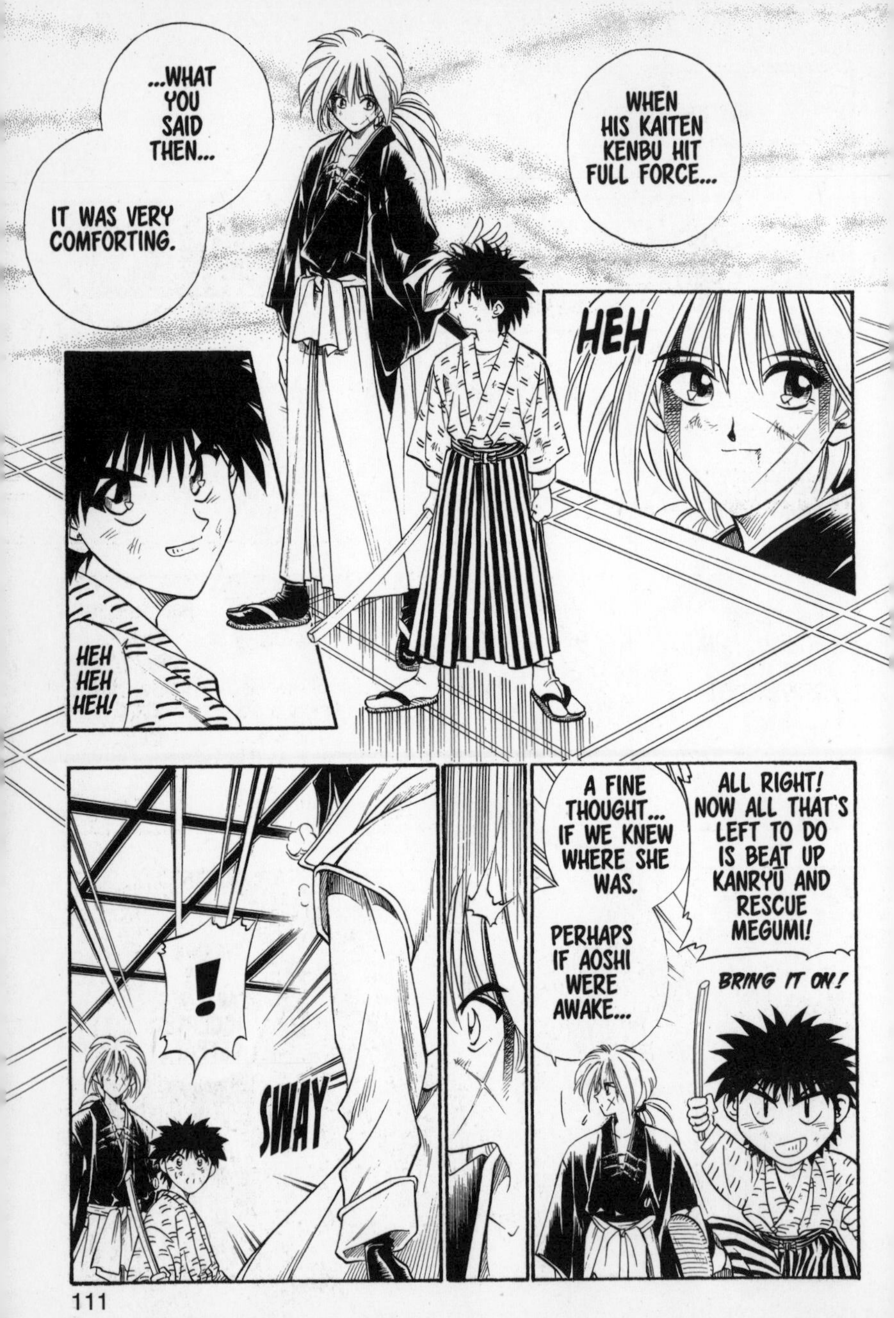
WHEN HIS KAITEN KENBU HIT FULL FORCE...
...WHAT YOU SAID THEN...
IT WAS VERY COMFORTING.
HEH
HEH HEH HEH!
ALL RIGHT! NOW ALL THAT'S LEFT TO DO IS BEAT UP KANRYŪ AND RESCUE MEGUMI!
BRING IT ON!
A FINE THOUGHT... IF WE KNEW WHERE SHE WAS.
PERHAPS IF AOSHI WERE AWAKE...
!
SWAY

READ THIS WAY

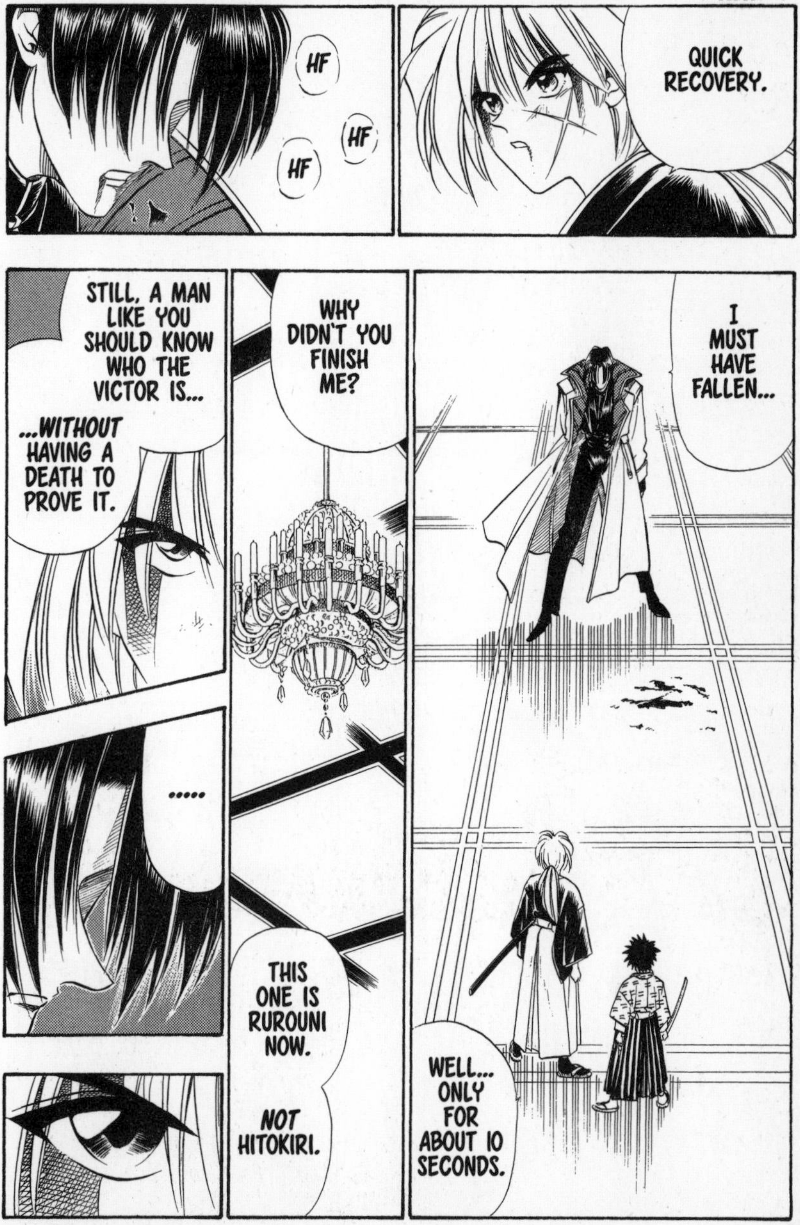
QUICK RECOVERY.
HF
HF
HF
I MUST HAVE FALLEN...
WELL... ONLY FOR ABOUT 10 SECONDS.
WHY DIDN'T YOU FINISH ME?
THIS ONE IS RUROUNI NOW.
*NOT* HITOKIRI.
STILL, A MAN LIKE YOU SHOULD KNOW WHO THE VICTOR IS...
...WITHOUT HAVING A DEATH TO PROVE IT.
.....

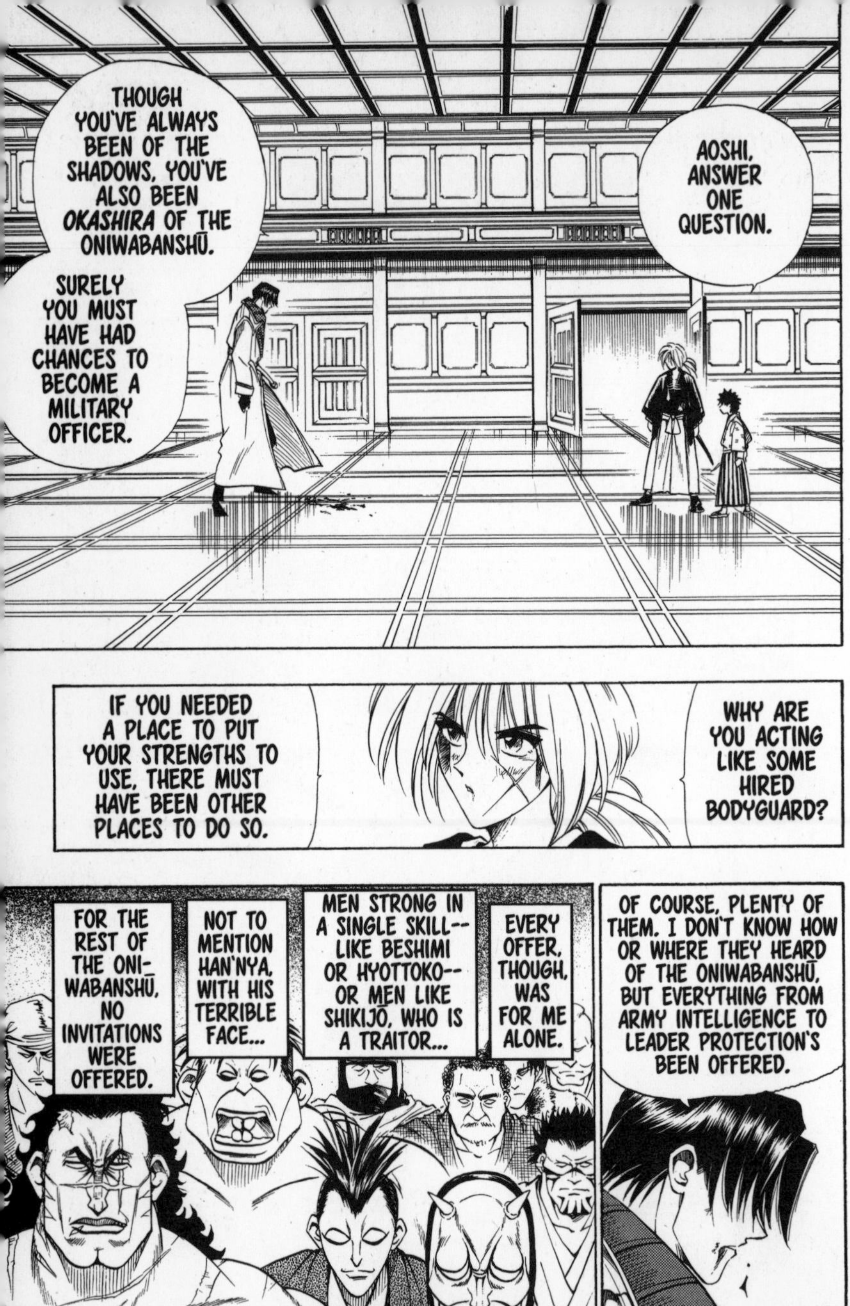
AOSHI, ANSWER ONE QUESTION.
THOUGH YOU'VE ALWAYS BEEN OF THE SHADOWS, YOU'VE ALSO BEEN *OKASHIRA* OF THE ONIWABANSHŪ.
SURELY YOU MUST HAVE HAD CHANCES TO BECOME A MILITARY OFFICER.
WHY ARE YOU ACTING LIKE SOME HIRED BODYGUARD?
IF YOU NEEDED A PLACE TO PUT YOUR STRENGTHS TO USE, THERE MUST HAVE BEEN OTHER PLACES TO DO SO.
OF COURSE, PLENTY OF THEM. I DON'T KNOW HOW OR WHERE THEY HEARD OF THE ONIWABANSHŪ, BUT EVERYTHING FROM ARMY INTELLIGENCE TO LEADER PROTECTION'S BEEN OFFERED.
EVERY OFFER, THOUGH, WAS FOR ME ALONE.
MEN STRONG IN A SINGLE SKILL-- LIKE BESHIMI OR HYOTTOKO-- OR MEN LIKE SHIKIJŌ, WHO IS A TRAITOR...
NOT TO MENTION HAN'NYA, WITH HIS TERRIBLE FACE...
FOR THE REST OF THE ONI-WABANSHŪ, NO INVITATIONS WERE OFFERED.

READ THIS WAY

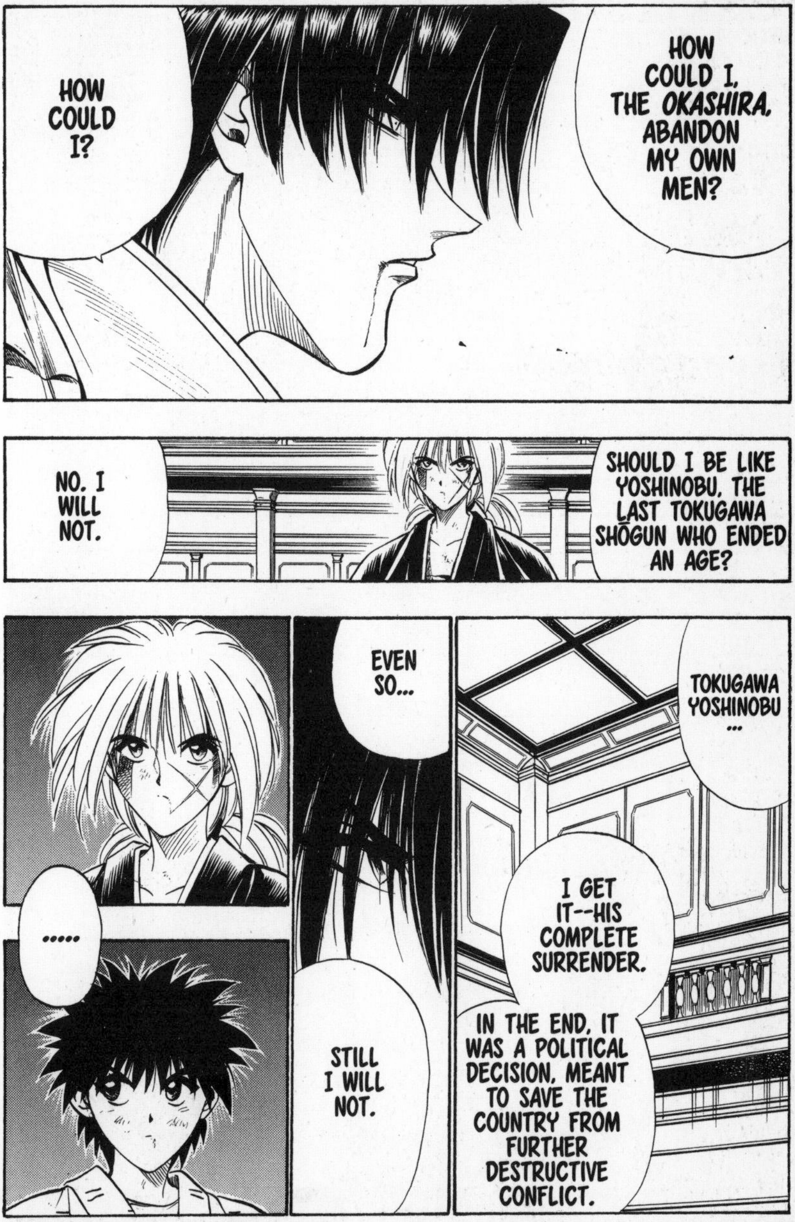

HOW COULD I, THE *OKASHIRA*, ABANDON MY OWN MEN?
HOW COULD I?
SHOULD I BE LIKE YOSHINOBU, THE LAST TOKUGAWA SHŌGUN WHO ENDED AN AGE?
NO. I WILL NOT.
TOKUGAWA YOSHINOBU...
I GET IT--HIS COMPLETE SURRENDER.
IN THE END, IT WAS A POLITICAL DECISION, MEANT TO SAVE THE COUNTRY FROM FURTHER DESTRUCTIVE CONFLICT.
EVEN SO...
STILL I WILL NOT.
.....

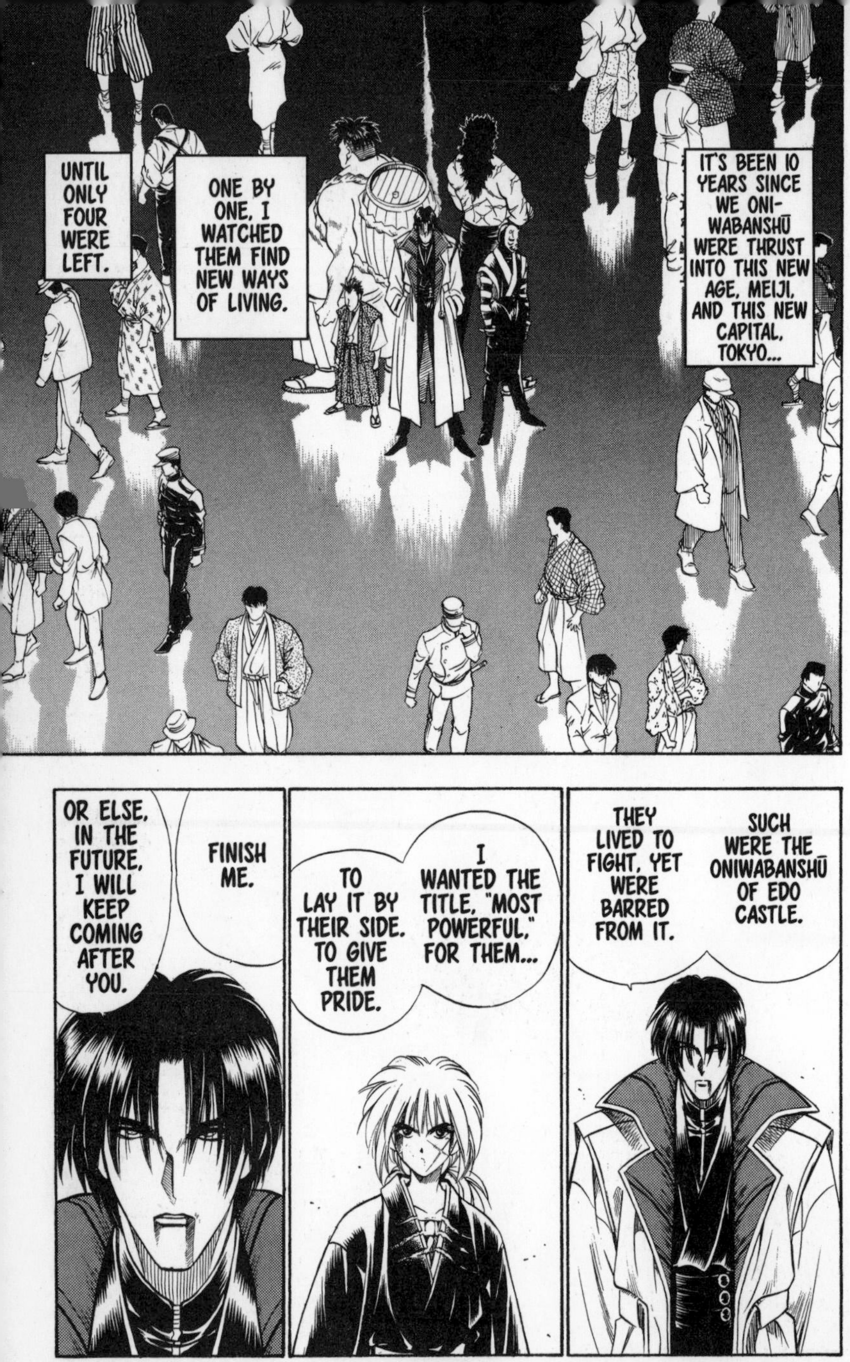
IT'S BEEN 10 YEARS SINCE WE ONIWABANSHŪ WERE THRUST INTO THIS NEW AGE, MEIJI, AND THIS NEW CAPITAL, TOKYO...
ONE BY ONE, I WATCHED THEM FIND NEW WAYS OF LIVING.
UNTIL ONLY FOUR WERE LEFT.
SUCH WERE THE ONIWABANSHŪ OF EDO CASTLE.
THEY LIVED TO FIGHT, YET WERE BARRED FROM IT.
I WANTED THE TITLE, "MOST POWERFUL," FOR THEM...
TO LAY IT BY THEIR SIDE. TO GIVE THEM PRIDE.
FINISH ME.
OR ELSE, IN THE FUTURE, I WILL KEEP COMING AFTER YOU.

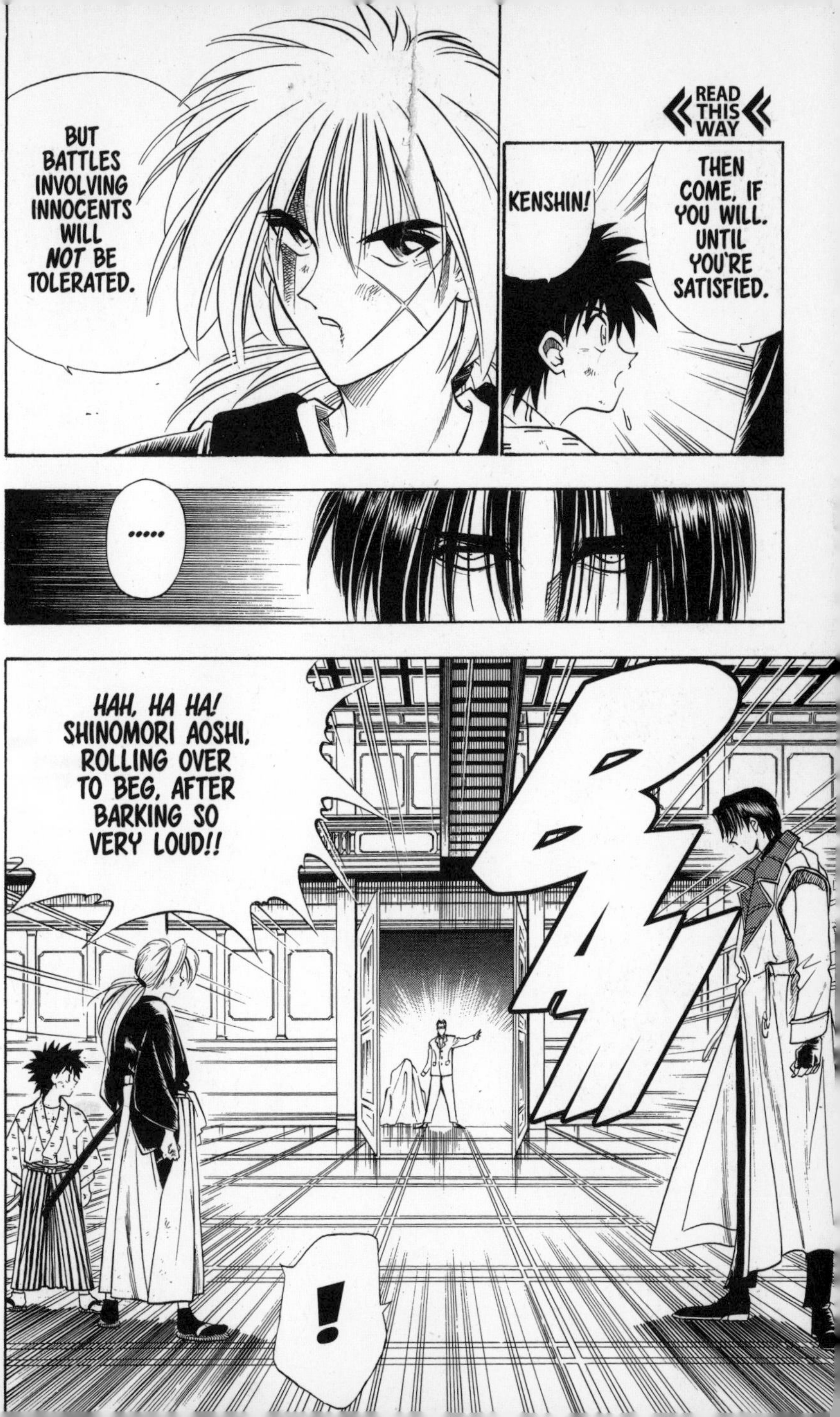
READ THIS WAY
THEN COME, IF YOU WILL. UNTIL YOU'RE SATISFIED.
KENSHIN!
BUT BATTLES INVOLVING INNOCENTS WILL *NOT* BE TOLERATED.
......
*HAH, HA HA!* SHINOMORI AOSHI, ROLLING OVER TO BEG, AFTER BARKING SO VERY LOUD!!
!

READ THIS WAY

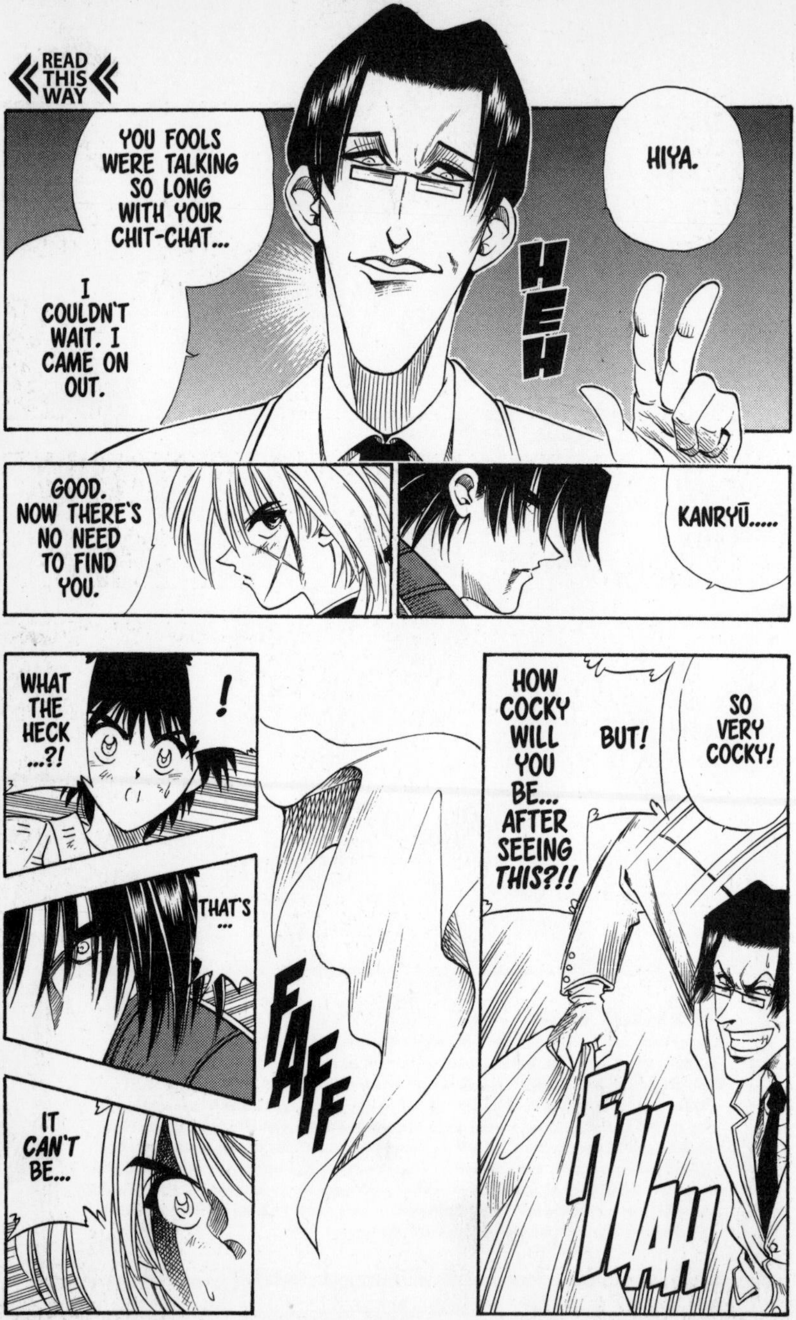
HIYA.
HEH
YOU FOOLS WERE TALKING SO LONG WITH YOUR CHIT-CHAT...
I COULDN'T WAIT. I CAME ON OUT.
KANRYŪ.....
GOOD. NOW THERE'S NO NEED TO FIND YOU.
SO VERY COCKY!
BUT!
HOW COCKY WILL YOU BE... AFTER SEEING *THIS*?!!
FWAH
FAFF
!
WHAT THE HECK ...?!
THAT'S ...
IT CAN'T BE...

READ THIS WAY

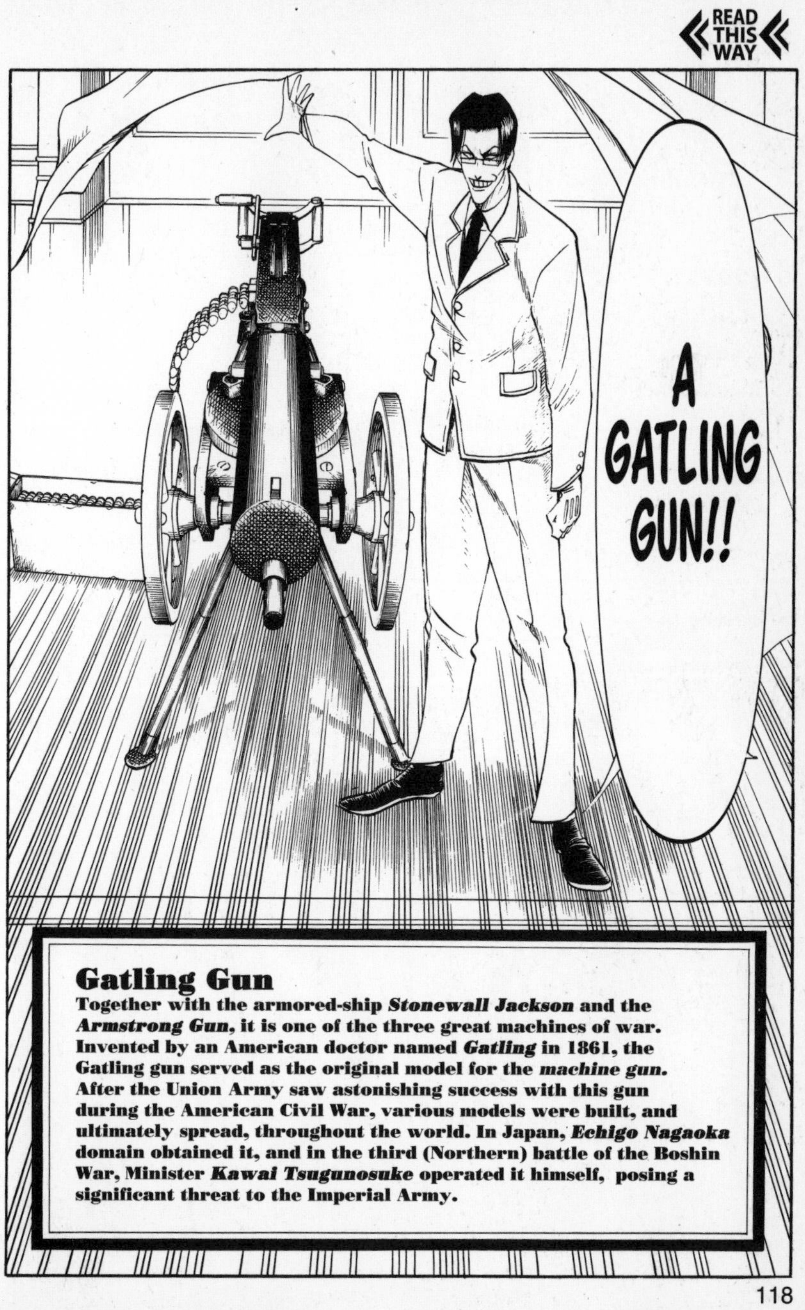
A GATLING GUN!!
Gatling Gun
Together with the armored-ship *Stonewall Jackson* and the *Armstrong Gun,* it is one of the three great machines of war. Invented by an American doctor named *Gatling* in 1861, the Gatling gun served as the original model for the *machine gun.* After the Union Army saw astonishing success with this gun during the American Civil War, various models were built, and ultimately spread, throughout the world. In Japan, *Echigo Nagaoka* domain obtained it, and in the third (Northern) battle of the Boshin War, Minister *Kawai Tsugunosuke* operated it himself, posing a significant threat to the Imperial Army.

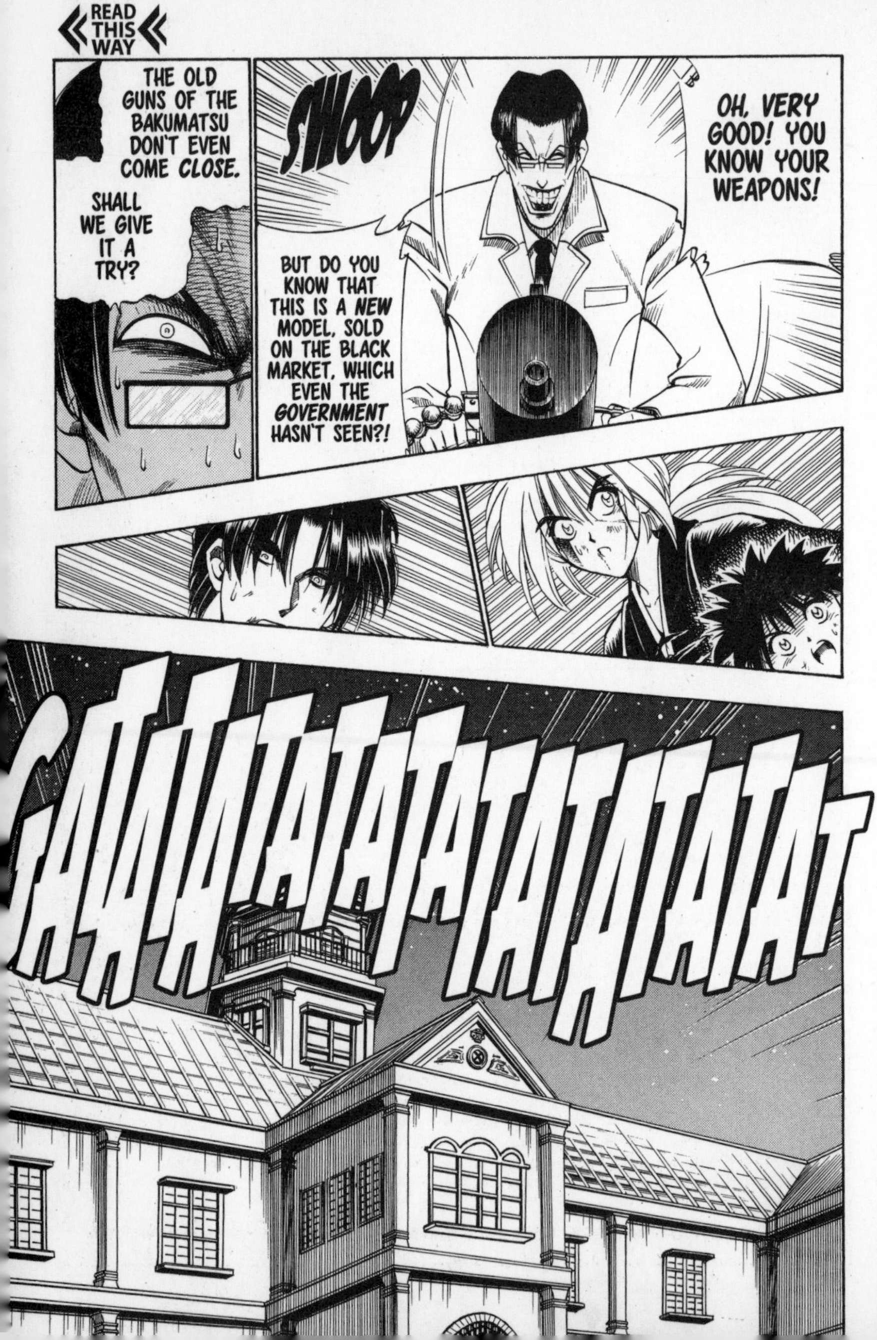
READ THIS WAY
OH, VERY GOOD! YOU KNOW YOUR WEAPONS!
SWOOP
BUT DO YOU KNOW THAT THIS IS A *NEW* MODEL, SOLD ON THE BLACK MARKET, WHICH EVEN THE *GOVERNMENT* HASN'T SEEN?!
THE OLD GUNS OF THE BAKUMATSU DON'T EVEN COME *CLOSE.*
SHALL WE GIVE IT A TRY?
GAGAGATATATATATATATATAT

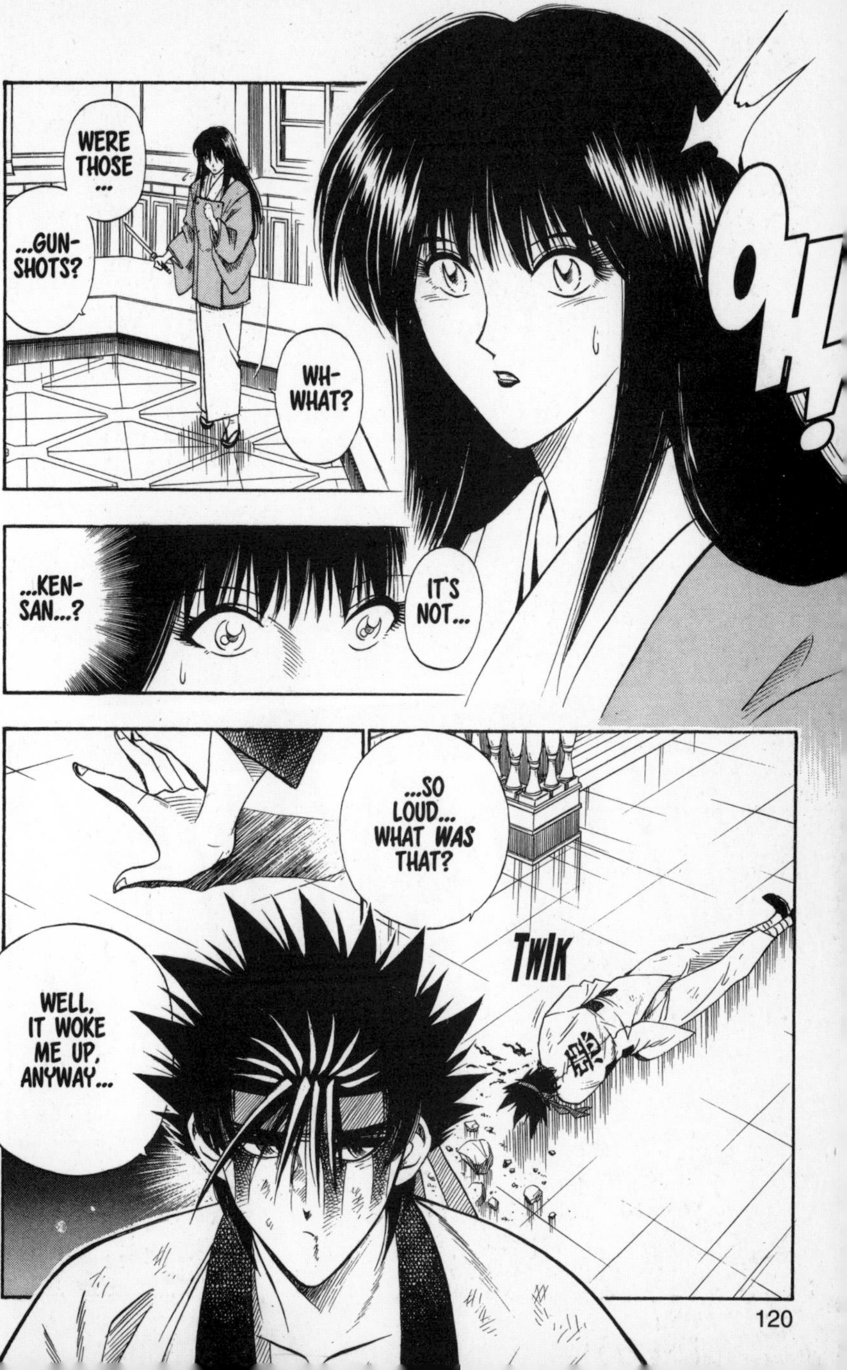

OH!
WH-WHAT?
WERE THOSE ...
...GUN-SHOTS?
IT'S NOT...
...KEN-SAN...?
...SO LOUD... WHAT WAS THAT?
TWIK
WELL, IT WOKE ME UP, ANYWAY...

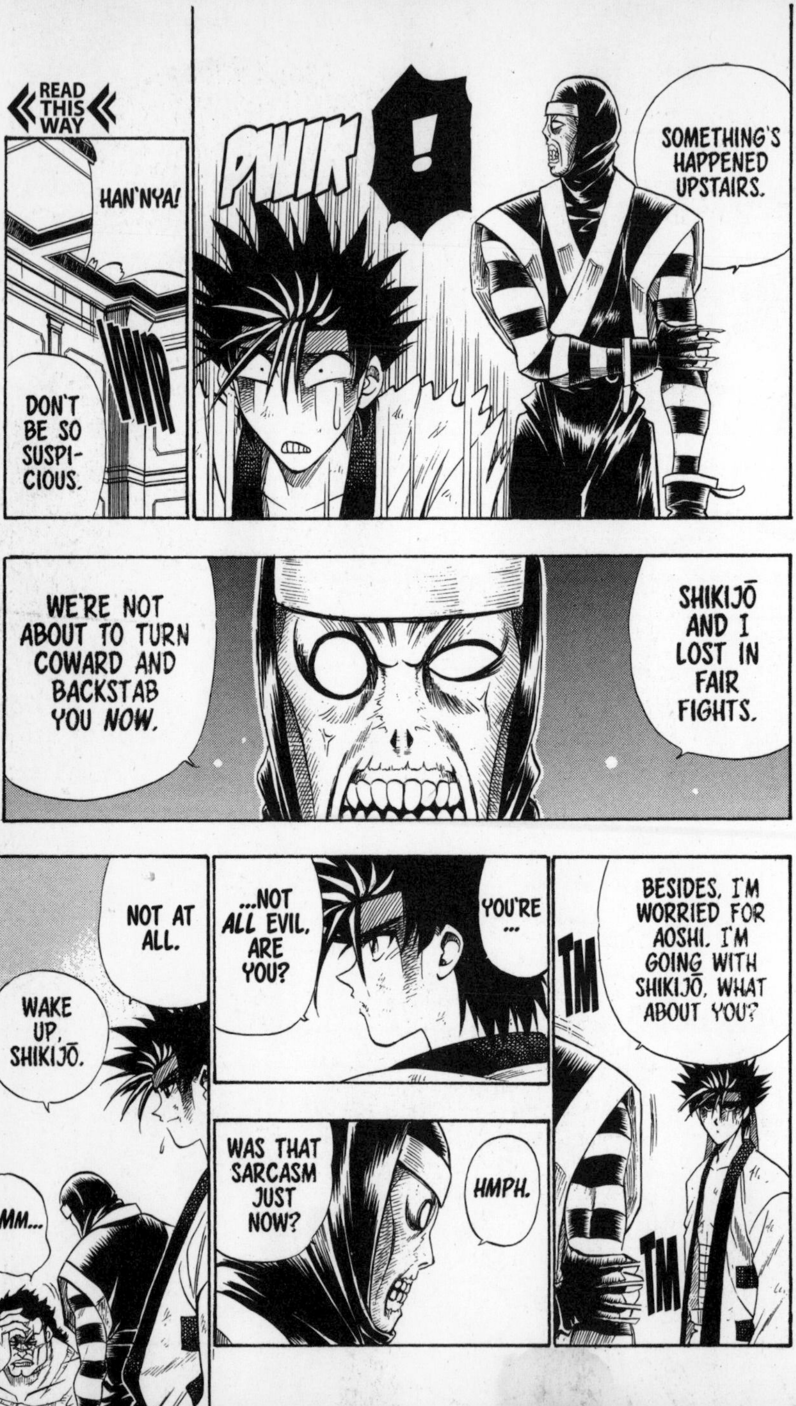
READ THIS WAY
SOMETHING'S HAPPENED UPSTAIRS.
PWIK
!
HAN'NYA!
VWIP
DON'T BE SO SUSPI-CIOUS.
SHIKIJŌ AND I LOST IN FAIR FIGHTS.
WE'RE NOT ABOUT TO TURN COWARD AND BACKSTAB YOU *NOW*.
BESIDES, I'M WORRIED FOR AOSHI. I'M GOING WITH SHIKIJŌ, WHAT ABOUT YOU?
TM
TM
YOU'RE ...
...NOT *ALL* EVIL, ARE YOU?
HMPH.
WAS THAT SARCASM JUST NOW?
NOT AT ALL.
WAKE UP, SHIKIJŌ.
MMM...

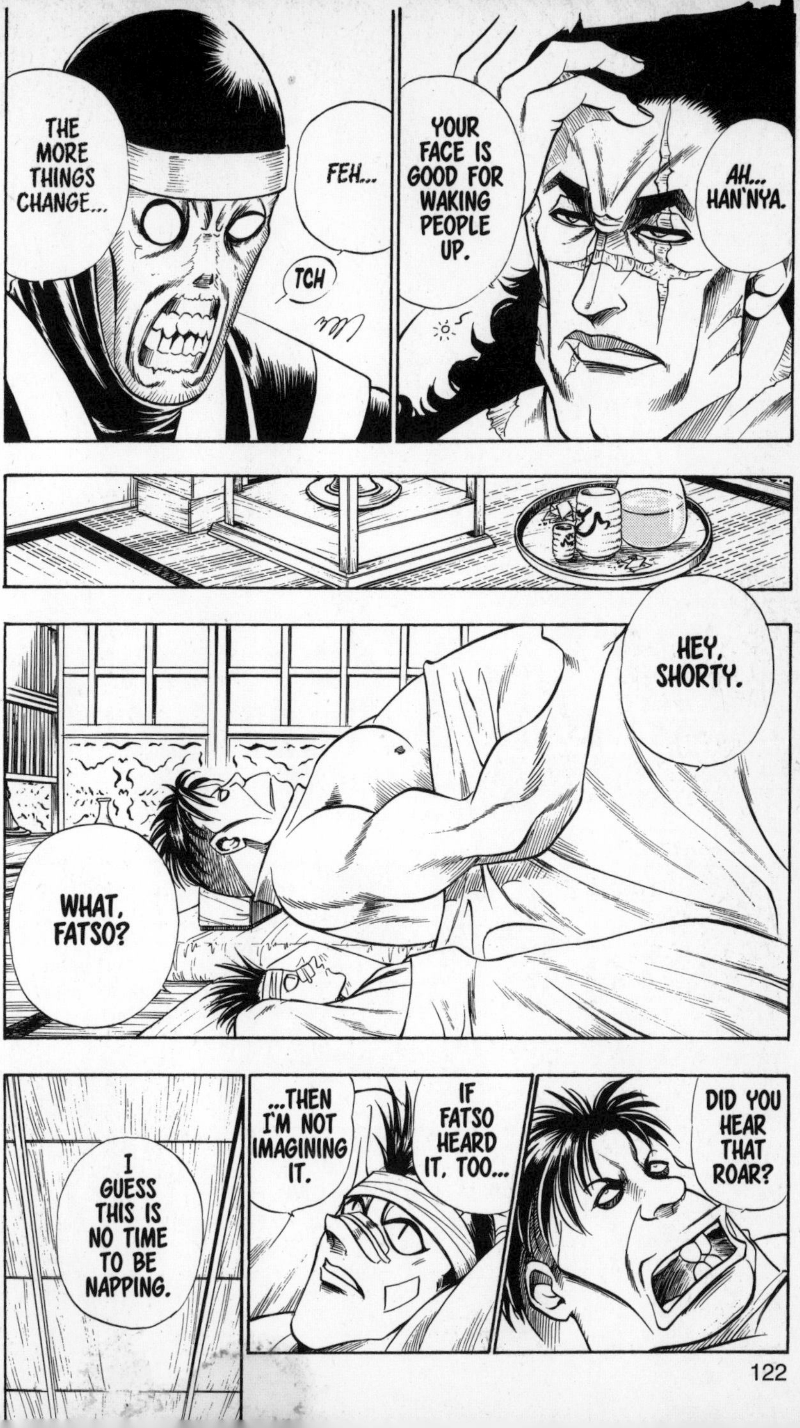
AH... HAN'NYA.
YOUR FACE IS GOOD FOR WAKING PEOPLE UP.
FEH...
TCH
THE MORE THINGS CHANGE...
HEY, SHORTY.
WHAT, FATSO?
DID YOU HEAR THAT ROAR?
IF FATSO HEARD IT, TOO...
...THEN I'M NOT IMAGINING IT.
I GUESS THIS IS NO TIME TO BE NAPPING.

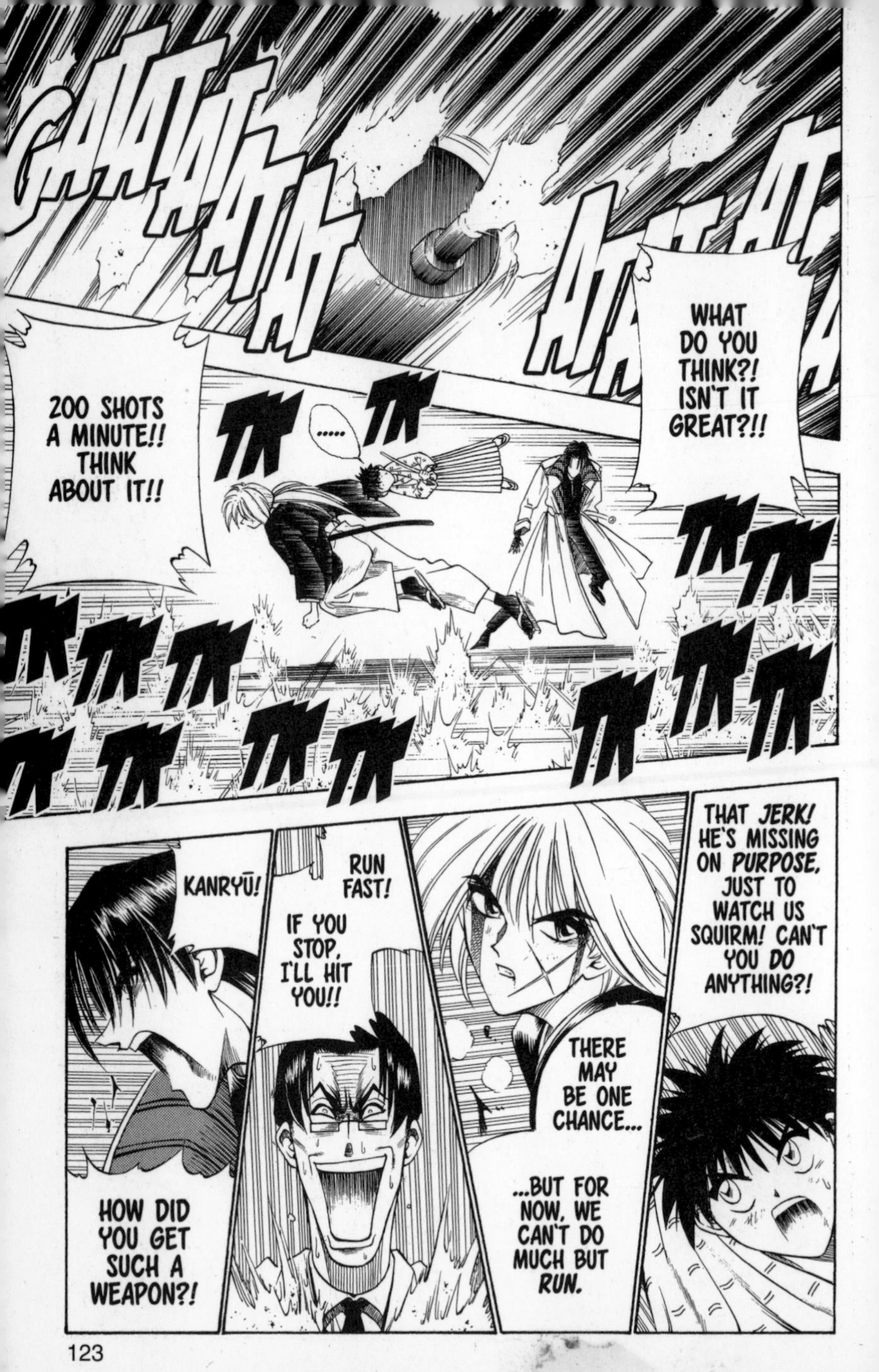
WHAT DO YOU THINK?! ISN'T IT GREAT?!!
200 SHOTS A MINUTE!! THINK ABOUT IT!!
.....
THAT JERK! HE'S MISSING ON PURPOSE, JUST TO WATCH US SQUIRM! CAN'T YOU DO ANYTHING?!
THERE MAY BE ONE CHANCE...
...BUT FOR NOW, WE CAN'T DO MUCH BUT RUN.
RUN FAST!
IF YOU STOP, I'LL HIT YOU!!
KANRYŪ!
HOW DID YOU GET SUCH A WEAPON?!

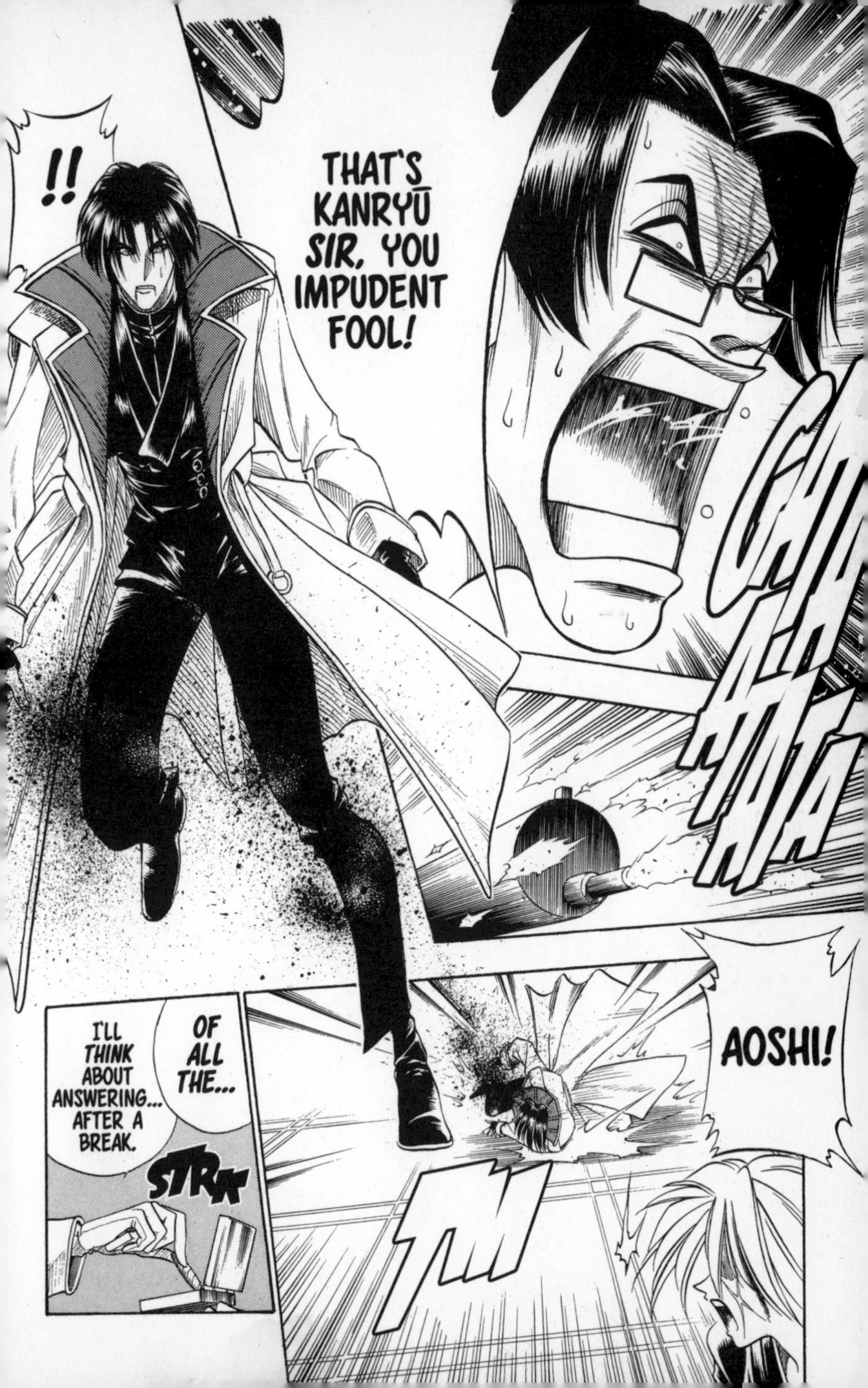
THAT'S KANRYŪ SIR, YOU IMPUDENT FOOL!
!!
AOSHI!
OF ALL THE...
I'LL THINK ABOUT ANSWERING... AFTER A BREAK.
STRK

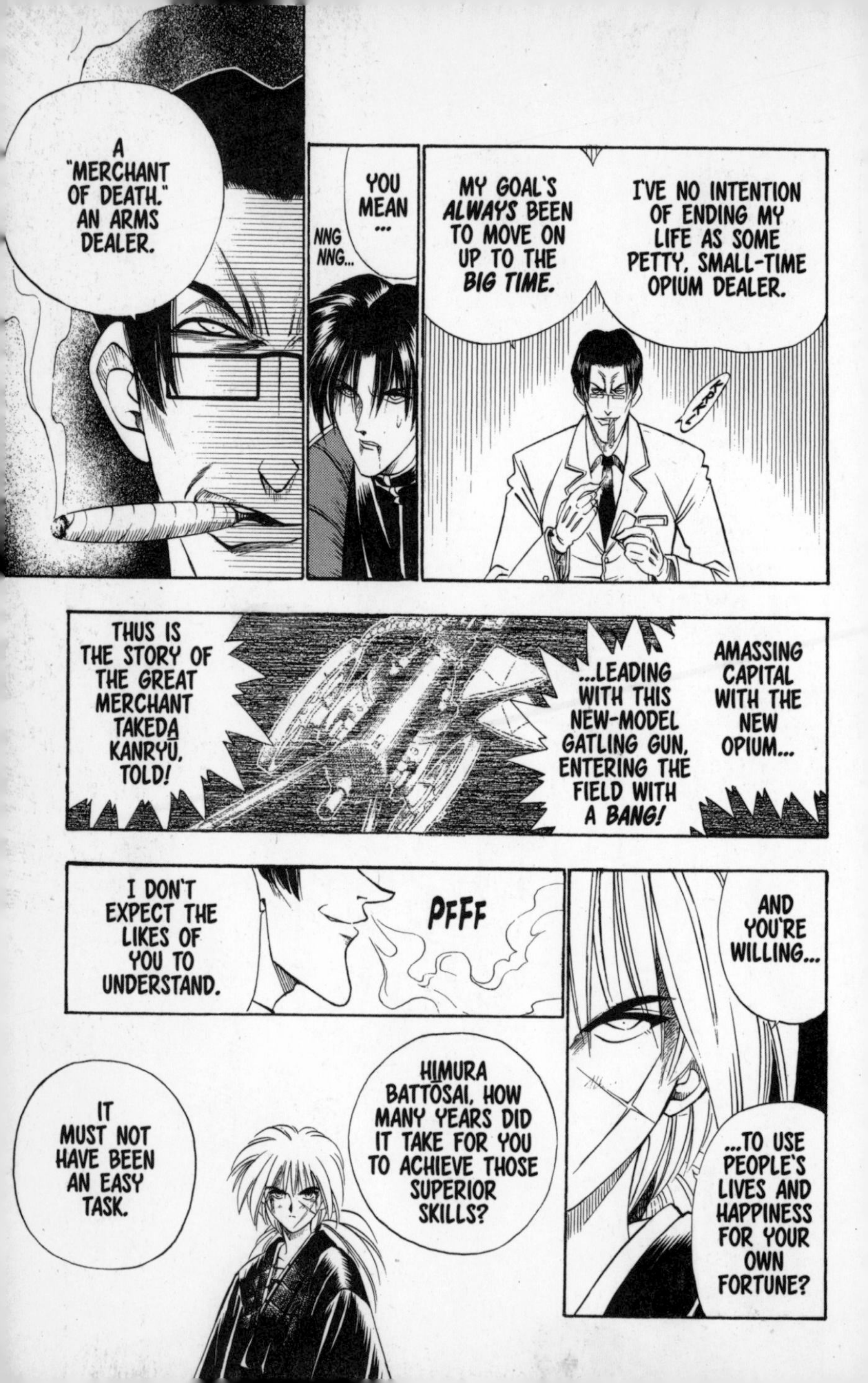
I'VE NO INTENTION OF ENDING MY LIFE AS SOME PETTY, SMALL-TIME OPIUM DEALER.
MY GOAL'S *ALWAYS* BEEN TO MOVE ON UP TO THE *BIG TIME.*
YOU MEAN ...
NNG NNG...
A "MERCHANT OF DEATH." AN ARMS DEALER.
AMASSING CAPITAL WITH THE NEW OPIUM...
...LEADING WITH THIS NEW-MODEL GATLING GUN, ENTERING THE FIELD WITH A *BANG!*
THUS IS THE STORY OF THE GREAT MERCHANT TAKEDA KANRYŪ, TOLD!
AND YOU'RE WILLING...
...TO USE PEOPLE'S LIVES AND HAPPINESS FOR YOUR OWN FORTUNE?
I DON'T EXPECT THE LIKES OF YOU TO UNDERSTAND.
PFFF
HIMURA BATTŌSAI, HOW MANY YEARS DID IT TAKE FOR YOU TO ACHIEVE THOSE SUPERIOR SKILLS?
IT MUST NOT HAVE BEEN AN EASY TASK.

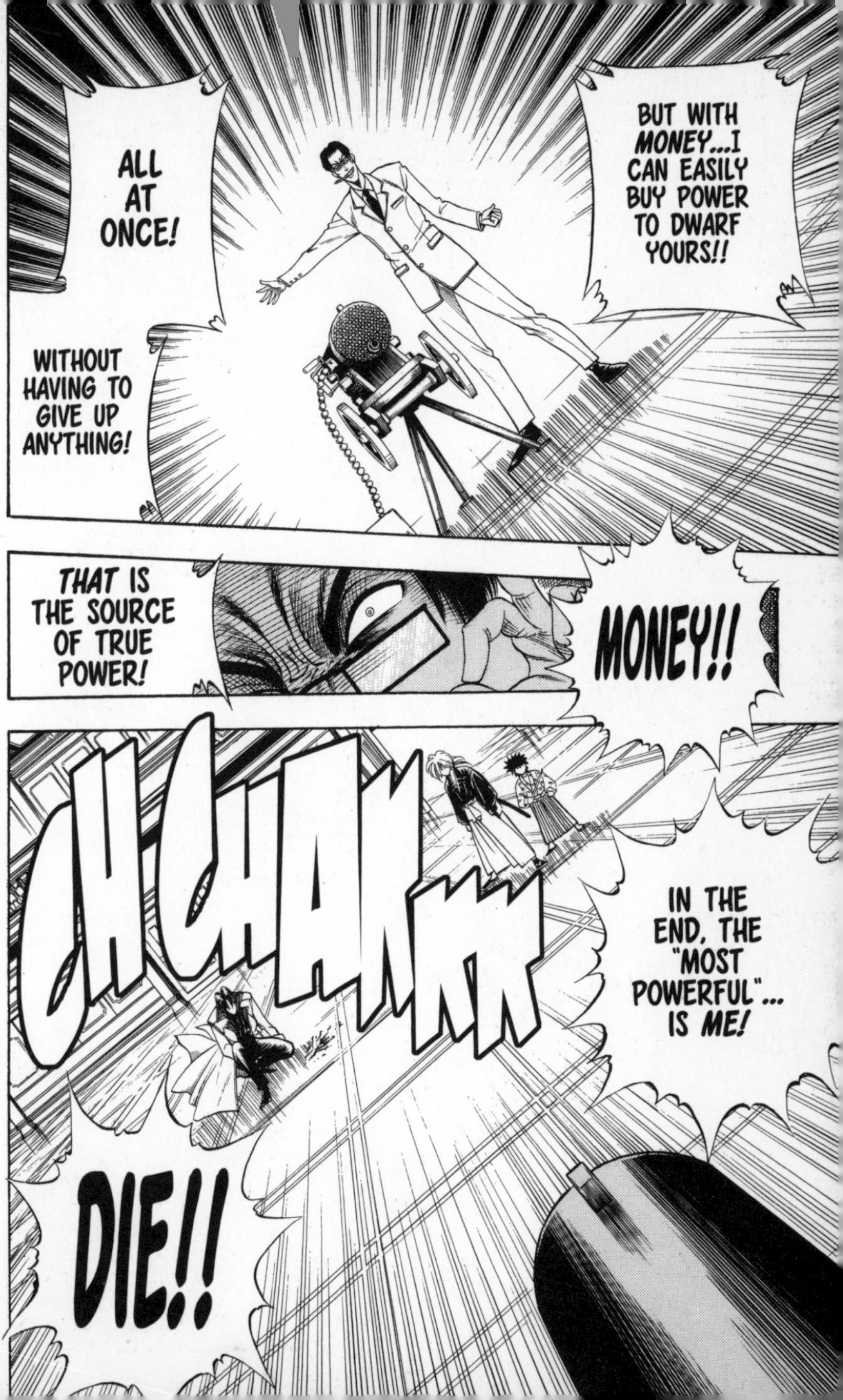
BUT WITH MONEY...I CAN EASILY BUY POWER TO DWARF YOURS!!
ALL AT ONCE!
WITHOUT HAVING TO GIVE UP ANYTHING!
MONEY!!
THAT IS THE SOURCE OF TRUE POWER!
IN THE END, THE "MOST POWERFUL"... IS ME!
CHCHAKKK
DIE!!

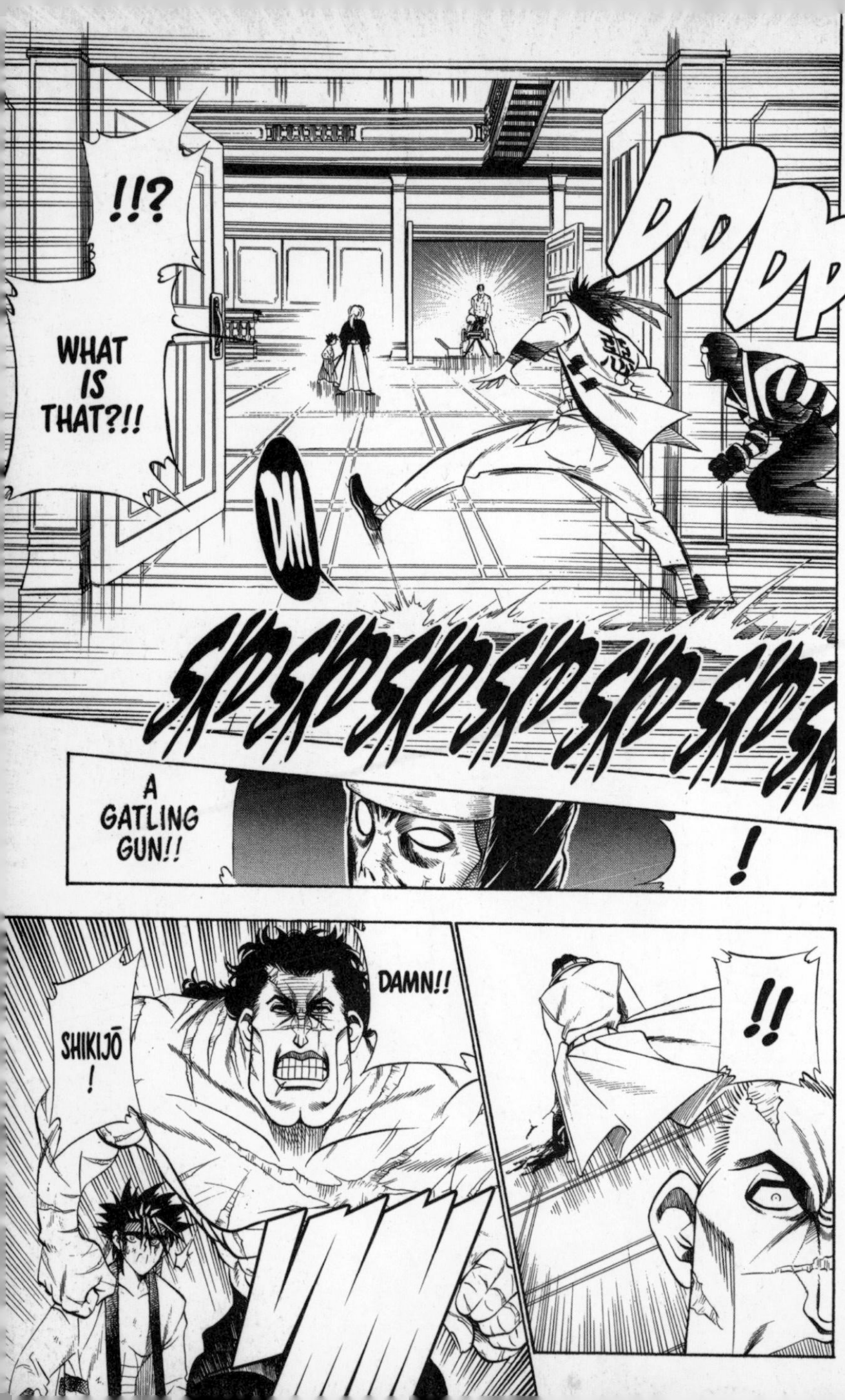
DDDD
!!?
WHAT IS THAT?!!
DM
SKID SKID SKID SKID SKID SKID SKID
!
A GATLING GUN!!
!!
DAMN!!
SHIKIJŌ!

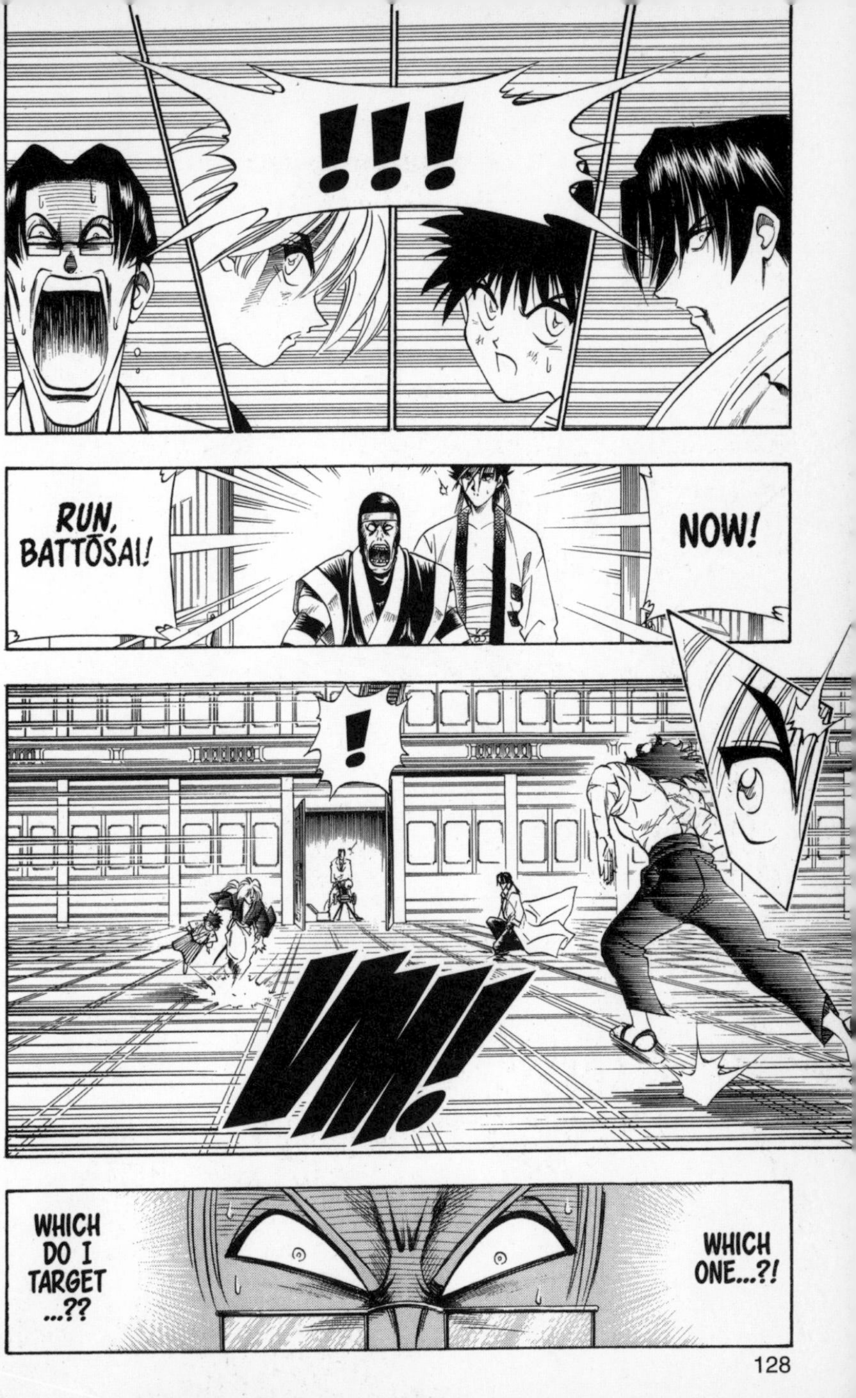
!!!
NOW!
RUN, BATTŌSAI!
!
VM!
WHICH ONE...?!
WHICH DO I TARGET ...??

READ THIS WAY

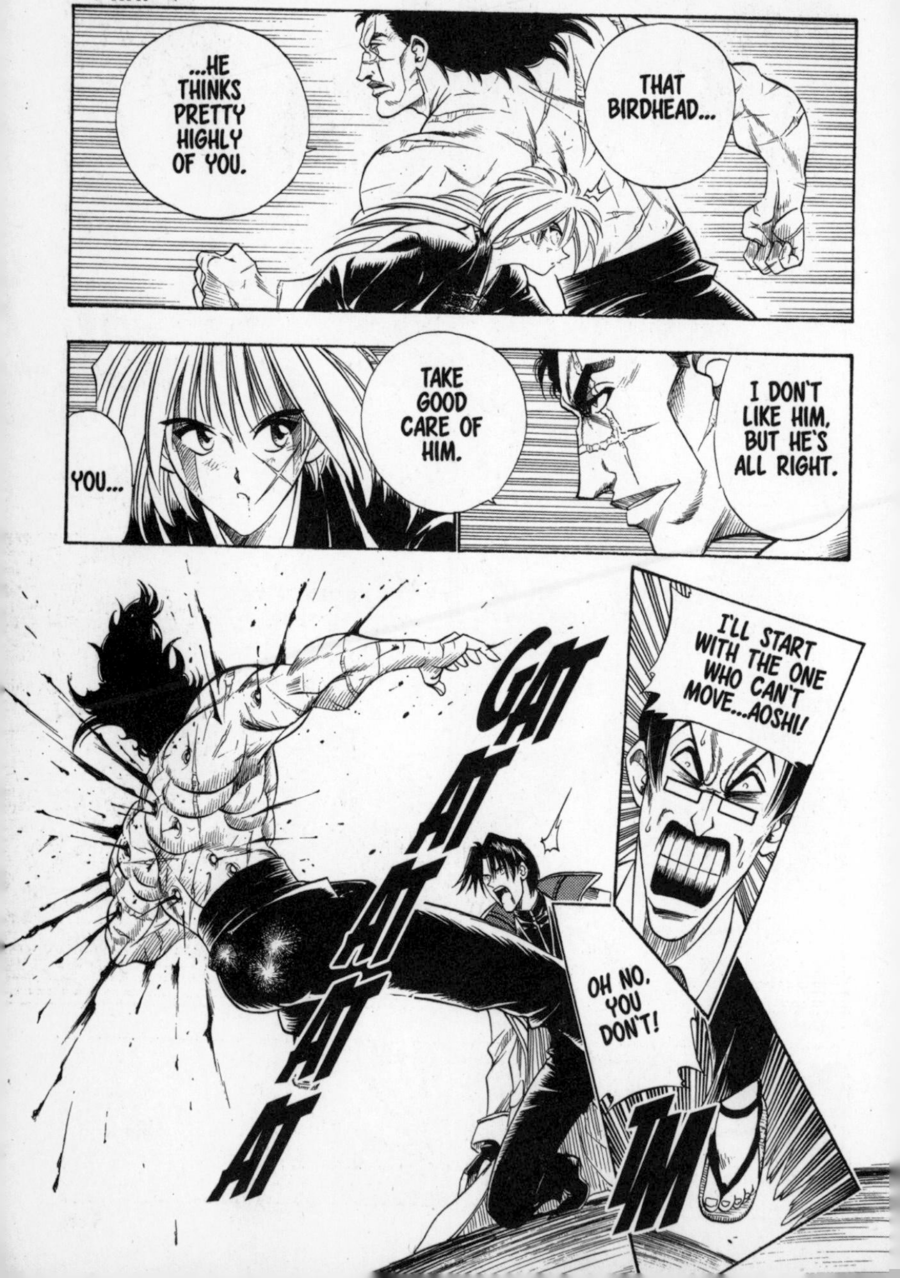

THAT BIRDHEAD...
...HE THINKS PRETTY HIGHLY OF YOU.
I DON'T LIKE HIM, BUT HE'S ALL RIGHT.
TAKE GOOD CARE OF HIM.
YOU...
I'LL START WITH THE ONE WHO CAN'T MOVE...AOSHI!
OH NO. YOU DON'T!
TM
GATATATATATAT

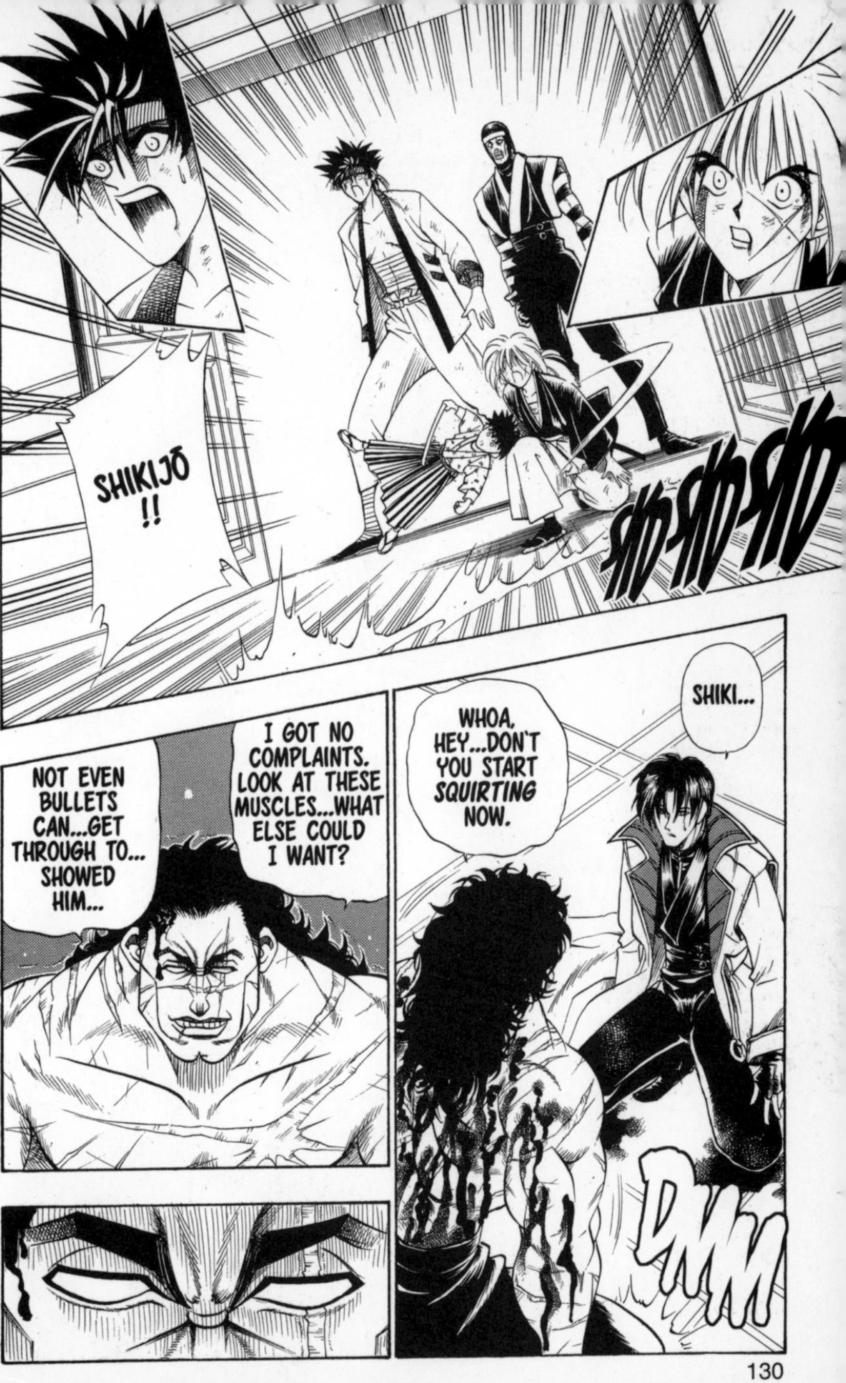
SHIKIJŌ !!
SHIKI...
WHOA, HEY...DON'T YOU START SQUIRTING NOW.
DMM
I GOT NO COMPLAINTS. LOOK AT THESE MUSCLES...WHAT ELSE COULD I WANT?
NOT EVEN BULLETS CAN...GET THROUGH TO... SHOWED HIM...

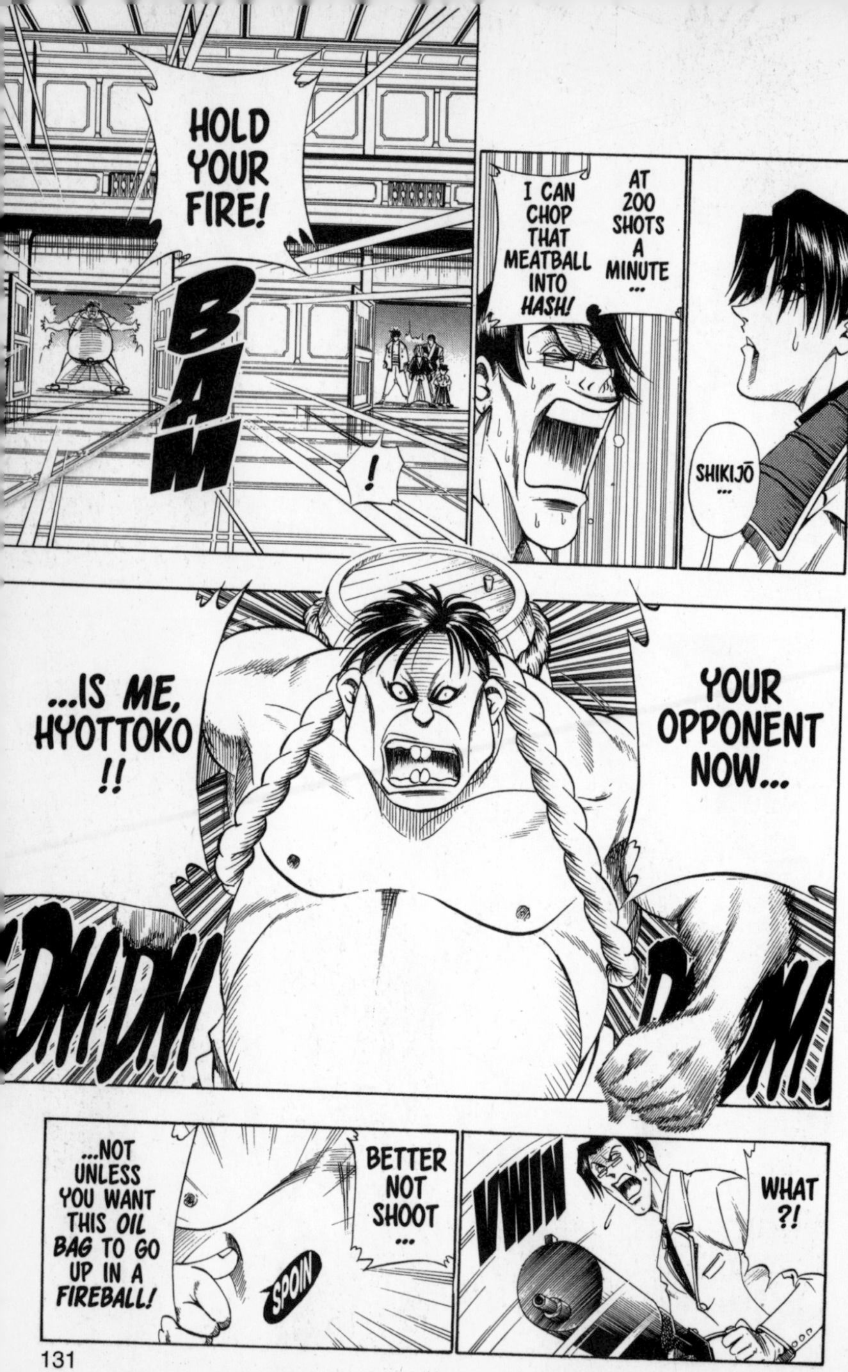

SHIKIJŌ ...
AT 200 SHOTS A MINUTE ...
I CAN CHOP THAT MEATBALL INTO HASH!
HOLD YOUR FIRE!
BAM
!
YOUR OPPONENT NOW...
...IS ME, HYOTTOKO !!
WHAT ?!
VWIN
BETTER NOT SHOOT ...
...NOT UNLESS YOU WANT THIS OIL BAG TO GO UP IN A FIREBALL!
SPOIN

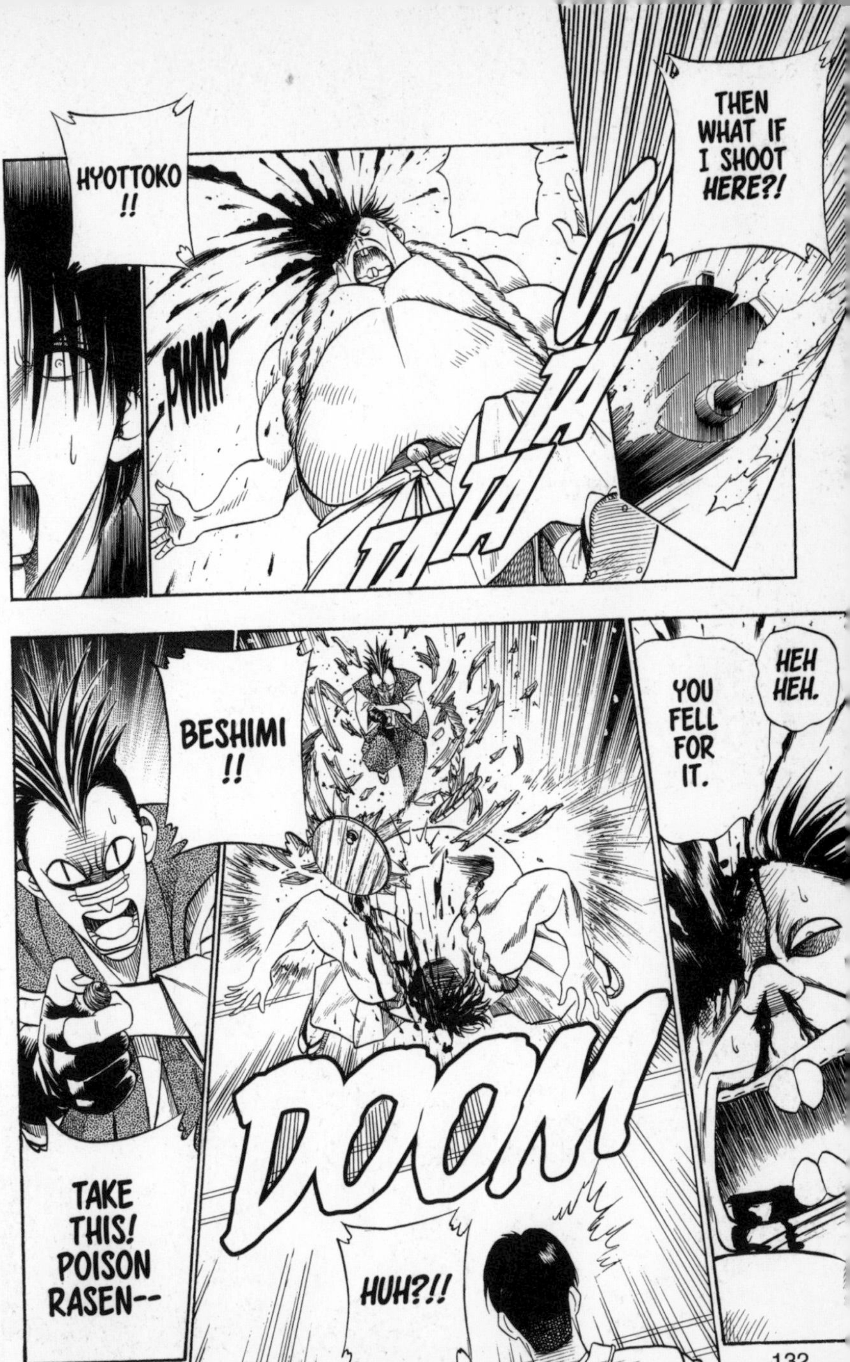
THEN WHAT IF I SHOOT HERE?!
CHATATA
PWMP
HYOTTOKO!!
HEH HEH.
YOU FELL FOR IT.
BESHIMI!!
DOOM
HUH?!!
TAKE THIS! POISON RASEN--

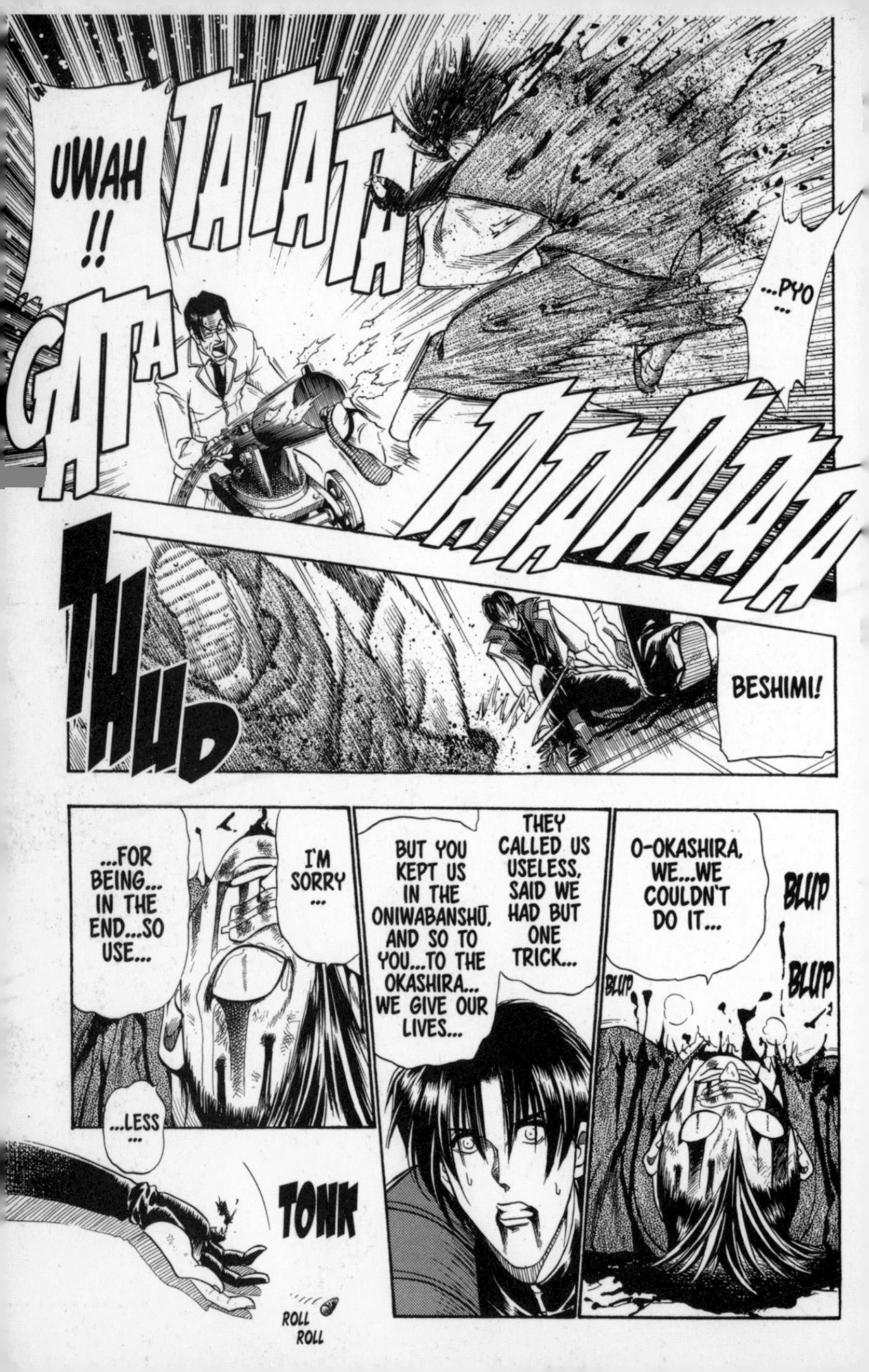

...PYO...
TATATA
UWAH!!
GATA
DADADADA
BESHIMI!
THUD
O-OKASHIRA, WE...WE COULDN'T DO IT...
BLUP
BLUP
BLUP
THEY CALLED US USELESS, SAID WE HAD BUT ONE TRICK...
BUT YOU KEPT US IN THE ONIWABANSHŪ, AND SO TO YOU...TO THE OKASHIRA... WE GIVE OUR LIVES...
I'M SORRY...
...FOR BEING... IN THE END...SO USE...
...LESS...
TONK
ROLL
ROLL

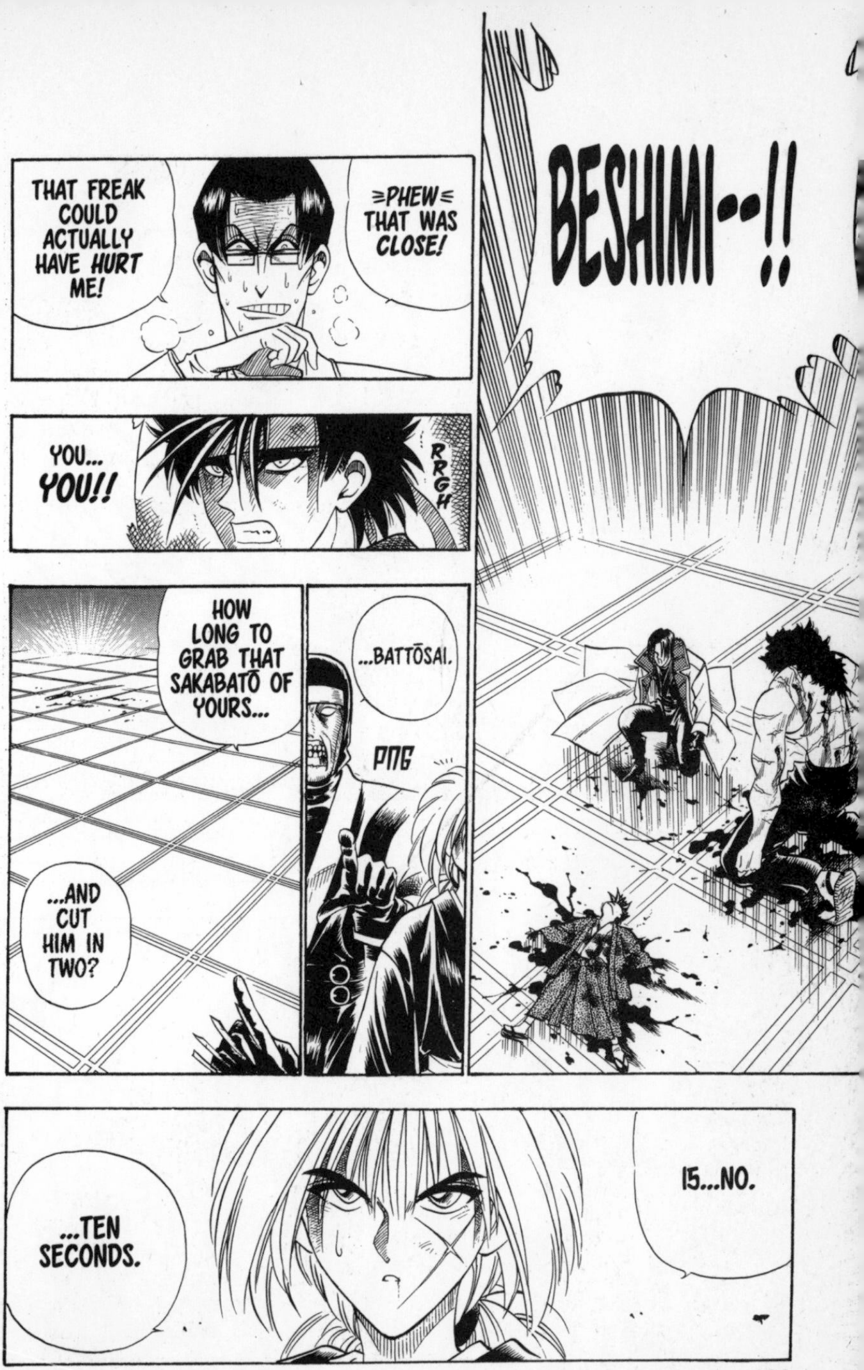
BESHIMI--!!
≡PHEW≡ THAT WAS CLOSE!
THAT FREAK COULD ACTUALLY HAVE HURT ME!
RRGH
YOU... YOU!!
...BATTŌSAI.
PNG
HOW LONG TO GRAB THAT SAKABATŌ OF YOURS...
...AND CUT HIM IN TWO?
15...NO.
...TEN SECONDS.

READ THIS WAY

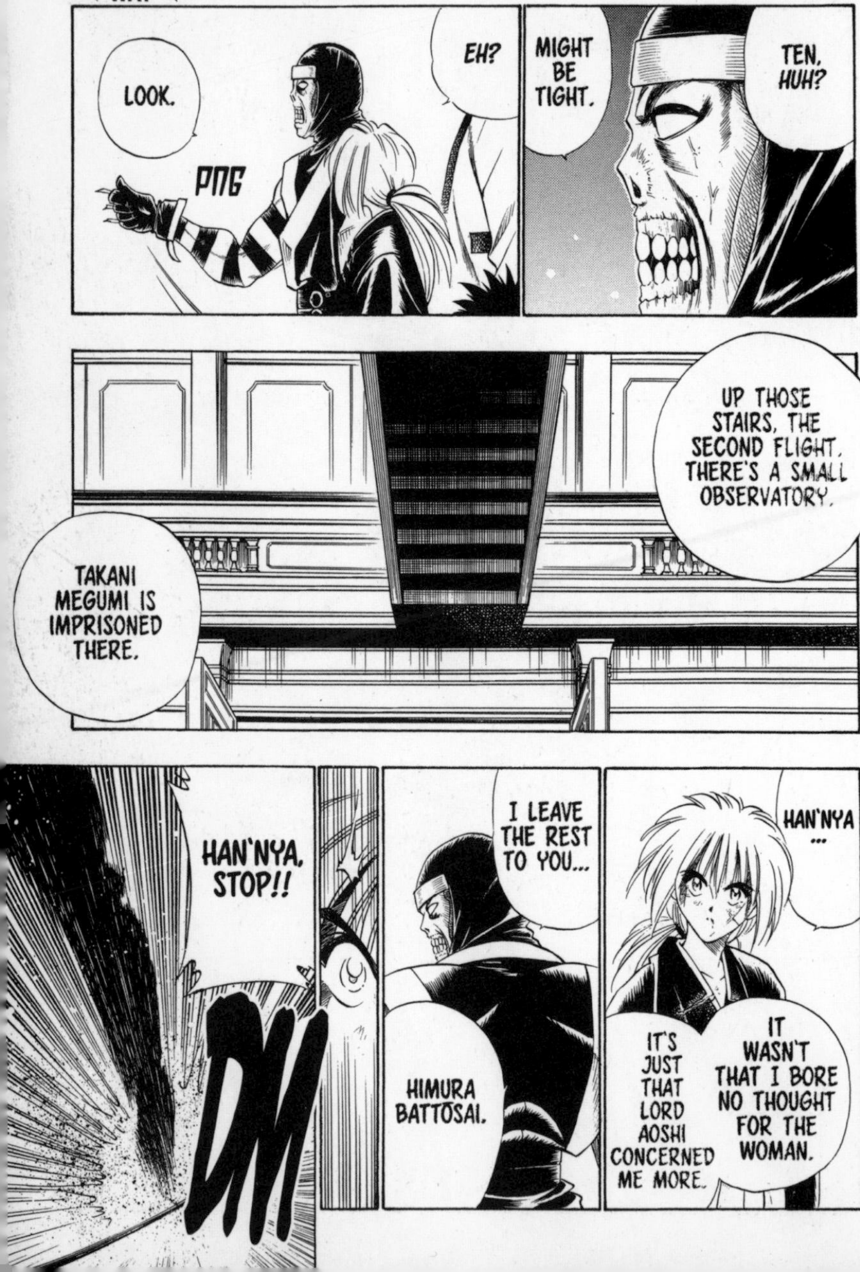
TEN, HUH?
MIGHT BE TIGHT.
EH?
LOOK.
PNG
UP THOSE STAIRS, THE SECOND FLIGHT. THERE'S A SMALL OBSERVATORY.
TAKANI MEGUMI IS IMPRISONED THERE.
HAN'NYA...
IT WASN'T THAT I BORE NO THOUGHT FOR THE WOMAN.
IT'S JUST THAT LORD AOSHI CONCERNED ME MORE.
I LEAVE THE REST TO YOU...
HIMURA BATTOSAI.
HAN'NYA, STOP!!
DM

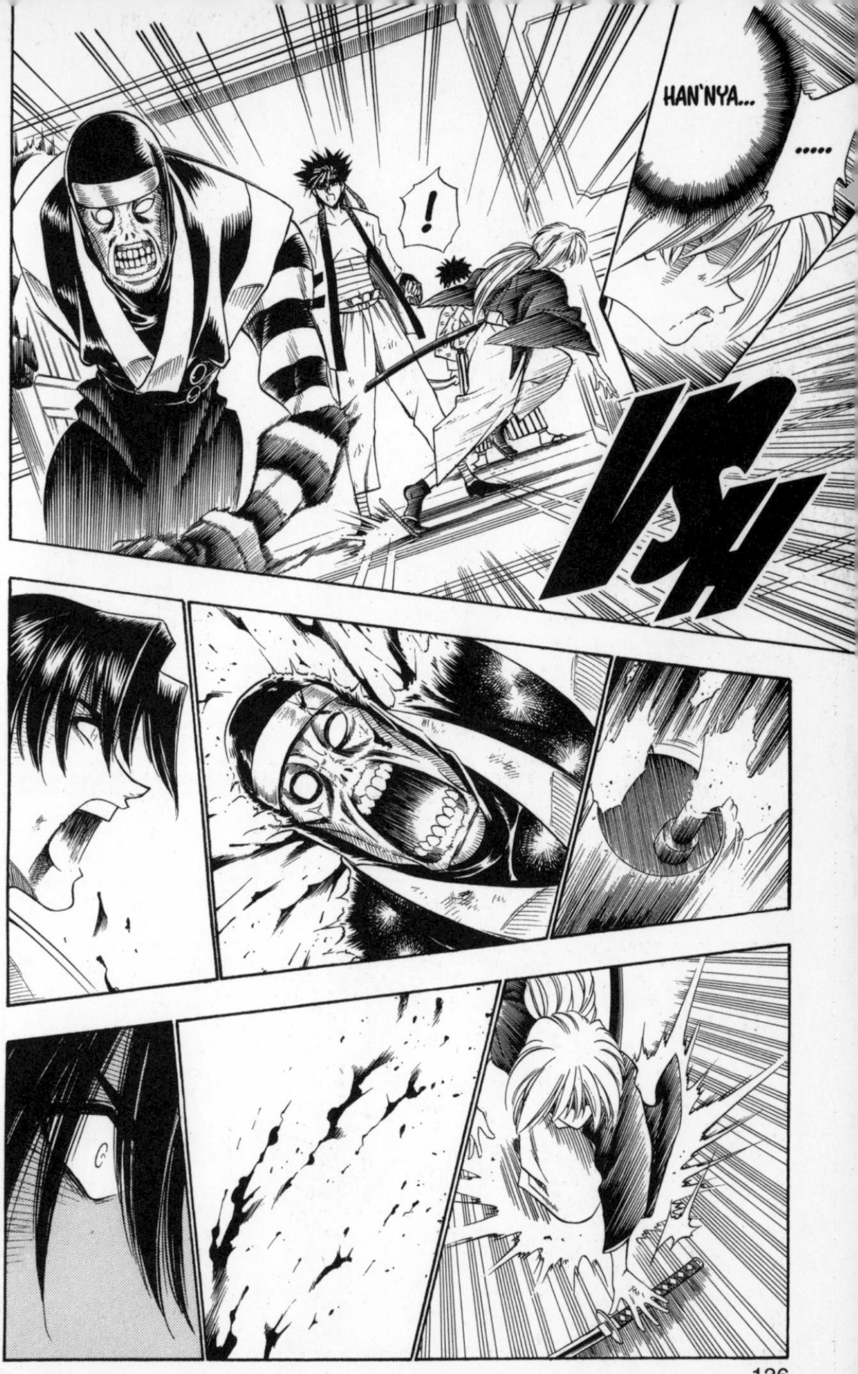
HAN'NYA...
......
!
VSH

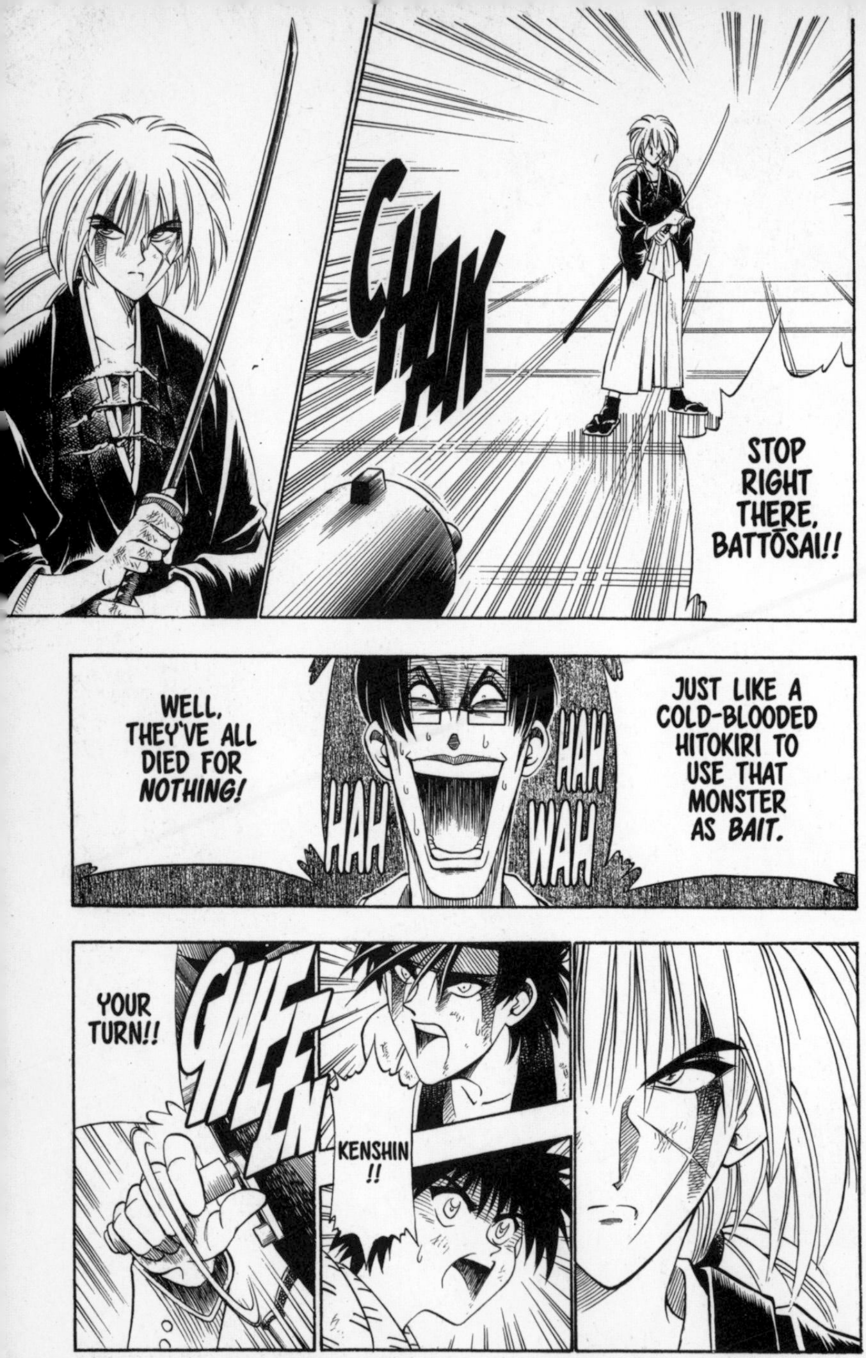
STOP RIGHT THERE, BATTŌSAI!!
CHAK
JUST LIKE A COLD-BLOODED HITOKIRI TO USE THAT MONSTER AS BAIT.
HAH WAH
HAH HAH
WELL, THEY'VE ALL DIED FOR NOTHING!
YOUR TURN!!
GYEEN
KENSHIN!!

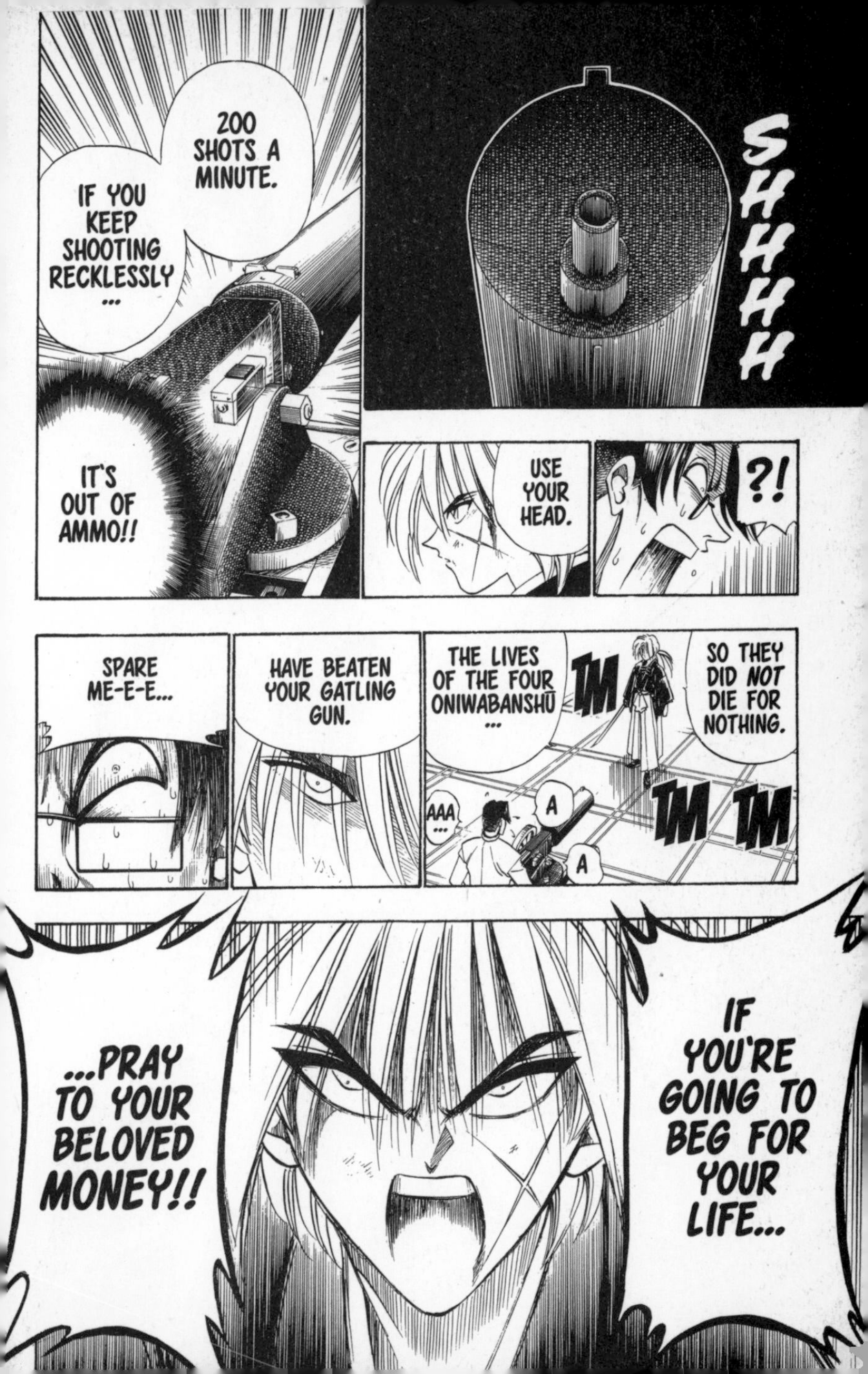
SHHHH
?!
USE YOUR HEAD.
200 SHOTS A MINUTE.
IF YOU KEEP SHOOTING RECKLESSLY ...
IT'S OUT OF AMMO!!
SO THEY DID NOT DIE FOR NOTHING.
THE LIVES OF THE FOUR ONIWABANSHŪ ...
TM
A
AAA ...
A
TM TM
HAVE BEATEN YOUR GATLING GUN.
SPARE ME-E-E...
IF YOU'RE GOING TO BEG FOR YOUR LIFE...
...PRAY TO YOUR BELOVED MONEY!!

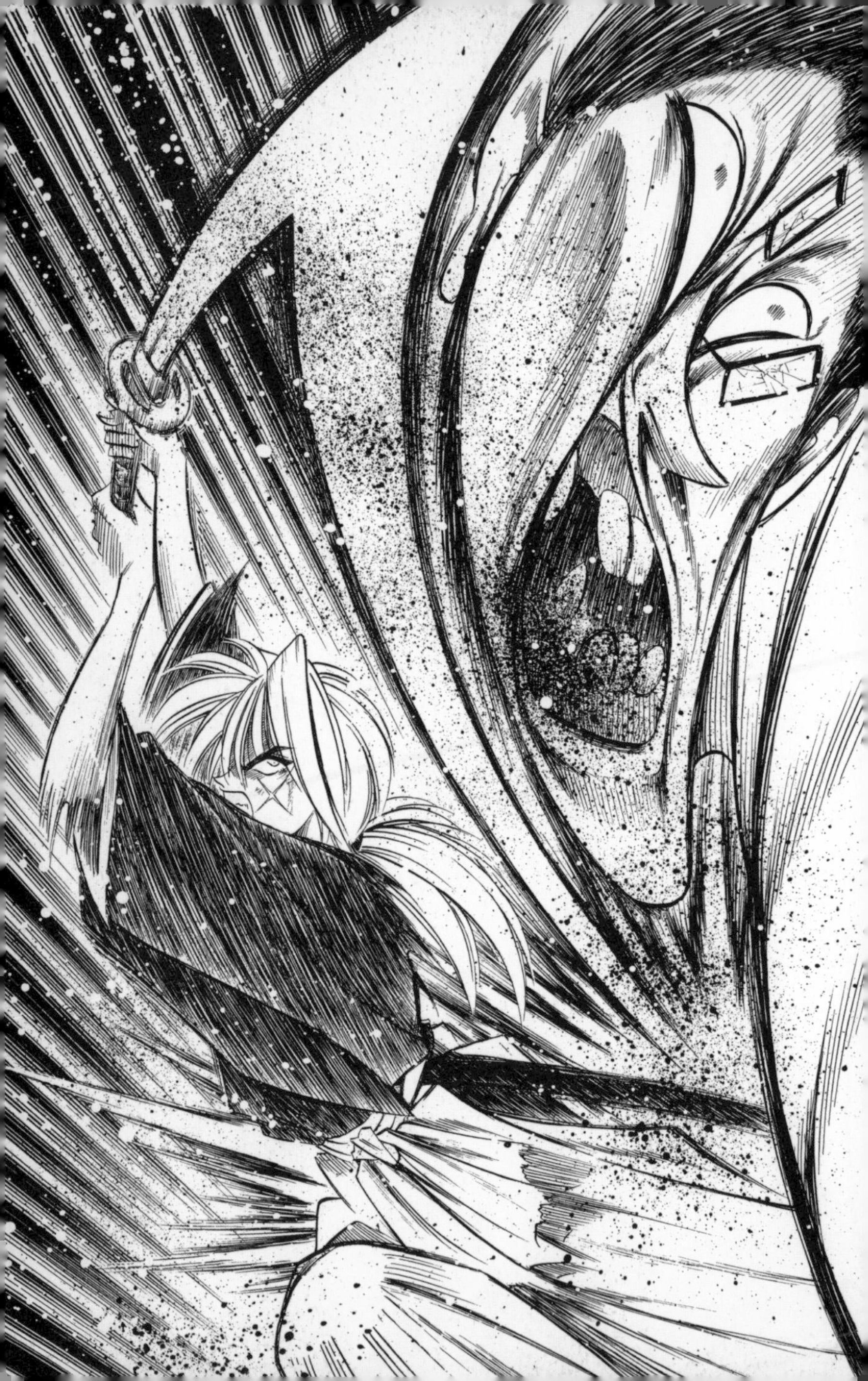

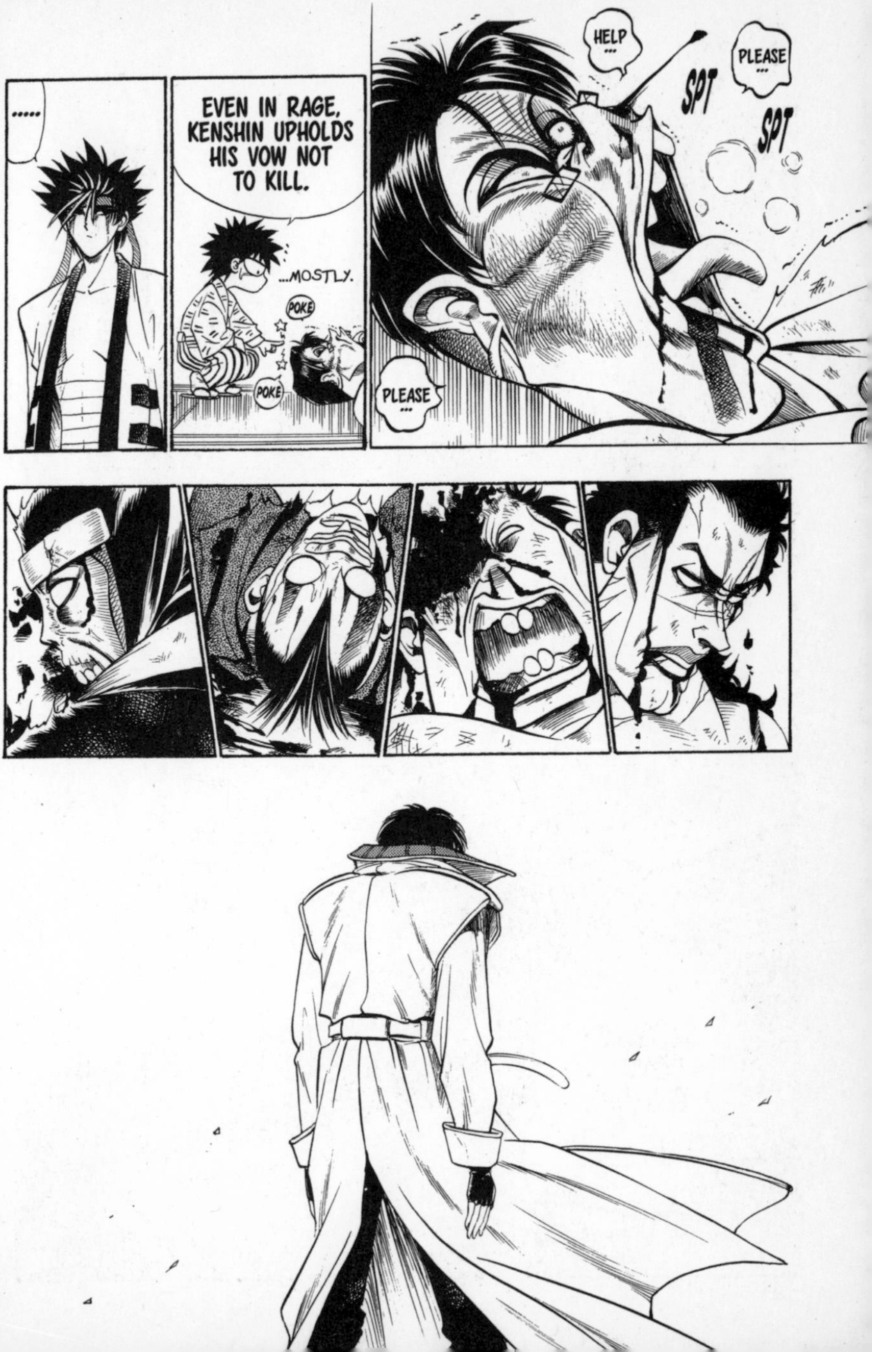
HELP ...
SPT
PLEASE ...
SPT
PLEASE ...
EVEN IN RAGE, KENSHIN UPHOLDS HIS VOW NOT TO KILL.
...MOSTLY.
POKE
POKE
......

READ THIS WAY

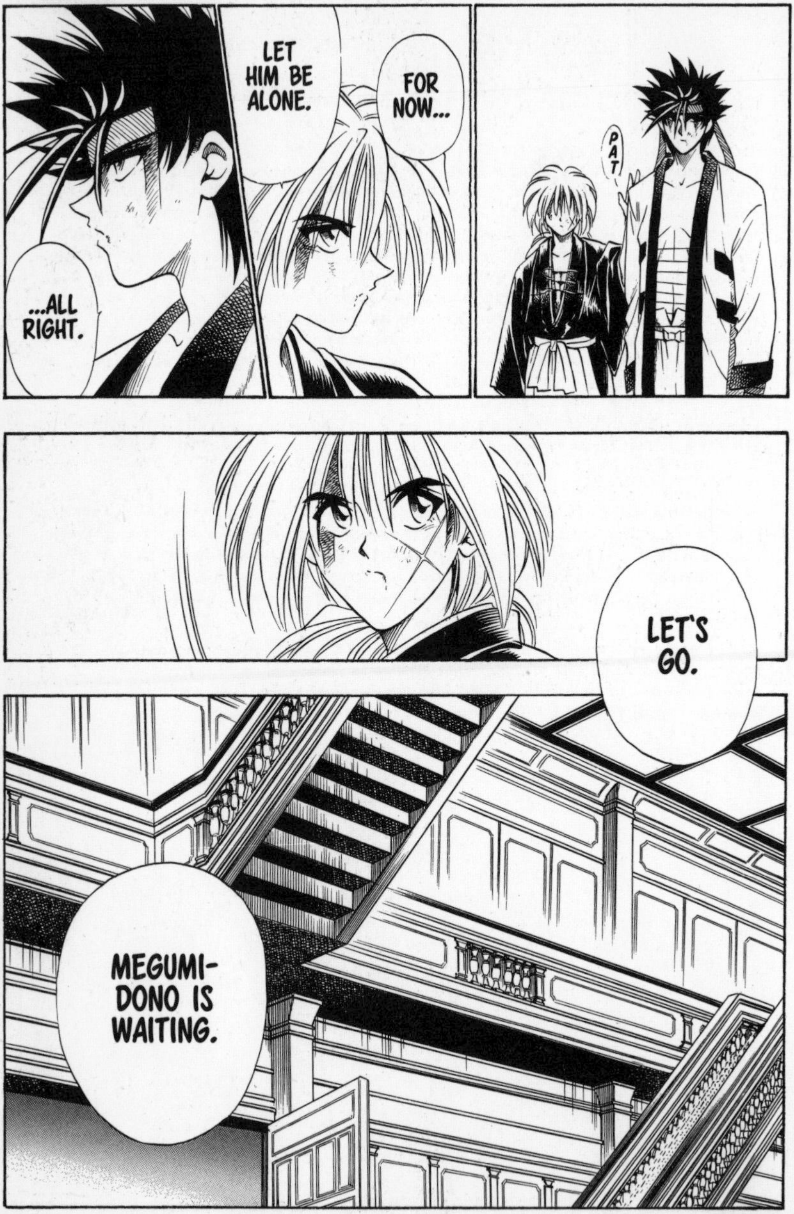
PAT
LET HIM BE ALONE.
FOR NOW...
...ALL RIGHT.
LET'S GO.
MEGUMI-DONO IS WAITING.

## The Secret Life of Characters (12)

# —Takeda Kanryū—

Just as they did with Sanosuke, Shinsengumi fans will recognize right off that Kanryū is based on the captain of the 5th unit of the Shinsengumi, Takeda Kanryūsai. A man who studied *Kōshū-ryū* war theory, Takeda Kanryūsai was a rare Shinsengumi intellectual. His personality, though, was bad—kissing up to superiors, being mean and sneaky to subordinates. Basically, he was jumping on the Shinsengumi bandwagon, and once the outlook started to turn grim, he tried to defect to Satsuma Prefecture but was found out. He was disciplined...and that was the end of him. The main characters of Shinsengumi novels are almost always the same gang of four: Serizawa Kamo, Yamanami Keisuke, Itō Kashitarō, Takeda Kanryūsai. The first three had their own beliefs and ways of life to provide narrative conflict, but as the "sincere fool," Takeda Kanryūsai had his own narrative value, and so I used him as a model here. I found myself putting so much emphasis on Megumi and the Oniwabanshū, though, that Takeda Kanryū never became the character I wanted him to be. That for me was a bit of a letdown.

Purely as a sidenote, the historical Kanryūsai Takeda is well-known as having been gay, and so of course I thought about that for my own Takeda. On top of it being irrelevant to the plot, though, it was thought that it might unnecessarily complicate things, and so it was dropped. I do wonder sometimes how the story might have gone, had we done it that way.

There is no real model in terms of design. Takeda Kanryū is a carry-over from Nishiwaki in the stand-alone *Rurouni* episodes, and wears white if only because, between Kenshin and Aoshi, there was too much black already. And that's all I have to say about that.

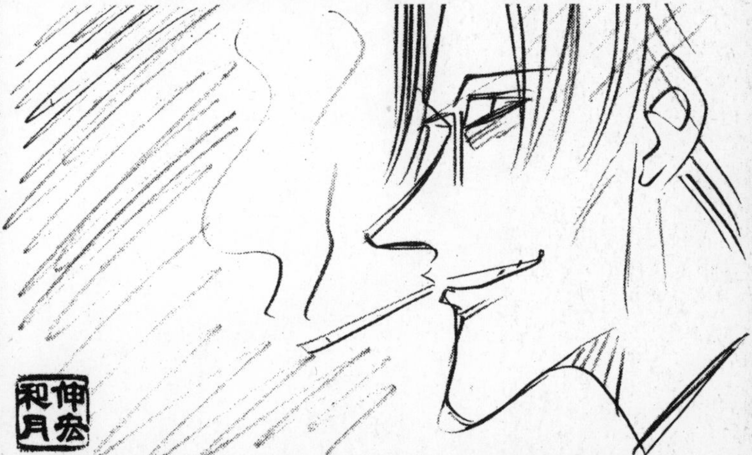

伸宏
和月

READ THIS WAY

# Act 29
# Dual Conclusions: Megumi

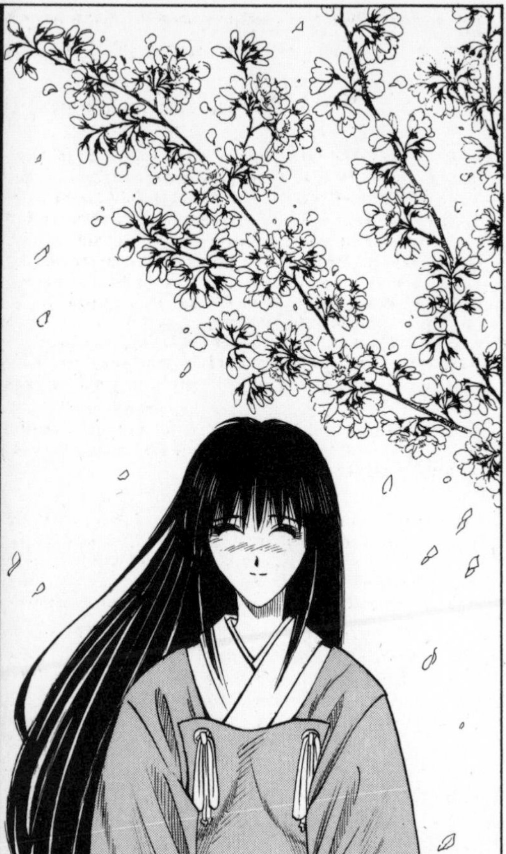

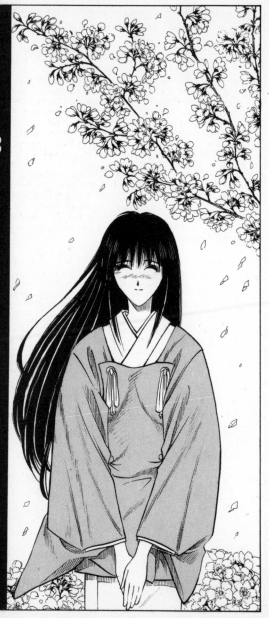

READ THIS WAY

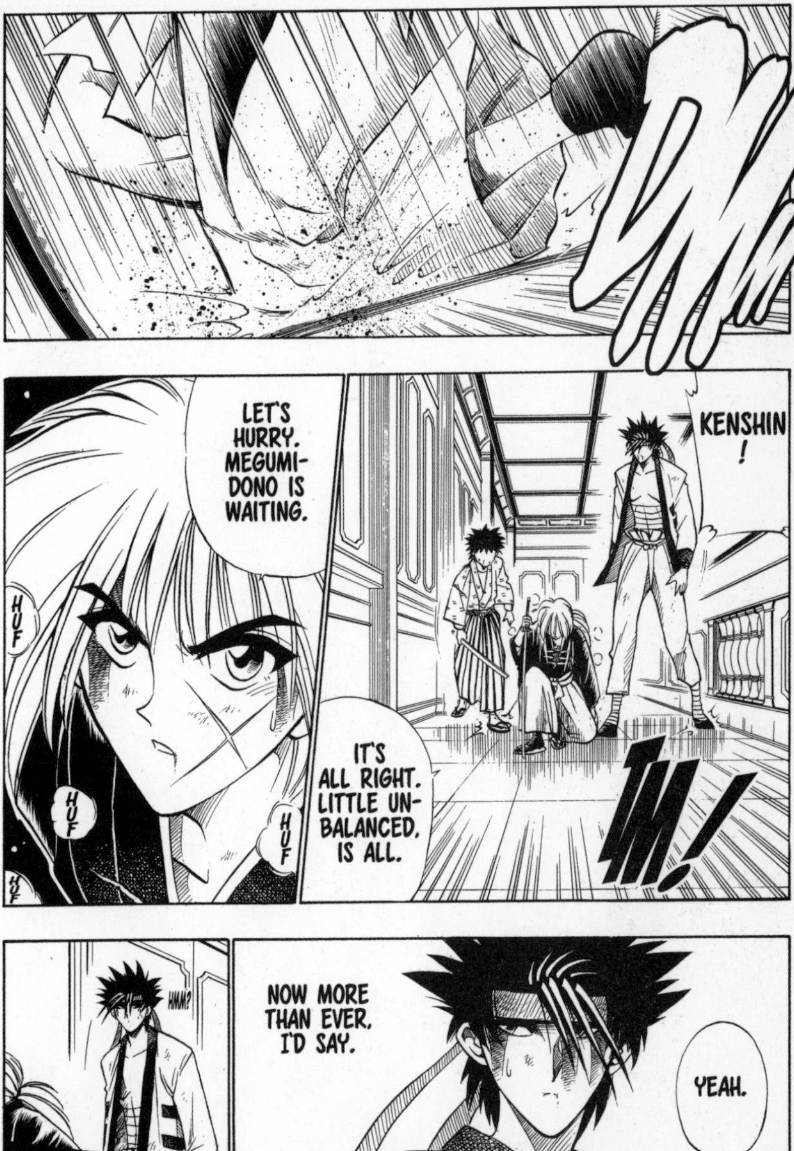
KENSHIN!
IT'S ALL RIGHT. LITTLE UN-BALANCED, IS ALL.
LET'S HURRY. MEGUMI-DONO IS WAITING.
HUF
HUF
HUF
HUF
NOW MORE THAN EVER, I'D SAY.
YEAH.
HMM?

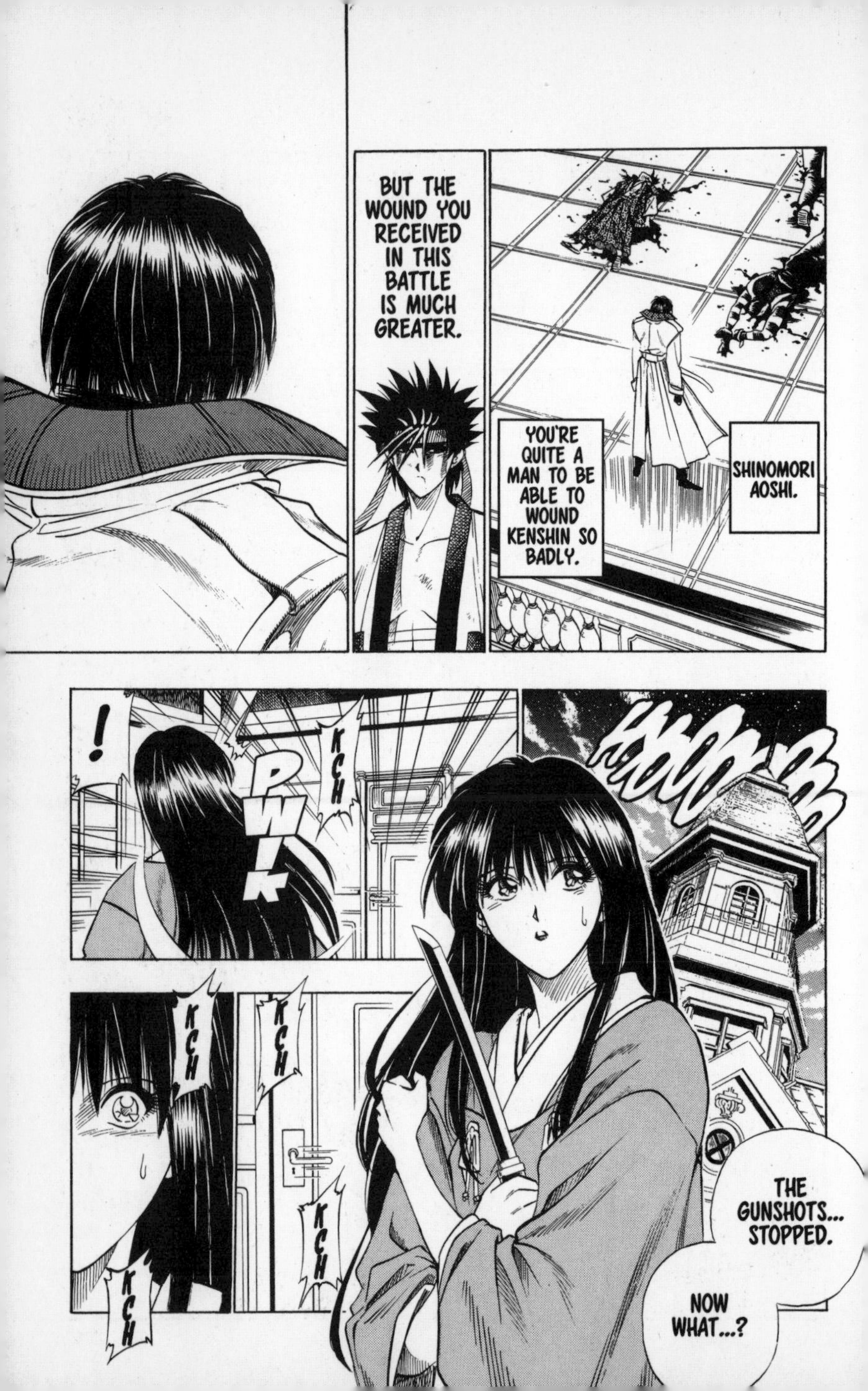
SHINOMORI AOSHI.
YOU'RE QUITE A MAN TO BE ABLE TO WOUND KENSHIN SO BADLY.
BUT THE WOUND YOU RECEIVED IN THIS BATTLE IS MUCH GREATER.
THE GUNSHOTS... STOPPED.
NOW WHAT...?
KCH
PWIK
!
KCH
KCH
KCH
KCH

READ THIS WAY

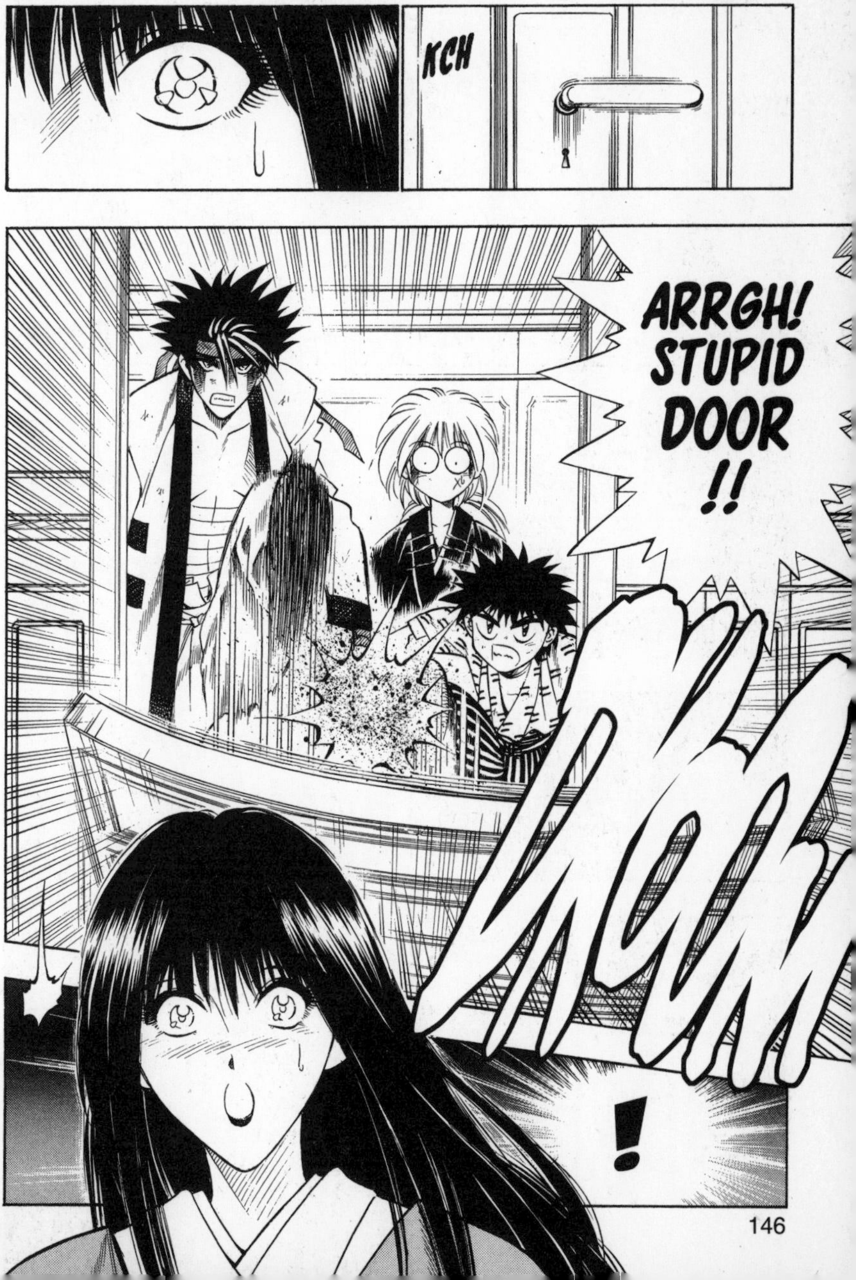
KCH
ARRGH! STUPID DOOR !!
!

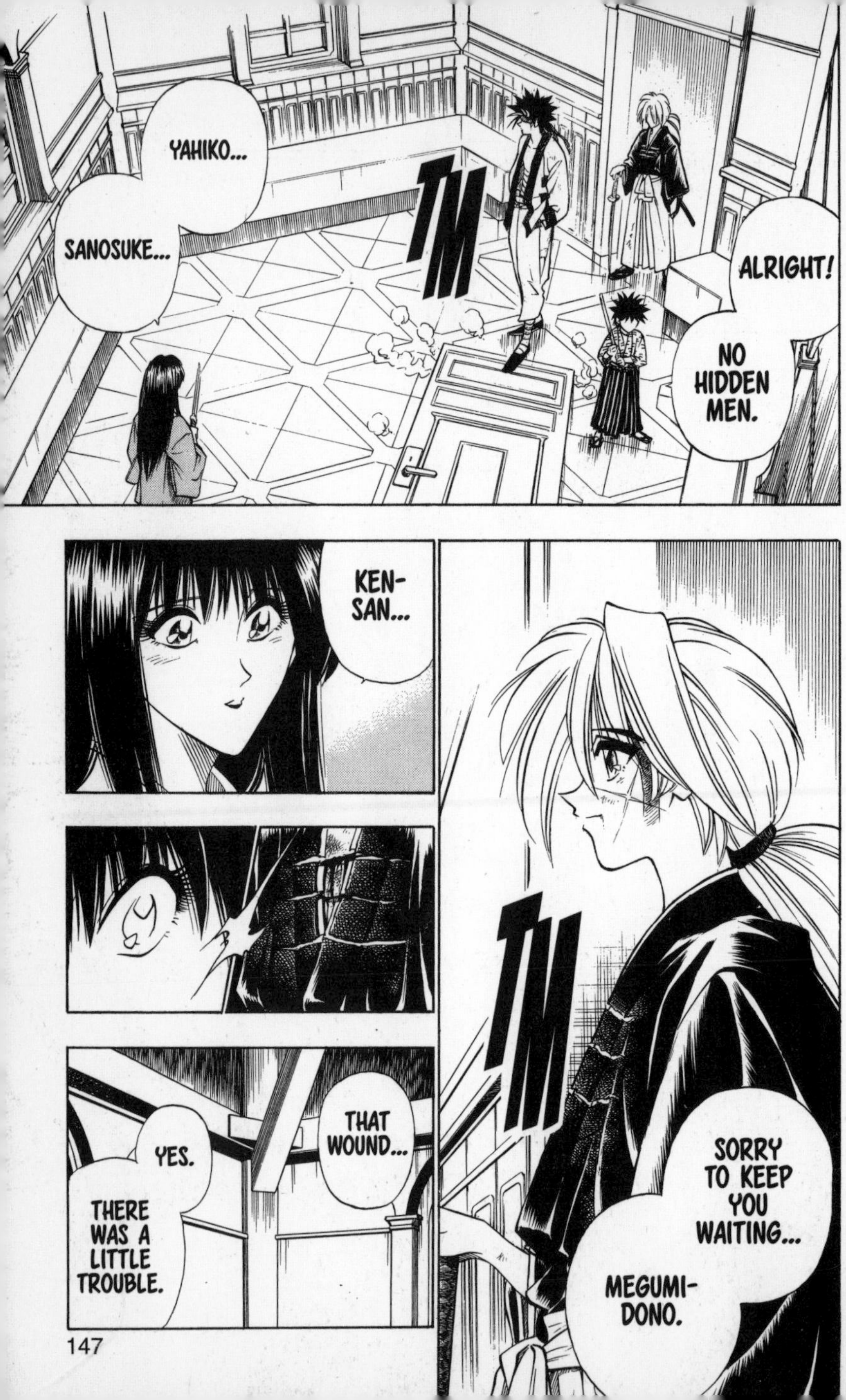
ALRIGHT!
NO HIDDEN MEN.
YAHIKO...
SANOSUKE...
SORRY TO KEEP YOU WAITING...
MEGUMI-DONO.
KEN-SAN...
THAT WOUND...
YES.
THERE WAS A LITTLE TROUBLE.

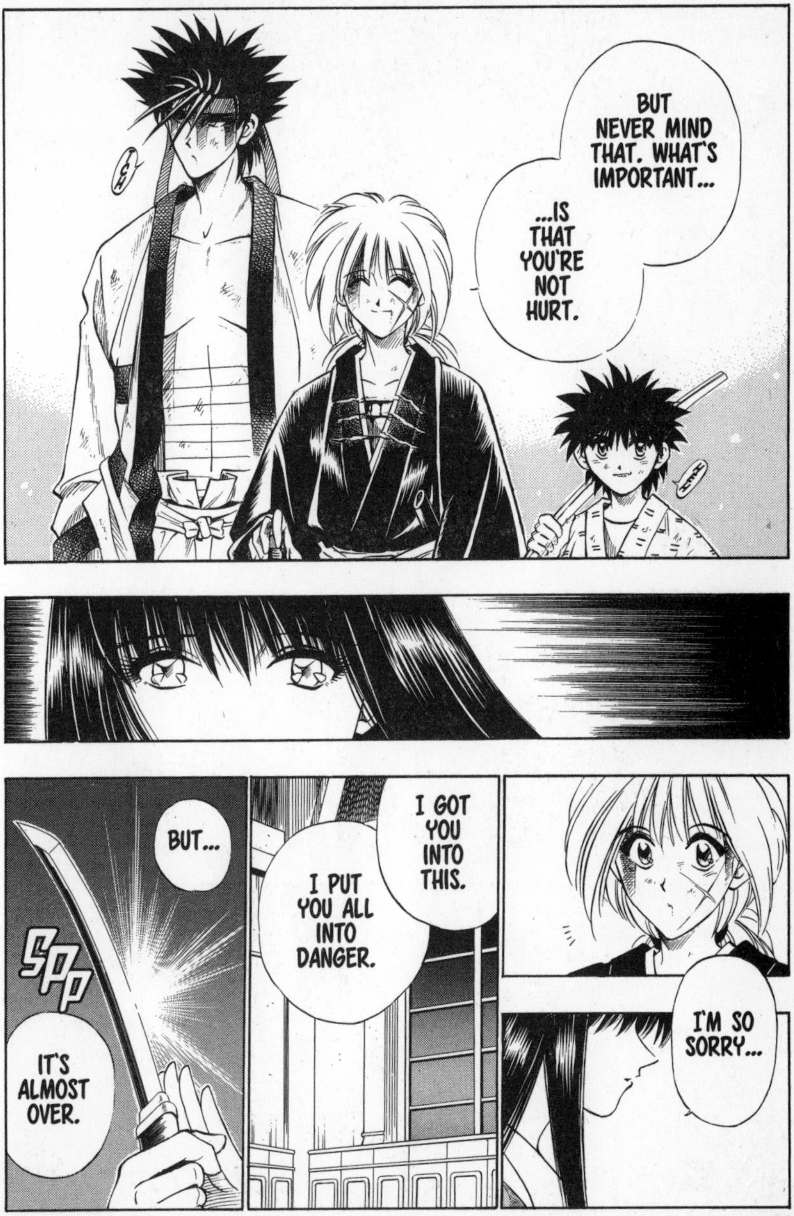
BUT NEVER MIND THAT. WHAT'S IMPORTANT...
...IS THAT YOU'RE NOT HURT.
TCH
HEH
I'M SO SORRY...
I GOT YOU INTO THIS.
I PUT YOU ALL INTO DANGER.
BUT...
SPP
IT'S ALMOST OVER.

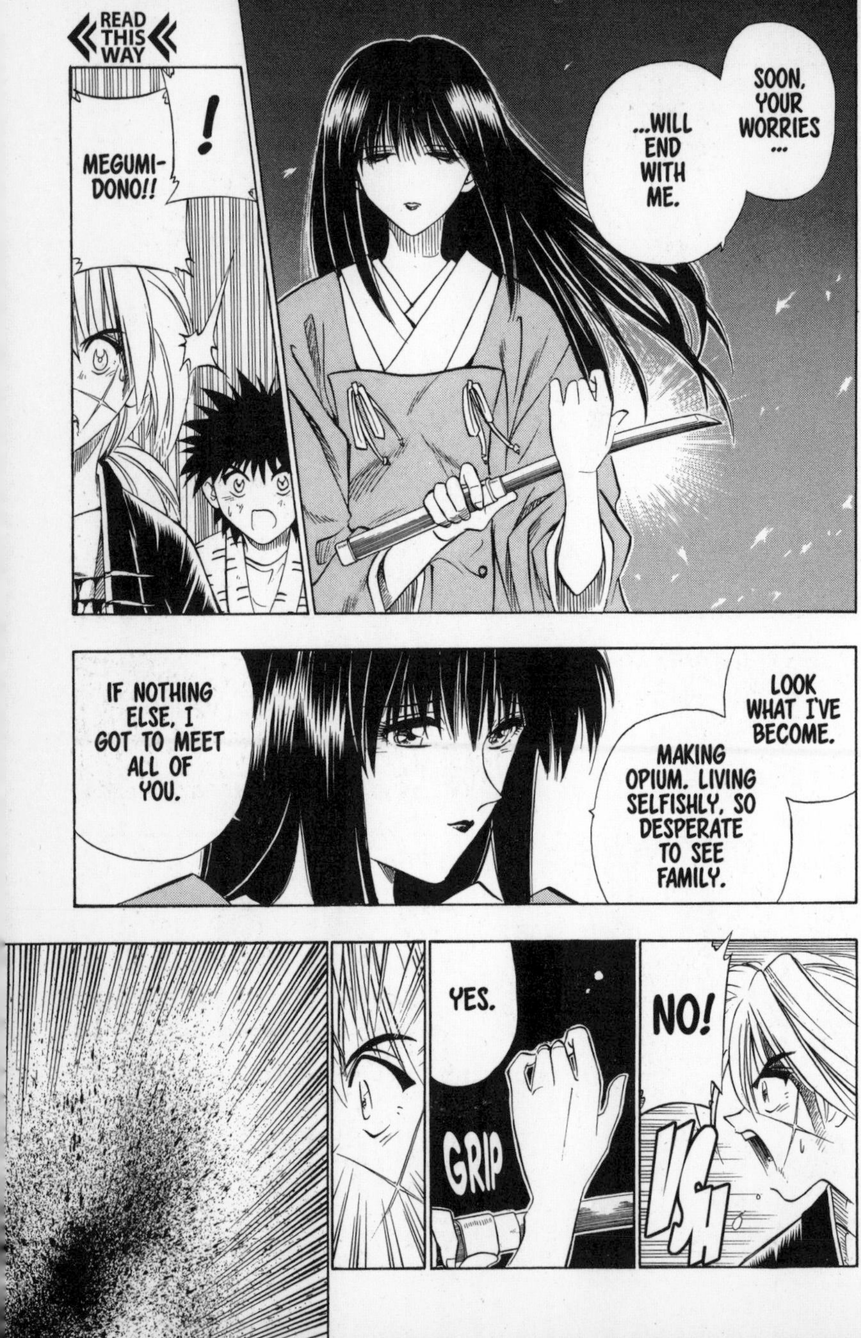
READ THIS WAY
SOON, YOUR WORRIES...
...WILL END WITH ME.
!
MEGUMI-DONO!!
LOOK WHAT I'VE BECOME.
MAKING OPIUM. LIVING SELFISHLY, SO DESPERATE TO SEE FAMILY.
IF NOTHING ELSE, I GOT TO MEET ALL OF YOU.
NO!
VSH
YES.
GRIP

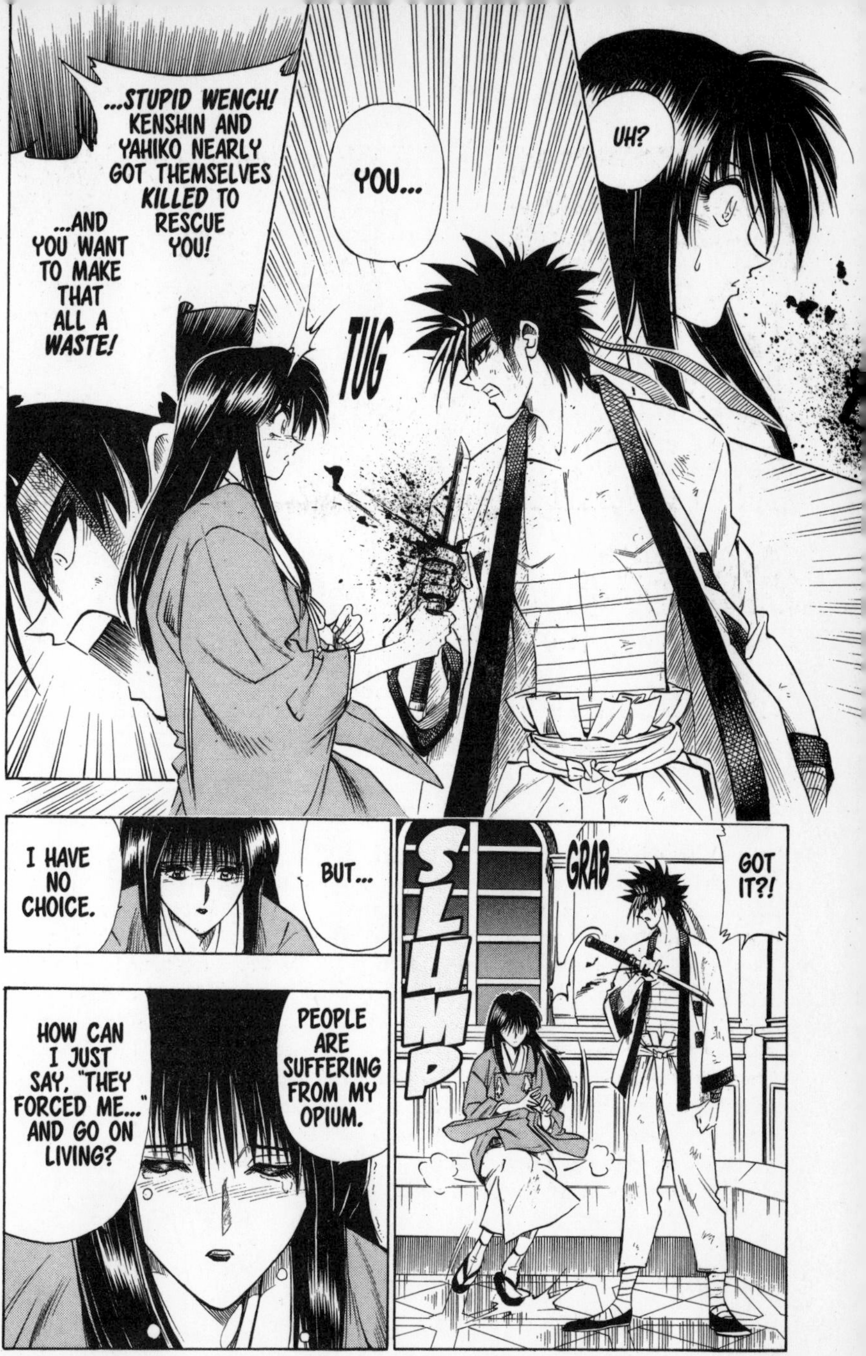
UH?
YOU...
...STUPID WENCH! KENSHIN AND YAHIKO NEARLY GOT THEMSELVES KILLED TO RESCUE YOU!
...AND YOU WANT TO MAKE THAT ALL A WASTE!
TUG
GOT IT?!
GRAB
SLUMP
BUT...
I HAVE NO CHOICE.
PEOPLE ARE SUFFERING FROM MY OPIUM.
HOW CAN I JUST SAY, "THEY FORCED ME..." AND GO ON LIVING?

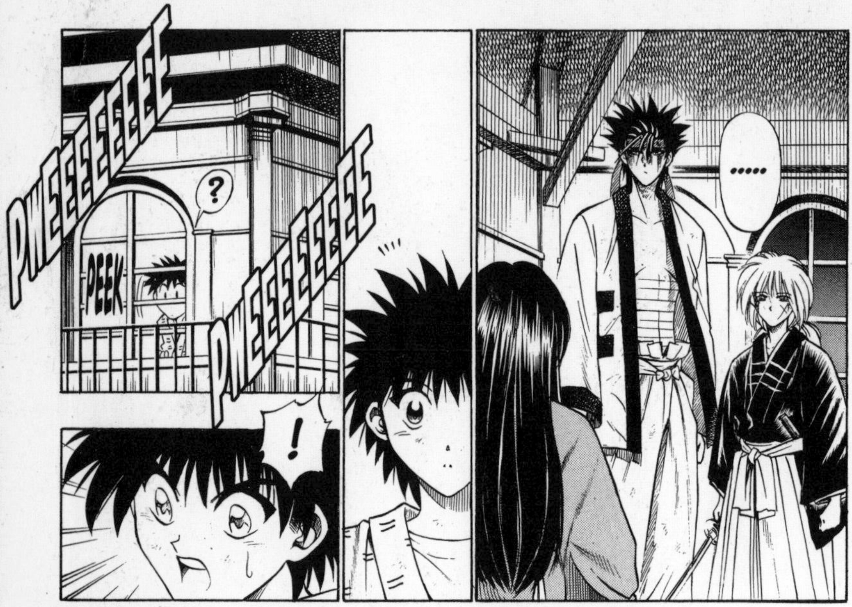

......
PWEEEEEEE
?
PEEK
PWEEEEEEE
!


Here's something I've noticed. I've been getting comments in letters lately along the lines, "I love the Shinsengumi, too! I hate the Ishin Shishi." Or, "I can't believe you like the Shinsengumi. What are you, an anti-shōgunate dog?" People, in other words, who acknowledge only one side of the conflict. This is a shame, if you ask Watsuki. One of the most interesting things about the Bakumatsu is that there were 100 different factions fighting for 100 different causes. They lived according to their own beliefs, not by some "this side not that side" mentality. Watsuki's personal favorite may be the Shinsengumi's Hijikata Toshizō, but his second favorite is (pro-Imperialist) Ōkubo Toshimichi. To those of you who've discovered an interest in the Meiji Restoration because of "RuroKen," keep reading! Keep enjoying! Remember, there wouldn't have been a revolution without the Imperialists and the Shōgunists. See you next volume!

Watsuki

和月伸宏

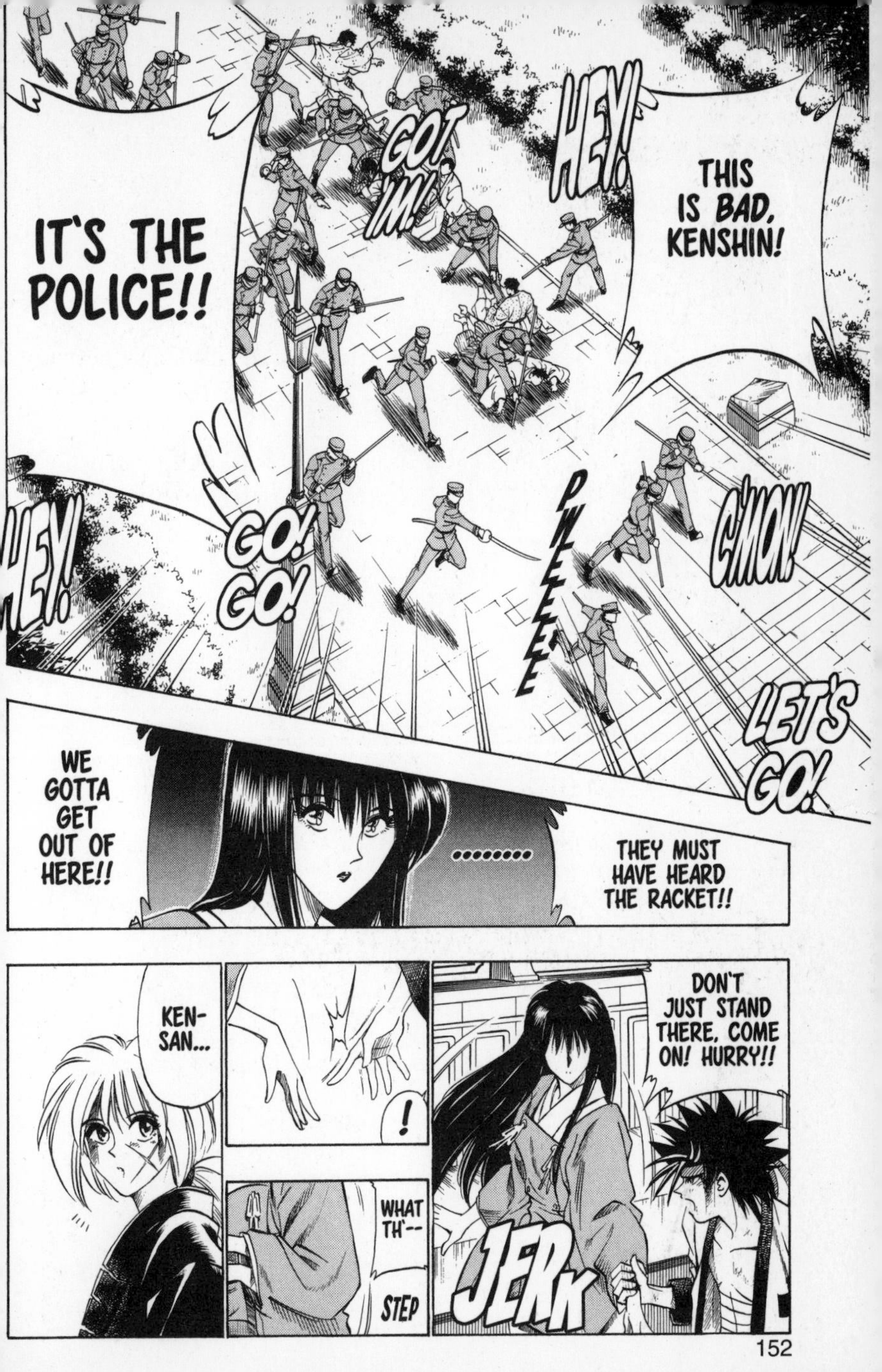
THIS IS BAD, KENSHIN!
HEY!
GOT 'IM!
IT'S THE POLICE!!
C'MON!
PWEEEEEE
GO! GO!
HEY!
LET'S GO!
THEY MUST HAVE HEARD THE RACKET!!
........
WE GOTTA GET OUT OF HERE!!
DON'T JUST STAND THERE, COME ON! HURRY!!
JERK
!
WHAT TH'--
STEP
KEN-SAN...

READ THIS WAY

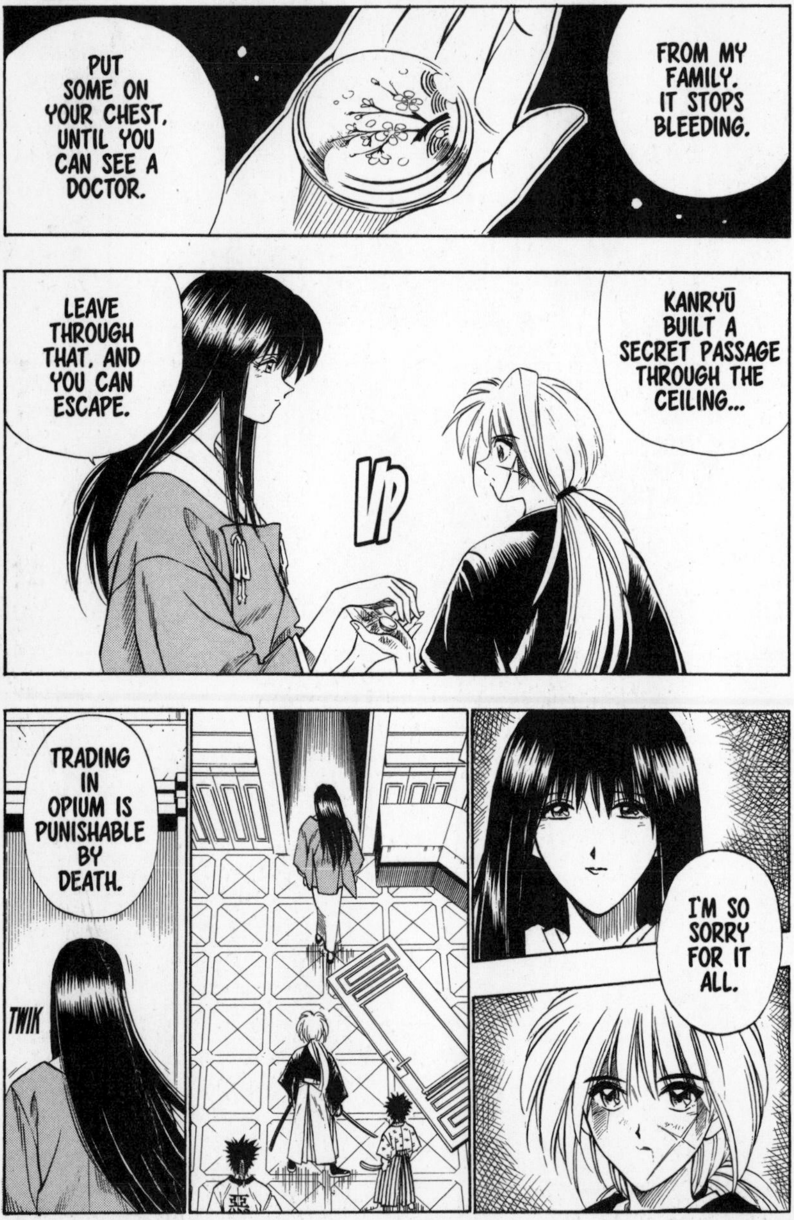
FROM MY FAMILY. IT STOPS BLEEDING.
PUT SOME ON YOUR CHEST, UNTIL YOU CAN SEE A DOCTOR.
KANRYŪ BUILT A SECRET PASSAGE THROUGH THE CEILING...
LEAVE THROUGH THAT, AND YOU CAN ESCAPE.
I'M SO SORRY FOR IT ALL.
TRADING IN OPIUM IS PUNISHABLE BY DEATH.
TWIK

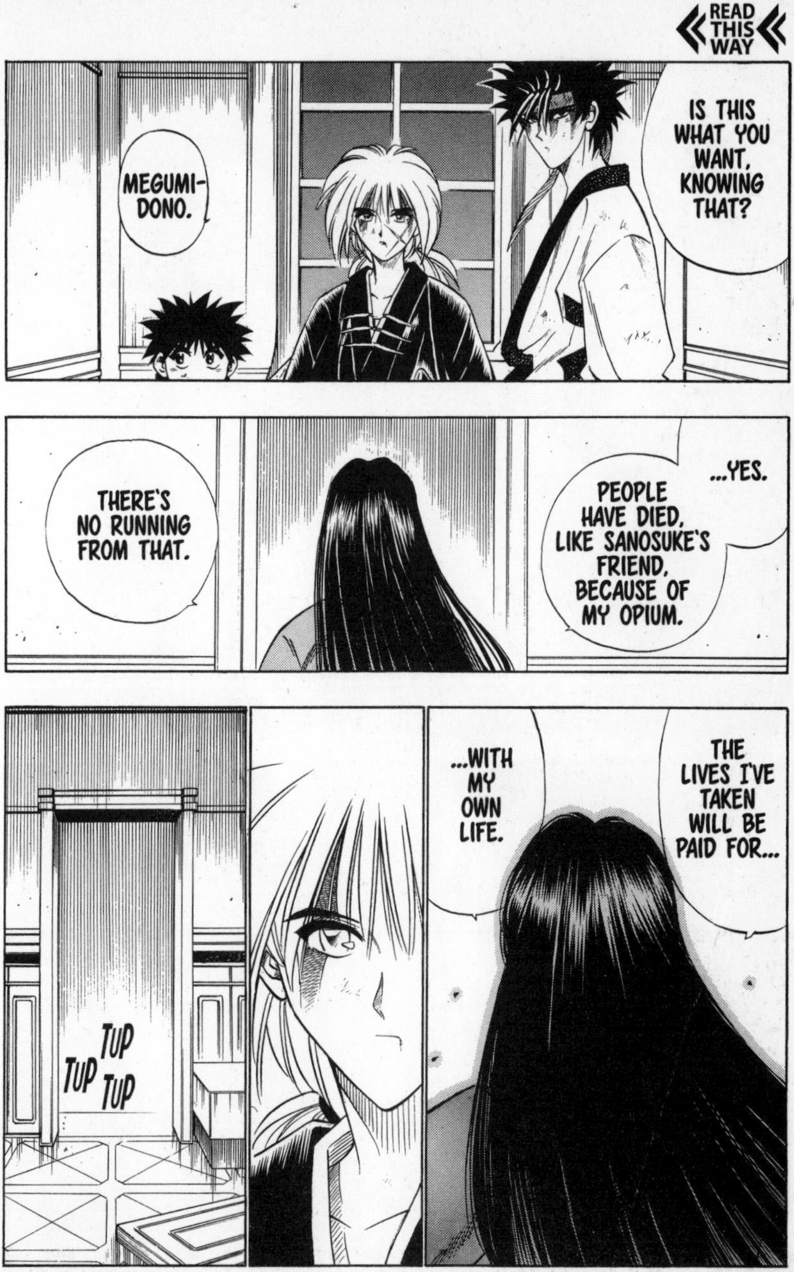
READ THIS WAY
IS THIS WHAT YOU WANT, KNOWING THAT?
MEGUMI-DONO.
...YES.
PEOPLE HAVE DIED, LIKE SANOSUKE'S FRIEND, BECAUSE OF MY OPIUM.
THERE'S NO RUNNING FROM THAT.
THE LIVES I'VE TAKEN WILL BE PAID FOR...
...WITH MY OWN LIFE.
TUP TUP TUP TUP

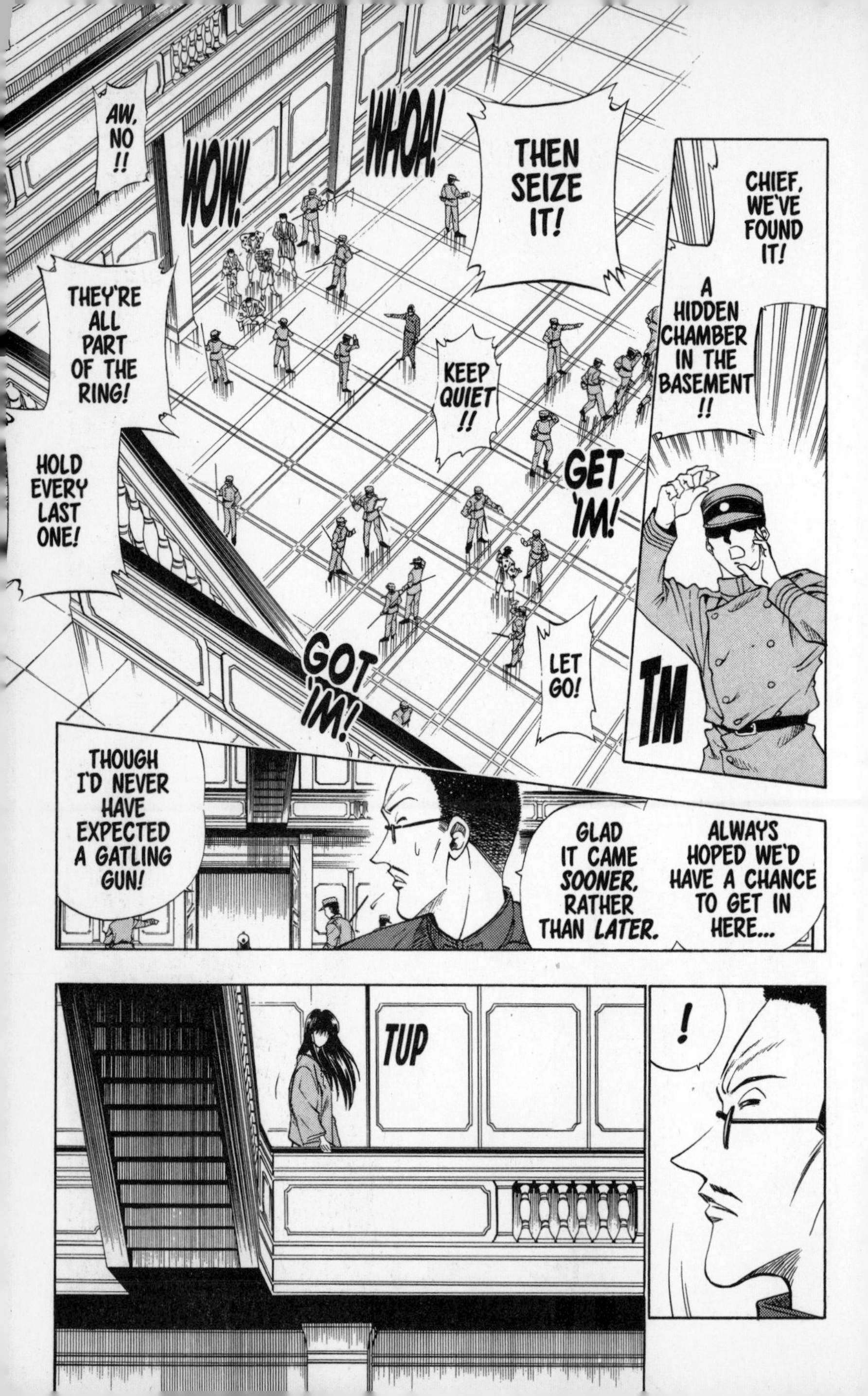
CHIEF, WE'VE FOUND IT!
A HIDDEN CHAMBER IN THE BASEMENT!!
TM
THEN SEIZE IT!
WHOA!
WOW!
AW, NO!!
THEY'RE ALL PART OF THE RING!
KEEP QUIET!!
GET 'IM!
HOLD EVERY LAST ONE!
LET GO!
GOT 'IM!
ALWAYS HOPED WE'D HAVE A CHANCE TO GET IN HERE...
GLAD IT CAME *SOONER*, RATHER THAN *LATER*.
THOUGH I'D NEVER HAVE EXPECTED A GATLING GUN!
!
TUP

READ THIS WAY

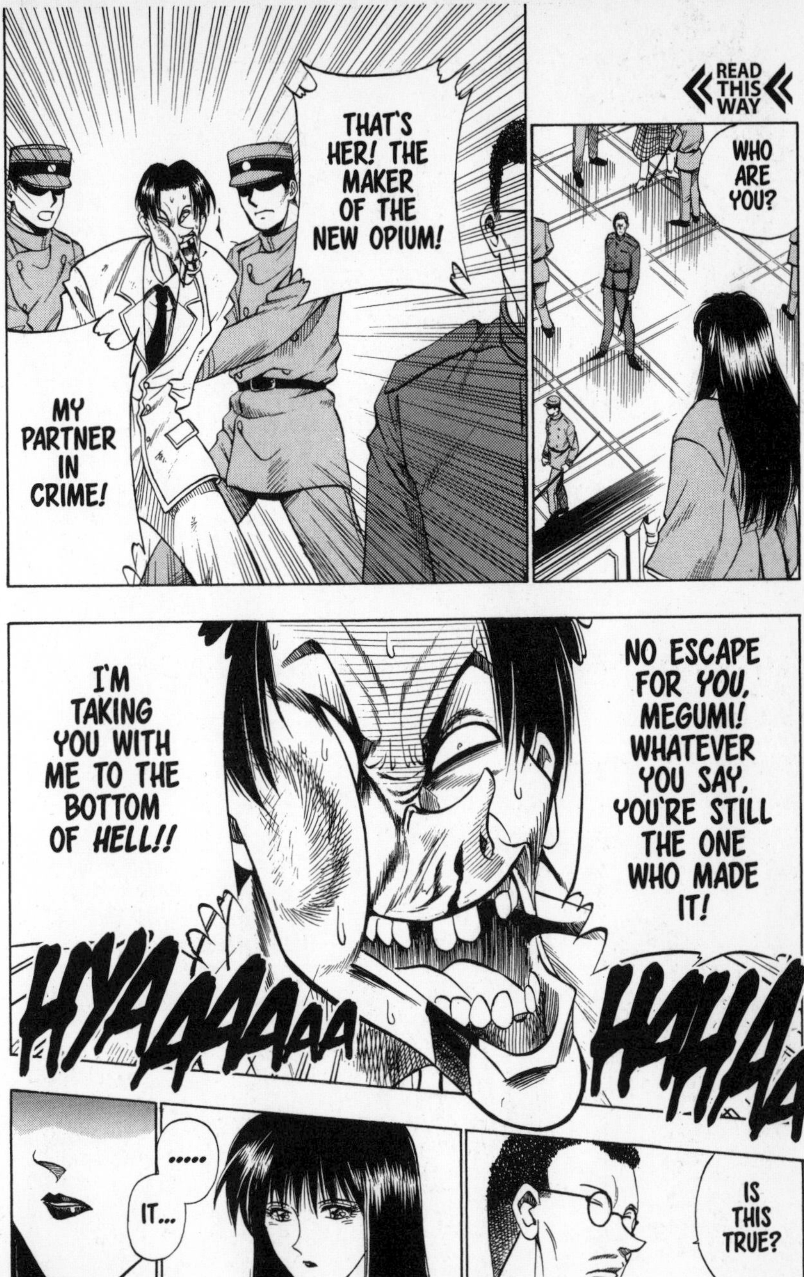

WHO ARE YOU?
THAT'S HER! THE MAKER OF THE NEW OPIUM!
MY PARTNER IN CRIME!
NO ESCAPE FOR YOU, MEGUMI! WHATEVER YOU SAY, YOU'RE STILL THE ONE WHO MADE IT!
I'M TAKING YOU WITH ME TO THE BOTTOM OF HELL!!
HYAAAAAAA HAHAA
IS THIS TRUE?
.....
IT...

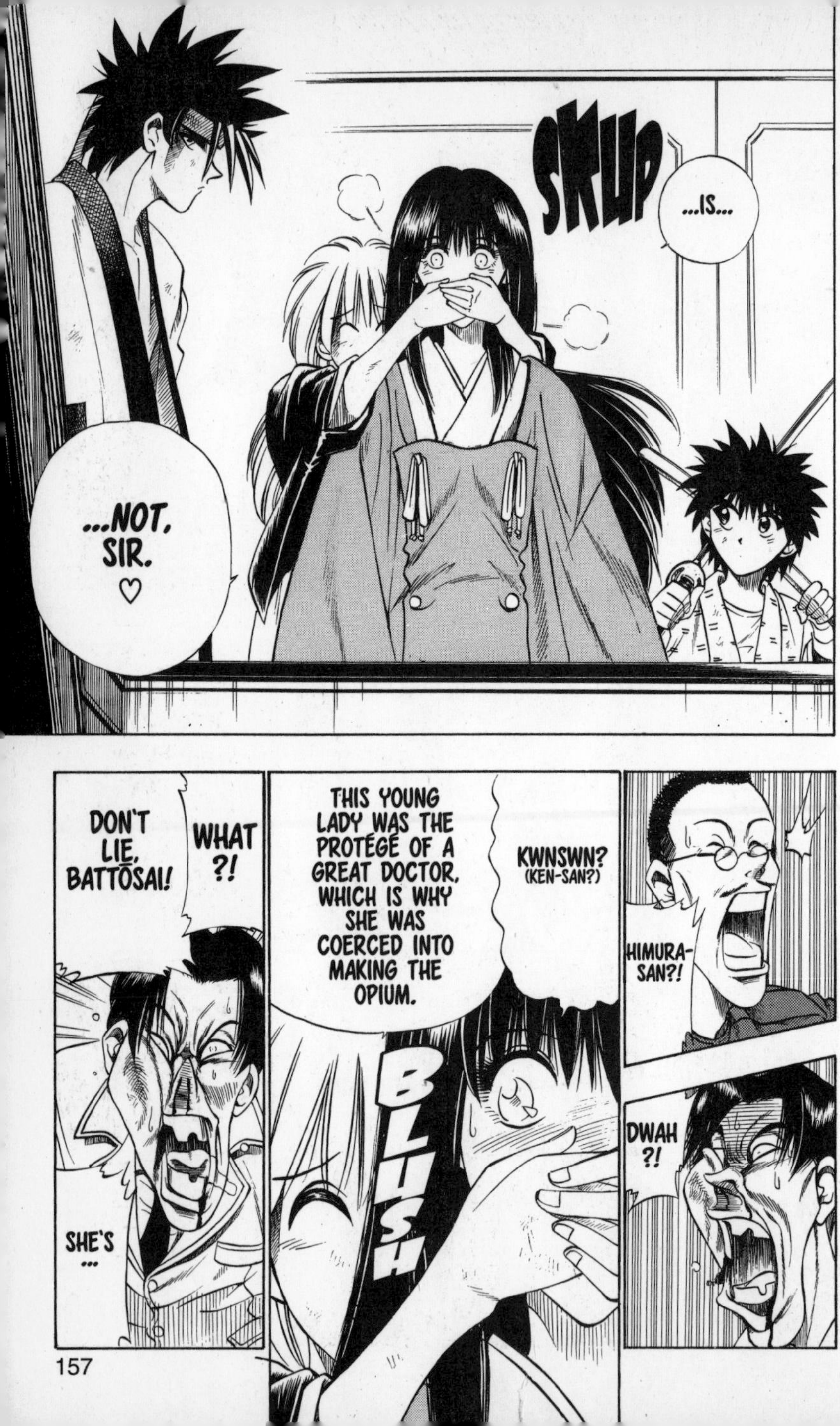
SKUP
...IS...
...NOT, SIR. ♡
HIMURA-SAN?!
DWAH ?!
KWNSWN? (KEN-SAN?)
THIS YOUNG LADY WAS THE PROTÉGÉ OF A GREAT DOCTOR, WHICH IS WHY SHE WAS COERCED INTO MAKING THE OPIUM.
BLUSH
WHAT ?!
DON'T LIE, BATTŌSAI!
SHE'S ...

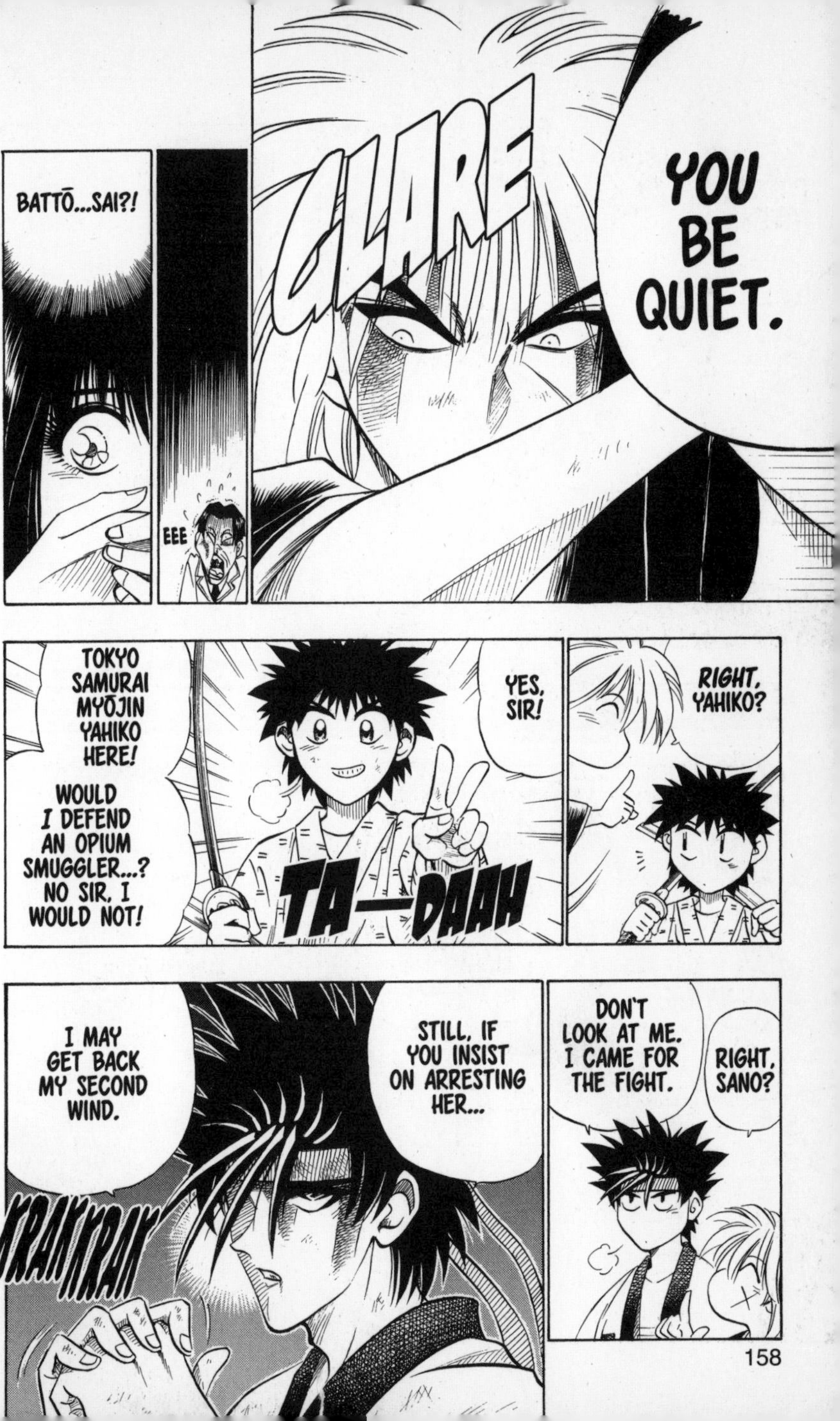
YOU BE QUIET.
GLARE
EEE
BATTŌ...SAI?!
RIGHT, YAHIKO?
YES, SIR!
TOKYO SAMURAI MYŌJIN YAHIKO HERE!
WOULD I DEFEND AN OPIUM SMUGGLER...? NO SIR, I WOULD NOT!
TA-DAAH
RIGHT, SANO?
DON'T LOOK AT ME. I CAME FOR THE FIGHT.
STILL, IF YOU INSIST ON ARRESTING HER...
I MAY GET BACK MY SECOND WIND.
KRAKKRAK

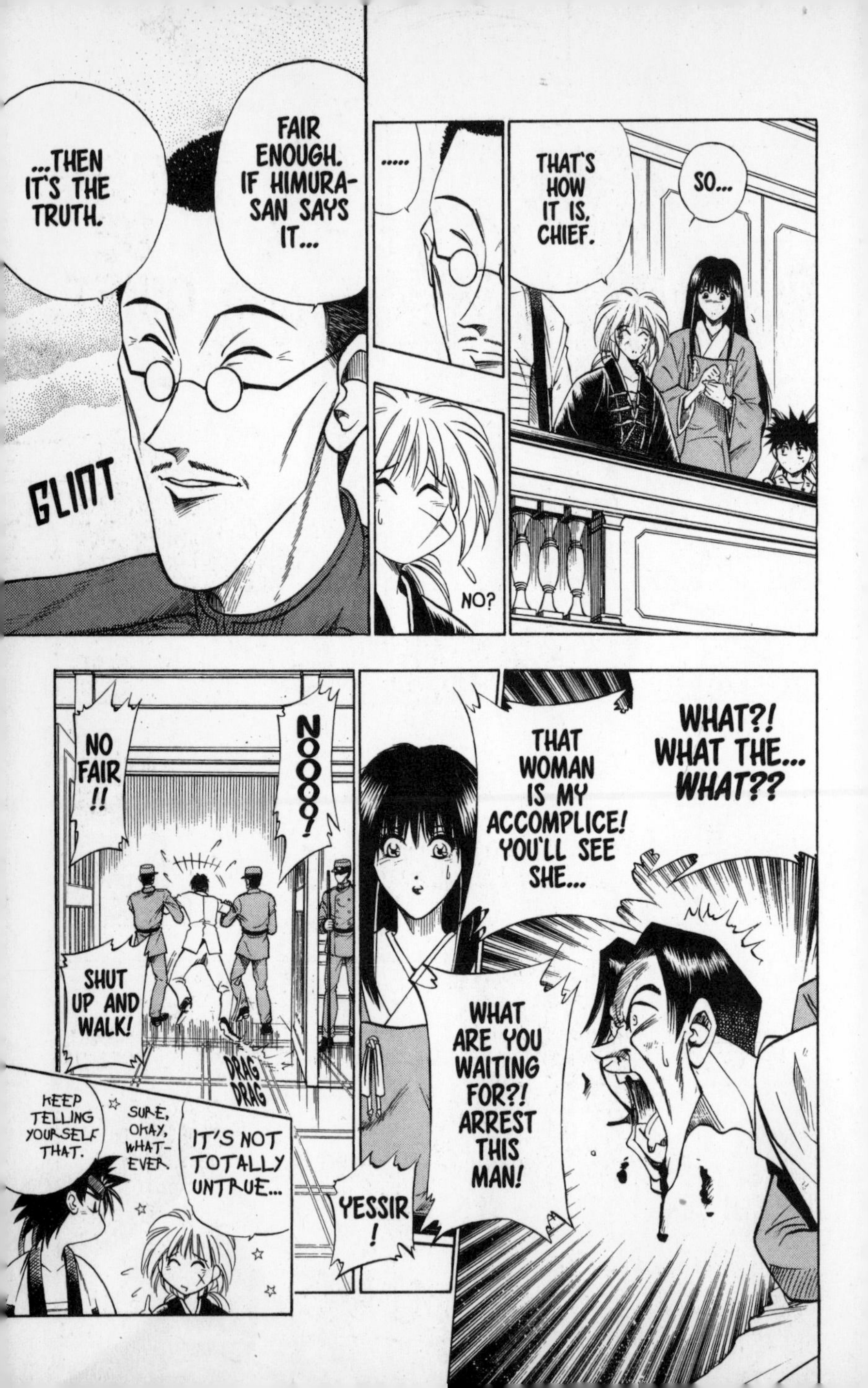
SO...
THAT'S HOW IT IS, CHIEF.
.....
NO?
FAIR ENOUGH. IF HIMURA-SAN SAYS IT...
...THEN IT'S THE TRUTH.
GLINT
WHAT?! WHAT THE... WHAT??
THAT WOMAN IS MY ACCOMPLICE! YOU'LL SEE SHE...
WHAT ARE YOU WAITING FOR?! ARREST THIS MAN!
YESSIR!
NOOOO!
NO FAIR!!
SHUT UP AND WALK!
DRAG DRAG
IT'S NOT TOTALLY UNTRUE...
SURE, OKAY, WHATEVER.
KEEP TELLING YOURSELF THAT.

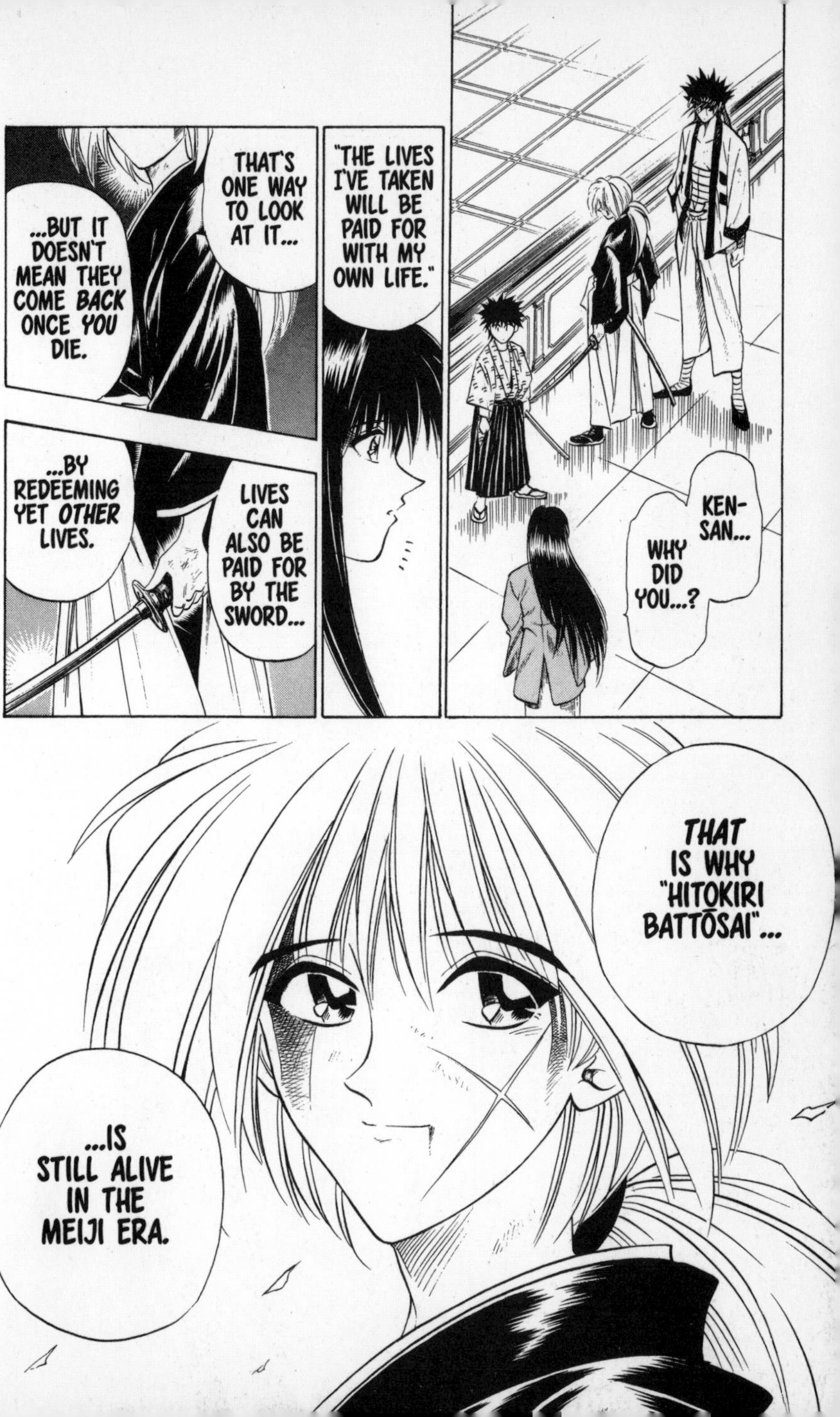
KEN-SAN...
WHY DID YOU...?
"THE LIVES I'VE TAKEN WILL BE PAID FOR WITH MY OWN LIFE."
THAT'S ONE WAY TO LOOK AT IT...
...BUT IT DOESN'T MEAN THEY COME BACK ONCE YOU DIE.
LIVES CAN ALSO BE PAID FOR BY THE SWORD...
...BY REDEEMING YET OTHER LIVES.
THAT IS WHY "HITOKIRI BATTŌSAI"...
...IS STILL ALIVE IN THE MEIJI ERA.

READ THIS WAY

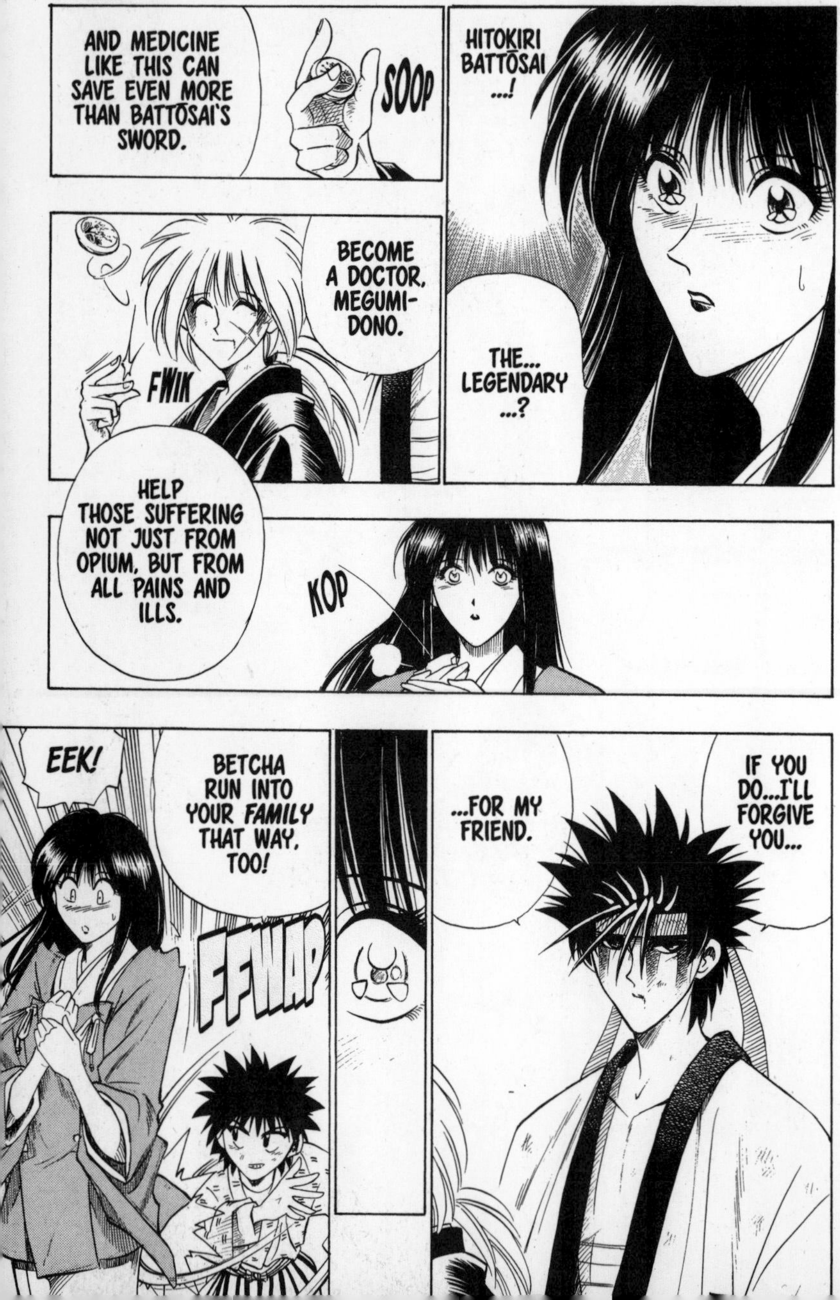

HITOKIRI BATTŌSAI ...!
THE... LEGENDARY ...?
AND MEDICINE LIKE THIS CAN SAVE EVEN MORE THAN BATTŌSAI'S SWORD.
SOOP
BECOME A DOCTOR, MEGUMI-DONO.
FWIK
HELP THOSE SUFFERING NOT JUST FROM OPIUM, BUT FROM ALL PAINS AND ILLS.
KOP
IF YOU DO...I'LL FORGIVE YOU...
...FOR MY FRIEND.
BETCHA RUN INTO YOUR *FAMILY* THAT WAY, TOO!
FFWAP
EEK!

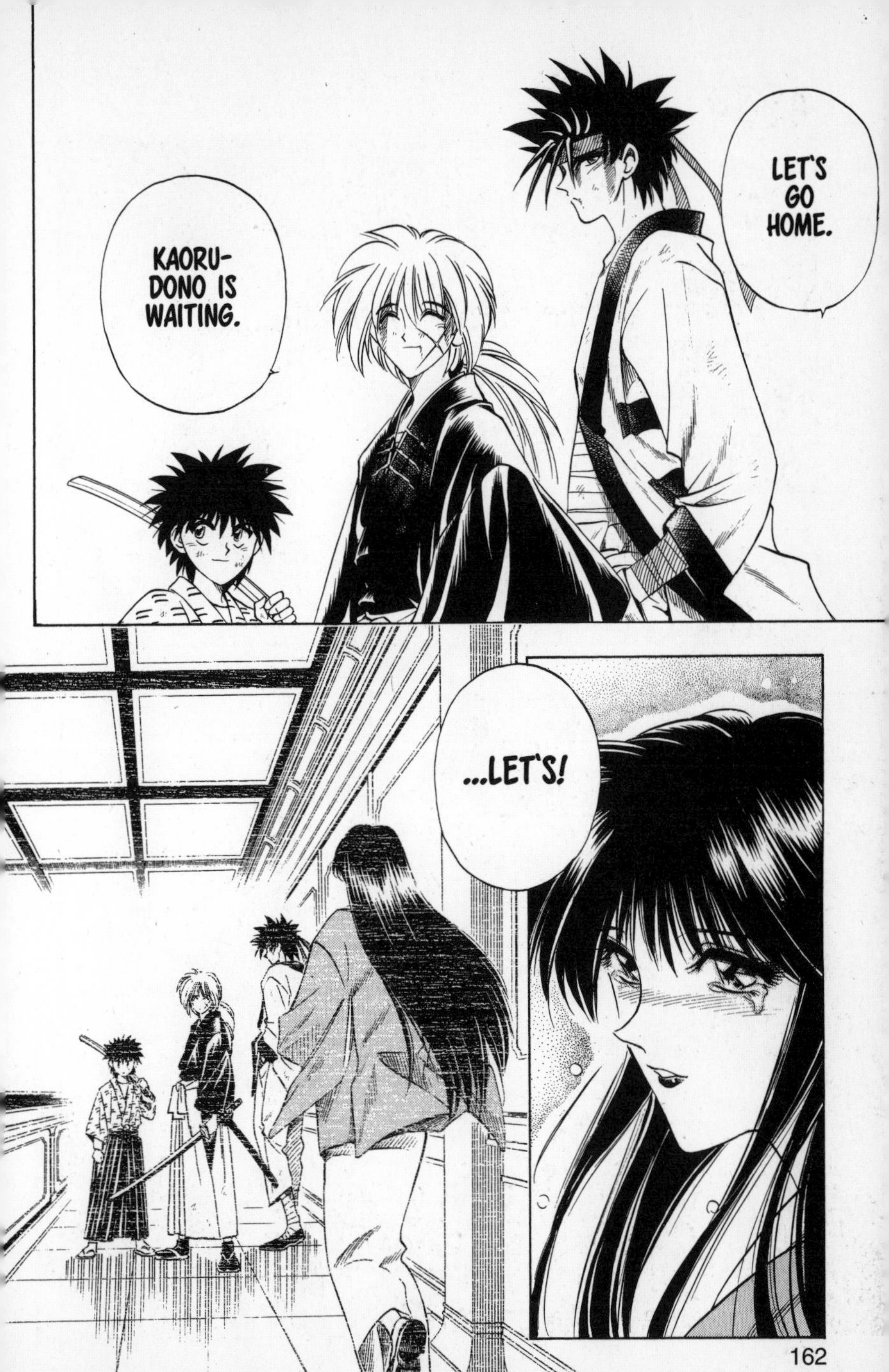
LET'S GO HOME.
KAORU-DONO IS WAITING.
...LET'S!

READ THIS WAY

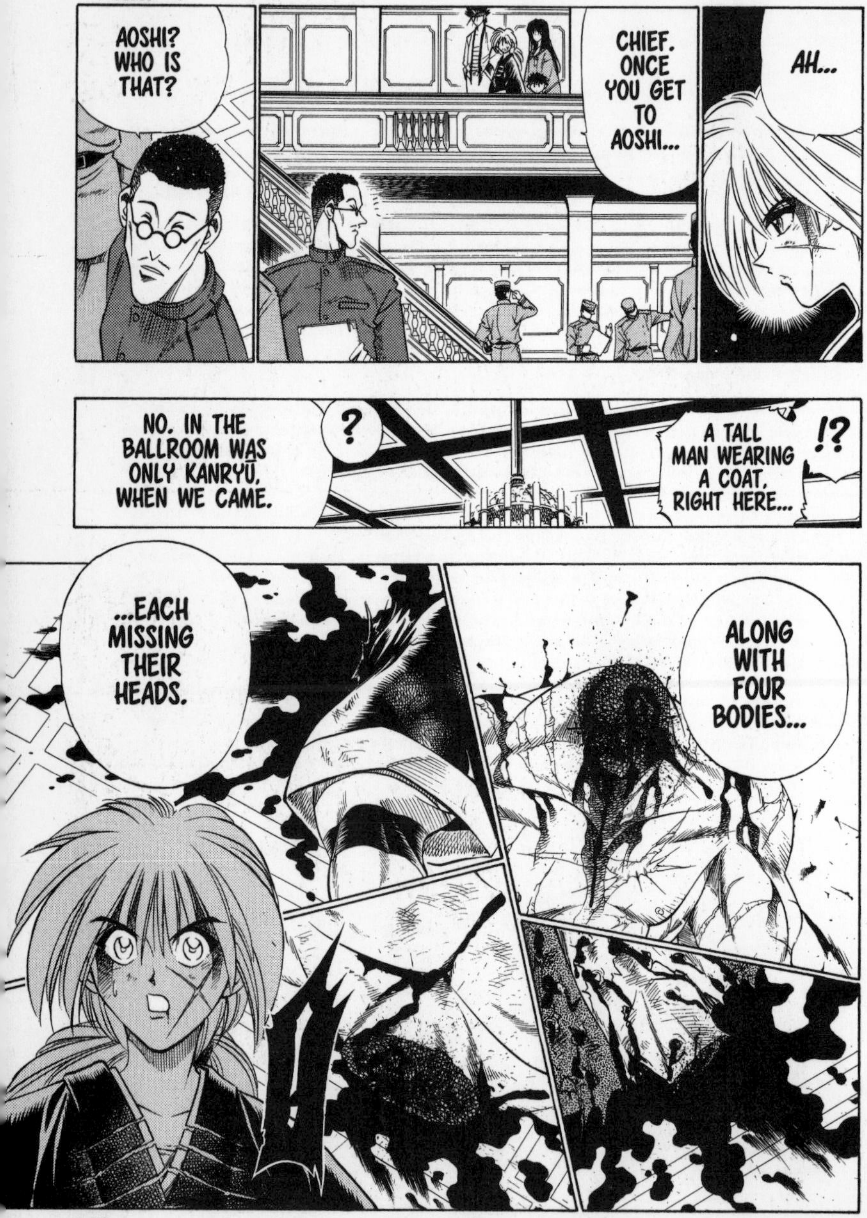
AH...
CHIEF. ONCE YOU GET TO AOSHI...
AOSHI? WHO IS THAT?
!?
A TALL MAN WEARING A COAT, RIGHT HERE...
?
NO. IN THE BALLROOM WAS ONLY KANRYŪ, WHEN WE CAME.
ALONG WITH FOUR BODIES...
...EACH MISSING THEIR HEADS.

## The Secret Life of Characters (13)

# —Takani Megumi—

**There's no real model, but when creating her I imagined a mature woman. Some of you were no doubt surprised to see how different she turned out here as compared to the stand-alone episodes (Volume 3) but, for me, they both spring from the same spirit and therefore aren't really that unalike.**

**The stand-alone Megumi did have a lighter quality to begin with, but that was because she didn't have as much to do. Once I realized that she would also appear in this series, I knew she had to make more of an impression and I therefore gave her a more earthy quality. It was my first time with this kind of character, though, and so there was a lot to learn. Looking back now, she isn't nearly what I'd wanted, and that's a bit disappointing. Still, the heart of the drama flows from her deepest inner spirit, and so I suppose that's to be expected.**

**Megumi was entertaining to draw—and is the one character who can talk "female-to-female" with Kaoru—so I plan to have her appear frequently as a secondary character. She also has the convenience of being a doctor. According to reader mail, two main opinions prevail: (1) "Megumi and Aoshi are suited for each other," and (2) "Megumi and Sano are suited for each other." Watsuki wonders if, in the case of the former, the "suited" part is meant intellectually, while the latter "suited" may be meant temperamentally. Just as with Kenshin and Kaoru, though, at this point I have no such plans for her future. The Megumi arc has "redemption for her crimes" as its theme, and I wanted to express through Megumi Kenshin's determination. (This second part, though, was really tough to pull off.) To write about Kenshin's redemption for his own crimes...thinking of that, I get a headache.**

**The model in terms of design is the young grandma appearing in Obata-*sensei's* "*Cyborg Ji'i-chan 'G'* (Cyborg Grandpa 'G')." That manga's given me ideas for a long time but, obviously, I can't draw as well as the *sensei,* and now his character has turned into my own rather lame Megumi. Sigh....**

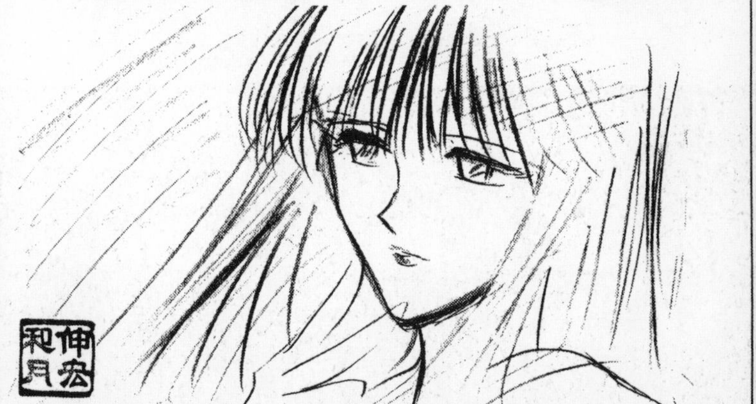
伸宏
和月

READ THIS WAY

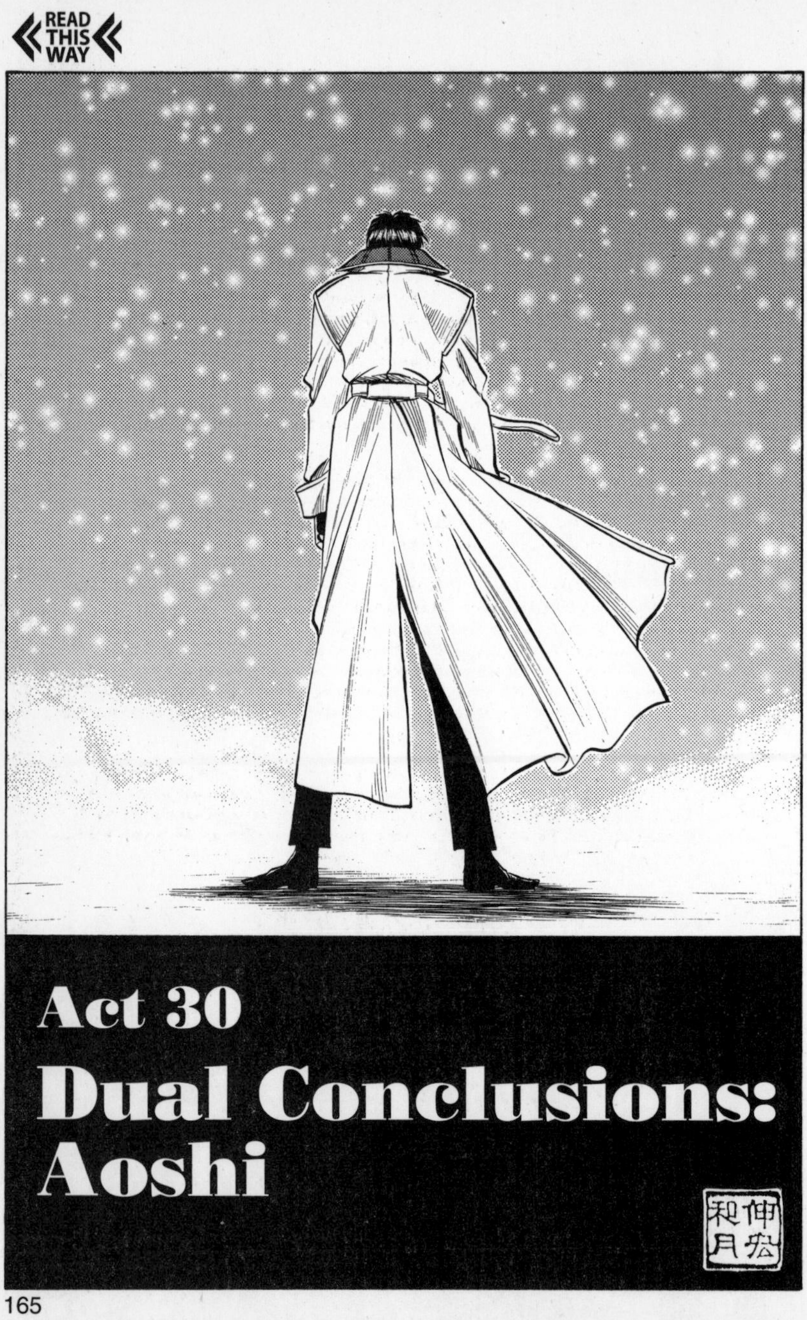

# Act 30
# Dual Conclusions: Aoshi

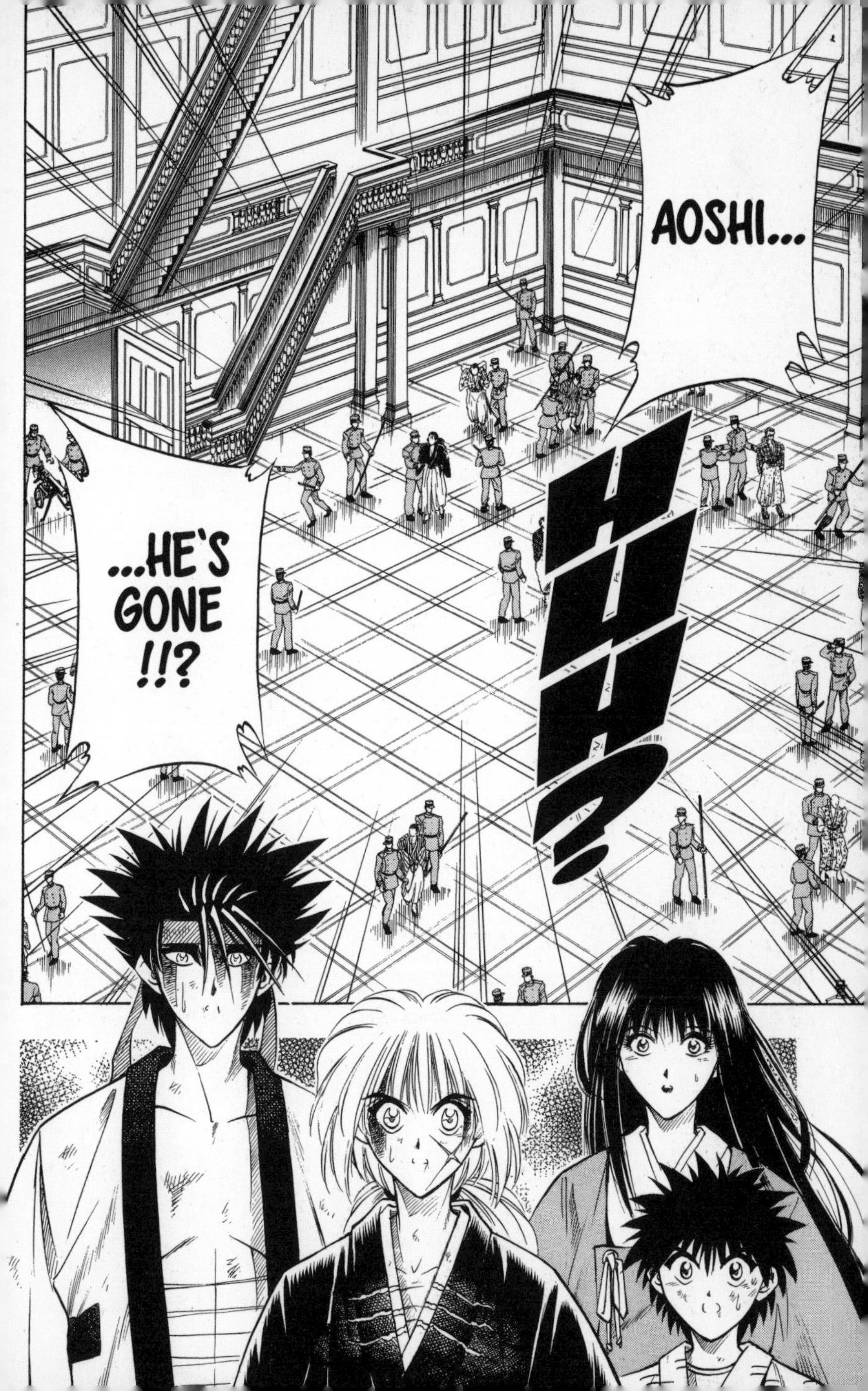
AOSHI...
HHH?
...HE'S GONE !!?

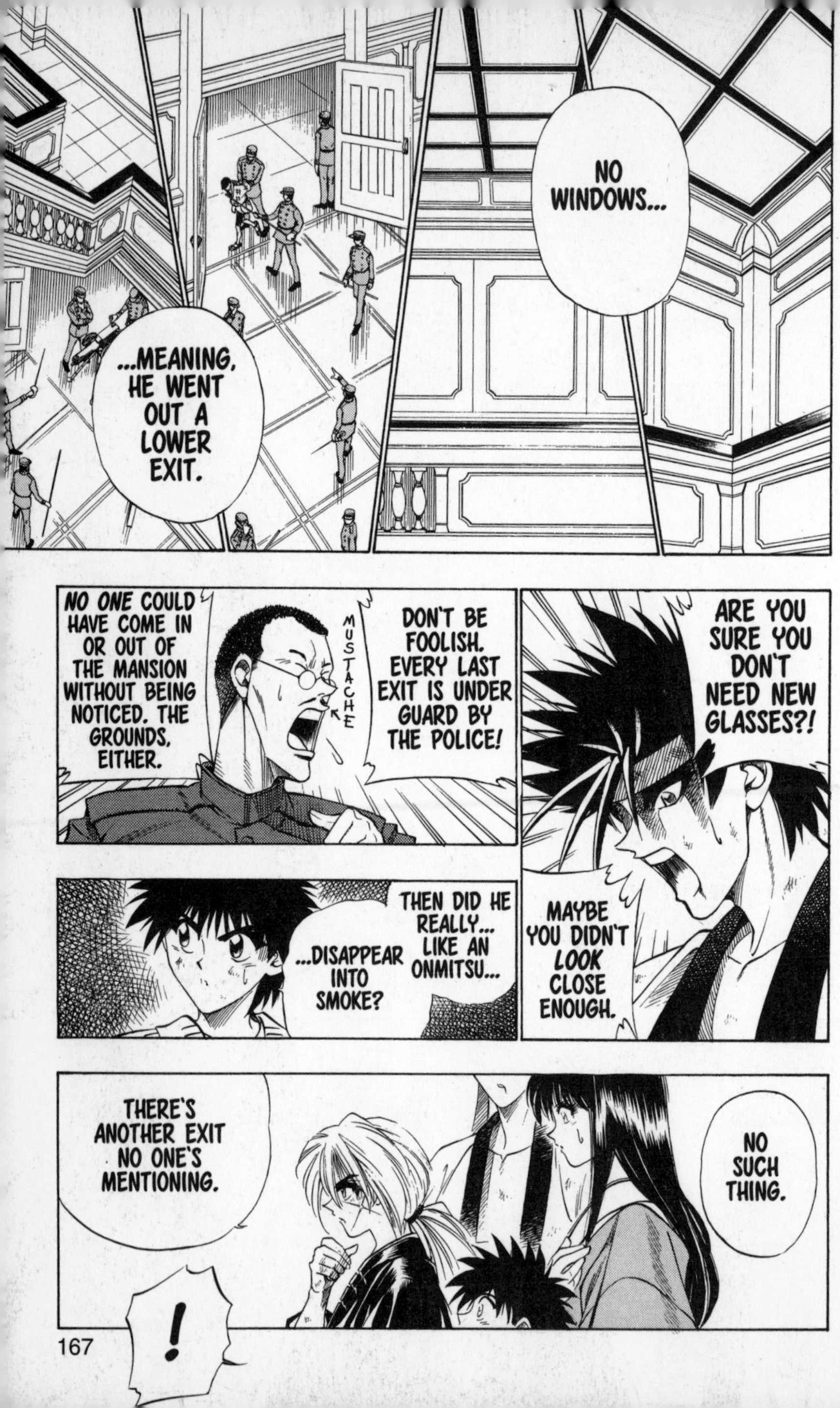
NO WINDOWS...
...MEANING, HE WENT OUT A LOWER EXIT.
ARE YOU SURE YOU DON'T NEED NEW GLASSES?!
MAYBE YOU DIDN'T *LOOK* CLOSE ENOUGH.
DON'T BE FOOLISH. EVERY LAST EXIT IS UNDER GUARD BY THE POLICE!
MUSTACHE
*NO ONE* COULD HAVE COME IN OR OUT OF THE MANSION WITHOUT BEING NOTICED. THE GROUNDS, EITHER.
THEN DID HE REALLY... LIKE AN ONMITSU...
...DISAPPEAR INTO SMOKE?
NO SUCH THING.
THERE'S ANOTHER EXIT NO ONE'S MENTIONING.
!

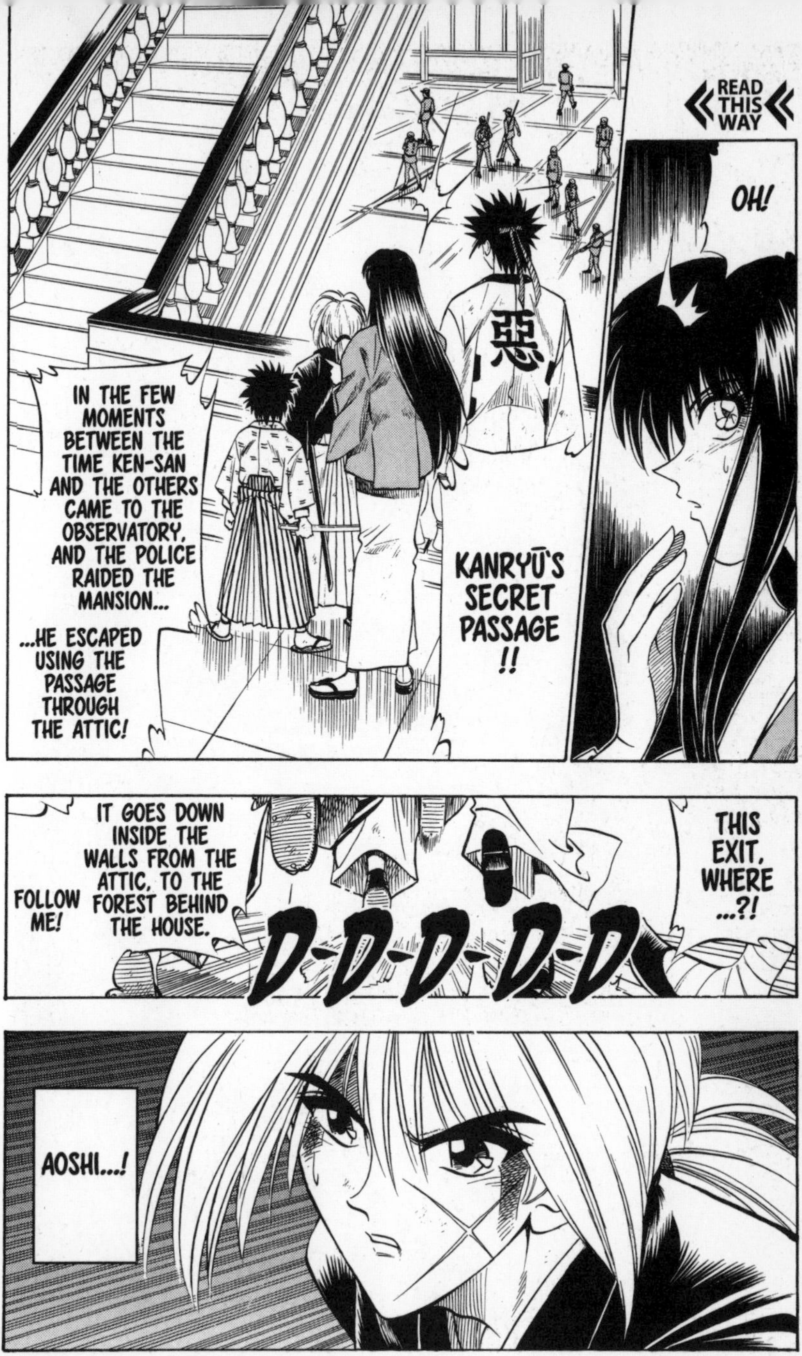
READ THIS WAY
OH!
KANRYŪ'S SECRET PASSAGE !!
IN THE FEW MOMENTS BETWEEN THE TIME KEN-SAN AND THE OTHERS CAME TO THE OBSERVATORY, AND THE POLICE RAIDED THE MANSION...
...HE ESCAPED USING THE PASSAGE THROUGH THE ATTIC!
THIS EXIT, WHERE ...?!
D-D-D-D-D
IT GOES DOWN INSIDE THE WALLS FROM THE ATTIC, TO THE FOREST BEHIND THE HOUSE.
FOLLOW ME!
AOSHI...!

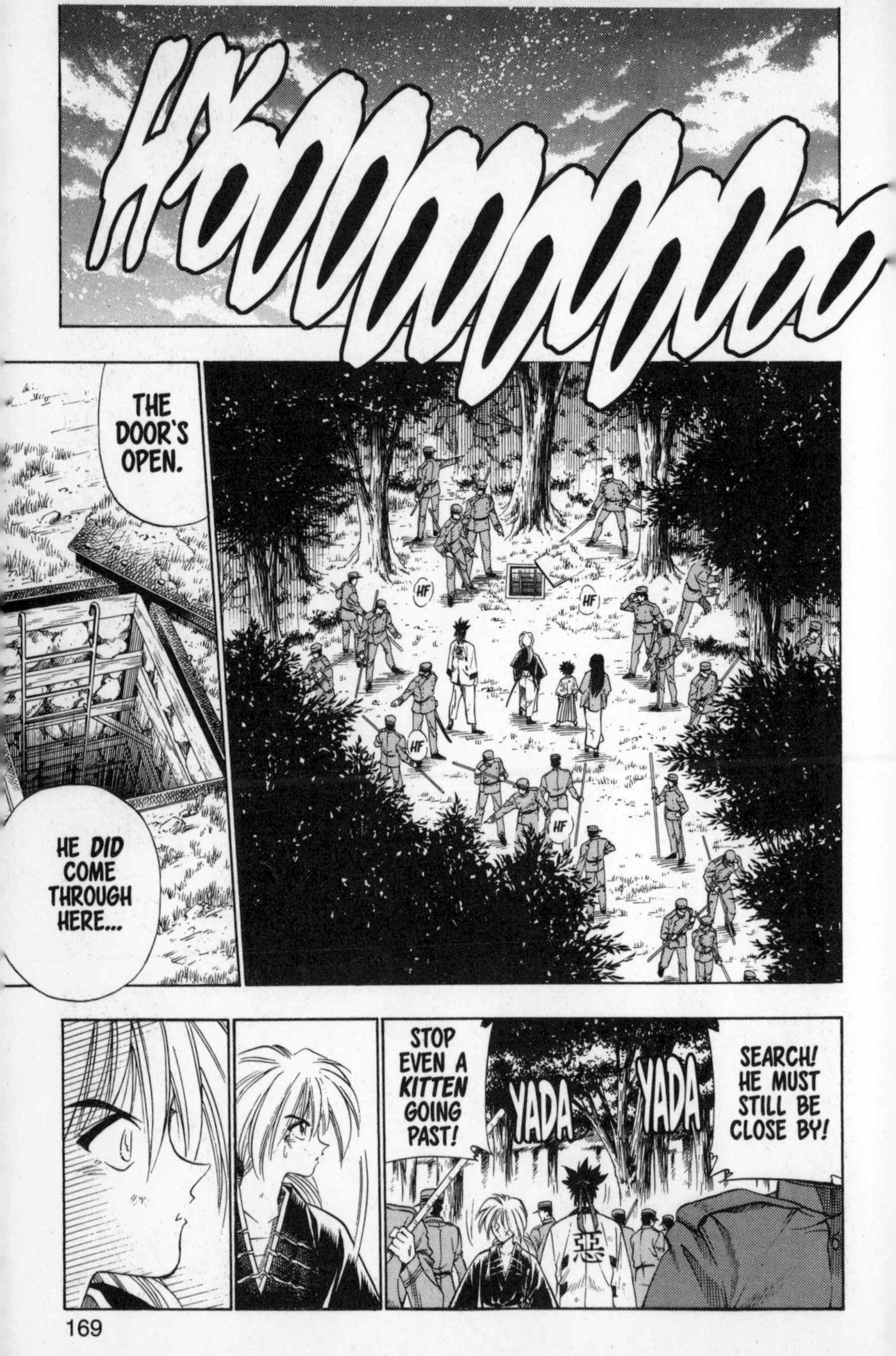
HF
HF
HF
HF
THE DOOR'S OPEN.
HE *DID* COME THROUGH HERE...
SEARCH! HE MUST STILL BE CLOSE BY!
YADA
YADA
STOP EVEN A *KITTEN* GOING PAST!
悪

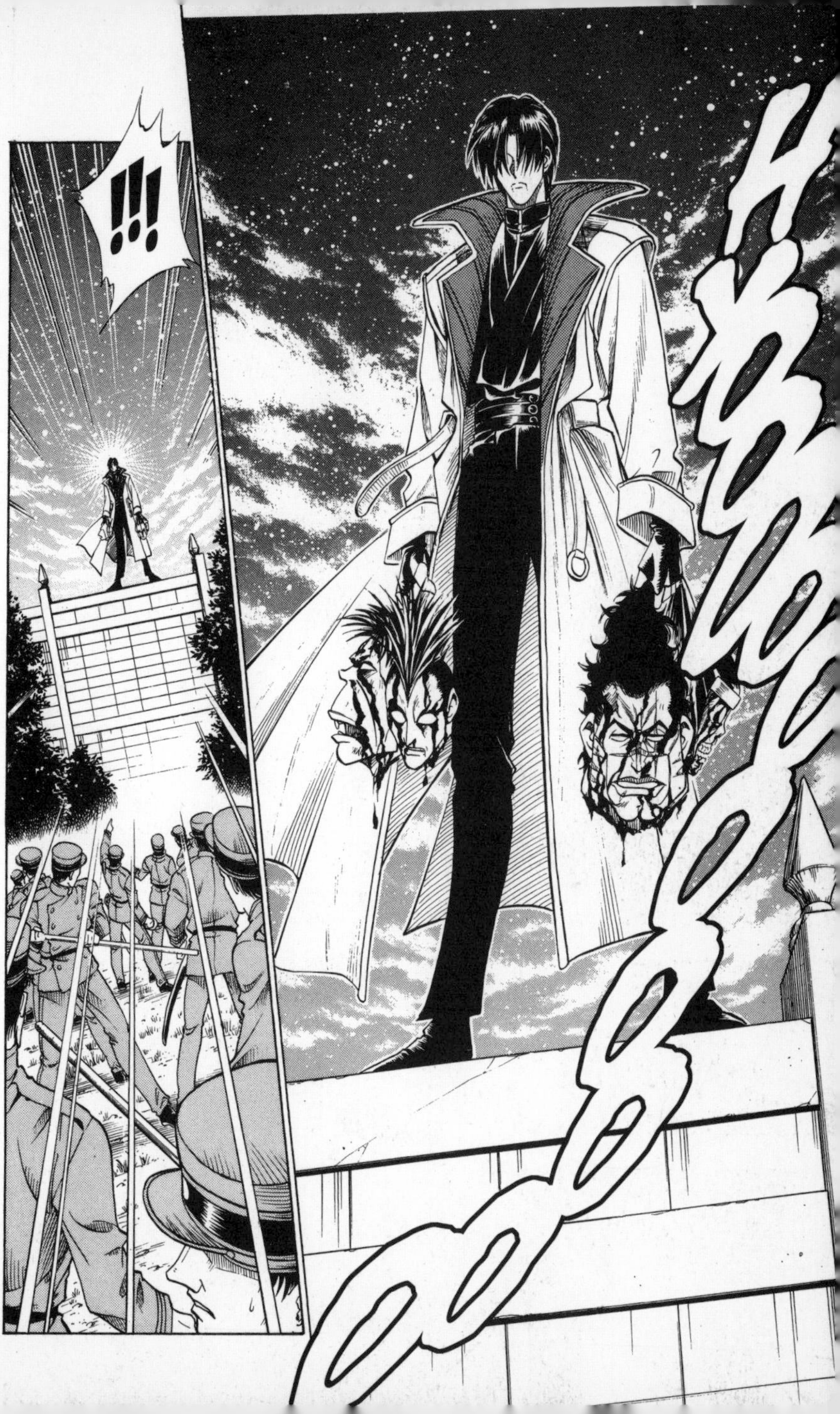
!!!

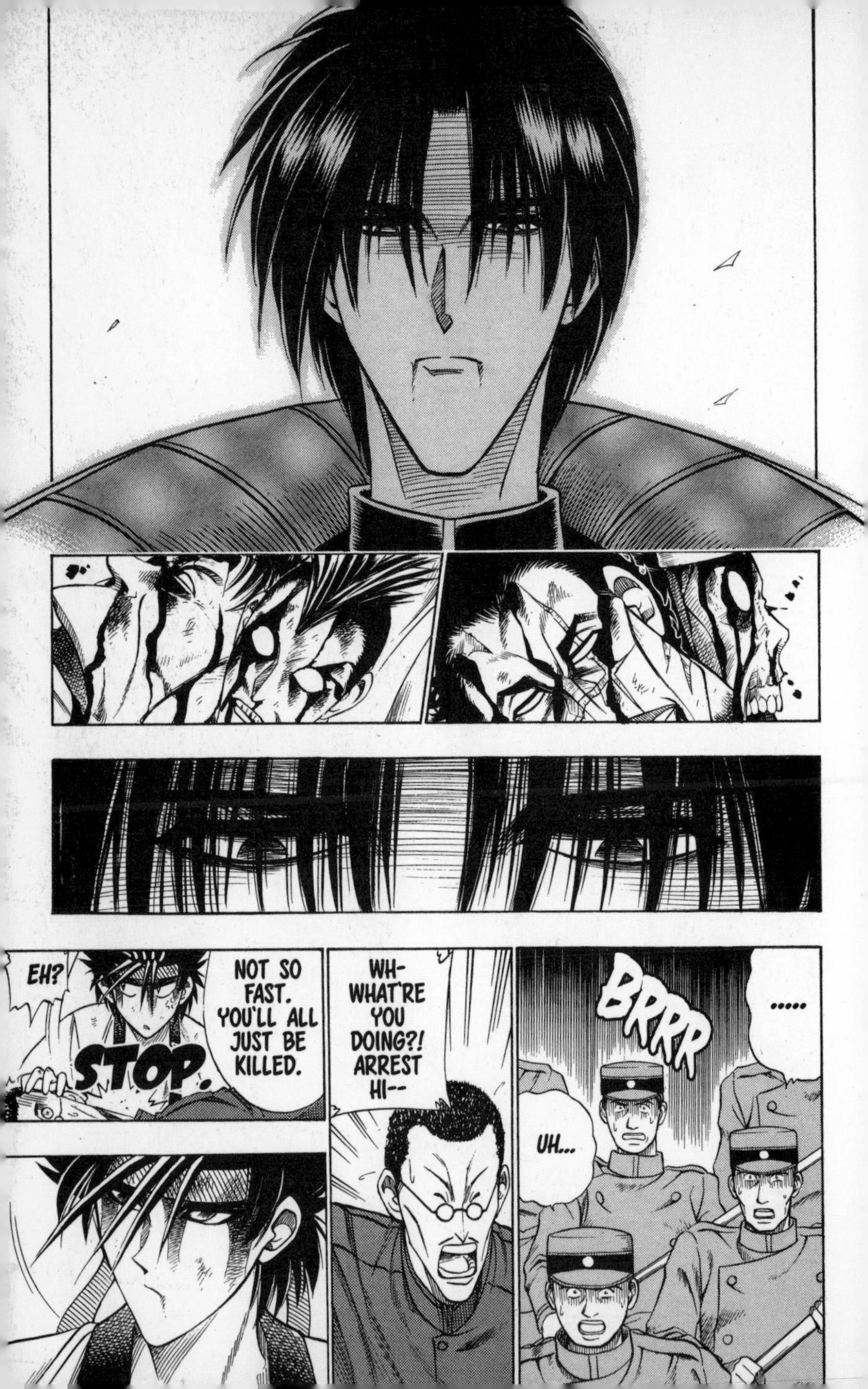

.....
BRRR
UH...
WH-WHAT'RE YOU DOING?! ARREST HI--
NOT SO FAST. YOU'LL ALL JUST BE KILLED.
EH?
STOP

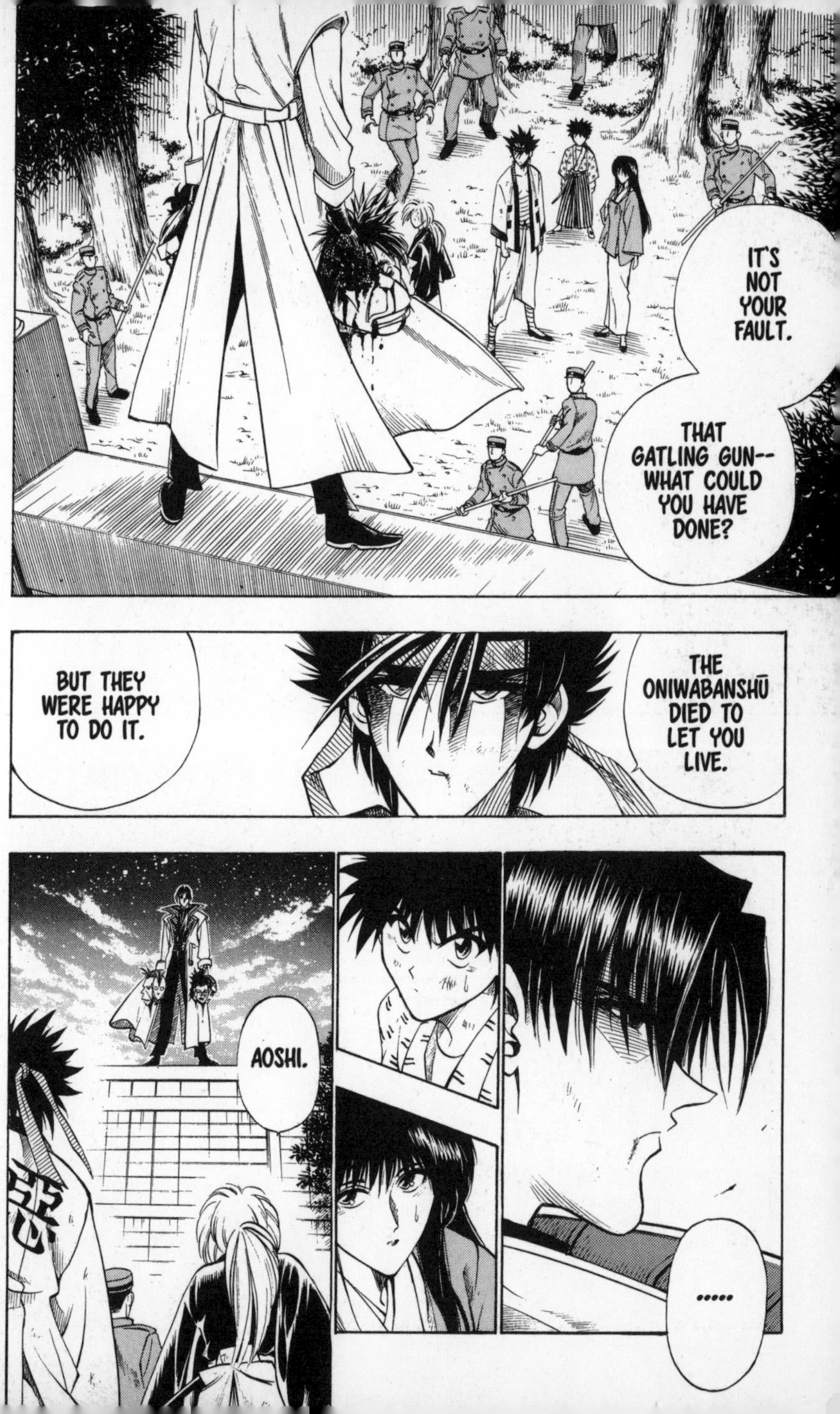
IT'S NOT YOUR FAULT.
THAT GATLING GUN--WHAT COULD YOU HAVE DONE?
THE ONIWABANSHŪ DIED TO LET YOU LIVE.
BUT THEY WERE HAPPY TO DO IT.
.....
AOSHI.

READ THIS WAY

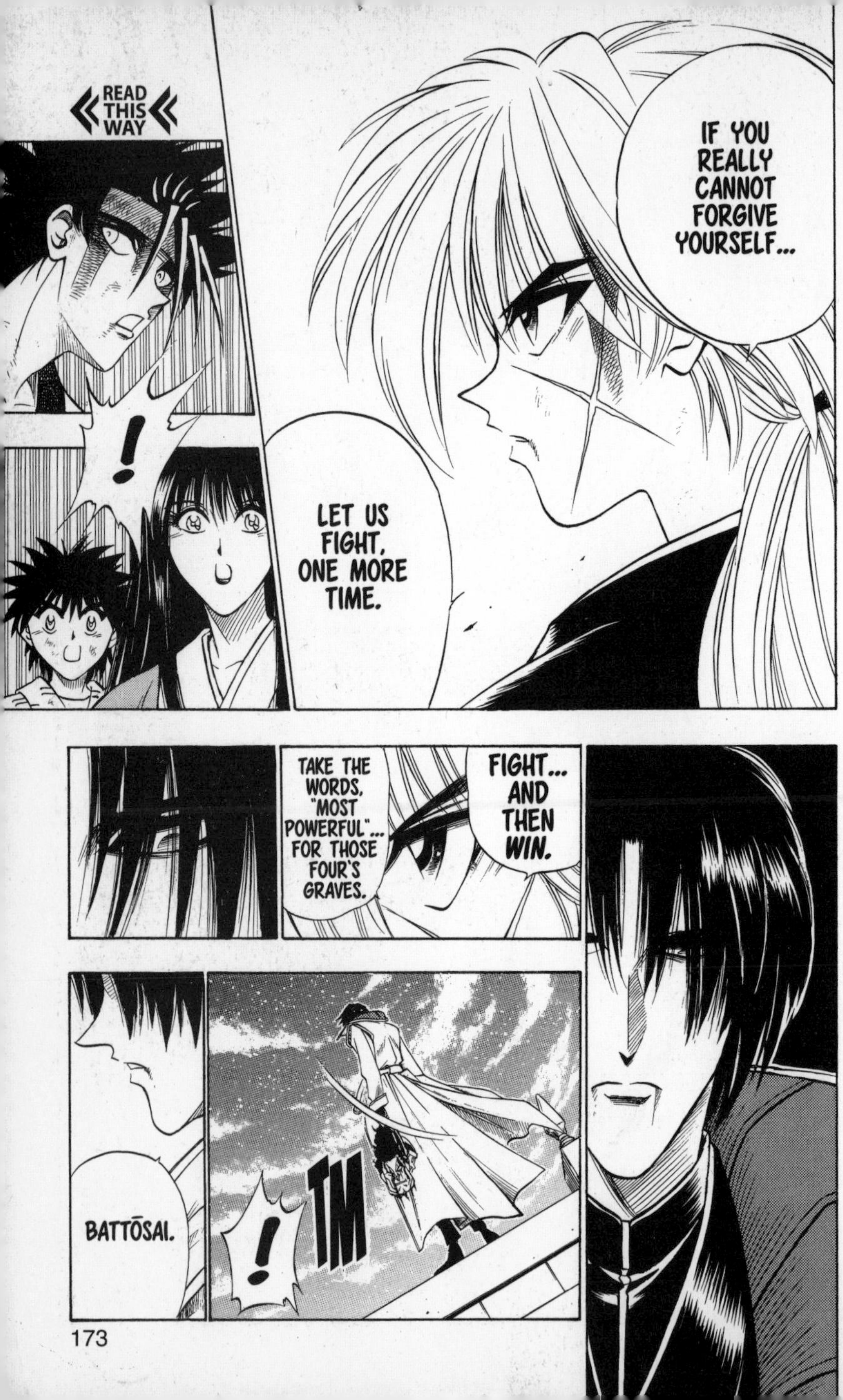
IF YOU REALLY CANNOT FORGIVE YOURSELF...
LET US FIGHT, ONE MORE TIME.
!
FIGHT... AND THEN WIN.
TAKE THE WORDS, "MOST POWERFUL"... FOR THOSE FOUR'S GRAVES.
TM
!
BATTŌSAI.

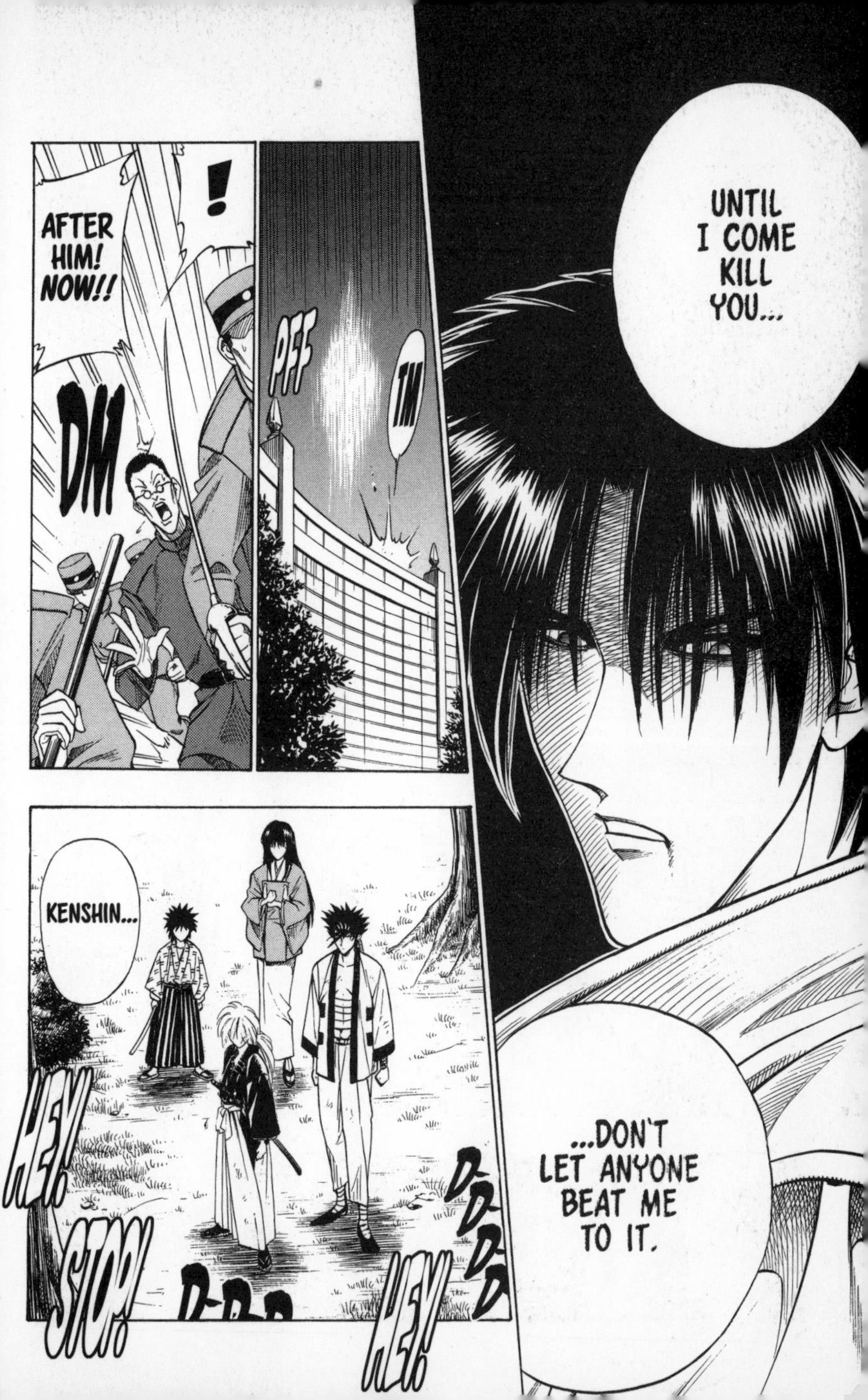
UNTIL I COME KILL YOU...
...DON'T LET ANYONE BEAT ME TO IT.
PFF
TM
!
AFTER HIM! NOW!!
DM
KENSHIN...
HEY!
STOP!
HEY!
DDDD

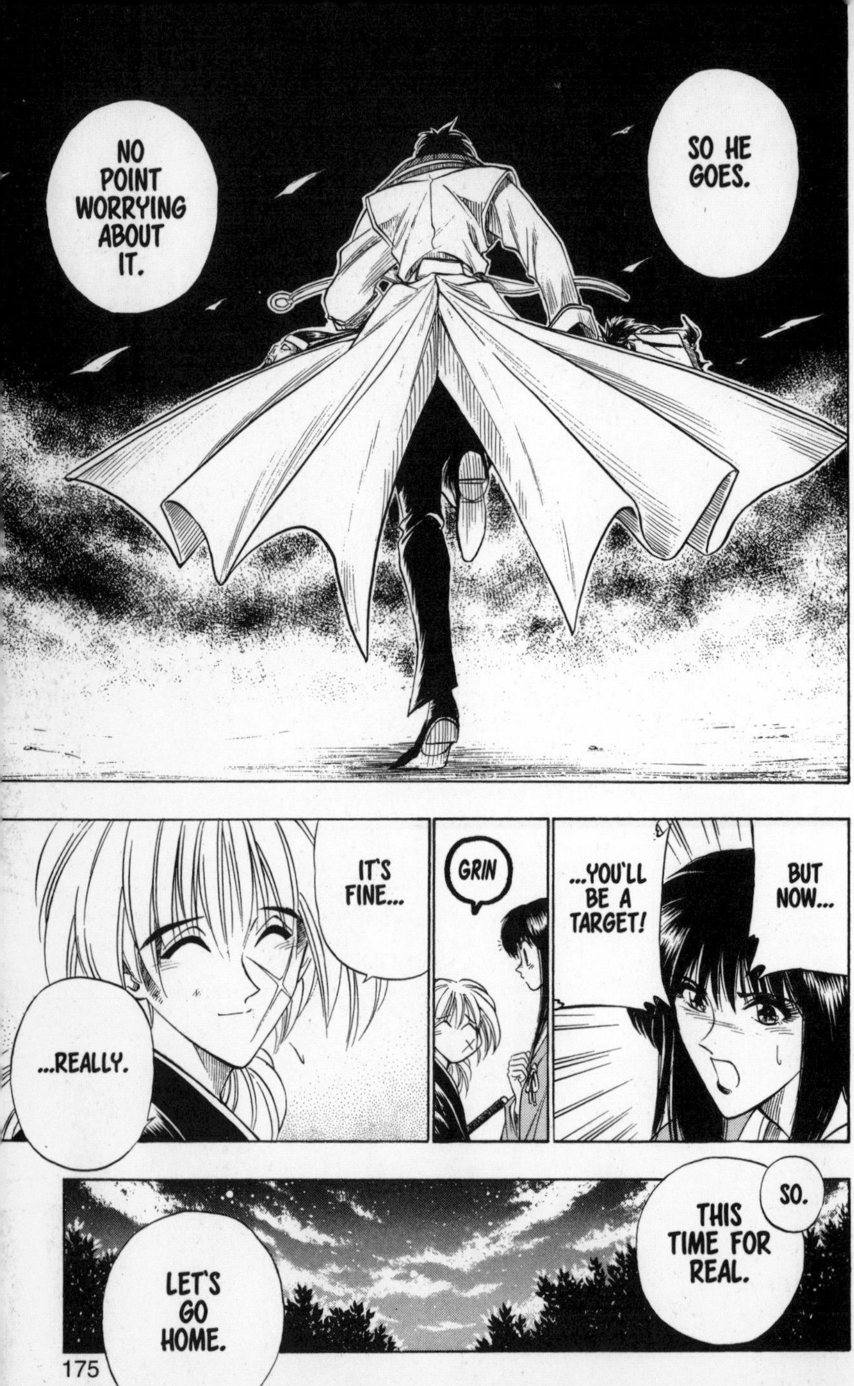
SO HE GOES.
NO POINT WORRYING ABOUT IT.
BUT NOW...
...YOU'LL BE A TARGET!
GRIN
IT'S FINE...
...REALLY.
SO.
THIS TIME FOR REAL.
LET'S GO HOME.

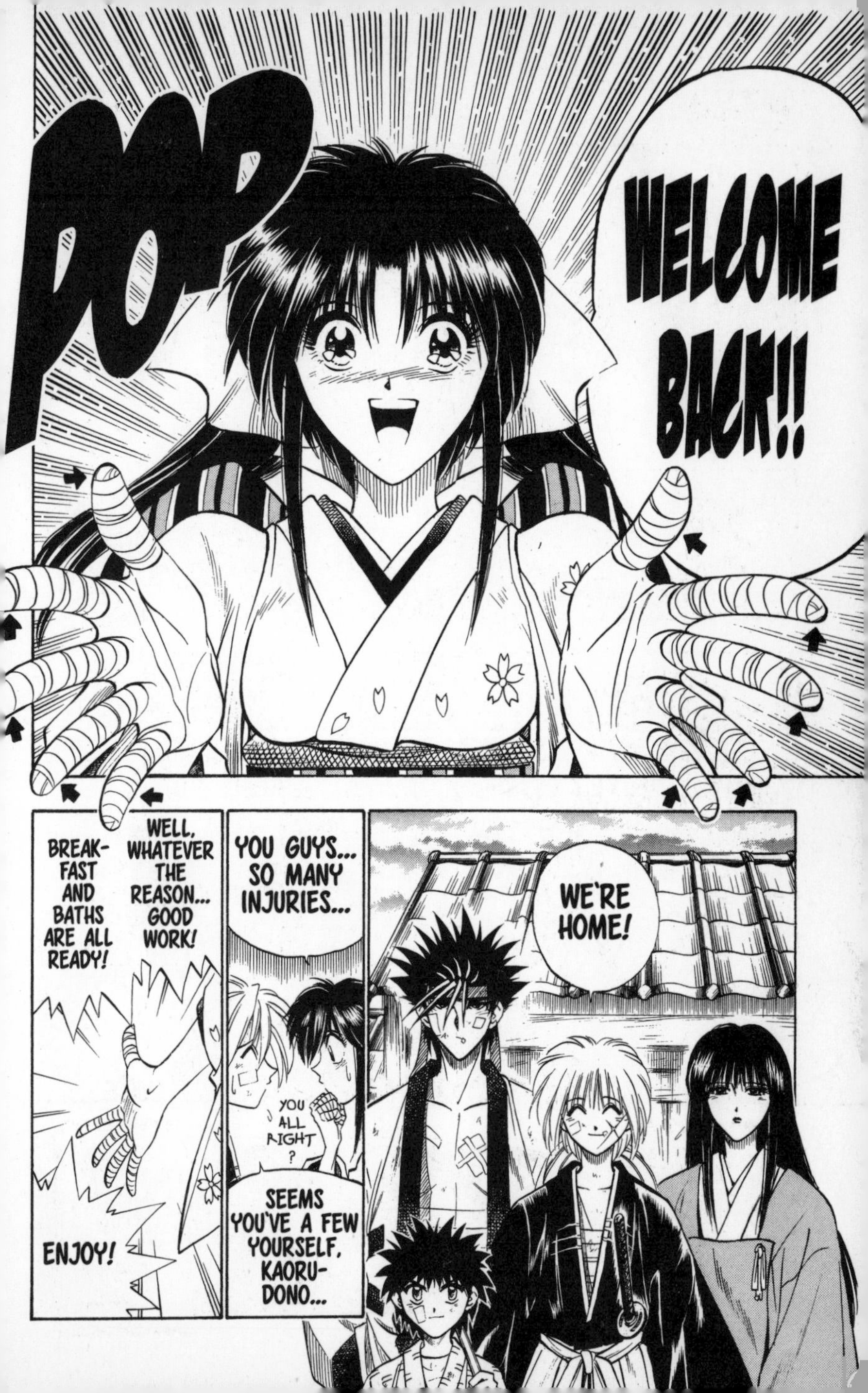
WELCOME BACK!!
POP
WE'RE HOME!
YOU GUYS... SO MANY INJURIES...
YOU ALL RIGHT?
SEEMS YOU'VE A FEW YOURSELF, KAORU-DONO...
WELL, WHATEVER THE REASON... GOOD WORK!
BREAK-FAST AND BATHS ARE ALL READY!
ENJOY!

READ THIS WAY

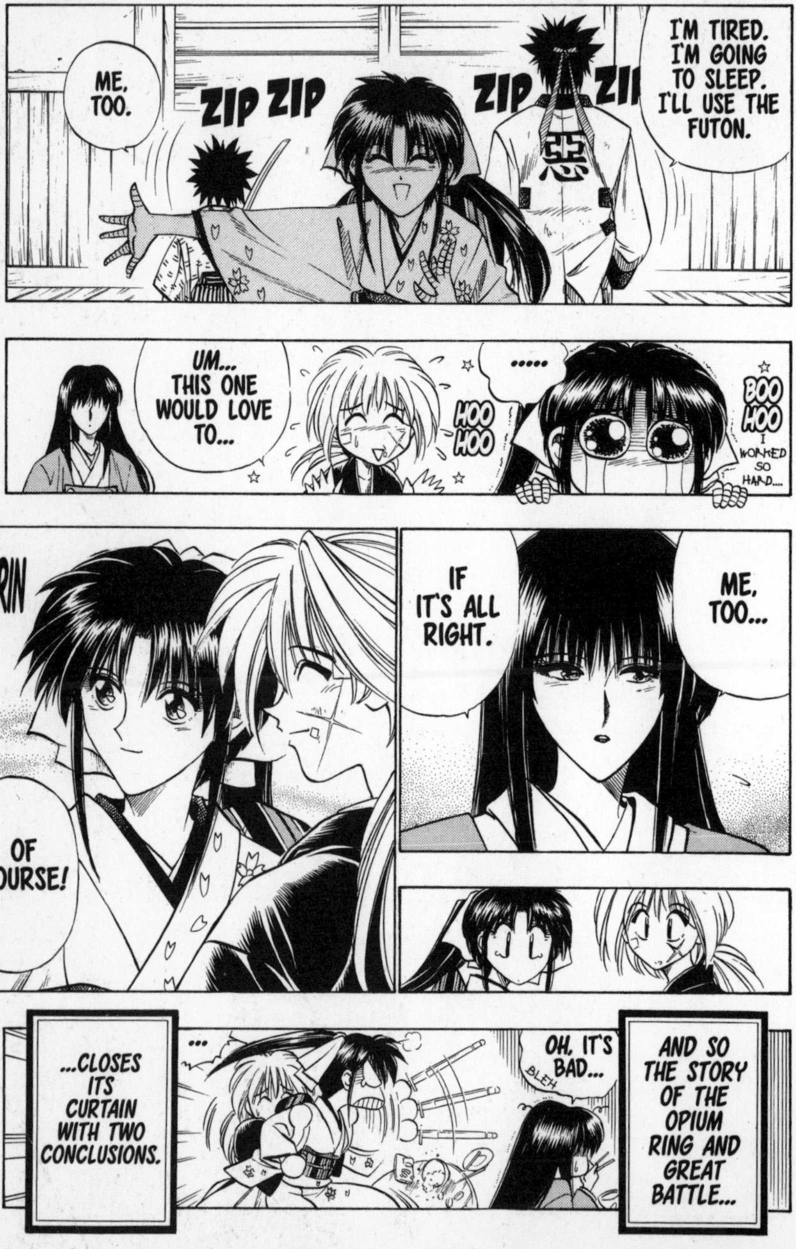

I'M TIRED. I'M GOING TO SLEEP. I'LL USE THE FUTON.
ZIP ZI
ZIP ZIP
ME, TOO.
BOO HOO
I WORKED SO HARD....
.....
HOO HOO
UM... THIS ONE WOULD LOVE TO...
ME, TOO...
IF IT'S ALL RIGHT.
GRIN
OF COURSE!
AND SO THE STORY OF THE OPIUM RING AND GREAT BATTLE...
OH, IT'S BAD...
BLEH
...
...CLOSES ITS CURTAIN WITH TWO CONCLUSIONS.

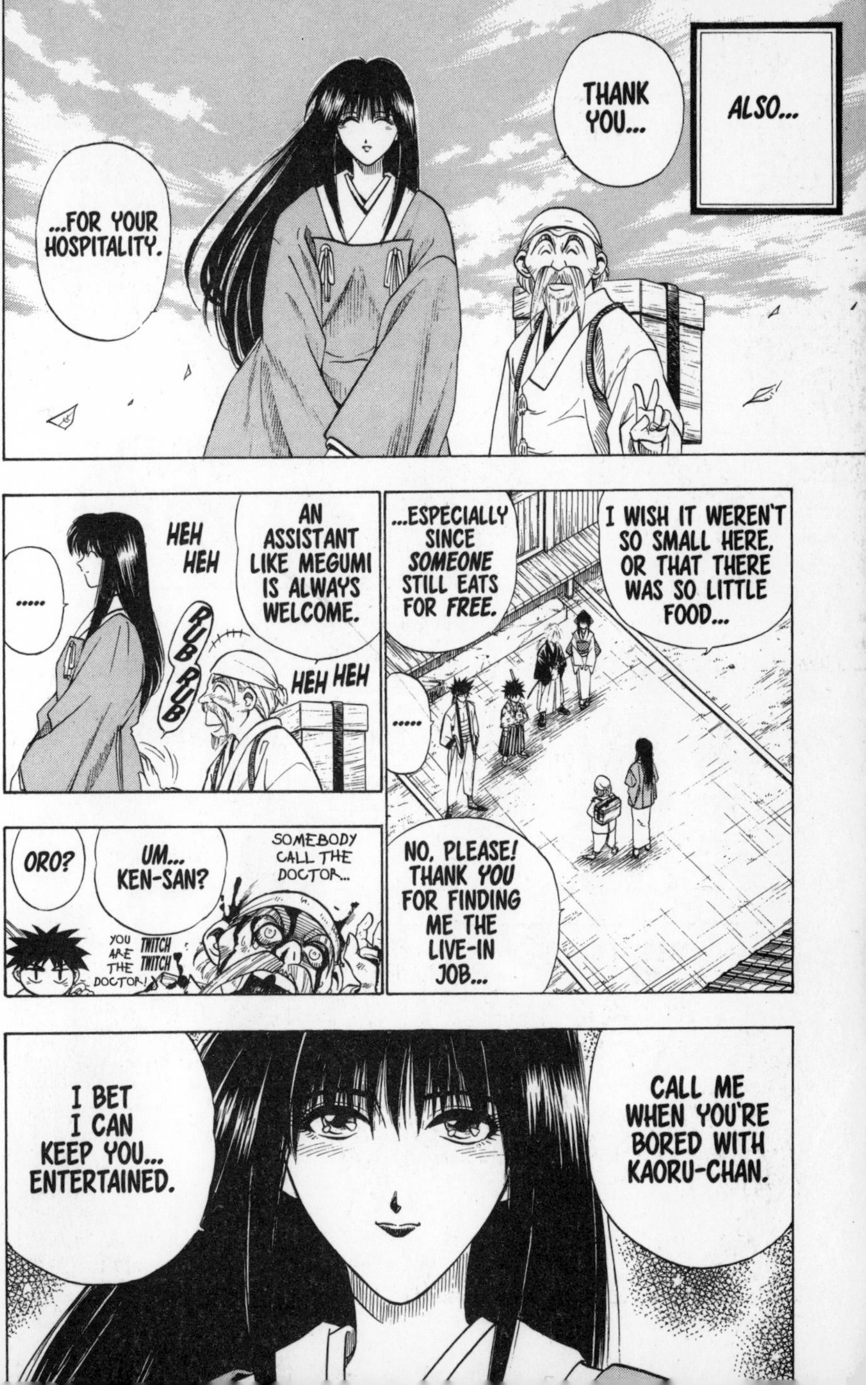
ALSO...
THANK YOU...
...FOR YOUR HOSPITALITY.
I WISH IT WEREN'T SO SMALL HERE, OR THAT THERE WAS SO LITTLE FOOD...
...ESPECIALLY SINCE SOMEONE STILL EATS FOR FREE.
.....
NO, PLEASE! THANK YOU FOR FINDING ME THE LIVE-IN JOB...
AN ASSISTANT LIKE MEGUMI IS ALWAYS WELCOME.
HEH HEH
RUB RUB
HEH HEH
.....
SOMEBODY CALL THE DOCTOR...
UM... KEN-SAN?
ORO?
TWITCH TWITCH
YOU ARE THE DOCTOR!
CALL ME WHEN YOU'RE BORED WITH KAORU-CHAN.
I BET I CAN KEEP YOU... ENTERTAINED.

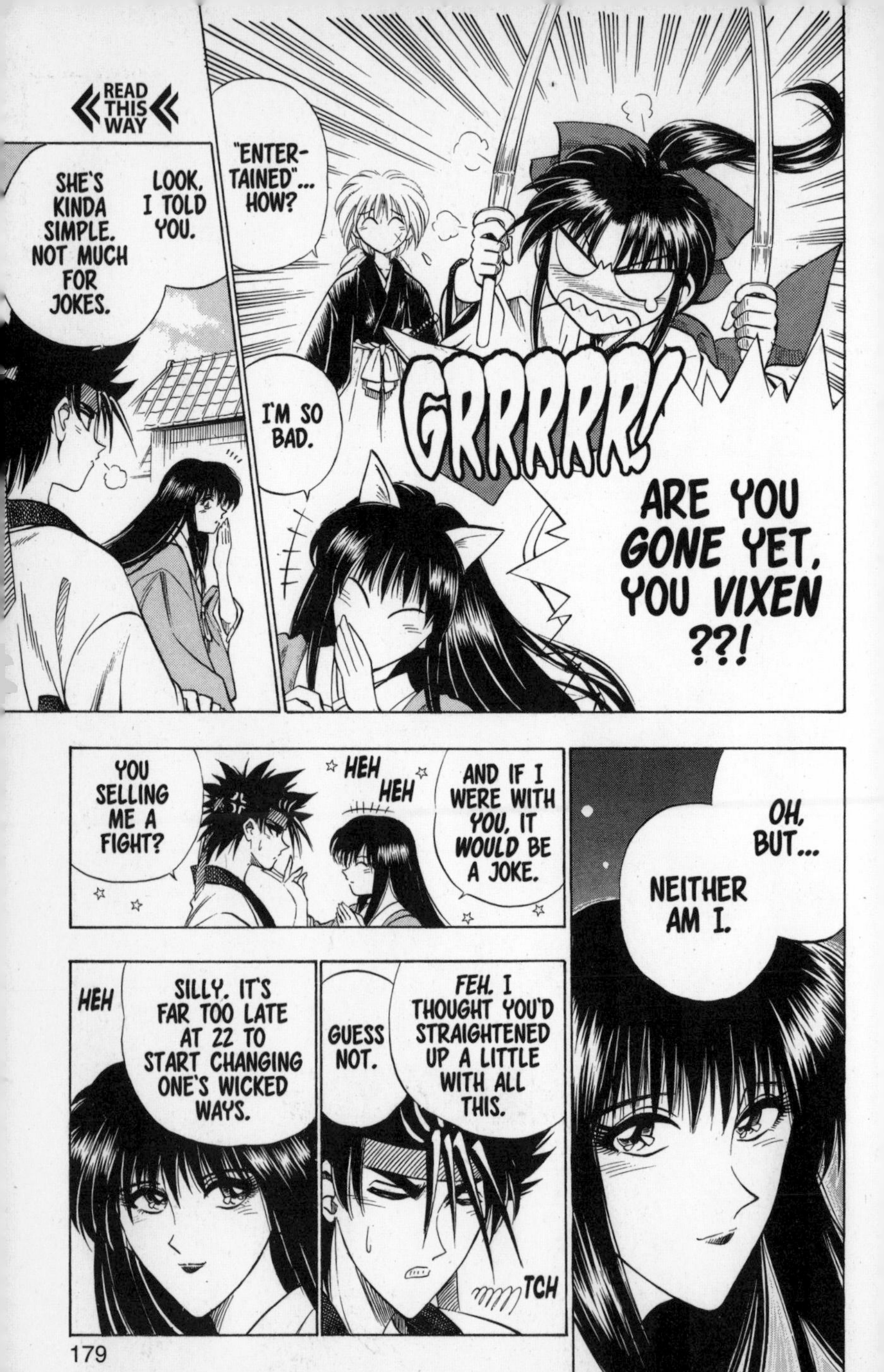
READ THIS WAY
"ENTER-TAINED"... HOW?
I'M SO BAD.
GRRRRR!
ARE YOU GONE YET, YOU VIXEN??!
LOOK, I TOLD YOU.
SHE'S KINDA SIMPLE. NOT MUCH FOR JOKES.
OH, BUT...
NEITHER AM I.
HEH HEH
AND IF I WERE WITH YOU, IT WOULD BE A JOKE.
YOU SELLING ME A FIGHT?
FEH. I THOUGHT YOU'D STRAIGHTENED UP A LITTLE WITH ALL THIS.
GUESS NOT.
TCH
SILLY. IT'S FAR TOO LATE AT 22 TO START CHANGING ONE'S WICKED WAYS.
HEH

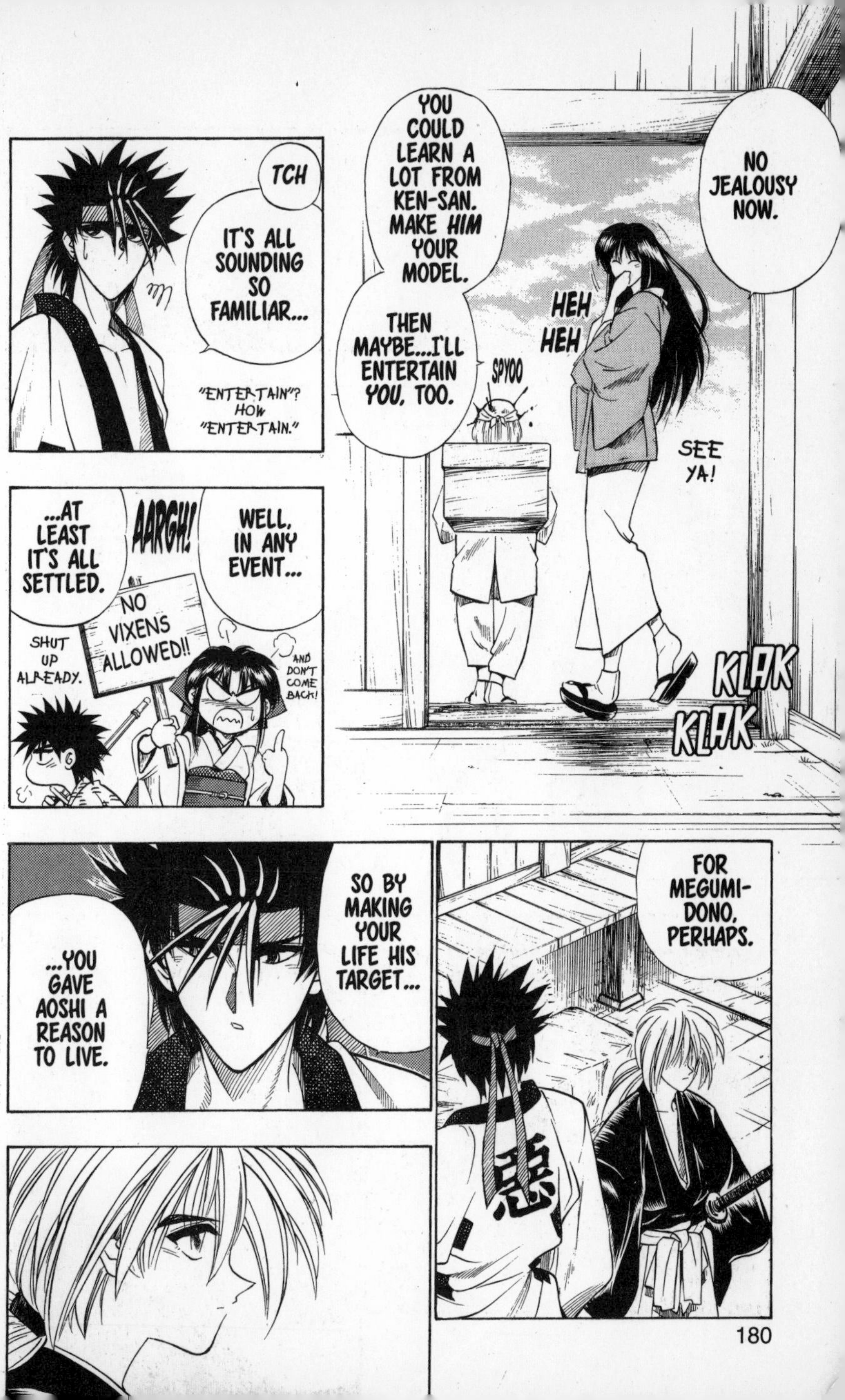
NO JEALOUSY NOW.
YOU COULD LEARN A LOT FROM KEN-SAN. MAKE *HIM* YOUR MODEL.
HEH HEH
THEN MAYBE...I'LL ENTERTAIN *YOU*, TOO.
SPYOO
SEE YA!
KLAK
KLAK
TCH
IT'S ALL SOUNDING SO FAMILIAR...
"ENTERTAIN"? HOW "ENTERTAIN."
WELL, IN ANY EVENT...
AARGH!
...AT LEAST IT'S ALL SETTLED.
NO VIXENS ALLOWED!!
AND DON'T COME BACK!
SHUT UP ALREADY.
FOR MEGUMI-DONO, PERHAPS.
SO BY MAKING YOUR LIFE HIS TARGET...
...YOU GAVE AOSHI A REASON TO LIVE.

READ THIS WAY

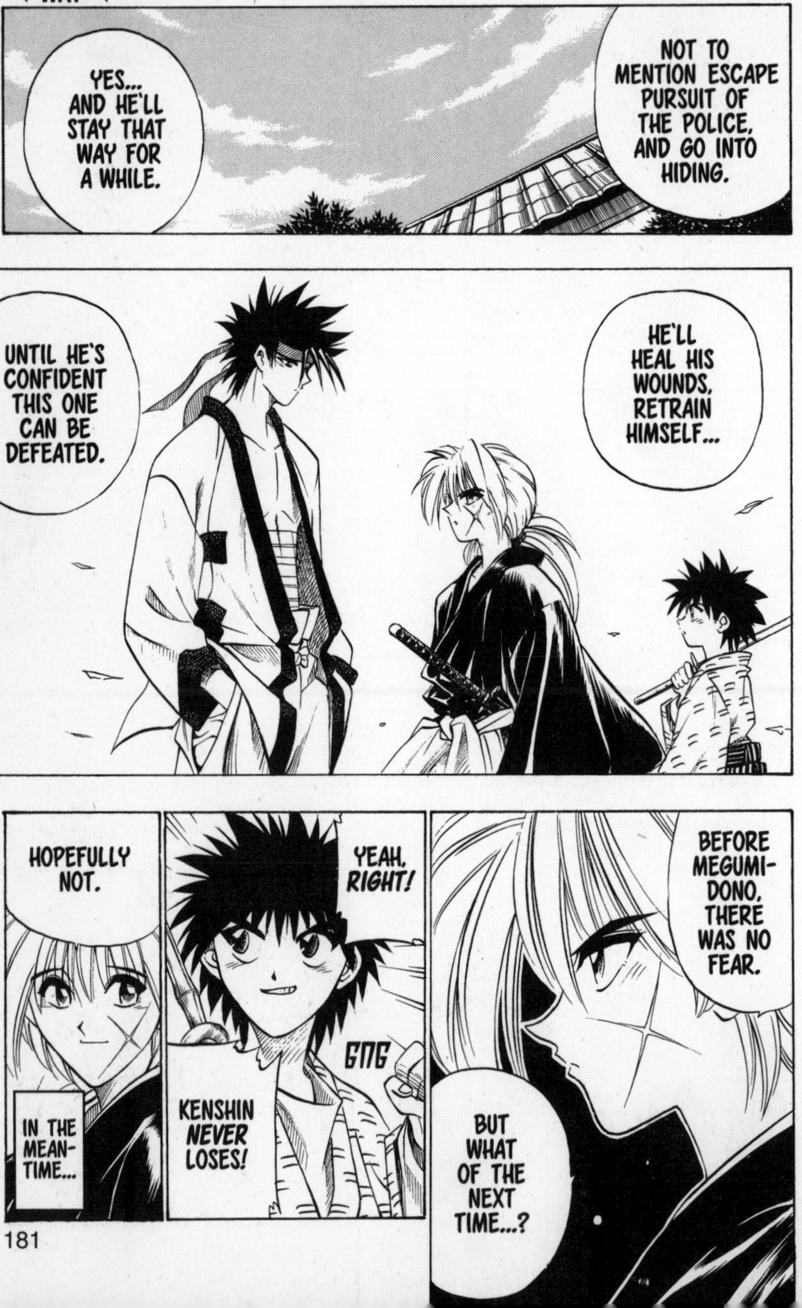
NOT TO MENTION ESCAPE PURSUIT OF THE POLICE, AND GO INTO HIDING.
YES... AND HE'LL STAY THAT WAY FOR A WHILE.
HE'LL HEAL HIS WOUNDS, RETRAIN HIMSELF...
UNTIL HE'S CONFIDENT THIS ONE CAN BE DEFEATED.
BEFORE MEGUMI-DONO, THERE WAS NO FEAR.
BUT WHAT OF THE NEXT TIME...?
YEAH, RIGHT!
GNG
KENSHIN NEVER LOSES!
HOPEFULLY NOT.
IN THE MEAN-TIME...

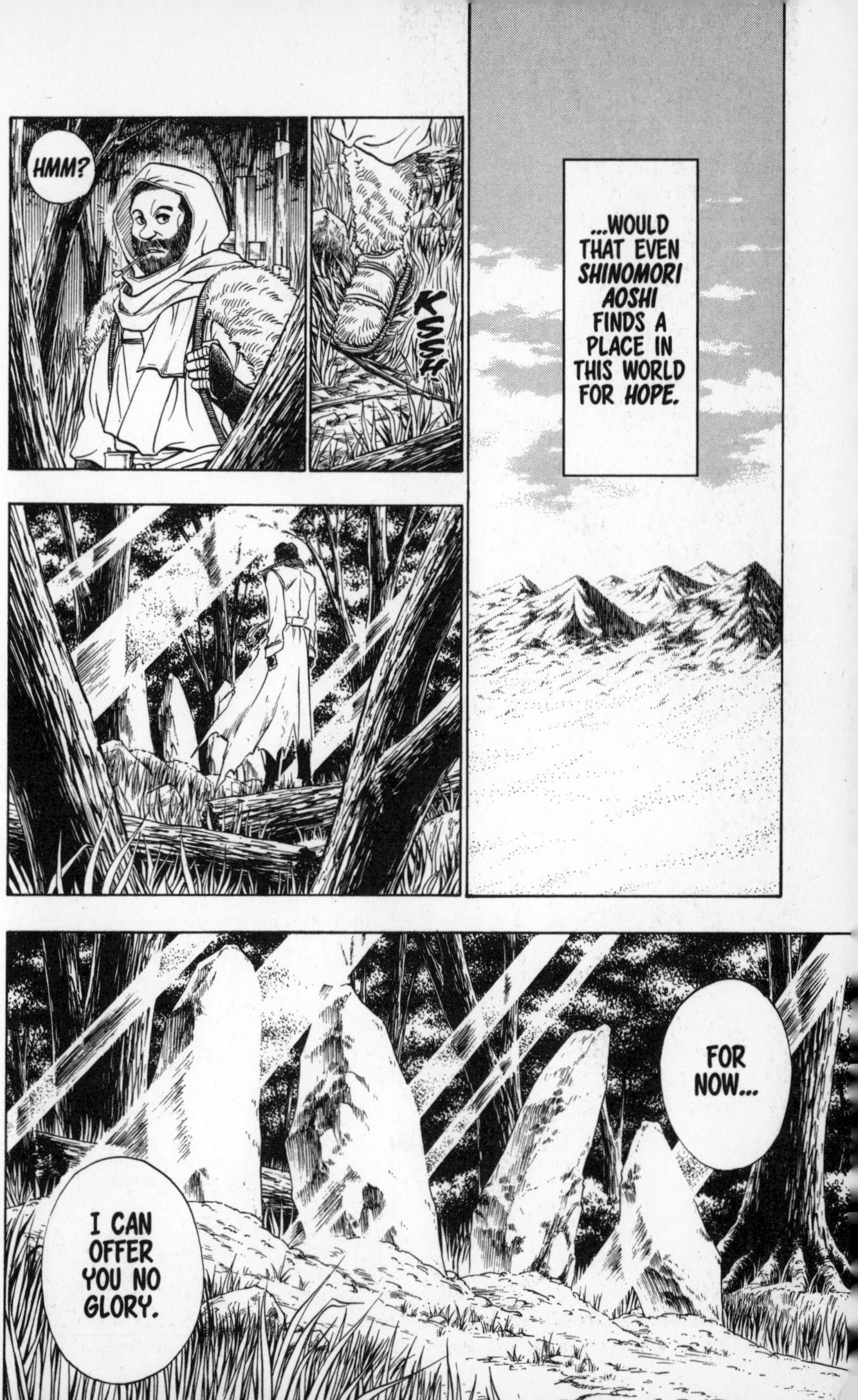
...WOULD THAT EVEN SHINOMORI AOSHI FINDS A PLACE IN THIS WORLD FOR HOPE.
KSSH
HMM?
FOR NOW...
I CAN OFFER YOU NO GLORY.

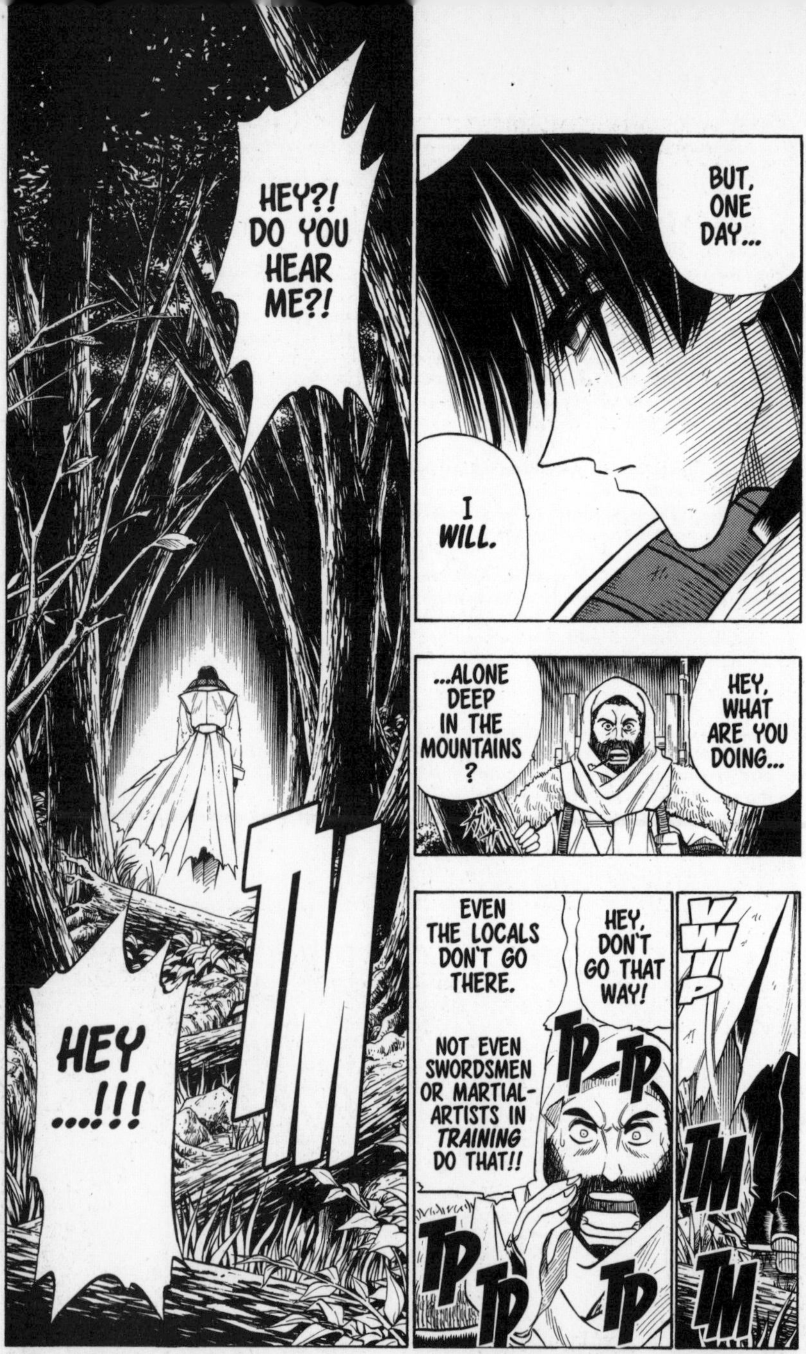
BUT, ONE DAY...
I WILL.
HEY, WHAT ARE YOU DOING...
...ALONE DEEP IN THE MOUNTAINS?
WHIP
TM
TM
HEY, DON'T GO THAT WAY!
EVEN THE LOCALS DON'T GO THERE.
NOT EVEN SWORDSMEN OR MARTIAL-ARTISTS IN *TRAINING* DO THAT!!
TP-TP
TP
TP
TP
HEY?! DO YOU HEAR ME?!
TM
HEY ...!!!

 To be continued in Volume 5: The State of Meiji Swordsmanship

## The Secret Life of Characters (14)

# —Okashira • Shinomori Aoshi—

**As mentioned previously in regard to Beshimi, the Oniwabanshū were tacked on at the last minute, and so when it was time for Aoshi to appear, I hadn't really worked out a concrete image and therefore had some trouble writing him. With time, though, the models for the Oniwabanshū became my favorite Shinsengumi, and Aoshi's model became the Assistant Chief of the Shinsengumi, Hijikata Toshizō. Even citing Hijikata as a reference, though, there's still two versions of him in the novels (you Shinsengumi hardcores know what I'm talking about).**

**One Hijikata is the one from "*Moeyo Ken* (Burn, O Sword)," a bundle of raw combat-instinct who keeps fighting until the very death (it's this Hijikata that Watsuki is a fan of). The other Hijikata is the one who hides his selfishness for the sake of the Shinsengumi, acting mercilessly but crying inside. (That's the one Aoshi has as his model.) "The Shinsengumi who could not fight..." In other words, they couldn't show their beliefs, honor, or abilities to the outside world, and so were labeled the defeated. The Asst. Chief who fought to keep his Oniwabanshū from hiding their lights beneath a bushel, that's Aoshi. I won't reveal here whether or not Aoshi will become an ogre-like warrior who fights to the death, but his reappearance isn't that far away.**

**There's no specific design-model for him. I first used a character I have in my sketchbook, but as the story went on, the image of Hijikata became stronger and stronger, causing me to add the bangs. When editing the (compiled) manga, I had the chance to change it, but that might seem kind of strange, so I let it be—I wouldn't want anyone to think Aoshi was wearing a rug or anything.**

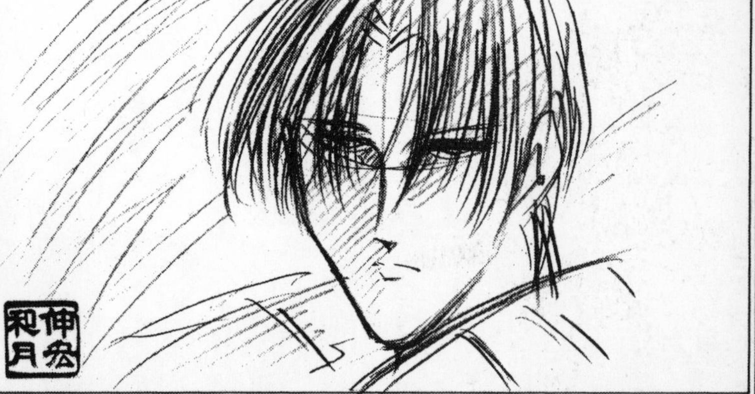
伸宏
和月

Rurouni Kenshin

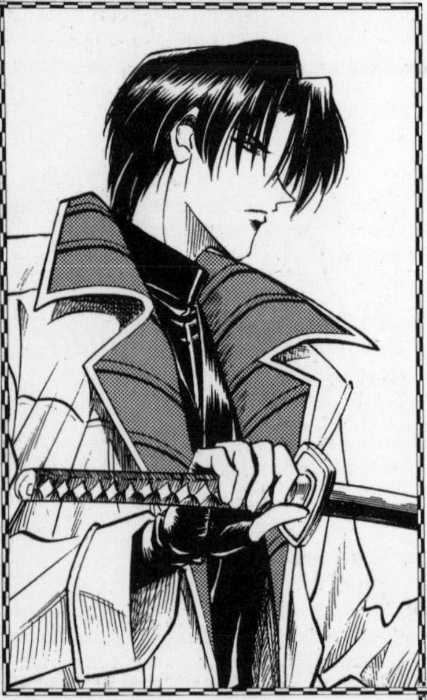

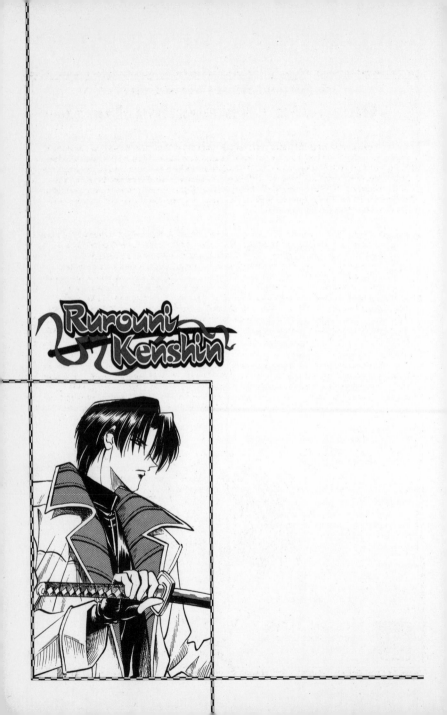

# GLOSSARY of the RESTORATION

*A brief guide to select Japanese terms used in **Rurouni Kenshin**. Note that, both here and within the story itself, all names are Japanese style—i.e., last or "family" name first, with personal or "given" name following. This is both because **Kenshin** is a "period" story, as well as to decrease confusion—were we to take the example of Kenshin's sakabatô and "reverse" the format of the historically established assassin-name "Hitokiri Battôsai," for example, it would make little sense to then call him "Battôsai Himura."*

**hitokiri**
An assassin. Famous swordsmen of the period were sometimes thus known to adopt "professional" names—**Kawakami Gensai**, for example, was also known as "Hitokiri Gensai"

**Ishin Shishi**
Loyalist or pro-Imperialist **patriots** who fought to restore the Emperor to his ancient seat of power

**Jôdan, Chûdan (Seigan), Gedan, Hassô, Wakigamae**
The five basic postures or "stances (*kamae*)" of kendô. **Jôdan**: Sword lifted overhead. **Chûdan** (Seigan): Cut to middle level. **Gedan**: Low-level, downward/sweeping block. **Hassô**: Sword held vertically, hands shoulder-level. **Wakigamae**: Horizontal (guard) position. In this story, Han'nya uses **Shinken**, a variant of **Seigan**, as noted (correctly) by Yahiko

**Kamiya Kasshin-ryû**
Sword-arts or **kenjutsu** school established by Kaoru's father, who rejected the ethics of **Satsujin-ken** for **Katsujin-ken**

**katana**
Traditional Japanese longsword (curved, single-edge, worn cutting-edge up) of the samurai. Used primarily for slashing; can be wielded either one- or two-handed

**Katsujin-ken**
"Swords that give life"; the sword-arts style developed over ten years by Kaoru's father and founding principle of **Kamiya Kasshin-ryû**

**Katsu Kaishû**
Founder of the Japanese navy. Described famously as "the greatest man in Japan," Katsu Kaishû was born the only son of an impoverished petty samurai in Edo in January 1823, and would one day become the most powerful man in the Tokugawa Shôgunate

**Bakumatsu**
Final, chaotic days of the Tokugawa regime

**bokutô**
Kendô ("sword-arts") weapon made of wood; also known as a "*bokken*"

**-chan**
Honorific. Can be used either as a diminutive (e.g., with a small child—"Little Hanako or Kentarô"), or with those who are grown, to indicate affection ("My dear...")

**dojo**
Martial arts training hall

**-dono**
Honorific. Even more respectful than **–san**; the effect in modern-day Japanese conversation would be along the lines of "Milord So-and-So." As used by Kenshin, it indicates both respect and humility

**Edo**
Capital city of the **Tokugawa Bakufu**, renamed **Tokyo** ("Eastern Capital") after the Meiji Restoration

**Himura Battôsai**
Swordsman of legendary skills and former assassin (**hitokiri**) of the **Ishin Shishi**

**Himura Kenshin**
Kenshin's "real" name, revealed to Kaoru only at her urging

**Hiten Mitsurugi-ryû**
Kenshin's sword technique, used more for defense than offense. An "ancient style that pits one against many," it requires exceptional speed and agility to master

**rurouni**
Wanderer, vagabond

**Saigô Takamori**
Commander of an Imperial Army 50,000 strong, at one time Saigô Takamori was the most powerful man in Japan. Described as a "quintessential samurai who cherished the words 'Love mankind, revere heaven,'" Saigô would eventually become a leader of disgruntled samurai opposing the rapid modernization of Japan (on which they blamed the demise of their own class)

**sakabatô**
Reversed-edge sword (the dull edge on the side the sharp should be, and vice-versa); carried by Kenshin as a symbol of his resolution never to kill again

**-san**
Honorific. Carries the meaning of "Mr.," "Ms.," "Miss," etc., but used more extensively in Japanese than its English equivalent (note that even an enemy may be addressed as "-san")

**Satsujin-ken**
"Swords that give death"; a style of swordsmanship rejected by Kaoru's father

**shôgun**
Feudal military ruler of Japan

**shôgunate**
See *Tokugawa Bakufu*

**Tokugawa Bakufu**
Military feudal government which dominated Japan from 1603 to 1867

**Tokyo**
The renaming of "*Edo*" to "*Tokyo*" is a marker of the start of the *Meiji Restoration*

**wakizashi**
Similar to the more familiar *katana*, but shorter (blade between 12 and 24 inches)

**Kawakami Gensai**
Real-life, historical inspiration for the character of *Himura Kenshin*

**kenjutsu**
The art of fencing; sword arts; kendô

**-kun**
Honorific. Used in the modern day among male students, or those who grew up together, but another usage—the one you're more likely to find in *Rurouni Kenshin*—is the "superior-to-inferior" form, intended as a way to emphasize a difference in status or rank, as well as to indicate familiarity or affection

**kodachi**
Medium-length sword, shorter than the *katana* but longer than the *wakizashi*. Its easy maneuverability also makes for higher defensive capability

**loyalists**
Those who supported the return of the Emperor to power; *Ishin Shishi*

**Meiji Restoration**
1853-1868; culminated in the collapse of the *Tokugawa Bakufu* and the restoration of imperial rule. So called after Emperor Meiji, whose chosen name was written with the characters for "culture and enlightenment"

**Okashira**
Literally, "the head"; i.e., leader, boss

**Oniwabanshû**
Elite group of *onmitsu* or "spies" of the *Edo* period. Note that while Watsuki acknowledges the "Oniwabanshû *onmitsu*" to be his own fictional creation, the Oniwabanshû do in fact seem to have a historical correlative as an information-gathering group, serving under the *shôgun*, who continued up until the *Bakumatsu* to conduct their investigations all over the country

**onmitsu**
Spies. Also known as "shinobi," or of course the more familiar "ninja"

**patriots**
Another term for *Ishin Shishi*…and when used by Sano, not a flattering one

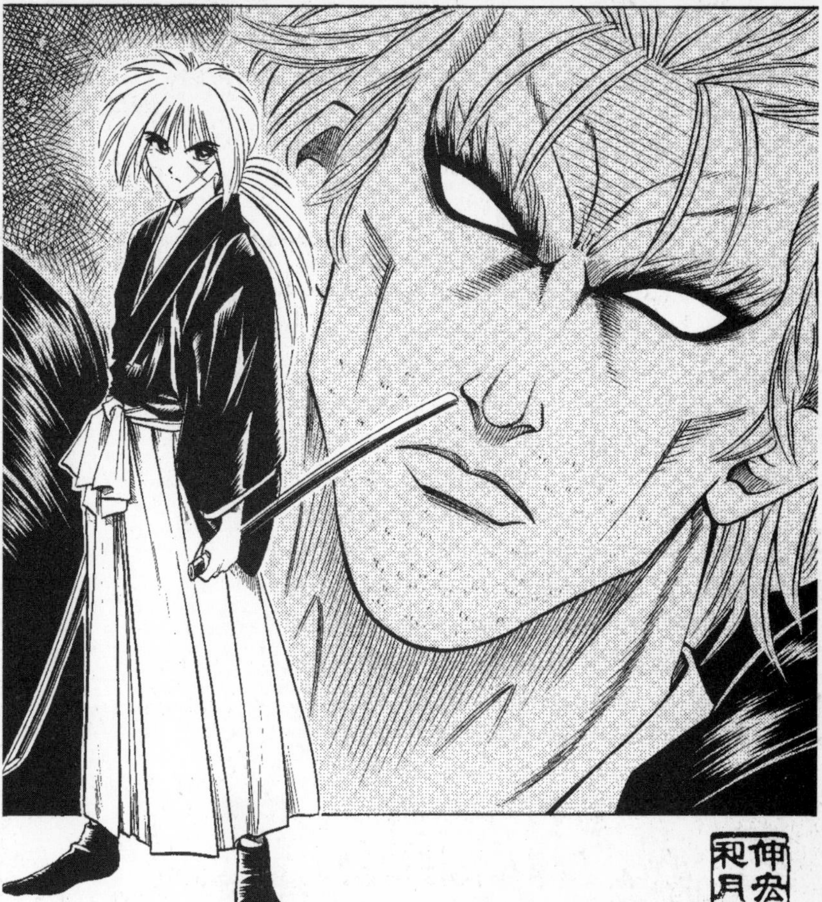
伸宏
和月

## IN THE NEXT VOLUME...

Yahiko's recent truancy at practice sessions is bothering Kenshin and Kaoru. When it's uncovered that Yahiko has been working part-time at a local eatery, Kenshin knows that something must be up. Eager to prove himself as a warrior, Yahiko attempts to save a troubled waitress from a gang of unruly *yakuza*. Kenshin and company offer their assistance, but Yahiko wants to fight the gang alone. Later, a trip to a neighboring school ends in disaster when Raijûta Isurugi, a fighter of incredible strength and speed, defeats the school's master, a close friend of Kaoru. Wishing to show the futile state of Meiji-era swordsmanship, Raijûta challenges Kenshin to a duel. Will Kenshin's antiquated style of fighting be his downfall?

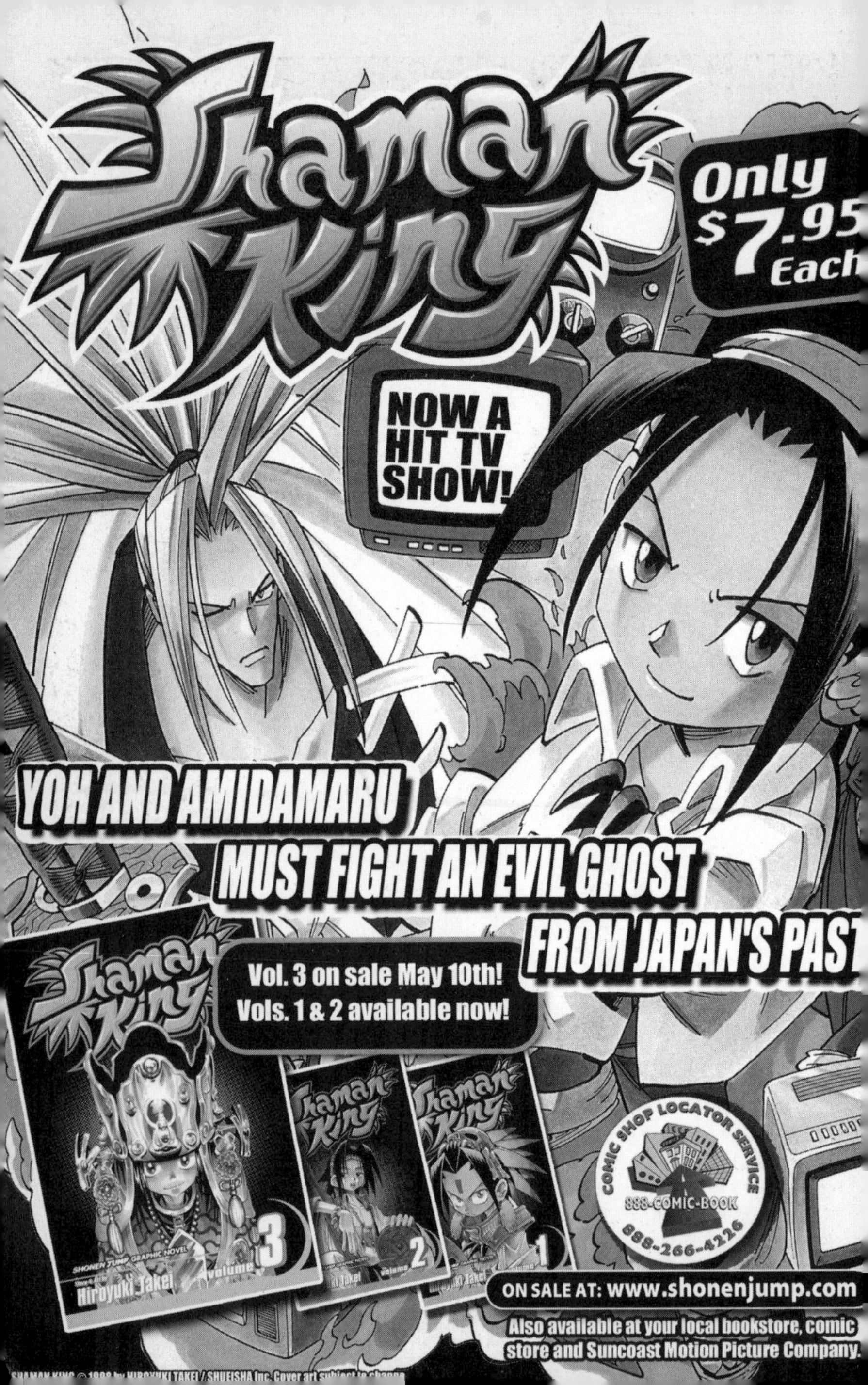
Shaman King
Only $7.95 Each
NOW A HIT TV SHOW!
YOH AND AMIDAMARU MUST FIGHT AN EVIL GHOST FROM JAPAN'S PAST
Vol. 3 on sale May 10th!
Vols. 1 & 2 available now!
Shaman King
SHONEN JUMP GRAPHIC NOVEL
Hiroyuki Takei
volume 3
volume 2
volume 1
COMIC SHOP LOCATOR SERVICE
888-COMIC-BOOK
888-266-4226
ON SALE AT: www.shonenjump.com
Also available at your local bookstore, comic store and Suncoast Motion Picture Company.
TAKEI / SHUEISHA Inc. Cover art

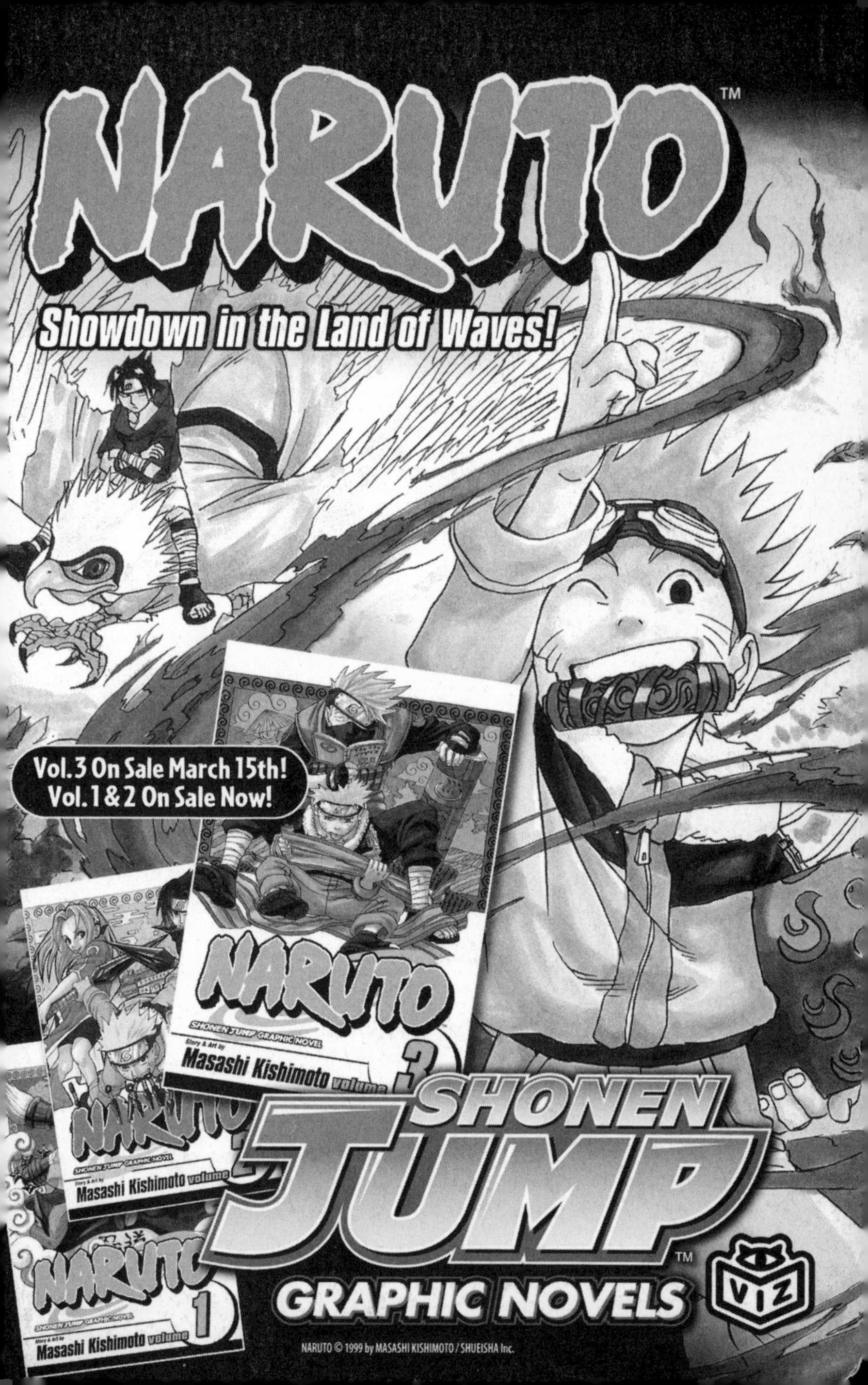
NARUTO™
Showdown in the Land of Waves!
Vol. 3 On Sale March 15th!
Vol. 1 & 2 On Sale Now!
NARUTO
SHONEN JUMP GRAPHIC NOVEL
Story & Art by
Masashi Kishimoto volume 3
Masashi Kishimoto volume
Masashi Kishimoto volume 1
SHONEN JUMP™
GRAPHIC NOVELS
VIZ
NARUTO © 1999 by MASASHI KISHIMOTO / SHUEISHA Inc.

# SHONEN JUMP
THE WORLD'S MOST POPULAR MANGA

## COMPLETE OUR SURVEY AND LET US KNOW WHAT YOU THINK!

☐ Please check here if you DO NOT wish to receive information or future offers from VIZ

**Name:** _____

**Address:** _____

**City:** _____ **State:** _____ **Zip:** _____

**E-mail:** _____

☐ Male ☐ Female    **Date of Birth** (mm/dd/yyyy): ___/___/___   ( Under 13? Parental consent required )

### What race/ethnicity do you consider yourself? (please check one)

☐ Asian/Pacific Islander    ☐ Black/African American    ☐ Hispanic/Latino

☐ Native American/Alaskan Native    ☐ White/Caucasian    ☐ Other: _____

### What SHONEN JUMP Graphic Novel did you purchase? (indicate title purchased)

_____

### What other SHONEN JUMP Graphic Novels, if any, do you own? (indicate title(s) owned)

_____

_____

### Reason for purchase: (check all that apply)

☐ Special offer    ☐ Favorite title    ☐ Gift

☐ Recommendation    ☐ Read in SHONEN JUMP Magazine

☐ Other_____

### Where did you make your purchase? (please check one)

☐ Comic store    ☐ Bookstore    ☐ Mass/Grocery Store

☐ Newsstand    ☐ Video/Video Game Store    ☐ Other:_____

☐ Online (site: _____)

**Do you read SHONEN JUMP Magazine?**

☐ Yes ☐ No **(if no, skip the next two questions)**

Do you subscribe?

☐ Yes ☐ No

If you do not subscribe, how often do you purchase SHONEN JUMP Magazine?

☐ 1-3 issues a year

☐ 4-6 issues a year

☐ more than 7 issues a year

**What genre of manga would you like to read as a SHONEN JUMP Graphic Novel?**
**(please check two)**

☐ Adventure ☐ Comic Strip ☐ Science Fiction ☐ Fighting

☐ Horror ☐ Romance ☐ Fantasy ☐ Sports

**Which do you prefer? (please check one)**

☐ Reading right-to-left

☐ Reading left-to-right

**Which do you prefer? (please check one)**

☐ Sound effects in English

☐ Sound effects in Japanese with English captions

☐ Sound effects in Japanese only with a glossary at the back

**THANK YOU! Please send the completed form to:**

VIZ Survey
42 Catharine St.
Poughkeepsie, NY 12601

**All information provided will be used for internal purposes only. We promise not to sell or otherwise divulge your information.**

# SHONEN JUMP
### THE WORLD'S MOST POPULAR MANGA

## COMPLETE OUR SURVEY AND LET US KNOW WHAT YOU THINK!

☐ Please check here if you DO NOT wish to receive information or future offers from VIZ

Name: _____

Address: _____

City:_____ State:_____ Zip:_____

E-mail: _____

☐ Male ☐ Female Date of Birth (mm/dd/yyyy): ___/___/_____ ( Under 13? Parental consent required )

**What race/ethnicity do you consider yourself?** (please check one)

☐ Asian/Pacific Islander ☐ Black/African American ☐ Hispanic/Latino

☐ Native American/Alaskan Native ☐ White/Caucasian ☐ Other: _____

**What SHONEN JUMP Graphic Novel did you purchase?** (indicate title purchased)

_____

**What other SHONEN JUMP Graphic Novels, if any, do you own?** (indicate title(s) owned)

_____

_____

**Reason for purchase:** (check all that apply)

☐ Special offer ☐ Favorite title ☐ Gift

☐ Recommendation ☐ Read in SHONEN JUMP Magazine

☐ Other_____

**Where did you make your purchase?** (please check one)

☐ Comic store ☐ Bookstore ☐ Mass/Grocery Store

☐ Newsstand ☐ Video/Video Game Store ☐ Other: _____

☐ Online (site: _____ )

**Do you read SHONEN JUMP Magazine?**

- ☐ Yes
- ☐ No **(if no, skip the next two questions)**

Do you subscribe?

- ☐ Yes
- ☐ No

If you do not subscribe, how often do you purchase SHONEN JUMP Magazine?

- ☐ 1-3 issues a year
- ☐ 4-6 issues a year
- ☐ more than 7 issues a year

**What genre of manga would you like to read as a SHONEN JUMP Graphic Novel?**
**(please check two)**

- ☐ Adventure
- ☐ Comic Strip
- ☐ Science Fiction
- ☐ Fighting
- ☐ Horror
- ☐ Romance
- ☐ Fantasy
- ☐ Sports

**Which do you prefer? (please check one)**

- ☐ Reading right-to-left
- ☐ Reading left-to-right

**Which do you prefer? (please check one)**

- ☐ Sound effects in English
- ☐ Sound effects in Japanese with English captions
- ☐ Sound effects in Japanese only with a glossary at the back

**THANK YOU! Please send the completed form to:**

VIZ Survey
42 Catharine St.
Poughkeepsie, NY 12601

**All information provided will be used for internal purposes only. We promise not to sell or otherwise divulge your information.**

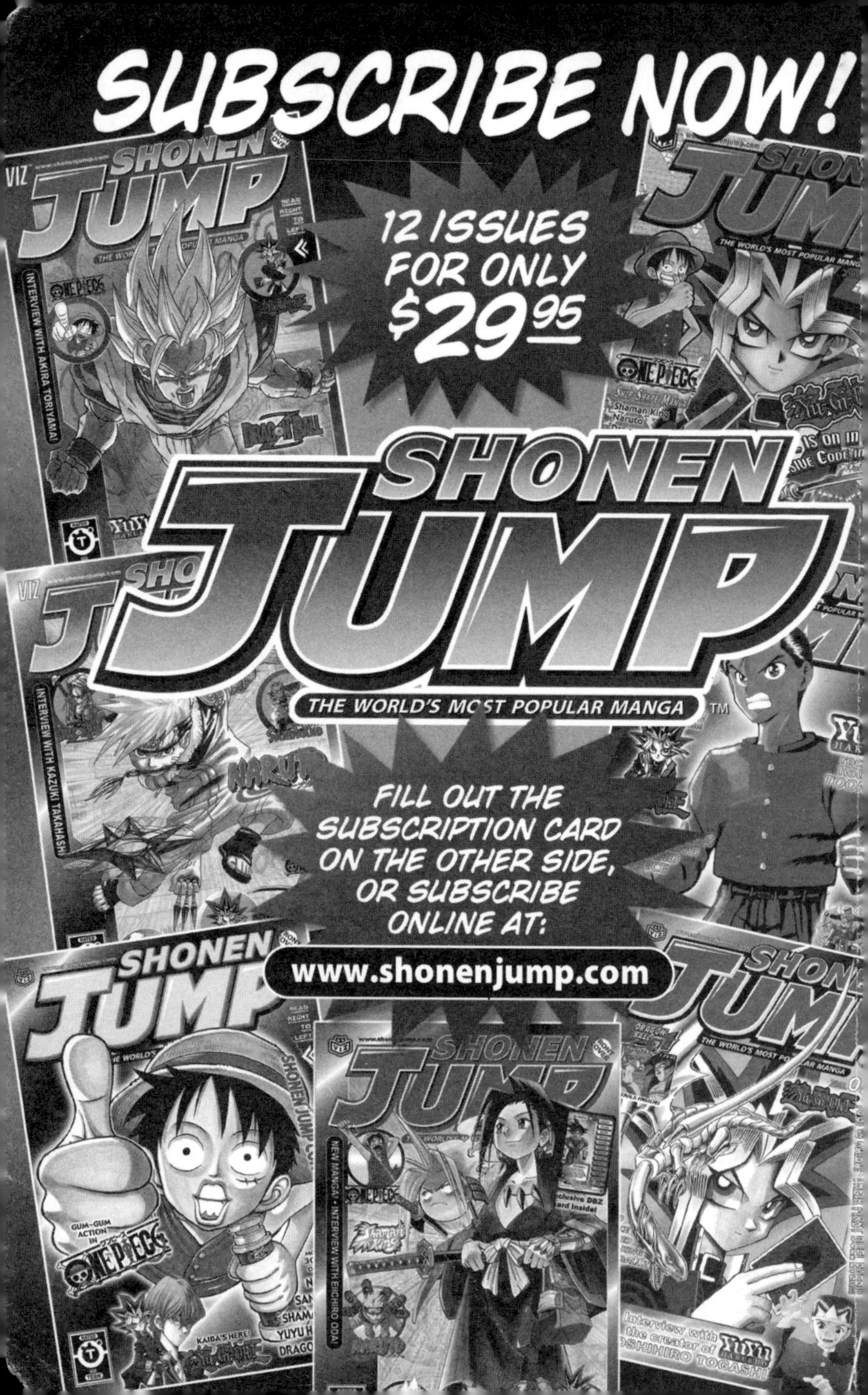

SUBSCRIBE NOW!
12 ISSUES FOR ONLY $29.95
SHONEN JUMP
THE WORLD'S MOST POPULAR MANGA
FILL OUT THE SUBSCRIPTION CARD ON THE OTHER SIDE, OR SUBSCRIBE ONLINE AT:
www.shonenjump.com

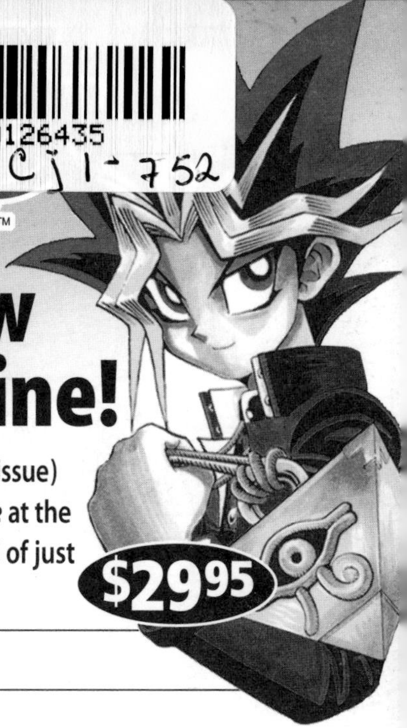